VOLUME THREE

ADVANCES IN TRANSPORT POLICY AND PLANNING

The Evolving Impacts of ICT on Activities and Travel Behavior

VOLUME THREE

ADVANCES IN TRANSPORT POLICY AND PLANNING

The Evolving Impacts of ICT on Activities and Travel Behavior

Edited by

ERAN BEN-ELIA

Department of Geography and Environmental Development, Ben-Gurion University of the Negev, Beer Sheva, Israel

ELSEVIER

ACADEMIC PRESS

An imprint of Elsevier

Academic Press is an imprint of Elsevier
50 Hampshire Street, 5th Floor, Cambridge, MA 02139, United States
525 B Street, Suite 1650, San Diego, CA 92101, United States
The Boulevard, Langford Lane, Kidlington, Oxford OX5 1GB, United Kingdom
125 London Wall, London, EC2Y 5AS, United Kingdom

First edition 2019

Notices
Knowledge and best practice in this field are constantly changing. As new research and experience broaden our understanding, changes in research methods, professional practices, or medical treatment may become necessary.

Practitioners and researchers must always rely on their own experience and knowledge in evaluating and using any information, methods, compounds, or experiments described herein. In using such information or methods they should be mindful of their own safety and the safety of others, including parties for whom they have a professional responsibility.

To the fullest extent of the law, neither the Publisher nor the authors, contributors, or editors, assume any liability for any injury and/or damage to persons or property as a matter of products liability, negligence or otherwise, or from any use or operation of any methods, products, instructions, or ideas contained in the material herein.

ISBN: 978-0-12-816213-2
ISSN: 2543-0009

For information on all Academic Press publications
visit our website at https://www.elsevier.com/books-and-journals

Publisher: Zoe Kruze
Acquisition Editor: Sam Mahfoudh
Editorial Project Manager: Shellie Bryant
Production Project Manager: James Selvam
Cover Designer: Alan Studholme

Typeset by SPi Global, India

Contents

Part III
Socio-technical and methodological evolutions

Contributors

Paulus Aditjandra
Newcastle University Business School, Newcastle upon Tyne, United Kingdom

Mike Bérénos
New Movements in Transport and Mobility NMTM, The Hague, The Netherlands

Hannah Budnitz
School of Geography, Earth & Environmental Sciences, University of Birmingham, Birmingham, United Kingdom

Yupo Chan
University of Arkansas at Little Rock, Little Rock, AR, United States

Lee Chapman
School of Geography, Earth & Environmental Sciences, University of Birmingham, Birmingham, United Kingdom

Giovanni Circella
School of Civil and Environmental Engineering, Georgia Institute of Technology, Atlanta, GA; Institute of Transportation Studies, University of California at Davis, Davis, CA, United States

Gonçalo Homem de Almeida Correia
Department of Transport and Planning, Delft University of Technology, Delft, The Netherlands; Department of Civil Engineering, University of Coimbra, Coimbra, Portugal

Rita Cyganski
German Aerospace Center, Institute of Transport Research, Berlin, Germany

Xianbiao Hu
Department of Civil, Architectural and Environmental Engineering, Missouri University of Science and Technology, Rolla, MO, United States

Viktoriya Kolarova
German Aerospace Center, Institute of Transport Research, Berlin, Germany

Yongsung Lee
School of Civil and Environmental Engineering, Georgia Institute of Technology, Atlanta, GA, United States

Barbara Lenz
German Aerospace Center, Institute of Transport Research; Geography Department, Humboldt-Universität zu Berlin, Berlin, Germany

Glenn Lyons
Mott MacDonald Professor of Future Mobility, Faculty of Environment and Technology, University of the West of England, Frenchay Campus, Bristol, United Kingdom

Qing Tang
Department of Civil, Architectural and Environmental Engineering, Missouri University of Science and Technology, Rolla, MO, United States

Emmanouil Tranos
School of Geography, Earth & Environmental Sciences, University of Birmingham, Birmingham, United Kingdom

Bart van Arem
Department of Transport and Planning, Delft University of Technology, Delft, The Netherlands

Peter van der Waerden
Urban Planning and Transportation Group, Eindhoven University of Technology, Eindhoven, The Netherlands

Yihong Wang
Department of Transport and Planning, Delft University of Technology, Delft, The Netherlands

Geert Wets
School for Transportation Sciences, Hasselt University, Hasselt, Belgium

Preface

Information and Communication Technologies (ICT) have been evolving for more than 5 decades at least. Hägerstrand (1970) in his seminal work "What about people in regional science?"—the forefather to Time Geography—was probably the first scholar to examine critically the impacts of telecommunications on the activity space and social and economic opportunities of human beings. Since then the question of how telecommunications shape activities and travel behavior has continued to provoke researchers and policy makers alike. Over time this question has become more complex as it has manifested that the interrelationships between ICT, activities, time use, and travel behavior have co-evolved while technology continues to develop together with the appearance of new forms of behavior. In this sense the complexity of the research question is tied to both ICT being a co-variate and a moving target, simultaneously (Ben-Elia and Zhen, 2018).

The simple linear relationships hypothesized by the so-called "substitution" school of thought—the idea that investments in telecommunications will replace the need to travel (as in telecommuting)—have been supplanted by the "complementarity" or generation school of thought, which suggests that technology opens up new opportunities to participate in activities and modifies the need to travel (Mokhtarian, 1990; Mokhtarian and Salomon, 1994; Mokhtarian and Tal, 2013). In parallel digital technology has been changing the quality of activity participation, namely while on the move, as identified in the important works on Travel Time Use that changed the way scholars and policy makers look at the value of travel time and infrastructural investments in travel time savings. From wasted time, travel, for some purpose (e.g., business) and travelers, has become valuable—a gift (Jain and Lyons, 2008). This revelation has had impacts on the valuation of investments in public transportation where travel time can be used both productively (i.e., work/business) and to improve the quality of life (socializing and entertainment) (Line et al., 2011; Varghese and Jana, 2018).

Perhaps the greatest change in the way research and policy have examined ICT is with the transition from sedentary devices (desktop PCs and landline telephones) to mobile devices (laptops and mobile phones) and in the last few years the merging of the computer and the telephone with the proliferation of the "smartphone" (Frith, 2018). This has changed the discourse on ICT and activity–travel behavior from a location-based to a person-based framework, introduced new participation concepts such as multitasking, and brought about increasing fragmentation of activity time space and blurring of the border between personal and professional life (Couclelis, 2009; Lenz and Nobis, 2007).

In parallel the information-based World Wide Web or Internet 1.0 has evolved to the information and communication-based Internet 2.0 that allowed social networks and social media to flourish with wide scale, even global, impacts on people's preferences, beliefs, behaviors, and habits (Tillema et al., 2010). This has also manifested in the ascendance of ICT-generated "Big Data" harvested from personal devices and accounts that people actively agree to share as part of corporate terms of service (Hasan et al., 2016). In addition a growing share of data is being generated passively not by people but by objects including phones and onboard devices like GPS transponders (Chen et al., 2016).

Data richness has contributed to the development of a new mobility paradigm known as MaaS (Mobility as a Service) where communication and information exchange are the key supporters of sustainable, smooth, and seamless transportation (Matyas and Kamargianni, 2018). Today we are in the midst of a third wave of technological change with the appearance of Internet 3.0—The Internet of Things (IoT)—that will also pave the way for the game-changing chimera of autonomous mobility where both the physical and digital dimensions are fused together creating one vast personalized mobility toolkit (Lyons, 2018; Shladover, 2018).

This is the third volume of the seminal series on "Advances in Transport Policy and Planning" and it points to the critical position in the field that ICT was chosen as the leading theme for this book. In it I have attempted to create a collage of 10 diverse and unique contributions to the ongoing discourse. The book is divided into three broad sections. Part I focuses on conceptual and theoretical evolutions, Part II on the evolution of Travel Time Use, and Part III on Methodological and sociotechnical evolutions. Each chapter is designed as an in-depth review of the literature with possible empirical underpinnings.

In Part I, van der Waerden et al. provide a refreshing discussion on the concept of communication. They contend that the motivation for mobility, be it physical or digital, is foremost a question of the need to maintain communication. They test this hypothesis in a preliminary case study. Aditjandra presents the MaaS (Mobility as a Service) concept and a discussion of the development of European research in this area. Budnitz et al. introduce the notion of weather in activity and travel behavior especially as a growing disruptive phenomenon. They continue the discussion on how ICT can contribute to create a more resilient transportation system. Wang et al., dwell on mobile phone usage patterns and in particular the possibility to use Internet browsing traces and duration in addition to standard Call Data Records (CDRs) logged by the Cellular provider to deduce activities and trip purposes. They demonstrate this approach on a small case study in the city of Shanghai. Finally, Lee and Circella present their research on millennials or "Generation Y" that grew up as adolescents in conjunction with the proliferation of digital technologies and how these impact their every day lives, activities and travel choices.

Part II focuses on the theme of Travel Time Use. Lyons presents an invigorating view of more than a decade of research on travel time use and the positive utility of travel time. He compares findings from various waves of studies in the United Kingdom and from there to postulate where the phenomenon is heading. Kolarova, Cyganski, and Lenz examine travel time use through the future lens of automated vehicles. They discuss how automation can change the way car travel will take place and how travel time may be perceived.

Part III examines more methodological advances. Tang and Hu discuss the literature on the use of incentives and information to change travel behavior. They examine what the role of ICT is in allowing sustainable behavior changes across various aspects of travel demand. Finally, Chan in a double contribution critically examines the important roles ICT have in supporting proactive travel management policies both from the supply and the demand side. In his first chapter, the discussion examines short-term predictable outcomes on supply and demand, whereas in his second chapter the door is opened to more speculative thoughts on how ICT and connected automated vehicles will reshape transportation in the farther future.

Before closing this introduction to the book I would like to pay special thanks to Prof. Bert van Wee, the Series Editor-in-Chief, for inviting me to edit this book—a wonderful personal opportunity for me to leave an ongoing legacy. My personal thanks go also to Sam Mahfoudh the Acquisition Editor and to Shellie Bryant the volume's Editorial Project Manager. Their dedication and constant attention to details helped me tremendously in accomplishing my role. Lastly, my personal gratitude to all the authors for providing these unique and diverse viewpoints and for cooperating in getting the production to the finish line in a timely and efficient manner.

Eran Ben-Elia
Department of Geography and Environmental Development,
Ben-Gurion University of the Negev, Beer Sheva, Israel
e-mail: benelia@bgu.ac.il

References

Ben-Elia, E., Zhen, F., 2018. ICT, activity space–time and mobility: new insights, new models, new methodologies. Transportation 45 (2), 267–272.

Chen, C., Ma, J., Susilo, Y., Liu, Y., Wang, M., 2016. The promises of big data and small data for travel behavior (aka human mobility) analysis. Transp. Res. C Emerg. Technol. 68, 285–299.

Couclelis, H., 2009. Rethinking time geography in the information age. Environ. Plan. A 41 (7), 1556.

Frith, J., 2018. Smartphones as Locative Media (Digital Media and Society), first ed. John Wiley & Sons.

Hägerstrand, T., 1970. What about people in regional science? Pap. Reg. Sci. 24 (1), 6–21.

Hasan, S., Ukkusuri, S.V., Zhan, X., 2016. Understanding social influence in activity-location choice and life-style patterns using geo-location data from social media. Front. ICT 3, 10.

Jain, J., Lyons, G., 2008. The gift of travel time. J. Transp. Geogr. 16 (2), 81–89.

Lenz, B., Nobis, C., 2007. The changing allocation of time activities in space and time by the use of ICT-fragmentation as a new concept and empirical results. Transp. Res. A 41 (2), 190–204.

Line, T., Jain, J., Lyons, G., 2011. The role of ICTs in everyday mobile lives. J. Transp. Geogr. 19 (6), 1490–1499.

Lyons, G., 2018. Getting smart about urban mobility—aligning the paradigms of smart and sustainable. Transp. Res. A Policy Pract. 115, 4–14. https://doi.org/10.1016/j.tra.2016.12.001.

Matyas, M., Kamargianni, M., 2018. The potential of mobility as a service bundles as a mobility management tool. Transportation, 1–18.

Mokhtarian, P.L., 1990. A typology of relationships between telecommunications and transportation. Transp. Res. Part A: Gen 24 (3), 231–242.

Mokhtarian, P.L., Salomon, I., 1994. Modeling the choice of telecommuting: setting the context. Environ. Plan. A 26 (5), 749–766.

Mokhtarian, P.L., Tal, G., 2013. Impacts of ICT on travel behavior: a tapestry of relationships. In: The SAGE Handbook of Transport Studies. vol. 14. SAGE, pp. 241–260.

Shladover, S.E., 2018. Connected and automated vehicle systems: introduction and overview. J. Intell. Transp. Syst. 22 (3), 190–200.

Tillema, T., Dijst, M., Schwanen, T., 2010. Face-to-face and electronic communications in maintaining social networks: the influence of geographical and relational distance and of information content. New Media Soc. 12 (6), 965–983.

Varghese, V., Jana, A., 2018. Impact of ICT on multitasking during travel and the value of travel time savings: empirical evidences from Mumbai, India. Travel Behav. Soc. 12, 11–22.

PART I

Theoretical and conceptual evolutions

CHAPTER ONE

Communication and its relationship with digital and physical mobility patterns—A review

Peter van der Waerden[a,*], Mike Bérénos[b], Geert Wets[c]
[a]Urban Planning and Transportation Group, Eindhoven University of Technology, Eindhoven, The Netherlands
[b]New Movements in Transport and Mobility NMTM, The Hague, The Netherlands
[c]School for Transportation Sciences, Hasselt University, Hasselt, Belgium
*Corresponding author: e-mail address: p.j.h.j.v.d.waerden@tue.nl

Contents

Abstract

With a new look on the phenomenon of mobility this chapter aims to contribute to the formulation of theories about people, society, and mobility. In this case, as traditionally used, the physical traffic and transportation system is not the starting point. It assumes

Advances in Transport Policy and Planning, Volume 3
ISSN 2543-0009
https://doi.org/10.1016/bs.atpp.2019.05.001

that not just physical infrastructures and modalities are involved. In order to understand mobility—and that includes also transport of goods—the starting point must be the so-called communicative system. "Man is a communicative being; he is not made to be alone" (Aristoteles, 400 years before Christ). Yes indeed, people need contacts and meetings to communicate with each other. A society without communication is unthinkable. This communication now evokes physical mobility, but also, what we call digital or virtual mobility. You do not have to go on the road or even travel at the desired moment to communicate with each other.

The communicative system is therefore the starting point for thinking about transportation and mobility. From this starting point, we provide a conceptual framework for understanding the phenomenon of mobility better. From there, the question arises how to quantify and test hypothesis. Our intention is to trace endogenous relationships—so within the communicative system—between the physical and digital mobility and to find out if there exists an interchange between these two subsystems, in search of planning instruments to diminish the number of undesirable physical mobility. We conducted a small, preliminary and indicative research on this, a first struggling, and highlight a veil on this.

Keywords: Communication, Physical, Digital, Mobility, Patterns

1. Introduction

In trying to fundamentally understand transportation and mobility, it could be better to take care of a sustainable and more vital mobile society. In trying to understand transportation and mobility, planners were only interested in physical traffic and mobility patterns and flows. Since a few decades transportation planners are also interested in the relationship between physical mobility and what is called telecommunication. It is well known that up till now there exists a fragmented landscape of this relationship. Various studies in this field were mainly focused on the interaction between the two communication systems (the physical traffic and transportation system and the digital communication system), and what effects telecommunication has on physical mobility. Four impacts are usually mentioned in this respect: substitution, neutrality, modification and complementarity (e.g., Mokhtarian, 1990).

When looking broader at mobility, it can be argued that the origin of mobility has its roots in the fact that people do not want to live isolated. People are continuously searching for contacts, want to meet other people, and therefore, want to communicate with one another in a certain way. For this, they want or need to move from A to B in a physical or digital way. In his book "On the Move," Cresswell (2006) identifies this move as a meaningful movement to achieve "a durable way of being." Communication with societal purposes is a basic need for people and society and causes physical and/or digital—also called virtual—mobility. Physical mobility refers to communication for which people travel from the spatially separated origin A to destination B to meet each other physically. Various attributes are connected to this physical mobility such as travel mode and travel distance. In the case of digital mobility, the meeting takes place through Information and Communication Technology (ICT) without a physical movement. ICT is a broad architecture comprised of software and hardware allowing computers and devices to facilitate communication of people and exchange information via the Internet. To this type of communication several attributes are connected as well, such as mode of digital communication, distances and personal communication network. The two types of mobility include a variety of similar attributes (frequency, location, duration, etc.). Both types are interesting on their own but also the relation and cohesion between the two types of mobility is of importance. Digital communication can replace or augment certain physical movements, while physical movements can be the results of digital communication.

For decades, studies have been conducted on the influence of telecommunication on physical mobility. In these studies, physical mobility is defined as traveling from an origin A to a destination B. In the hope that telecommunication can also help to solve the problems that physical mobility evokes such as congestion and pollution. The image that these studies produce is not fully clear. There are many contradictory outcomes, fragmented and ad hoc approaches and there is little consistency between the study outcomes. This is due to the complexity, bi-directional influences, moving targets and probably also due to the sometimes insufficient background of theories and concepts about travel and mobility in respect to this.

All together many unknowns still lurk about the relationship between physical-digital mobility. The knowledge gained is often ad hoc and not very consistent. Also interesting details like the exact location of the person one is calling are often missing. In this chapter we try to answer the following two research questions "*How does the communication between people looks like in terms of physical and digital mobility?*" and "*How can we measure these so called communication patterns?*" The *aim* of this paper is to develop a theoretical framework around communication and thus physical and digital mobility patterns. It is our intention to give a starting conceptual framework and basic handles on how to measure communication patterns.

The remainder of this chapter continues with Section 2 where a literature review is presented. The section is divided into studying the important review papers before 2010 and after 2010 on this theme. In the section attention is paid to some formalized ideas concerning the relationship between telecommunication and transportation, data collection methods including investigated dependent and independent variables, findings from previous studies, and interesting future research topics suggested in these previous studies. After this we give in Section 3 our view on mankind, society and mobility. This must be seen as a starting point for understanding transportation and mobility. In Section 4 we explain some findings of a first, explorative, and indicative study on communication patterns. Finally, in Section 5 we give an overview of our findings, the benefits of the new approach and posit a proposal for a research agenda.

2. Literature review

2.1 Introduction

In their foreword, Pawlak et al. (2015) stated that "since the 1980s, transportation professionals have been tackling the issue of how information and communication technology (ICT) affects physical mobility." This attention resulted into a series of research reports and policy documents. During these 30 years of interest, several reviews are published presenting the state of art at a specific moment in time (Aguiléra et al., 2012; Andreev et al., 2010; Ben-Elia et al., 2018; Mokhtarian, 1990, 2003; Pawlak et al., 2015). This section gives a brief overview of the findings of some former reviews and adds the latest insights regarding the relationship between ICT and physical mobility. The section starts with a basic taxonomy of the relationship between ICT and physical mobility presented by Mokhtarian (1990) and extended by Pawlak et al. (2015). Next, various specifications of telecommunication and transportation as dependent variable and some findings regarding the relationship will be presented. The section ends with suggested research topics from the literature.

2.2 Taxonomy

After investigating many linkages identified in the literature, Mokhtarian (1990) defined a "robust" conceptual framework for the relationship between telecommunication and transportation. Fig. 1 shows a simplified view of this framework. The framework consisted of four basic components:

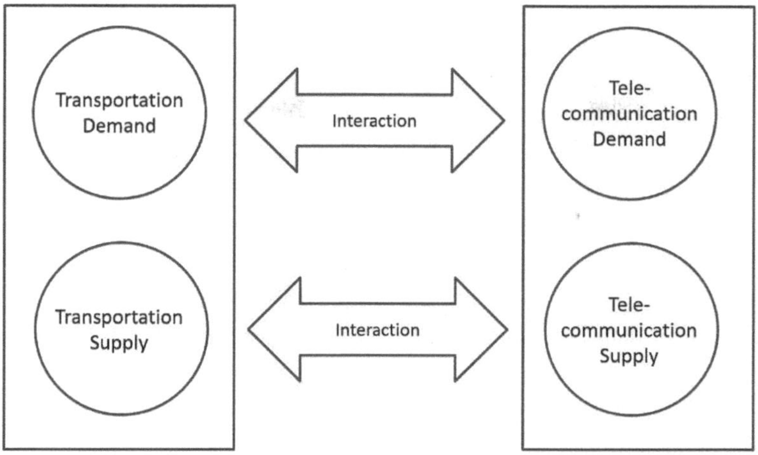

Fig. 1 Simplified view of the relationship between telecommunication and transportation.

transportation demand, telecommunications demand, transportation supply, and telecommunications supply. Between the components several relations exist. The vertical boxes represent traditional relationships for a single topic (transportation or communication based). The horizontal arrows focus on cross-category relationships. The arrow at the top of Fig. 1 describes the substitution (replace one by another) and complementarity (add one to another) effect. Mokhtarian also indicated that stimulation effect can arise in several ways: short-term direct (accessible information can stimulate people to travel or participate in an activity), short-term indirect (time saved for one trip can be used for another trip) and long-term (changes in land use patterns).

In 2003, Mokhtarian formalized several findings in literature in a taxonomy regarding the ICT-physical mobility interactions. She identified the following cross-mode relationships: Substitution (replacing one means of communication for another means of communication); Complementarity (increase use of alternative mode of communication); Modification (one communication mode modifies something about the use of another mode) and Neutrality (use of one mode leaves other mode unaffected). In Mokhtarian and Tal (2013) a revised version of the taxonomy is presented including replacement of traditional activity (substitution), displacement of new ICT activity (substitution), multitasking (neutrality), reallocation of resources to other activities (substitution), and using ICT as facilitator of activities (modification). More recently, Pawlak et al. (2015) introduces a subdivision of lower and higher order relationships. They connect the cross-mode relationships identified by Mokhtarian (1990) to the lower level indication of the short term (or direct) impacts; substitution, modification, complementarity, and neutrality. The higher level relationships focus on the indirect influence of ICT on other aspects of life that are connected to travel. After some time these influences might trigger modifications of travel behavior patterns due to changes in for example residential location, smart infrastructure, and accepted social and professional norms. Recently, Ben-Elia et al. (2018) discusses the complexity of the relationship between ICT and travel behavior. In their epilogue they emphasizes two different alternatives for causality: a two-way causality in two directions and a unidirectional causality with the existence of an unobserved confounding factor. They conclude that it is inadequate to understand the relationship with "single-equation models."

The discussion regarding ICT and physical mobility covers many activities. Mokhtarian (1990) identified eight groups of tele-activities mainly based on studies that focus on the substitutionary potential of telecommunication: telecommuting, teleconferencing, teleshopping, telebanking, tele-entertainment, tele-education, tele-medicine and tele-justice. In their study, Andreev et al. (2010) focused more on the individual motivations or purpose to engage in an activity. They came up with three groups of activities: mandatory activities (like work), maintenance activities (like shopping) and discretionary activities (like sporting and leisure). To each group of activity different tele-activities are connected: mandatory (telecommuting and teleconferencing), maintenance (teleshopping and teleservice) and discretionary (tele-leisure).

2.3 Data collection and analyses

In the past various data collection approaches are elaborated. Most often used data collection approach is an online or pencil and paper based household survey (Calastri et al., 2017; Carrasco, 2011; Delbosc and Mokhtarian, 2018; Hong et al., 2019; Jamal and Habib, 2017; Kroesen and Handy, 2015; Nobis and Lenz, 2009). Often, this approach is used for cross-sectional data collection. More extensive (longitudinal) data collection approaches use travel and/or activity diaries covering one or more days of the week to investigate the relationship between ICT and travel behavior (Andreev et al., 2010; Kenyon, 2010; Le Vine et al., 2014, 2016; Sasaki and Nishii, 2010; Van den Berg et al., 2012, 2013). The generated datasets commonly include different aspects of an individual's travel behavior, use of telecommunication means, activity participation, and personal characteristics. With this information various relationships are investigated in more detail. Beside several other aspects, the following relationships are investigated:

- Correlation between mobile phone use and travel frequency (Jamal and Habib, 2017; Nobis and Lenz, 2009);
- Internet use and activity participation (Kenyon, 2010; Suel et al., 2018);
- The number of telecommunications in terms of sent/received call and mails and the number of trips (Sasaki and Nishii, 2010);
- ICT availability and use related to frequency of face-to-face interaction (Carrasco, 2011);
- The contact frequency and communication modes (Van den Berg et al., 2012);
- The use of ICT and social travel distance (Hong et al., 2019; Van den Berg et al., 2013);
- The amount of time spent on online activities and car mileage (Le Vine et al., 2014);
- The use of internet and social network sites and meeting with friends/attending concerts (Kroesen and Handy, 2015);
- The amount of time spend on online activities and time spend at out-of-home activities (Le Vine et al., 2016);
- Personal characteristics and the use of different means of communication (Calastri et al., 2017);
- The frequency of digital interaction (using phone, email, texting and social media) and the monthly frequency of out-of-home interactions (Delbosc and Mokhtarian, 2018);
- The influence of ICT on activity fragmentation (Ben-Elia et al., 2014; Hubers et al., 2008).

A totally different approach to investigate the relationship between ICT and physical mobility is followed by Bris et al. (2017) who composed a dataset based on various national datasets including households' transport expenditures and various control variables. They investigated the relationship between ICT access at home and households' transport expenditure.

A varied set of control (or independent) variables are included in the investigation of the relationships mentioned above. Most common control variables are an individual's age, gender, income, educational level, employment status, profession, civil status, and availability of driving license and car. More specific control variables are availability of internet and smartphone, social network size and composition, household composition, living environment (Carrasco, 2011; Delbosc and Mokhtarian, 2018; Jamal and Habib, 2017; Kroesen and Handy, 2015; Le Vine et al., 2014, 2016; Van den Berg et al., 2013). Other control related variables are associated with an individual's activity pattern: day of the week, use of internet, time spent at home, activity participation, and use of social network sites (Andreev et al., 2010; Carrasco, 2011; Kenyon, 2010; Kroesen and Handy, 2015; Le Vine et al., 2014). Regarding to the extent of the use of internet, Le Vine et al. (2014) defined five types of internet users based on the average number of internet activity classes users are involved in: none, narrow, moderate, broad without leisure, and broad with leisure internet users. Besides characteristics of individuals (egos), Carrasco (2011), van den Berg et al. (2012) and Calastri et al. (2017) also included characteristics of alters such as type of relationship between ego and alter (family, neighbor, and friend), distance between ego and alter (in terms of living in neighborhood, city, region), duration of relationship between ego and alter, and communication topic (ask for help, discuss problems, and both). Delbosc and Mokhtarian (2018) also included in their research personality; introversion and extraversion. Finally, Hong et al. (2019) focused on individuals' level of numeracy and financial literacy (math related literacy).

As mentioned before, Bris et al. (2017) used a different data collection approach as the studies presented above. They included several control variables that cover similar topics as the previous studies internet access, income per household, household size, urbanization, population density, rate of unemployment, and car ownership level. In addition they looked at more general variables such as consumption expenditure, transportation network density, retail diesel price, and cost of fixed-broadband sub-basket.

2.4 Findings from previous studies

The findings regarding the relationship between ICT and physical mobility show a diverse picture. The review papers indicated that the relationship is sometimes unclear (Aguiléra et al., 2012; Andreev et al., 2010; Mokhtarian, 1990, 2003; Pawlak et al., 2015). Based on various empirical studies, Mokhtarian (1990, 2003) concluded that "the most important impact of telecommunications may not be that it increases or decreases the amount of travel that takes place, but that it permits a great deal of flexibility in whether, when, where and how to travel." She also noticed a lack of empirical evidence to confirm the causality between ICT and physical mobility. She stated that most studies focus on a single application and often found substitution effects. According to Mokhtarian (2003), these studies are incomplete and likely to miss the more subtle, indirect, and long-term effects. Based on an extensive literature review (about 100 studies), Andreev et al. (2010) concluded that substitution is mostly prevailed in the context of telecommuting, while complementarity is most often noticed for teleshopping and tele-leisure. Aguiléra et al. (2012) concluded that the relationship between travel demand and ICT is still unclear; sometimes saved trips generate other trips. The "powerful determinants" of travel demand mostly are not affected by the rise of ICT. They expect that there might be changes in trip frequency, trip purpose, travel mode, and used route, but the trips themselves stay the same. They also state that the link between ICT and trips has to be considered in combination with organizational, economic and societal context. In more general terms, Pawlak et al. (2015) stated that empirical results frequently contradict one another and that many results are descriptive with little formal theory. Still, they noticed some consistency in research findings: the need for physical participation in activities will remain; the role of ICT in mode choices is secondary, but decrease time use when traveling; and the interaction of ICT and physical mobility seems to differ between demographic groups and countries.

The other studies included in this literature review are more focused on one specific topic (see before). Also in these studies the findings are diverse. Some studies did not find a clear relationship between ICT and physical mobility. Kenyon (2010) concluded that there is no evidence of a link between physical mobility and virtual mobility. In contrast, Suel et al. (2018) found that "having shopped online since the last shopping trip significantly reduces the probability of undertaking a physical shopping trip." This finding suggests the presence of substitution effect. In addition, Carrasco (2011) found that more frequent ICT interaction is more related to socializing interaction than to face-to-face interaction. Kroesen and Handy (2015) concluded that the trend in digitization of society does not play a major role in the downward trend in car mobility. Finally, Calastri et al. (2017) stated that a strong underlying preference for face-to-face contact remains.

There are also several studies that found some evidence of a relationship between ICT and physical mobility. Nobis and Lenz (2009) found that individuals with an increase of mobile phone use show a decrease of travel frequency. Sasaki and Nishii (2010) noticed a negative relation between the number of telecommunications and the average time of trips over 1 day. Van den Berg et al. (2012) concluded that a complementary relationship exists between contact frequencies and different communication modes. The study of Le Vine et al. (2014) showed that spending a large amount of time on online activities is associated with less car driving mileage. Later, Le Vine et al. (2016) found that internet usage correlates positively with both time spent traveling and time spent at out-of-home activities. The study of Bris et al. (2017) showed that transport expenditure is negatively associated with internet expenditure. Most recent findings come from Delbosc and Mokhtarian (2018) who concluded that more frequent virtual interaction was associated with more frequent face-to-face interaction (or at least not less) and from Hong et al. (2019) who found that math related literacy is directly associated with internet use and total travel distance.

2.5 Research agenda retrieved from literature

In the review papers a variety of research needs are suggested to be included in future studies regarding the interaction between ICT and physical mobility. Mokhtarian (2003) identified several research needs such as focusing on the wide range of tele-related activities (see before), quantifying communications, and collecting data from individuals on their communications activities by various modes.

Aguiléra et al. (2012) identified four major limits when linking ICT use to the number of trips. The first limit concerns the difficulty to take into account possible cross effects (generation for some trips and substitution for others). The second limit includes the difficulty to separate long-term effects from short term effects where different measurement scales (individual and household) might be relevant. The third limit deals with the fact that relationship between travel demand and ICT is a two-way relationship (chicken-egg problem?). The fact that changes in travel behavior may depend on many parameters in addition to ICT is acknowledge as fourth limit. All these limitations make that the link between ICT and physical mobility is very a complicated one also because the link has to be considered as a "moving target" because technology and social practices related to it change over time (Ben-Elia et al., 2018). Consequently, Aguiléra et al. (2012) advice to consider the relationship from various aspects of an individual's daily live with an emphasis on the effect on temporal and spatial organization of everyday activities. They suggest the following research directions.

- Focus on nature of travel demand (including the spatial-temporal organization of trips) instead of number of trips;
- Focus on relationship between mobile ICT usage and the perception of travel and spaces;

- Focus on the way travel demand influences the use of mobile ICT and the need for new services;
- Focus on the use of many types of mobile ICTs by individuals;
- Focus on data collection methods: adapting existing travel survey to capture data regarding the above topics.

Pawlak et al. (2015) suggest looking in more detail to the higher-level relationships (indirect impacts), to new methodologies to analyze and collect data, to empirically establish the nature of the relationship based on disaggregate analyses, and to private sector decisions in combination with policy measures. They also suggest quantification of ICT use in terms of frequency of access or total time spent on it.

Also the more specialized studies discussed in this section, came up with several recommendations for future research. The most relevant suggestions are presented below. Some authors suggest using longitudinal (panel) data more to discover the impact of virtual mobility on activity participation and personal travel (Bris et al., 2017; Kenyon, 2010; Van den Berg et al., 2013). Kenyon (2010) recognizes the following benefits of the use of longitudinal panel based research versus cross-sectional based research: overcome problems with retrospective recall and likeliness of uncover strength and form of relationships between variables over time. Also more attention is asked for the capturing of information regarding online activities (Le Vine et al., 2016) and for a more adequate indicator of communication contents considering the differences in communications tools (Sasaki and Nishii, 2010; Van den Berg et al., 2013). Ettema (2018) emphasize the great variety of ICT devices and tools, and suggests to focus on individual Apps as more or less independent agents. Some authors propose to extent the research to various racial or immigration based social contexts (Carrasco, 2011), to include cross-national comparisons (Le Vine et al., 2014) or to distinguish between different social structure (Ettema, 2018). Finally, based on their experiences regarding the international symposium on "ICT, Activity, Time Use and Travel," Ben-Elia et al. (2018) indicate that it is very important to collaborate in multidisciplinary research designs that allow both qualitative and quantitative research questions to be addressed.

3. The communicative system

3.1 Introduction

When we talk about transportation and mobility, much emphasis has so far been placed on physical mobility that is moving geographically from a certain origin to a certain destination. That has everything to do with the history of mobility and the corresponding discipline of transportation. This discipline has its roots in the road management field. Road authorities are responsible for managing the physical infrastructure (roads). In addition to maintenance/management, the use of the infrastructure is also in their interest. So, the use arises when traffic is on its way from origin A to destination B. In the beginning, when the primacy lies with the engineers, they mainly focused on the use of infrastructure by motorized traffic. The flow and safety of traffic played an important role similar to the accessibility of destinations. Mobility is then seen as the fact that people move from an origin to a destination and that people make agreements about moving goods from an origin to a destination.

3.2 A new approach

The primacy of mobility still lies with the transportation agencies and the road authorities. You can discuss whether this is correct. Indeed, if we look at mobility from the need of people to contact, meet and communicate with each other with social goals, the basis of mobility could look very different. This communication need of people leads to mobility whenever there is a spatial geographical distance to bridge. The need for communication can be seen as the origin of mobility. So far there is no physical infrastructure at issue yet. This need to communicate—*Communication Need*—evokes as said before mobility and transport. However, in the mobility of people, this mobility does not always have to involve physical mobility. There is also something like "digital mobility" when people want to communicate with each other. You do not have to go on the road or even travel at the desired moment when you want to communicate with someone else. Digital mobility takes place via digital networks and with the help of for example apps, devices and interfaces; precisely, with the help of ICT.

The basis of transportation and mobility is therefore not the physical traffic and transportation system, but what we could call the *Communicative System* (Fig. 2). This communicative system includes two important, inseparably connected subsystems, namely, the physical traffic and transportation system and the digital communication system. These two subsystems are therefore not separate systems, but part of one and the same communicative system. Hence, it is an inseparably connectivity. So, there has to be a profession with the communicative system as an object of study. This profession stands for the task of facilitating communication—with social goals—when the spatial component is at issue. Of course, the profession has to take

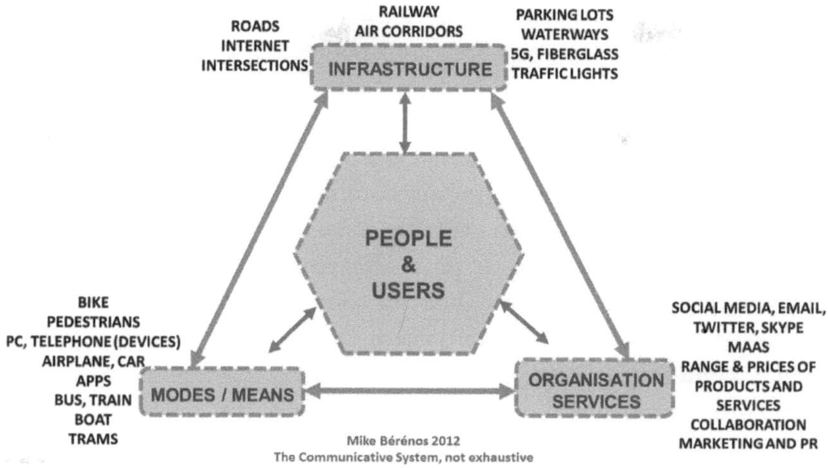

Fig. 2 The communicative system—physical and digital.

Table 1 Comparing the two subsystems (not exhaustive).

Components	Traffic and transportation system	Digital communication system
Infrastructure	Roads, junctions, traffic lights, waterways, air-corridors, etc.	Internet, Fiberglass, 5G, etc.
Modes/means	Bicycle, car, walk, boat, plane, etc.	Mobile phone, computer, interfaces, etc.
Organization	Mobility as a Service, Uber, etc.	Social media, Twitter, Skype, Mobility as a Service etc.

into account the negative aspects of physical mobility like unsafety, uncertain travel times and air pollution. So the base of this profession is not alone managing the physical traffic and transportation system, but facilitating the communication need of people. This look at communication continues on the idea of Couclelis (2009) who introduced virtual communication in time geography where the three-dimensional space has to be replaced by a multidimensional space.

If we subdivide the communicative system into three components, namely (1) infrastructure, (2) means and modes, and (3) organization of supply and demand, with people and users at the center, then we see that the two subsystems—the physical traffic and transportation system and the digital communication system—have the same structure (Fig. 2 and Table 1). In both subsystems there is infrastructure, means/modes, and organization of supply and demand. For example, infrastructure within the physical traffic and transportation system includes among other things bicycle roads, and within the digital communication system for example 5G network (Table 1). For some new developments like Mobility as a Service (MaaS), it is clear that it currently is considered as a physical variant of communication. Given the fact that the base of our communicative system is a physical or digital movement, MaaS also could be considered in the digital communication system, for instance in providing telephone possibilities, social media options, twitter and so on. This is a completely new look at mobility that now is based on communication needs, communicative system with the two subsystems physical traffic and transportation system and digital communication system, and communication patterns for both subsystems, looking for a *System Shift* based on insight in these communication patterns. More details of this system shift between physical and digital mobility are presented in Section 5.

The explanatory variables involved are also the same for the two subsystems. There are always variables like origins, destinations, frequency, modes, motives, time, costs, and route. So, in both subsystems there are so-called "travel" patterns. We should call this *Communication or Mobility Patterns*, because travel mainly refers on physical mobility. The communicative system therefore shows communication patterns, which can be split up into physical communication patterns (which we traditionally call travel) and digital communication patterns with the help of ICT tools such as apps, devices, interfaces, and social media. Viewed from the perspective of the societal communication need of people, it is obvious, and also possible and perfect that traffic and transportation professionals and ICT professionals together have the communicative system as object of study (Fig. 2). In addition to the traditional ways of investigating mobility, it is desirable to investigate the use ICT tools to do research on communication patterns and to search for the interchangeability of physical and digital mobility. With the mobile phone, for example, these patterns have actually already been recorded for physical mobility patterns. The ownership and accessibility of these data is different question.

Our suggested conceptual framework is presented in Section 5. Origin and destination studies in both physical and digital mobility are the main parts of the communication patterns. Research into the interchangeability between both types of mobility based on these communication patterns is still in its infancy. In the next section a start has been made to get insight in as we see the relationship between physical end digital mobility.

4. First empirical insights

4.1 Introduction

The aim of the empirical study is to provide some first insights into the composition of both physical and digital communication of individuals (Shaker, 2017). Because the conceptual framework we present in this section was not yet fully developed the study had more or less an exploratory character. So for the time being, the analyses focus on a description of the communication patterns and a few other things that has to do with these patterns. Based on a literature review a limited list of variables were included in the empirical study. The variables include frequency of communication, means of physical respectively digital communication, distance between the respondents and their social network (family, friend, and colleagues) and type of social media. In addition, some propositions are including covering issues as time and money issues. Finally, some personal characteristics were collected like age, gender, level of education, and country of origin. Special attention is paid to the role of digital communication means (in this study mobile phone, smartphone, laptop, and desktop) and social network (Facebook/Twitter, Skype, WhatsApp, and email).

To obtain more insight into individuals' communication patterns an online questionnaire was designed. The questionnaire focused on three types of information: (i) general information regarding the respondents' communication; (ii) information regarding a respondents' physical and digital communication patterns; and (iii) information regarding respondents' personal characteristics. Questions regarding the respondents' communication patterns are subdivided into three groups: communication with family members, communication with friends, and communication with colleagues. For each distinguished group a set of questions was included in the questionnaire to describe both the physical and digital communication pattern. The online questionnaire was distributed among students and staff members of Hasselt University, Belgium, and various social networks. In total, 405 respondents completed the questionnaire. Based on the personal characteristics, it could be concluded that the sample is not really representative but that the sample consists of a variety of respondents.

4.2 Some first results

Before coming to some details regarding the respondents' communication pattern a brief description of the sample will be provided. In general, it seems that almost all respondents own a smartphone (96.3%) and more than two-third (69.6%) of the respondents has access to internet with their smartphone. In addition, some personal characteristics of the sample are given in Table 2. It appears that distribution across gender and educational level follows general expectations. In contrast, the respondents are relatively young and mainly from Belgium.

Because of the availability of data from the empirical study, we focus on the so-called Mobility Balance when presenting some preliminary results (Fig. 3). The mobility balance represents the communication patterns of individuals by a ratio of the numbers of digital and physical trips. In total, 1135 communication patterns are used to produce the results shown below.

The mobility balance includes five classes. The first class includes communication patterns only covering digital trips. In the second class, the number of digital trips is higher than the number of physical trips. The third class consists of communication patterns where the numbers of digital and physical trips are equal. The fourth class consists of patterns where the number of digital trips is less than the number of physical trips. Finally, the fifth class includes communication patterns with only physical trips. Fig. 4 shows the distribution of the 1135 communication patterns across the five classes.

Table 2 Characteristics of the sample.

Characteristics	Levels	Frequencies	Percentages
Gender	Male	218	53.8
	Female	187	46.2
Age	26 years or younger	263	64.9
	27 years or older	142	35.1
Educational level	Undergraduate/graduate	185	45.7
	Masters	165	40.7
	Doctorate/post-doctorate	55	13.6
Country of origin	Belgium	214	52.8
	Pakistan	81	20.0
	Other western countries	56	13.8
	Other non-western countries	54	13.4
Total		405	100.0

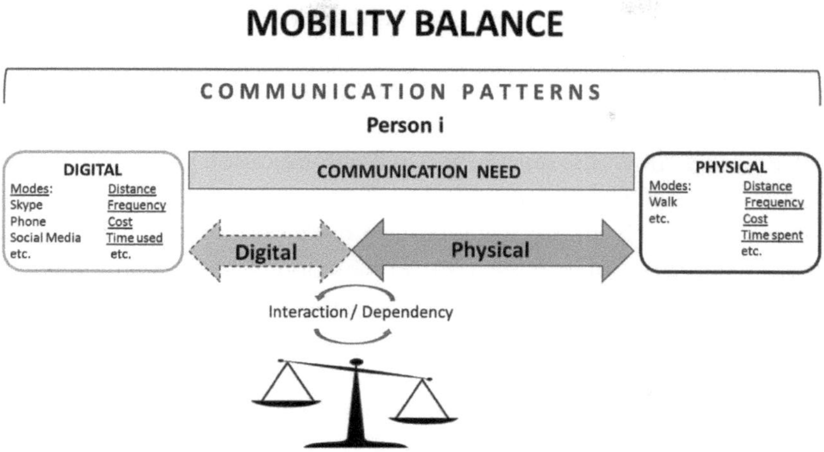

Fig. 3 The mobility balance as representative of communication patterns.

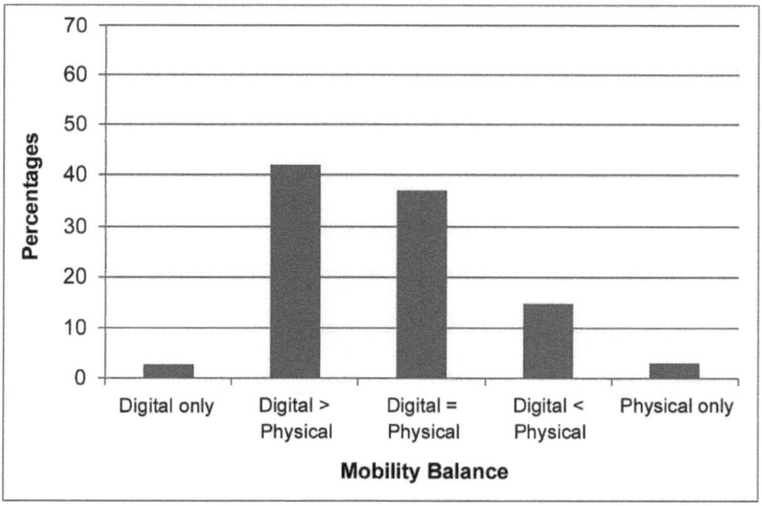

Fig. 4 Mobility balance based on 1135 communication patterns.

It appears that more than 40% of the communication patterns include more digital trips than physical trips. The amount of communication patterns where the number of digital and physical trips is equal is approximately 35%. The class where the number of digital trips is smaller than the number of physical trips covers about 15%. The two remaining classes with only digital trips and only physical trips cover only a limited number of communication patterns.

In addition to a general view of communication patterns, some specific views are generated. From the literature review it came out that distance between individuals and their contacts, and type of relation (e.g., family, friends, and colleagues) are interesting topics in the context of communication patterns. Fig. 5 shows the distribution of communication patterns across different classes. The figure shows for two distance classes, the percentages of the various classes. It appears that for longer distances (more than 20 km), the amount of digital mobility is greater than the amount of physical mobility. In the case of shorter distances (20 km and less), the share of physical mobility is equal to or greater than the digital mobility.

In addition Fig. 6 shows that the communication patterns of respondents with Family and friends more or less follow the same pattern; a high share of the classes with more digital than physical trips. In contrast, the communication with colleagues shows a different picture; the amount of physical mobility is equal to or greater than the amount of digital mobility.

With the results shown above, it is possible to identify the distribution between physical and digital mobility of certain groups or even individuals. This information gives insights into what different target groups have to be considered when trying to move physical trips toward digital trip. Of course, the highest profit can be achieved in the case of the classes "Digital < Physical" and "Physical only."

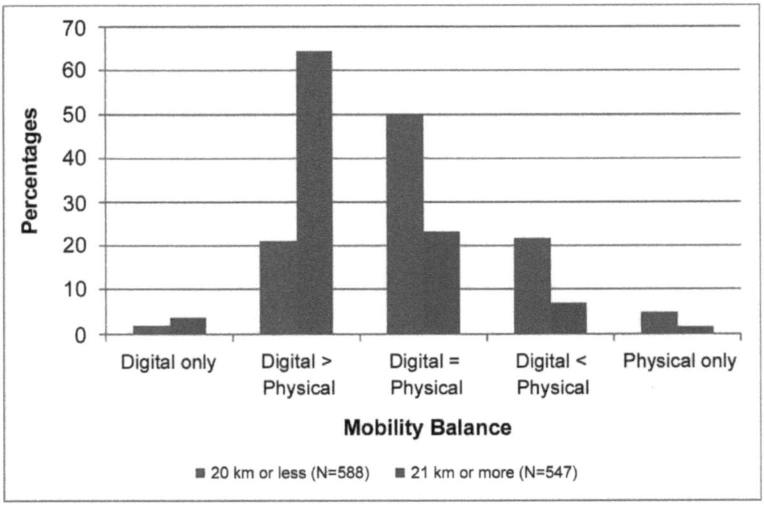

Fig. 5 Overview mobility balance and distances.

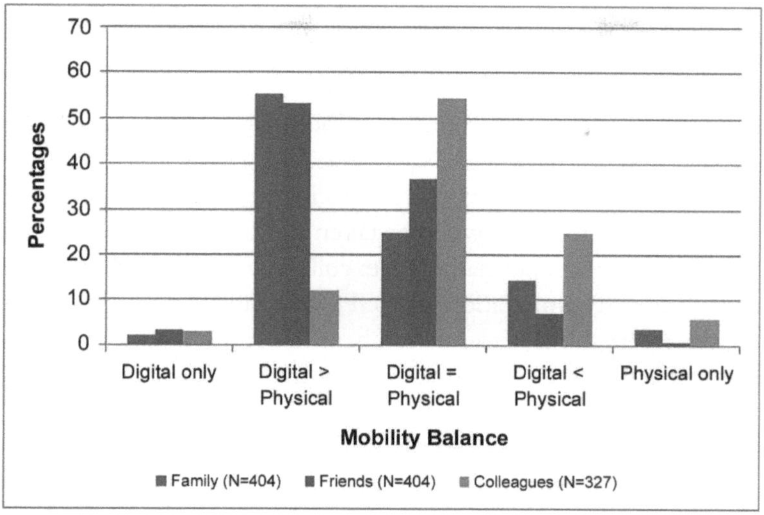

Fig. 6 Overview mobility balance and social network relation.

5. Conclusions, recommendations and research agenda

This section deals with conclusions arising from the literature review. Furthermore, it shows our new look at mobility (10 pillars), and thus what is really new in our opinion. In addition to this new look, a conceptual framework is introduced. Finally, we present some recommendations for a future research agenda.

5.1 Conclusions literature review

In the past decades, much has been done to better understand the influence of telecommunications on physical mobility. This period is characterized by many ad hoc studies. All together these studies were very fragmented, illuminating pieces of the veil, but hardly based on a theoretical framework or concepts. The studies resulted into fragmented and often contradictory insights that are highly depending on the lack of a well sound theory about physical and digital mobility. In recent years, some theoretical frameworks have been prompted, including Mokhtarian (1990), in the "Conceptual framework of the relationship between telecommunication and transportation."

Whereas in the past there was a focus on the four cross mode relationships of telecommunications on physical mobility, Mokhtarian (1990) already indicated that "the most important impact of telecommunications may not be that it increases or decreases the amount of travel that takes place, but that it permits a great deal more flexibility in whether, when, where and how to travel." So, a plea therefore is to look at things in a much broader context.

It is proclaimed that, as with travel, also in the world of digital mobility the spatial-temporal aspects have to be taken into account. This broadening requires quite a bit more specialized data collection for example using smart phone usage data in combination with GPS data. In addition, the difficulties and limits put forth in the literature still have to cope with. These are among others the cross-modes effects, long-term and short-term aspects, the higher order relationships between physical and digital mobility, and the two-way relationship physical and digital mobility.

5.2 A new look at mobility

We can summarize our new look at mobility and show how we dive into the subject with the following 10 pillars.

1. The start is the communication need of people as a basic need for a dynamic and livable society.
2. The need for communication leads to mobility, physical, and/or digital. So the origin of mobility is the communication need.
3. The communication need depends on individuals' social network.
4. Communication also evokes freight transport which is a different issue but has to be considered as well.
5. There is one basic communicative system that is divided into two inseparable and interconnected subsystems: the traffic and transportation system and the digital communication system.
6. It is important to first investigate the system shift: the choice of individuals for the traffic and transportation system versus the digital communication system.
7. Insight in individuals' physical and digital communication patterns is needed to understand the individuals' system shift and mobility balance.
8. We hypothesize that there is an interchange between the two subsystems within the communicative system.
9. If the hypothesis stands, it should be possible to substitute certain physical mobility into digital mobility. This means less traffic but not less communication.

10. The individual communication patterns depend on the social networks and the possibilities of communication influence the social network.

The 10 pillars come together in our conceptual framework that is presented in Fig. 7.

The upper part of Fig. 7 is about people, society and mobility, and indicates how one should get out of the starting blocks. The mid part is about supply and demand, where physical and digital mobility have to be seen as one communicative system. In the lower part, insight is given in the search of several relationships and most interesting, especially from a policy point of view, the shift to be explained between the two subsystems. This lower part needs, and when necessary also the other parts of Fig. 7, a further deepening toward a conceptual framework on its own and so looking for hypotheses around the system shift, based on the idea of communication patterns. So, if there are means, services and products, especially in the digital communication system, to influence the mobility balance of people, this is politically highly interesting and has some value in regulating physical mobility in a desired direction. Involving ICT and its impact on communication patterns, i.e., the mobility balances can result into social desired physical mobility patterns (column part right). Ultimately, the presented conceptual framework is not what the relationship between telecommunication and physical mobility is, but how we can find instruments in de digital communication system to influence the physical mobility in a desired, sustainable, vital and mobile society.

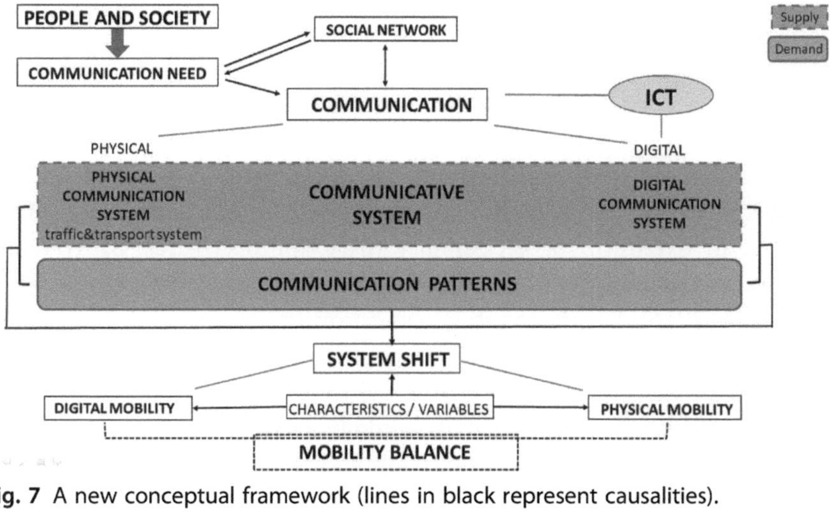

Fig. 7 A new conceptual framework (lines in black represent causalities).

The new approach continues on the activity based approach (e.g., McNally and Rindt, 2007) as it explains the reasons why people participate in certain activities. The approach not only focuses on physical trips as in most activity based applications but also details digital trips. We are aware of the fact that some activities are not initiated by a need for communication such as delivering packages and walking the dog. These trips, which do not fit in the suggested approach, cover a very small part of the large number of activities and trips people make. In addition, the exchangeability of this latter group of physical trips into digital trips (system shift) is much more relevant for policy makers.

5.3 Research agenda—A start

Looking at mobility in the way we suggested, there are two important points that can determine the extent of the innovative character and possible new areas in the field of transportation and mobility research. On the one hand, it is the way in which the relationship between telecommunication (digital mobility) and traffic and transportation (physical mobility) is measured, and on the other hand what concepts are used about this relationship or the question of how the world looks like in terms of transport mobility.

The last issue, concepts/theories, is displayed in Fig. 7. Much research must be done in verifying the different propositions and hypotheses. The step toward measuring mobility patterns also means mapping the "movements" of digital mobility, in addition and similar to the familiar measurement of physical mobility. The latter—in the traditional way with travel based (with origin and destination, purposes, modes, etc.) or activity based research—is increasingly being done with the help of ICT instruments, for example, with the smartphone (Thomas et al., 2018). It would be welcome if this is also possible for measuring digital mobility patterns by at least adding more detailed origin-destination information (e.g., exact location). This could be an extension of accessibility diary approach used by Kenyon (2010) or the pseudo diary of online activities approach used by Le Vine et al. (2014, 2016). So, thorough investigation still has to be done.

It is also important to distinguish at least between family, close friends, acquaintances and colleagues. Once a valid connection between physical and digital mobility is determined, it should be possible to search for instruments in the digital communication system to influence physical mobility in a desired direction. This is an important part of a research agenda and a challenging task for the world of ICT. Moreover, these insights can stimulate and promote a mind setting of individuals and help to find what kind of information and tools on communication should be given to specific population groups.

Once the interchangeability of physical and digital trips is clear and valid, it is possible to search for instruments, particularly in the digital communicative system, to achieve the shift from less desirable physical mobility to digital mobility. Here lies an enormous task and challenge for the ICT world and the ICT professionals, together with the transportation and mobility professionals. Which ICT products, resources and instruments are there or need to be developed in order to achieve a mobility shift from less physical to more digital communication? Obviously, this is also politically highly interesting, given the problems that physical mobility and its problems increasingly encounters our society, and cannot be solved with traditional approaches alone.

So in an era of enormous technological developments especially in the field of ICT, the "C" in ICT brings physical and digital communication closer together, for example, by the introduction of Mobility as a Service. These types of developments—organization and services—provide new challenges for researching the interaction between physical and digital mobility and corresponding components as infrastructure, modes/means and organization.

Acknowledgment

The authors want to thank Muhammad Shaker, master student Transportation Sciences of Hasselt University, for his contribution to the empirical part of this chapter.

References

Aguiléra, A., Guillot, C., Rallet, A., 2012. Mobile ICTs and physical mobility: review and research agenda. Transp. Res. A 46, 664–672.

Andreev, O., Salomon, I., Pliskin, N., 2010. Review: state of tele-activities. Transp. Res. C 18, 3–20.

Ben-Elia, E., Alexander, B., Hubers, C., Ettema, D., 2014. Activity fragmentation, ICT and travel: an exploratory path analysis of spatiotemporal interrelationships. Transp. Res. A 68, 56–74.

Ben-Elia, E., Lyons, G., Mokhtarian, P.L., 2018. Epilogue: the new frontiers of behavioral research on the interrelationships between ICT, activities, time use and mobility. Transportation 45, 479–497.

Bris, M., Pawlak, J., Polak, J., 2017. How is ICT use linked to household transportation expenditure? A cross-national macro analysis of the influence of home broadband access. J. Transp. Geogr. 60, 231–242.

Calastri, C., Hess, S., Daly, A., Maness, M., Kowald, M., Axhausen, K., 2017. Modelling contact mode and frequency of interactions with social network members using the multiple discrete-continuous extreme value model. Transp. Res. C 76, 16–34.

Carrasco, J.A., 2011. Personal network maintenance, face-to-face interaction, and distance: role of availability and use of information and communication technologies. Transp. Res. Rec. 2231, 120–128.

Couclelis, H., 2009. Rethinking time geography in the information age. Environ. Plan. A 41, 1556–1575.

Cresswell, T., 2006. On the Move: Mobility in the Modern Western World. Taylor & Francis Group, Oxon, UK.

Delbosc, A., Mokhtarian, P., 2018. Face to Facebook: the relationship between social media and social travel. Transp. Policy 64, 20–27.

Ettema, D., 2018. Apps, activities and travel: a conceptual exploration based on activity theory. Transportation 45, 273–290.

Hong, J., Thakuriah, P.V., Mason, P., Lido, C., 2019. The role of numeracy and financial literacy skills in the relationship between information and communication technology and travel behavior. In: Paper Presented at the TRB 2019 Annual Meeting, Washington DC, USA.

Hubers, C., Schwanen, T., Dijst, M., 2008. ICT and temporal fragmentation of activities: an analytical framework and initial empirical findings. Tijdschr. Econ. Soc. Geogr. 99, 528–546.

Jamal, S., Habib, M.A., 2017. Mobile ICT and travel: does the dependency on smartphone applications stimulate social trips or not? In: Paper Presented at the TRB 2017 Annual Meeting, Washington DC, USA.

Kenyon, S., 2010. The impacts of internet use upon activity participation and travel: results from a longitudinal diary-based panel study. Transp. Res. C 18, 21–35.

Kroesen, M., Handy, S.L., 2015. Is the rise of the E-society responsible for the decline in car use by young adults? Results from the Netherlands. Trans. Res. Rec. 2496, 28–35.

Le Vine, S., Latinopoulos, C., Polak, J., 2014. Establishing the links between online activity and car use: evidence from a combined travel diary and online-activity pseudo-diary data set. Trans. Res. Rec. 2405, 68–77.

Le Vine, S., Latinopoulos, C., Polak, J., 2016. Analysis of the relationship between internet usage and allocation of time for personal travel and out of home activities: case study of Scotland in 2005/6. Travel Behav. Soc. 4, 49–59.

McNally, M.G., Rindt, C.R., 2007. The activity-based approach. In: Hensher, D.A., Button, K.J. (Eds.), In: Handbook of Transport Modelling (Handbooks in Transport), vol. 1. Emerald Transport eBook Collection, pp. 55–73.

Mokhtarian, P., 1990. A typology of relationships between telecommunications and transportation. Transp. Res. A 24, 231–242.

Mokhtarian, P., 2003. Telecommunications and travel. J. Ind. Ecol. 6, 43–57.

Mokhtarian, P.L., Tal, G., 2013. Impacts of ICT on travel behavior: a tapestry of relationships. In: Rodrigue, J.-P., Notteboom, T., Shaw, J. (Eds.), The SAGE Handbook of Transport Studies. Sage Publications Ltd, Los Angeles, USA, pp. 241–272.

Nobis, C., Lenz, B., 2009. Communication and mobility behavior—a trend and panel analysis of the correlation between mobile phone use and mobility. J. Transp. Geogr. 17, 93–103.

Pawlak, J., Le Vine, S., Polak, J., Sivakumar, A., Kopp, J., 2015. ICT and Physical Mobility: State of Knowledge and Future Outlook. Institute for Mobility, London, UK.

Sasaki, K., Nishii, K., 2010. Measurement of intention to travel: considering the effect of telecommunications on trips. Transp. Res. C 18, 36–44.

Shaker, M., 2017. Communication Patterns: Physical Versus Digital. (Master thesis). School for Transportation Sciences, Hasselt University, Hasselt, Belgium.

Suel, E., Daina, N., Polak, J.W., 2018. A Hazard-based approach to modelling the effects of online shopping on intershopping duration. Transportation 45, 415–428.

Thomas, T., Geurs, K.T., Koolwaaij, J., Bijlsma, M., 2018. Automatic trip detection with the Dutch mobile mobility panel: towards reliable multiple-week trip registration for large samples. J. Urban Technol. 25, 143–161.
Van den Berg, P.E.W., Arentze, T.A., Timmermans, H.J.P., 2012. A multilevel path analysis of contact frequency between social network members. J. Geogr. Syst. 14 (2), 125–141.
Van den Berg, P., Arentze, T., Timmermans, H., 2013. A path analysis of social network, telecommunications and social activity-travel patterns. Transp. Res. C 26, 256–268.

CHAPTER TWO

Review of international journey planning system to welcoming MaaS

Paulus Aditjandra*
Newcastle University Business School, Newcastle upon Tyne, United Kingdom
*Corresponding author: e-mail address: paulus.aditjandra@ncl.ac.uk

Contents

Abstract

Mobility as a Service (MaaS) is a concept for the future of mobility. It attracts transportation researchers in recent times and invites businesses to test its market feasibility. The key aspect of MaaS is the integration of multimodal transport information services, which remind us of a project from years ago about journey planning systems. This chapter offers to revisit an FP7 funded project with survey of journey planning system and assesses it against the current state-of-play of journey planning systems as referred in MaaS. Much development such as dynamic data supply, multimodality information and digital map presentations have improved with technologies such as broadband generation and personal mobile devices' capabilities. However, the challenge for MaaS market

Advances in Transport Policy and Planning, Volume 3
ISSN 2543-0009
https://doi.org/10.1016/bs.atpp.2019.07.001

uptake remains as similar to journey planning system products. Simply said, the product or service on offer from a trip planning is perhaps not as attractive as the function of the trip: to arrive at destination.

Keywords: Journey planning system, International scale, Intelligent transport service, MaaS

1. Introduction

There has been great interest in the transportation research communities with the rise of Mobility as a Service (MaaS) concept toward the future of transport, see, for example, a number of research articles published in well-known transportation research journals such as *Transport Reviews, Transportation Research Part A, Research in Transportation Business & Management, Travel Behaviour and Society*, to name a few. This is also evident with the support given to a number of EU funded projects under the Horizon 2020 framework program, e.g., the "MaaS4EU" project[a] the "MyCorridor," project[b] and CIVITAS initiated projects.[c,d,e] There is also a research group dedicated to MaaS based in the University College London. MaaS was dubbed as a newly trendy concept for mobility management services where the customer interface and the business back office are fully integrated (Mulley, 2017), and this is especially in the context of promoting non-private car services (Kamargianni et al., 2016) and non-ownership-based transport system (Jittrapirom et al., 2017). MaaS was said to have originated in the Nordic countries such as Finland and Sweden and popularized by the European Road Transport Telematics Implementation Coordination Organization—ERTICO, an Intelligent Transportation System (ITS) organization in Europe that promotes research and defines ITS industry standards (Liimatainen and Mladenovic, 2018). ITS as a technology element is key to the development of MaaS and especially within the integration of transport services via a single digital interface. Some scholars associated MaaS with ride-sharing services such as *Uber,* see, for example: Suatmadi et al. (2019), even though both MaaS and ride-sharing services share different histories. The ride-sharing mobility innovation provides solutions for reduced cost and time and opportunities for new

[a] https://cordis.europa.eu/project/rcn/210133/factsheet/en

[b] https://cordis.europa.eu/project/rcn/210137/factsheet/en

[c] https://cordis.europa.eu/project/rcn/204150/factsheet/en

[d] https://cordis.europa.eu/project/rcn/204474/factsheet/en

[e] https://cordis.europa.eu/project/rcn/204144/factsheet/en

business models (Cramer and Krueger, 2016), sustainable modal shift (Rayle et al., 2016), and road congestion relief (Hensher, 2018), although along with its complex transport policy implication (Cohen, 2018). However, those opportunities were realized with research funding granted toward looking for opportunities beyond a convenient taxi-hailing service.

The EU funded MyCorridor project (2017–20), attempts to address the seamlessness of interconnected public and private transportation services of international journeys, for instance, the need to visit a number of websites to plan for one holiday journey can be optimized into just one go—One Stop Shop—, to save time and money. Similarly, the MaaS4EU project (2017–20), aims to provide quantifiable evidence, frameworks and tools, to enable the MaaS concept viability to users/customers with, for example, understanding the business models. Initial evidence from the project demonstrates adoption of mobility packages' approach by a number of European cities toward different shared transportation modes: public transit, bike sharing, car-sharing and taxi (Esztergár-Kiss and Kerényi, 2019). In addition, it was understood that city stakeholders were motivated to engage with MaaS partnership for increasing market share and revenues, while end users perceived MaaS as an integrated smartphone application to support individual travel trip (Polydoropoulou et al., 2018).

Sochor et al. (2018) defined MaaS by four levels from no integration of information services (level 0) up to integration of societal goals (level 4). Multimodal travel planners, including price info, fall within level 1 of the typology developed (Sochor et al., 2018). These web-based services are also known as mobility platforms or mobility solutions (Willing et al., 2017). It is a form of digital platform services' distribution that connects, for instance (public) transit service providers with (passenger) travelers, via Information and Communication Technologies (ICT), provided by technology providers (Ben-Elia and Avineri, 2015; Ben-Elia and Zhen, 2018). Recent developments of shared mobility concepts, such as MaaS, and its link to technologies' development lead to appreciation of the potential of shared automated vehicle systems and electrification (Shaheen and Cohen, 2019). An appreciation that suggest a future mobility revolution (Lyons et al., 2019).

When seeing the MaaS development above, the case of previous funded projects under the 7th EU framework research program (FP7) comes to mind. For example, the Wide Scale network of *E*-Systems for Multimodal Journey Planning and Delivery of Trip Intelligent Personalized data (WISETRIP),[f] funded between 2008 and 2010. Despite the lag of time

[f] https://cordis.europa.eu/project/rcn/89641/reporting/en

between that project with the hype of MaaS studies, multimodal mobility platforms are yet considered to be in their infancy (Willing et al., 2017). This chapter aims to re-assess the journey planning system study into a discussion welcoming MaaS. The basis of this paper stems from an international survey of journey planning (JP) systems conducted then as part of the WISETRIP project. The outline of the paper consists of a literature review, review of EU projects relevant to JP system, international survey of internet-based JPs, discussion and assessment about the challenges and barrier of the JP toward MaaS. This original script was presented at ITS World Congress 2009 in Stockholm, documented in Aditjandra et al. (2009), and revised substantially to feature the book chapter.

2. Journey planning system: A review

Most existing internet-based public transport information systems cover either urban journeys or single mode long distance trips (e.g., through train) and provide static information (i.e., routes, schedules, and fares) and trip planning services. In particular, many metropolitan public transport organizations have developed urban trip planners which aim to identify the itinerary that departs or arrives at a given time and minimizes one of the three criteria: en-route time, number of transfers, or the walking time. On the other hand, the corresponding trip planners for long distance journeys refer to a single mode. A series of European Commission (EC) research projects have focused on the development of advanced information systems for providing users (travelers and/or tourists) with dynamic travel information and multimodal trip planning services. While such services were emerging across some neighboring countries within the European Union (EU), there was no evidence as yet of journey planning services linking non-neighboring countries within or even outside EU. While this was the main rationale behind the past funded multimodal journey planning project such as in the WISETRIP project, the same problem is still being used to make the case in the on-going MaaS project, such as in the MyCorridor project.

The past funded multimodal journey planning project, aimed at enhancing the present (then) type of journey planning service by developing a service for planning cross-border multimodal journeys by taking into account multiple criteria and complex scheduling constraints. The objective was to make a fundamental contribution through the personalization engine based on multiple personal criteria either defined before the trip or based on real-time data and events to provide instant information to the users. A common platform built on top of existing Journey Planners (JP) was developed to integrate the results from diverse JPs and so enhanced the information availability to the end user by providing additional details on destination services. The key feature was to deliver a uniform information service drawing on the current and future needs of travelers.

Previous research highlighted the importance of accurate, good quality information for journey planning (Kenyon and Lyons, 2003). The availability of comprehensive information for the traveler can engender knowledge and confidence, foster positive attitudes toward the service provider and create favorable perceptions of efficiency and security. Indeed, information has become such a vital commodity that one can argue that informed travelers are the key to successful future transport service provision. One of the responses to the need for informed travel planning and execution has been the development of internet-based journey planners. The EU FP6 funded eMOTION[g] (2006) project was one of the earlier studies that used the specification of a system architecture to enable integration of existing information services in order to develop a European multimodal on-trip (via devices like Personal Digital Assistance (PDA)/Smart Phones or in-car system) traffic information service.

Planning a journey constitutes a common decision faced by many travelers. The major complexities of this type of decision related to:

(1) the lack of information on the schedule and the routes of the public transport services,

(2) the difficulty in determining feasible itineraries within the dense urban and/or long distance public transport network, and

(3) the intensive task of assessing alternative feasible itineraries in terms of multiple traveling criteria.

The provision of real-time journey planning services through an on-line advanced public transport information system may lighten the difficulties listed above (Adler and Blue, 1998; Peng and Huang, 2000) and contributed to:

(1) the enhancement of the usability and accessibility of the system by accommodating the users' need for guidance,

(2) the increase of the level of transport services by identifying transit options complying with the travelers' preferences, and

(3) the integration of the public transport services by identifying multimodal journeys.

[g] https://cordis.europa.eu/project/rcn/85633/factsheet/en

In the last two decades many advanced public transportation systems have been developed providing journey planning services with the objective of determining the shortest itineraries in terms of the en-route time or the cost (Casey et al., 1996; Horn, 2003; Modesti and Sciomachen, 1998; Wong and Tong, 1998). Furthermore, journey planning services have been directly accessible to travelers while on the move by on-line web-based applications (Peng and Huang, 2000). One example is Helsinki City Transport and Helsinki Metropolitan Area Council who were piloting a mobile Internet connection in selected buses and trams to test the feasibility of a Flash-OFDN mobile network as a general communications channel for all information transferred in and out of the vehicle. The public Wi-Fi connection allows passengers to access schedule and real-time information including a map of the line they are currently on with current location and names of the next stops with estimated arrival times (Lehmuskoski, 2007). Another service using Near Field Communication (NFC) delivers real-time information to mobile phones, provides the option of buying a mobile ticket and future options include the provision of news, event information, weather forecasts, etc. In a survey of 50 key stakeholders (of public transport operators and city-transport authorities) across 7 North Western European countries, multimodal door-to-door trip planning was ranked first out of 10 of the most used ITS-based solutions (Nelson and Aditjandra, 2011).

Journey planning and the wider context of passenger information provision are moving forward rapidly. The increasing diffusion of information and communication technologies (ICT) offers potential for providing better multimodal transport information potentially available for query at any place or time. Furthermore, the opportunity to increase the number of service providers is facilitating the development of cross-modal journey planning and guidance. Crucially, the concept of "service provision" need no longer be restricted to transport services but can now be understood to embrace activity management for which there is a mobility dimension.

On the demand side, advances in personalized information driven by technology changes means that passenger activity management makes travel appear more seamless. However, ICT have the opportunity to raise the expectations of passengers for higher and better services which may not be matched by the network of services provided. The issues of meeting and managing passenger/customer expectation must not therefore be overlooked in the quest to provide citizens with user-friendly, user-empowered and efficient information. There is also rising expectation from the point of view of the customer for instant information, which in turn requires increasing system complexity. This was the area where multimodal journey planning system research projects seek to make a fundamental contribution. A second customer expectation is for information to be provided free of charge while new technology often exerts a heavy price tag (Van Leperen and Cappaert, 2006). A selection of relevant previous EU projects are examined next.

A series of previous EU funded research projects have focused on the development of advanced information systems for providing users (mainly travelers focused on accessing transport services and/or tourists with an interest in multi-service/activity information) with dynamic travel information and multimodal trip planning services; e.g., IMAGE, CRUMPET,[h] WH@M, ADAMANT,[i] eMOTION,[j] IM@GINE-IT,[k] EU-Spirit and ITISS.[l] All of the projects targeted tourism and transport users within various service sectors (private/public transport/urban/inter-urban/single modes/intermodal, etc.). The media used were varying from mobile services, Location Based Service (LBS), PDA and web services. eMOTION, IM@GINE-IT, EU-Spirit and ITISS had high relevance to the multimodal journey planning system.

IMAGE and EU FP5 CRUMPET (2000 – 02) focused on the development of intelligent agents' platforms for providing personalized tourism and travel information. The work in both projects, however, was oriented toward tourism while travel information was limited to urban trips through public transport. The objective of the EU FP5 WH@M project (2000 – 03) was the development of an innovative suite of software modules and services for:

(1) gathering multi-source (public, private, sponsored) information (tourism, travel, weather),
(2) disseminating this information, through the web and personal mobile services, and
(3) customizing the information dispatched by means of advanced user profiling techniques.

EU FP5 ADAMANT's contribution (2002–05) was on the interurban trip planning through the air transport network. EU FP6 eMOTION project (2006–08) proposed a traveler information system which provided the

[h] https://cordis.europa.eu/project/rcn/56840/factsheet/en
[i] https://cordis.europa.eu/project/rcn/63300/reporting/en
[j] https://cordis.europa.eu/project/rcn/85633/factsheet/en
[k] https://cordis.europa.eu/project/rcn/71146/factsheet/en
[l] https://www.keep.eu/project/1211/itiss-intermodal-traveller-information-systems

following services: real-time traffic information to road and public transport users, dynamic road routing services, urban public transport trip planning, and other traveler information services such as tourist information via on-trip-devices like PDA/Smart Phones or in-car-systems. The technical specification of the eMOTION system, which was useful for the categorization of data sources. Such specifications include architecture and data model, Geography Markup Language (GML) application scheme and the service interfaces (eMOTION, 2008).

EU FP6 IM@GINE IT aims were the development of an information system through a single access point that provides intermodal transport information, mapping, routing and navigation services in an urban and interurban environment through multiple modes including car. The proposed system provided a step-by-step interurban multi-legged journey planning service through a Personal Computer (PC) (connected to the Internet) or a mobile while on the move. The interurban trip planning services of the system were operated separately from the corresponding urban services (by car or public transport).

A useful classification was offered by EU FP6 IM@GINE-IT project (2004) which observed that (then) relevant projects could be divided into three main categories:

- Projects focus on mobile and/or LBS targeting tourist users
- Projects focus on drivers' users and in-vehicle services
- Projects focus on generic navigation/routing and public transport information.

Among the European projects which looked at cross-border journey planning systems, the EU Spirit and ITISS projects showed similarity to the WISETRIP project except on the geographical coverage and the media service offered. While these two projects covered European countries, the proposed multimodal journey planning system service offer were expected to reach Far-East Asian countries. The EU Spirit project, started some years ago, attempted to develop a collaborative intermodal journey planning system between cross-border European countries. The service continues for a fee and could be seen as a catalyst to demonstrate the need for such a concept to be expanded and extended. The more recent ITISS project showed that application of cross-border intermodal journey planning system could be challenging. The markets of different European countries, the standardization of data and the different co-ordinate systems that are used across Europe (Solotruk and Kristofic, 1980) were some of the challenges revealed from the project.

3. International survey of journey planners

An international survey of Internet based journey planning systems was conducted to identify gaps in the (then) current practices and highlighted opportunities. The survey resulted in information being provided for a total of 25 Journey Planners from a number of European countries (UK, Italy, Spain, Finland, Germany, Denmark, Greece and the Netherlands) plus China and Japan.

Overall, 11 main features of existing journey planning systems have been identified and information on each feature was captured through the survey questionnaire. The main variations in the features of each system are highlighted and the key priorities for further development identified by those responding to the survey are summarized below. It should be noted that some of the journey planners are not exist anymore, for example, Transport Direct (UK), which was closed in 2014; and ENOSIS (Greece). But others, such as The Trainline (UK) and Google transit (now well integrated with Google Maps) are still in operation with enhanced features.

3.1 Mode type covered

Half the responses received related to single mode journey planners. JPs, which deal only with one motorized mode, were considered as single mode even if they included walking times at the start and end of journeys or at interchange points. Most single mode JPs provided information on bus services although there were examples of rail and private car single mode JPs provided. There appeared to be two groups of multimode JPs; those offering public transport solutions by a variety of possible modes and those which offer private car journey information in addition to public transport options to enable car owners to make informed decisions about whether to drive or not. Car parking information was also provided by some JPs, e.g., Transport Direct (UK).

3.2 Information provided to user

Route information was provided by all JPs responding to the survey and schedule information for all but one. Availability of information on fares appeared to depend on the mode as well as national regulation. For instance, fare information was common for rail based JPs and also long distance bus travel but local bus fare information was less commonly available. The estimated cost of a car journey can be obtained from several JPs offering private car journey information. Walking times were generally provided for the start and end of the journey and for any interchange required except for some single mode JPs and for private car only JPs. It was noticeable that the JPs described for China lack this piece of information despite including public transport modes.

Some JPs also offered information on CO_2 emissions for a car or public transport for a specified journey. Although some local JPs only provided information in the local language, most national JPs provided information in at least the local language as well as English and in some cases in the languages of neighboring countries.

3.3 Geographic coverage

Almost ¾ of the JPs reviewed provided information at the local or regional level and less than half provided information on a national basis. Less than a ¼ claimed to be international, although most of these related to JPs in relatively small countries which has integrated transport networks with neighboring countries. A notable exception to this is The Trainline JP in the UK, which provided rail information across Europe.

3.4 Information display

Map based information supported by tabulated results were the most common means of presenting the results to the end users. In a number of cases this was accompanied by route diagrams. Only one JP (Google Transit Firenze in Italy) utilized Google Maps to display the information.

3.5 Criteria to calculate itineraries

Almost all JPs reviewed calculated itineraries based on minimizing en-route time as well providing the option of minimizing number of transfers. The Finnish, German Danish and Japanese JPs also allowed minimizing walk time. A couple of UK JPs which allowed rail based ticket booking also provided itinerary optimization based on minimizing cost. Three particularly interesting JPs regarding criteria used to calculate itineraries are: the ENOSIS Urban Journey Planner from Greece in which lexicographic ordering was used in order to determine the optimal itinerary using all the criteria simultaneously; the Intermodal Journey Planner from Germany generated automatically the fastest connections based on personalized user specified criteria including transfers, walking speed, exclusion of means of transport, barrier-free routing; Transport Direct from the UK could calculate car routes based on minimum en-route time accounting for predicted traffic levels at different times of the day so the user could make informed decisions about when to travel.

3.6 Other content features

Many respondents stated that real-time information was provided but this often related to travel news updates on traffic conditions and delays for presentation on the JP web-site but did not provide real time data used in the JP route optimization or to "alert" users of real time delays to previous journey details. Notable exceptions to this were: The ENOSIS Urban Journey Planner from Greece provided real-time information available via SMS or *E*-mail (according to the user's profile) about delays or cancellations for air routes to Athens International Airport and ferries at Heraklion port; Greek City Journey Planners provided real-time forecast for urban bus arrivals and departures; the Dutch 9292ov JP provided real-time congestion and delays for public transport; Yahoo, Route Selection in Japan used on-line real-time information according to the actual operational status of all modes of transportation covered by the JP (bus, rail and air).

Just over a third of the JPs reviewed stated they provided other services. These often took the form of travel agency information, point of interest tourist information and links to other tourist services. Weather forecast information is available via a few JPs.

The Traveline JP also provided the txt2traveline service allowing texting an 8-digit bus stop reference code to return the departure times of the next few buses from traveler chosen stop. The message could be customized to allow choice of destination, specific bus service, time period or date. The service was automated and operated 24 h-a-day, every day.

Page landing wizard was another interesting development in the use of journey planners. This enabled third party websites to embed the JP planner onto their sites. This was provided by the Traveline JP (UK) and Rejseplanen JP (Denmark).

Other interesting features included a carbon calculator to enable users to see how much traveling by train can help to reduce their carbon footprint in the The Trainline JP (UK). However, this feature is apparently no longer available and seemed to be abandoned by the JP provider at the time this book chapter has been written.

Dynamic travel information was only provided in 4 out of the 25 JPs surveyed. In the German Intermodal Journey Planner dynamic information was provided based on their Content Management System. Latest information on blocked routes and route diversions could be given route-, trip-, and direction-related. Alternative routes were provided in addition to notes showing restrictions of normal service.

Ticket booking was only available at a fifth of the JPs reviewed and related to only rail travel or long distance bus travel in the case of the Megabus JP (UK) where only one operator was involved. Where ticket booking was available the JP must also provide itinerary storage and update facility.

The Trainline JP (UK) provided the Mobitix system allowing customers to receive their tickets directly to their mobile phone. The tickets contained a number of visual security checks and could be inspected using handheld ticket checkers. The Print@home system allowed tickets to some train operators to simply buy their ticket via The Trainline and printed it on ordinary plain A4 paper.

3.7 Other media for accessing info

The journey planners reviewed from UK, Finland, Germany, Denmark, Greece and the Netherlands generally enable communication and information exchange via SMS, while those from Italy, Spain, China and Japan did not. Kiosks or terminals were rarely used in the countries with more established mobile communication infrastructure, however, these were still found in China where the mobile penetration rates and internet connections were relatively low, but growing rapidly. Telephone call centers still formed an important part of the JP package in more than half the responses received. This human interface was viewed as essential for large sections of the population who were not PC literate or have access to internet and mobile technologies.

3.8 Limitations of surveyed JPs

The main limitations for many of the JPs reviewed related to difficulties experienced in the supply of data. Problems mentioned included: differing data formats provided by different suppliers of data; gaps in service data provided to the data manager; unwillingness of some transport operators to provide data; difficulties of updating and maintaining large quantities of data from many different sources; frequency with which changes in service data occur. A lack of real time up-to-date of information was also mentioned as a problem.

3.9 Key priorities of JPs

In general, real-time information were sought by most JPs as the major priority, followed by dynamic data supply, multimodality information and digital map presentation. Table 1 shows the priorities from each of the

Table 1 Key priorities for JPs services in the next 5 years (period between 2009 and 2014).

Country	Key priorities	Assessment to the current state of JP
Italy	Improvements of cartography to reduce time spent to adapt to new environment and increase data quality supply	Google Maps has been extensively addressed the cartography aspects of its services and as time goes by with improvement of broadband allows congestion free of information services. 10 years ago, the broadband service is generally the first generation while now it is already moving to 5G
UK	Development of smartcard technology to make ticket purchase simpler and less labor intensive; multimodal JPs	Google Maps has integrated all sort of information that suit different topics/issues such as traditional travel options and other location based information such as businesses and markets, e.g., info about restaurants, hotels, bars, coffee, etc. where at each of the information portal, there are links to businesses entities that can then link to services on offer. Some of this offer include smartcard technology, such as London's Oyster card (well-integrated public transport service) and multimodal JP. 10 years ago Oyster card in London is already exist but Google Maps integrated information services were not
Finland	Integration of dynamic data and inclusion of all modes including DRT; real-time data and storage	Google Maps has used dynamic data with real time information (This was only at the early stage 10 years ago). Demand Responsive Transport (DRT) is not included within the transport mode choices. Where there is a case of DRT, the information goes within transit option

Continued

Table 1 Key priorities for JPs services in the next 5 years (period between 2009 and 2014).—cont'd

Country	Key priorities	Assessment to the current state of JP
German	Use of real-time info; dynamic creation of network route maps, stop index and location maps; and GPS-routing for mobile device	Google Maps has covered all of this now. Information about personalized travel plan is also easily accessible with mobile devices
Denmark	Real-time implementation; personalized information for before, during and after the journey	Google Maps allows personalized information with real data at all time, so the estimate time of before, during and after the journey can well be monitored
Greece	Full scale multimodality; real-time travel time updates; dynamic routing; instructions to guide travelers during mode interchanges; and simple ticket reservation	Google Maps ticked the boxes for all that information. However, for international multimodal information, there is limited integration with long distance transport services
The Netherlands	Real-time and reliable information to travelers en-route	Real time information service is certainly no issue these days with Google Maps
Japan	Develop rail JP	There is less information given using Google Maps in Japan but information on transit services are partially available. Cross-countries transport information inbound and outbound is also limited to air traffic
China	Map display and fare information	Google Maps have little access to Chinese transport information but there are other services that provide similar features

JPs involved in this study and then assessed against the current state of practice of the current Google Maps as JP that has been heavily used globally, especially for car travel and transit services information in many Western countries. Google Maps was chosen due to its popularity use in UK, other available JPs and its typology can be seen in Willing et al. (2017).

From Table 1, it can be drawn that Google Maps has covered the journey planning system agenda extensively in European countries but less in the Far East. The need for real time information system has certainly been addressed with dynamic data information services and digital map presentation. The aspect of multimodality information has also been well covered with clear choices for travelers to make. The integration with ticketing is somehow still not there yet but the choices are there for travelers to decide. Despite that, an interesting development now is the additional features of digital market places that allow further interaction between travelers and their trip purpose. As principally travel is a derived demand, the trip purpose will weigh more for the traveler to decide rather than the decision on how the trip is made (mode choices). In UK Google Maps, the options of places to go are well integrated with local businesses and this allows interaction between customers and suppliers, creating benefit of a rather solely JP system. This is especially the case of using Google Maps locally, for instance, when a traveler is based in Newcastle upon Tyne, then all options prompted to the traveler's smartphone are local attraction hotspots with various information about destination choices.

Cross-border journey information within Europe is quite well covered in Google Maps and this was not the case when multimodal journey planning system projects were carried out back then. This perhaps is the reason why many local JPs are abandoned or discontinued as Google Maps has been perfecting its system to serve the mass.

4. Conclusion

Review of multimodal journey planning system research projects shows that the public transport information systems can include a number of critical components (Solotruk and Kristofic, 1980) where among those things "data," "techniques" and "people/actors" were central to running of the system (eMOTION, 2006). "Data" could be considered as the sort of travel information that should be provided. "Technique" represented the way in which travel information was provided and "people/actors" mainly concerned the customers and operators. While the desired quality of integrated multimodal travel information in public transport was well documented from the customer's side (demand) (Grotenhuis et al., 2007), the survey of JPs' practices demonstrates the needs perceived by the JP Services' Operators (supply). This chapter shows the-state-of-practice of international journey planners with particular emphasis on the travel information service provision.

Different transport modes require different data to be provided by JPs. To acknowledge the customer needs for different data at different stages in a journey (i.e., pre-trip—the favorite stage to collect multimodal travel information especially public transport; wayside—the timing to catch the right public transport on-route; and on-board—the timely arrival time at interchanges in order to catch connecting modes) (Grotenhuis et al., 2007), the multimodal journey planning system would need to be sensitive to all the potential data provided from the individual JPs in order to feed the customers with selected information in a timely fashion. The highlighted features from the survey included mode and geographic coverage, information provision and display and criteria to calculate itineraries. The key priorities identified include map display, smartcard technology, real time data information and storage, full-scale multimodality. The survey also showed that some countries were more advanced than the other. Fig. 1 illustrates the key features of a journey planning system envisioned by the surveyed respondents.

The current most used journey planning system in Europe can be generally demonstrated by Google Maps where travelers can choose the type

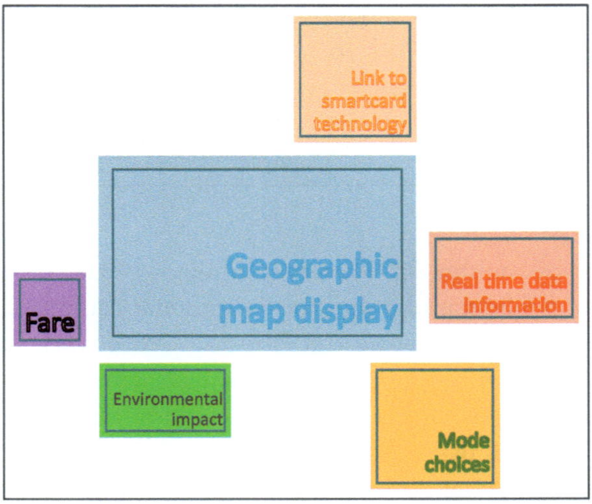

Fig. 1 Key features of a journey planning system. *Source: This study.*

of transport they wish to go with and then detail information about the route choices with distance and time were given. Where the public transport/transit choice picked, the information given would include information about the available services, such as bus/light rail/metro numbers and next departure time. This information is somehow not much different to that with we already have explored in the multimodal journey planning system project launched back 10 years or so ago. The most improvement made was through the application of dynamic real-time information services fed to travelers and the advancement of broadband technology and mobile devices. In terms of ticketing integration, there is still limited evidence with the JP. However, the provision of e-market places piggybacking the JP is of interesting development and open opportunities for added value products as highlighted in the literature (Willing et al., 2017). The packaging of the services with innovative solutions, such as rural mobility services (Eckhardt et al., 2018) or monthly subscription plans (Matyas and Kamargianni, 2018) are envisaged to attract users.

The multimodal journey planning system study, WISTRIP case, of information integration demonstrates the application of the first level of MaaS as described in Sochor et al. (2018), and only touches the second level agenda with booking and payment integration vision. The development with the current JP, in Google Maps, has not shown much development made to the second level. This is possibly the challenge for marketing MaaS where selling an integrated trip product is not an easy business. The cross-border journey planning product as what MyCorridor project attempts to address is in fact still using the same paradigm of long-distance journey planning problem encountered in many multimodal journey planning studies back a number years then. While the development has progressed through the realization of mobility package and its business models as reported in Kamargianni et al. (2016) and Esztergár-Kiss and Kerényi (2019), the use of the service is somehow still limited with the way people generally perceive how they do their travel. It is considered as rather an evolutionary importance than a technological intervention innovation as argued by Lyons et al. (2019). Aligning with this perspective, perhaps the phase of the change will take a number of generation before MaaS product can take into the mass as the same way Electric Vehicle attempts to replace fuel based vehicle.

Acknowledgment

This chapter benefited from the comments of Steve Wright on its first draft.

References

Aditjandra, P.T., Nelson, J.D., Wright, S.D., 2009. A multi-modal international journey planning system: a case study of WISETRIP. In: Paper Presented at the 16th World Congress on Intelligent Transport Systems and Services, Stockholm, Sweden.

Adler, J.L., Blue, V.J., 1998. Toward the design of intelligent traveller information systems. Transp. Res. C 6, 157–172. https://doi.org/10.1016/S0968-090X(98)00012-6.

Ben-Elia, E., Avineri, E., 2015. Response to travel information: a behavioural review. Transp. Rev. 35 (3), 352–377. https://doi.org/10.1080/01441647.2015.1015471.

Ben-Elia, E., Zhen, F., 2018. ICT, activity space-time and mobility: new insights, new models, new methodologies. Transportation 45 (2), 267–272. https://doi.org/10.1007/s11116-018-9870-y.

Casey, R.F., Labell, L.N., Holmstrom, R., LoVecchio, J.A., Schweiger, C.L., Sheehan, T., 1996. Advanced Public Transportation Systems: The State of the Art Update '96. US Department of Transportation, (Retrieved from).

Cohen, T., 2018. Being ready for the next Uber: can local government reinvent itself? Eur. Transp. Res. Rev. 10 (57), 1–11. https://doi.org/10.1186/s12544-018-0330-8.

Cramer, J., Krueger, A.B., 2016. Disruptive change in the taxi business: the case of Uber. Am. Econ. Rev. 106 (5), 177–182. https://doi.org/10.1257/aer.p20161002.

Eckhardt, J., Nykänen, L., Aapaoja, A., Niemi, P., 2018. MaaS in rural areas—case Finland. Res. Transp. Bus. Manag. 27, 75–83. https://doi.org/10.1016/j.rtbm.2018.09.005.

eMOTION, 2006. Requirements and Service Analysis. Deliverable D1. Retrieved from https://www.yumpu.com/en/document/read/18700439/d1-requirements-and-service-analysis-appendix-1.

eMOTION, 2008. eMOTION System-Technical Specification. Deliverable D6. Retrieved from https://www.yumpu.com/en/document/read/18745543/emotion-d6-appendix-1.

Esztergár-Kiss, D., Kerényi, T., 2019. Creation of mobility packages based on the MaaS concept. Travel Behav. Soc. https://doi.org/10.1016/j.tbs.2019.05.007. In Press.

Grotenhuis, J.-W., Wiegmans, B.W., Rietveld, P., 2007. The desired quality of integrated multimodal travel information in public transport: customer needs for time and effort savings. Transp. Policy 14, 27–38. https://doi.org/10.1016/j.tranpol.2006.07.001.

Hensher, D., 2018. Tackling road congestion—what might it look like in the future under a collaborative and connected mobility model? Transp. Policy 66, A1–A8. https://doi.org/10.1016/j.tranpol.2018.02.007.

Horn, M.E.T., 2003. An extended model and procedural framework for planning multi-modal passenger journeys. Transp. Res. B 37 (7), 641–660. https://doi.org/10.1016/S0191-2615(02)00043-7.

IM@GINE-IT, 2004. Use Cases and User/Vehicle Profile Requirements. Deliverable D1.1. Retrieved from, https://cordis.europa.eu/project/rcn/71146/factsheet/en.

Jittrapirom, P., Caiati, V., Feneri, A.-M., Ebrahimigharehbaghi, S., González, M.J.A., Narayan, J., 2017. Mobility as a service: a critical review of definitions, assessments of schemes, and key challenges. Urban Plan. 2 (2). https://doi.org/10.17645/up.v2i2.931.

Kamargianni, M., Li, W., Matyas, M., Schäfer, A., 2016. A critical review of new mobility services for urban transport. Transp. Res. Proc. 14, 3294–3303.

Kenyon, S., Lyons, G., 2003. The value of integrated multimodal traveller information and its potential contribution to modal change. Transp. Res. F 6, 1–21. https://doi.org/10.1016/S1369-8478(02)00035-9.

Lehmuskoski, M., 2007. Mobile internet in Helsinki public transport. Public Transp. Int. 56, 32–33.

Liimatainen, H., Mladenovic, M.N., 2018. Understanding the complexity of mobility as a service. Res. Transp. Bus. Manag. 27, 1–2.

Lyons, G., Hammond, P., Mackay, K., 2019. The importance of user perspective in the evolution of MaaS. Transp. Res. A 121, 22–36. https://doi.org/10.1016/j.tra.2018.12.010.

Matyas, M., Kamargianni, M., 2018. The potential of mobility as a service bundles as a mobility management tool. Transportation 1–18. https://doi.org/10.1007/s11116-018-9913-4.

Modesti, P., Sciomachen, A., 1998. A utility measure for finding multiobjective shortest paths in urban multimodal transportation networks. Eur. J. Oper. Res. 111 (3), 495–508. https://doi.org/10.1016/S0377-2217(97)00376-7.

Mulley, C., 2017. Mobility as a services (MaaS)—does it have critical mass? Transp. Rev. 37 (3), 247–251. https://doi.org/10.1080/01441647.2017.1280932.

Nelson, J.D., Aditjandra, P.T., 2011. Bridging the mobility gap: the role of ITS. In: Grieco, M., Urry, J. (Eds.), Mobilities: New Perspectives on Transport and Society. Ashgate, pp. 331–345.

Peng, Z.-R., Huang, R., 2000. Design and development of interactive trip planning for web-based transit information systems. Transp. Res. C 8, 409–425. https://doi.org/10.1016/S0968-090X(00)00016-4.

Polydoropoulou, A., Pagoni, I., Tsirimpa, A., 2018. Ready for Mobility as a Service? Insights from stakeholders and end-users. Travel Behav. Soc. https://doi.org/10.1016/j.tbs.2018.12.004. In Press.

Rayle, L., Dai, D., Chan, N., Cervero, R., Shaheen, S., 2016. Just a better taxi? A survey-based comparison of taxis, transit, and ridesourcing services in San Francisco. Transp. Policy 45, 168–178. https://doi.org/10.1016/j.tranpol.2015.10.004.

Shaheen, S., Cohen, A., 2019. Shared ride services in North America: definitions, impacts, and the future of pooling. Transp. Rev. 39 (4), 427–442. https://doi.org/10.1080/01441647.2018.1497728.

Sochor, J., Arby, H., Karlsson, I.C.M., Sarasini, S., 2018. A topological approach to mobility as a service: a proposed tool for understanding requirements and effects, and for aiding the integration of societal goals. Res. Transp. Bus. Manag. 27, 3–14.

Solotruk, M., Kristofic, M., 1980. Increasing the degree of information system integration and developing and integrated information system. Inf. Manag. 3 (5), 207–212. https://doi.org/10.1016/0378-7206(80)90015-4.

Suatmadi, A.Y., Creutzig, F., Otto, I.M., 2019. On-demand motorcycle taxis improve mobility, not sustainability. Case Stud. Transp. Policy 7, 218–229. https://doi.org/10.1016/j.cstp.2019.04.005.

Van Leperen, J., Cappaert, S., 2006. Intelligent public transport systems: the key to better mobility. Public Transp. Int. 55, 6–11.

Willing, C., Brandt, T., Neumann, D., 2017. Intermodal mobility. Bus. Inf. Syst. Eng. 59 (3), 173–179. https://doi.org/10.1007/s12599-017-0471-7.

Wong, S.C., Tong, C.O., 1998. Estimation of time-dependent origin-destination matrices for transit networks. Transp. Res. B 32 (1). https://doi.org/10.1016/S0191-2615(97)00011-8.

CHAPTER THREE

Weather, travel behavior, and the influence and potential of ICT to improve resilience

Hannah Budnitz*, Lee Chapman, Emmanouil Tranos
School of Geography, Earth & Environmental Sciences, University of Birmingham, Birmingham, United Kingdom
*Corresponding author: e-mail address: hannahbudnitz@gmail.com

Contents

Abstract

Weather has always influenced travel behavior and choices of mode, route, and timing, including cancelation, but climate change and the increasing occurrence of severe weather events which result in frequent and extensive transport disruption add urgency to the task of better understanding the existing and potential resilience of travel behaviors. Meanwhile, new and complex travel behavior trends are emerging, in part due to the development and spread of Information and Communication Technologies (ICT) but also in response to other external influences and to technological change within the transport sector. These trends may better be understood through a more holistic view of accessibility: online and via transport modes, in time and in space. This chapter reviews the literature exploring the influence of both daily weather parameters and severe weather events on travel behavior and activity participation. It then considers the parallels and interdependencies between the ICT and transport sectors, and finally reframes existing research into the impact of ICT on productivity, lifestyles, and travel behavior in order to demonstrate the potential for ICT to reduce the level of risk from severe weather impacts for different groups and individuals, increase their ability and propensity to choose more resilient options, and improve adaptation.

Advances in Transport Policy and Planning, Volume 3
ISSN 2543-0009
https://doi.org/10.1016/bs.atpp.2019.03.001

Keywords: Weather, Travel behavior, ICT, Resilience, Accessibility, Climate change, Recovery

1. Introduction

Information and Communication Technologies (ICT) have changed the way people work, shop, socialize and participate in other activities, both spatially and temporally. Travel behaviors are changing as a result, creating new and complex trends. These trends are influenced by not only the spread of ICT, but also by economic, cultural, demographic, and environmental circumstances (Chatterjee et al., 2018; Le Vine et al., 2017). This chapter is concerned with the latter, namely, interactions between weather and transport, and how such interactions are changing or could change due to Internet accessibility. There is substantial literature on how weather affects travel behavior, transport infrastructure, and activity participation, a selection of which is reviewed in the next two sections. This literature, as shown in Fig. 1, can be divided into three broad areas of research: studies of the influence of daily meteorological parameters on travel, reviews and case studies of the impacts of severe weather events on transport services and infrastructure, and forecasts of the risks presented by climate change to transport delivery. Some studies assess the vulnerabilities and dependencies between

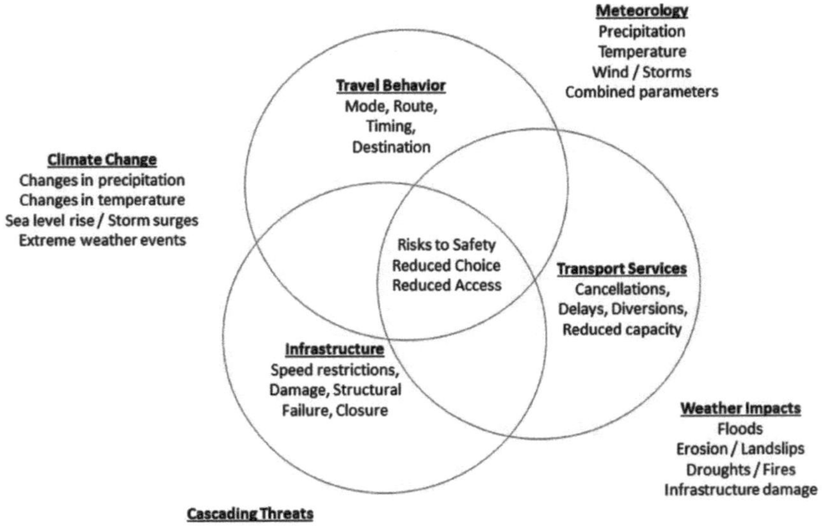

Fig. 1 The study of Weather and Transport interactions.

transport and other infrastructures, including ICT, to identify cascading threats, a concept which will be briefly explored in the third section of this chapter.

Both vulnerabilities from climate change and weather, as well as technological change produce uncertainties which may be better addressed by scenario-based approaches to research, analysis, planning, investing, and policy-making for future accessibility and adaptation options rather than traditional forecasting (Bonsall, 2004; Goodwin, 2012; Jaroszweski et al., 2010; Marsden et al., 2018; Rohr et al., 2016). The next three sections of this chapter review the evidence for scenarios that maximize the opportunities presented by ICT to increase the spatial and temporal flexibility of access and thus the resilience of travel behavior.

"Dynamic accessibility" offers a useful framework for analyzing future scenarios and levels of flexibility, particularly those concerned with the interactions between weather, travel, and ICT. This framework developed out of the call to research "time geography" and how "space-time paths" define personal movement (Hagerstrand, 1970; Miller, 2005). Conceptually, these constraints include a person's *capability* to undertake activities at a current location or move elsewhere within the time available, as no individual can corporeally be two places at once; by the need for coordination with others or *coupling*; and by whether *authorities* make particular spaces available at particular times for the duration of the activities in those spaces (Hagerstrand, 1970; Miller, 2005; Schwanen and Kwan, 2008). Within this framework, both transport and ICT are the means to overcome these constraints, rather than activities in and of themselves, and the parallels between ICT and transport infrastructure and services are manifold. Both are comprised of networks of links and nodes that create hierarchies of opportunities for interaction, but also have the potential to exclude some socio-demographic groups (Blank et al., 2018; Tranos et al., 2013). Both are "general purpose" technologies that are integral to many sectors of the economy, catalyze innovation in those sectors, and change the geography of activities people want to access (Karlsson et al., 2010). Both are industries of "derived demand," providing access to satisfy desires for goods, services, employment, leisure, and information, while minimizing the costs in terms of time and distance and balancing preferences and attitudes, ignoring any "undirected" travel (Banister, 2008; Mokhtarian and Salomon, 2001; Van Acker et al., 2010). This view ignores cases where transport or ICT are activities in their own right, such as running for exercise or reading social media without interacting with anyone. However, as ICT and its use evolve, the choice between travel and online access becomes more flexible, and even interchangeable, and influences all future scenarios (Lyons, 2015).

Dynamic accessibility considers the constraints people and communities face by nature of who they are, as represented by their personal timeline, who they need to interact with, as well as where they live, where they want to go, and what transport options are available to get them there. Therefore, it is not surprising that ICT changes the nature of these constraints—the original conceptualization of time geography noted this possibility (Hagerstrand, 1970). Thus, there is much academic speculation around whether ICT "dematerializes" various goods and activities, making distance and geography less important in consumer choices and awareness of far-flung options, from residential location to social connections, or whether the fragmentation and dynamism it introduces could increase the desire for dense, urban living and have a complementary impact on urban agglomeration and growth (Circella and Mokhtarian, 2017; Lyons, 2015; Qin et al., 2016; Tranos and Ioannides, 2015). Internet access, both fixed and mobile, relaxes some constraints, particularly temporal ones, but also can create new constraints and needs, for example, expectations of multi-tasking or being "on-call" or always available (Felstead and Henseke, 2017; Schwanen and Kwan, 2008). For this review, however, dynamic accessibility helps put into perspective the altered access challenges faced by different groups and individuals in both time and space during severe weather and disruption to transport networks, and how ICT can overcome some of those challenges.

Furthermore, while ICT mean travel behavior may be more flexible than in the past, there is still the need for conscious design of places and technologies that both offer "safe, affordable, accessible and sustainable transport systems for all" and motivate people to choose more sustainable travel behaviors (Headicar, 2015; Lyons, 2018; United Nations, 2015). Sustainable travel behaviors have usually been depicted as those that mitigate the impacts of transport on climate, as the sector is a major source of air pollution and greenhouse gas emissions, accounting for almost a quarter of total global emissions, which in the United Kingdom, for example, makes it the largest sectoral emitter (Bell et al., 2016; Sims et al., 2014). However, sustainable travel behaviors are also those that can adapt alongside infrastructure to the uncertainties arising from climate change, including a range of predictions for future precipitation levels, temperatures and increasingly frequent weather extremes and events, in order to enable continued accessibility in space and time by transport and/or ICT (Cox et al., 2011; Jaroszweski et al., 2014; Wang, 2015). The resilience of transport systems has been investigated in terms of how reliable or vulnerable infrastructure is and whether, instead of simple repair, proactive redesign might aim for robustness, redundancy, or quick recovery and stabilization (Mattson and Jenelius, 2015; Rogers et al., 2012; Wang, 2015). Yet the interaction of transport infrastructure and services with patterns of human behavior, mobility, and ICT use means that physical adaptation of transport systems is only part of the solution, and mitigation, coordination, and communication might offer more flexible, immediate ways to respond to disruption caused by weather or other events (Cox et al., 2011; Jaroszweski et al., 2014; Rogers et al., 2012).

If resilience hinges upon the ability to avoid or minimize delay, disruption, and risk to personal safety and property, ideally maintaining an acceptable level of accessibility to intended activities, then ICT has a number of roles to play, as shown in Fig. 2. ICT has enabled a step-change in the provision of travel information, making it an essential part of coordination and communication between the public and those with responsibility for transport services and for contingency/emergency planning during disruption from severe weather. ICT has changed how, when, and where people access activities, which can mitigate the risks and enable some to avoid disruption through online access or temporal and spatial flexibility. Finally, ICT trends have resulted in the delivery of new transport services,

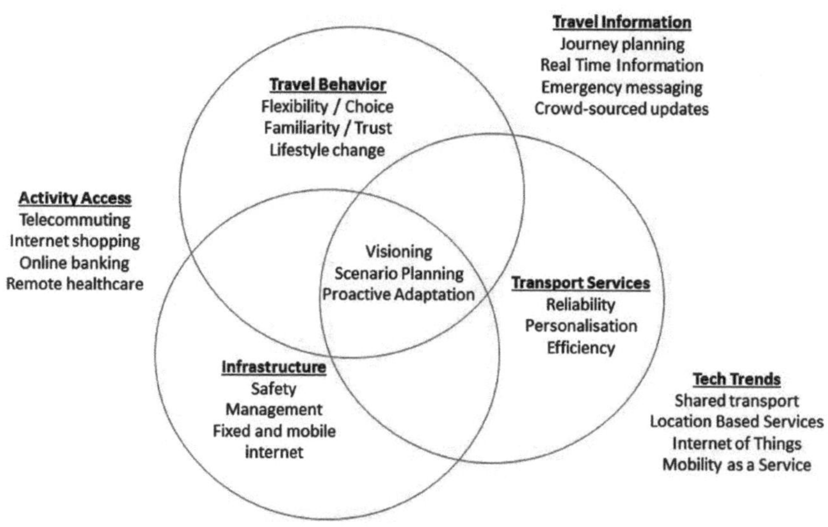

Fig. 2 The study of ICT and Transport interactions.

facilities, and interactions, which could speed and enhance recovery following disruption. The influences and impacts of ICT on information, flexibility, productivity, lifestyles, transport services, and travel behavior have been growing areas of research.

This chapter aims to bring together the two areas of research depicted in Figs. 1 and 2 in order to better understand the interactions between travel behavior, Internet accessibility and the weather. The next section reviews the literature on the influence of weather on travel behavior. Some of these use data sources derived from ICT, including those which are built into transport systems, but few consider the impact of ICT directly. Section 2.2 explores the vulnerabilities, resilience, and inter-dependencies of transport and ICT, particularly as risk assessed under future climate change scenarios. Sections 3.1–3.3 consider the ways in which ICT influence travel behavior as shown in Fig. 2 and offer insights into how these different influences might have potential benefits and applications in terms of weather resilience, particularly if incorporated into long-term planning. The final section concludes with a discussion of how better integration of transport and ICT in research, policy and decision-making could contribute to achieving more resilient and sustainable futures.

2. The relevance of weather

2.1 Impacts of weather on travel behavior

Among the external influences on travel behavior and the availability and reliability of transport networks and services, the impact of weather parameters such as precipitation, temperature and wind-speed, has long been recognized by researchers. Studies have used a wide variety of statistical modeling techniques, socio-demographic and other explanatory variables, and meteorological measurements in relative or absolute terms at daily, monthly or seasonal scales, to test how weather variations empirically affect travel patterns (Böcker et al., 2013). A few studies use stated and revealed preference techniques to assess whether and how people change their travel choices in response to not only the weather, but also weather forecasts (Cools and Creemers, 2013; Kilpelainen and Summala, 2007; Meng et al., 2016). Some surveys go even further, using extensive questionnaires to investigate travel behavior more generally, focusing on how travelers respond to a combination of weather and travel information, and the influence of socio-demographic characteristics and work situation, such as flexible hours (De Palma and Rochat, 1999; Khattak and De Palma, 1997).

Although these surveys might be described as traditional research methods, big data analysis techniques mean that many years of travel diaries, or records from sources covering millions of trips, such as traffic cameras, electronic ticketing transactions, mobile phones, and social media can be matched to weather observations and long-term patterns explored.

Most of the research questions from these studies are hypotheses about the impact of weather on safety, mode choice, and trip volumes, with only a few investigating the subtleties of changes to route or travel timing, e.g., leaving more time to travel or postponing travel until weather changes (Cools and Creemers, 2013; De Palma and Rochat, 1999; Khattak and De Palma, 1997; Koetse and Rietveld, 2009; Sabir et al., 2010). Pedestrians are disproportionately impacted by the weather and various studies focus on "active travel" and outdoor activities (Böcker et al., 2013). Researchers have used cyclist counts, travel diaries and route-side surveys to determine that rain, and to a lesser extent, temperature—both extreme heat and cold, and strong winds can reduce the amount of cycling for utility or leisure, although the size of any switch to other modes is dependent upon the share of bicycle travel in the area of study (Böcker et al., 2013; Meng et al., 2016; Saneinejad et al., 2012). There are indications that public transport ridership decreases in bad weather and increases in good weather, and although the percentage changes are small when studying large datasets from electronic fare collection, a wide selection of tests have shown statistically significant shifts in ridership and switches from bus to rail in adverse weather, the latter of which may be related to the facilities available, such as shelter at stops and stations, although public transport can also be affected by the discomfort of the active travel leg at the start or end of a journey (Guo et al., 2007; Hofmann and O'Mahony, 2005; Kalkstein et al., 2009; Singhal et al., 2014; Stover and McCormack, 2012). On the other hand, it is less clear whether the changes in travel behavior by public transport users result in more or less dynamic accessibility, as different public transport services have different capacities and the impacts up- or down-stream are rarely fully considered (Cats and Jenelius, 2014).

Most studies of road traffic have focused on the effects of precipitation. The influence of rain has been measured in multiple ways, with well-documented reductions in traffic speed, more frequent although less severe accidents, and increased congestion and resultant delays, particularly in denser, urban areas during already congested peak hours (Böcker et al., 2013; Cools et al., 2009; Hooper et al., 2014; Jaroszweski et al., 2014; Sabir et al., 2008; Snelder and Calvert, 2016; Tsapakis et al., 2013).

Research shows that where road networks are already operating close to capacity, such as in urban areas during rush hours, the impacts of even normal weather variations are much greater than in areas with spare capacity. This is not surprising, considering the amount of congestion relief that is delivered daily by public transport services even controlling for weather in urban areas where car use is relatively low (Adler and van Ommeren, 2016). Yet although congestion increases, there is evidence that rain can reduce the level of road traffic demand, dependent upon the mode shares of active or unsheltered travel that switch to private vehicles, the amount and intensity of the rain, and how weather parameters are modeled (Böcker et al., 2013; Cools et al., 2009; Sabir et al., 2010; Snelder and Calvert, 2016).

Much more obvious effects are attributed to snowfall and accumulation. Observations, simulations, and stated/revealed preference surveys, the latter of which offer a multi-modal view of travel behavior, all indicate that trip cancelations are most likely to occur when snow is forecast or occurring, although less so in regions where snow is most common (Böcker et al., 2013; Cools and Creemers, 2013; Kilpelainen and Summala, 2007; Kim et al., 2013; Sabir et al., 2010). This is not surprising, as snow is known to have significant negative impacts upon the resilience of physical assets and infrastructure, causing costly damage which can take some time to repair, and making it, along with flooding, a priority for transport authorities' scrutiny and review (Brown et al., 2014; Chatterton et al., 2016; Quarmby et al., 2010). Furthermore, as well as the risks snow and ice pose to the safety and availability of transport networks, the social impacts, of school closures, for example, also have a major impact on travel behavior (Marsden et al., 2016). Finally, some of the multi-modal studies provide evidence that strong winds might be one of the more significant weather parameters reducing travel demand by 2% overall and public transport demand by 22%, while warmer weather, at least in the temperate climates studied, may induce modal shift from vehicular to active travel (Cools et al., 2010; Sabir et al., 2010).

Yet the extent to which ICT accessibility replaces or modifies travel during severe weather events is largely unknown. Many studies focus on a single mode, there are relatively few investigations into responses such as changing destinations or canceling trips, and even fewer into the use of ICT for telecommuting or other activities during severe weather events or over the longer term as experience of disruption increases (Cools and Creemers, 2013; Kaufman et al., 2012; Koetse and Rietveld, 2009; Marsden et al., 2013). One reason such responses are included in so few of the studies cited in this section is that this area of literature includes many more longitudinal studies that track the relationships over time between rainfall, wind speeds, and other weather parameters and changes in trip numbers, vehicle speeds, and modal splits. While longitudinal data from weather records may correlate to flooding or fallen trees, identifying quantitative thresholds of weather variables that cause sufficient transport disruption often enough in the timeline studied to be statistically significant is challenging even if issues like time of day, the "intensity of use, the availability of alternatives and the economic importance of the route or service" are considered (Brown et al., 2014, p. 9; Mitsakis et al., 2014). Thus, longitudinal studies may struggle to capture both where and when specific impacts such as road closures, rail cancelations, and other disruptions occur that may affect space-time constraints and make online access more necessary.

The alternative approach is to assess the response to a case study of an identified weather event in a particular place where known disruption occurred. This approach is commonly pursued by governments following major weather events, where estimates of the direct and indirect impacts, including the "welfare costs" of delays, closures, cancelations, incidents, lost productivity, and any lengthy repair and recovery periods are calculated (Beiler et al., 2016; Brown et al., 2014; Chatterton et al., 2016; Quarmby et al., 2010). There are also academic case studies undertaken over various geographies, such as one that calculated the total impact of the UK-wide storms on 28 June 2012 upon the national rail and road networks (Jaroszweski et al., 2015), while another focused on the urban area of Newcastle-upon-Tyne on that day, measuring traffic flows on the network to locate critical points and possible mitigation scenarios (Pregnolato et al., 2016). Other examples track the impacts of hurricanes in the United States (Kaufman et al., 2012; Lee et al., 2009), or natural disasters around the world (Wang and Taylor, 2016). Often, such studies make assumptions about how people were affected during extreme weather using comparisons to an "average" day or transport models built to represent "average" daily mobility, rather than consider how people might change their behavior (Brown et al., 2014; Chatterton et al., 2016). Thus, the engineering solutions for redundancy or recovery, the operational changes, and strategic and emergency planning coordination, ranging from the identification of diversion routes to flood defenses and raising or moving infrastructure tend to be based on similar assumptions (Beiler et al., 2016; Suarez et al., 2005).

However, many would agree that the severity of the impacts is dependent upon patterns of human behavior, the time and location at which the event and disruption occurs, how they are perceived, and whether and when information about the weather event or disruption is available (Beiler et al., 2016; Dawson, 2016; Marsden et al., 2013). There is a recognition of the importance of developing a messaging strategy to keep the public informed and instill behavioral resilience, even within studies modeling simulated travel during severe weather without the benefit of real-life observation from either qualitative survey methodologies after known disruption or the exploration of alternative indicators and thresholds (Beiler et al., 2016; Kim et al., 2013; Snelder and Calvert, 2016; Suarez et al., 2005). Future scenario planning for resilience to severe weather and disruption must include options both for the physical re-design of infrastructure, and also for strategies addressing behavioral resilience and response, with decision-makers able to choose what will best enable adaptation or recovery in specific communities (Jaroszweski et al., 2014; Rogers et al., 2012). In either case, ICT is critical.

2.2 A comparison of infrastructure resilience

The importance of ICT to resilience, both infrastructural and behavioral, is most obvious when it is not available. In Lancaster, UK, the floods caused by storms and ground saturation in December 2015 not only cut major transport links, including a motorway junction and central bridges, but also resulted in a power outage that rendered all fixed Internet access as well as the base stations that enable mobile access in the area inoperable, except for a few buildings with emergency generators, like the hospital and the local radio station (Ferranti et al., 2017). This is an example of the cascading threat to the "system of systems," where the interdependencies within and between infrastructure networks mean that failure in one area instigates failure in another, not only in relation to various transport networks, but also to electricity, water and ICT systems, which is a major risk of climate change (Chapman et al., 2013; Horrocks et al., 2010). Cascading threats can also affect behavioral resilience, even if there is a lack of consideration of traveler reactions and demand-based measures in many of the climate change risk analyses (Mattson and Jenelius, 2015). In Lancaster, the local radio, plus a few public payphones, became for many the sole source of updates and information from emergency services and others (Ferranti et al., 2017). Therefore, local residents struggled to learn what services and infrastructure were still operational, and had no ability to substitute online access if transport access was unavailable. In this case, ICT could not help coordinate the emergency response, provide information on unaffected transport links, nor enable the participation in work and other activities. The resilience of ICT in the area, and its importance in the resilience of other infrastructure networks had not been considered. Fortunately, however, systems theory also means that there are always multiple ways to improve resilience (Rogers et al., 2012), including optimizing the inherent resilience of ICT infrastructure and its lower vulnerability to cascading threats as shown in Fig. 3.

Although dependent upon energy infrastructure for uninterrupted operation as in the case described above, ICT infrastructure and topology is generally more robust, at least at a strategic level, than transport infrastructure to both weather events and a changing climate (Chapman et al., 2013). Some reasons are the international design of many components built for weather extremes rarely seen in temperate climates, the frequent asset replacement as a result of the speed of technological development, and the often built-in redundancy between fixed and mobile services and competing providers (Fu et al., 2016; Horrocks et al., 2010; OfCom, 2014). Indeed, the majority of faults for telephone and broadband infrastructure tend to be local and residential due to built-in redundancy at the strategic

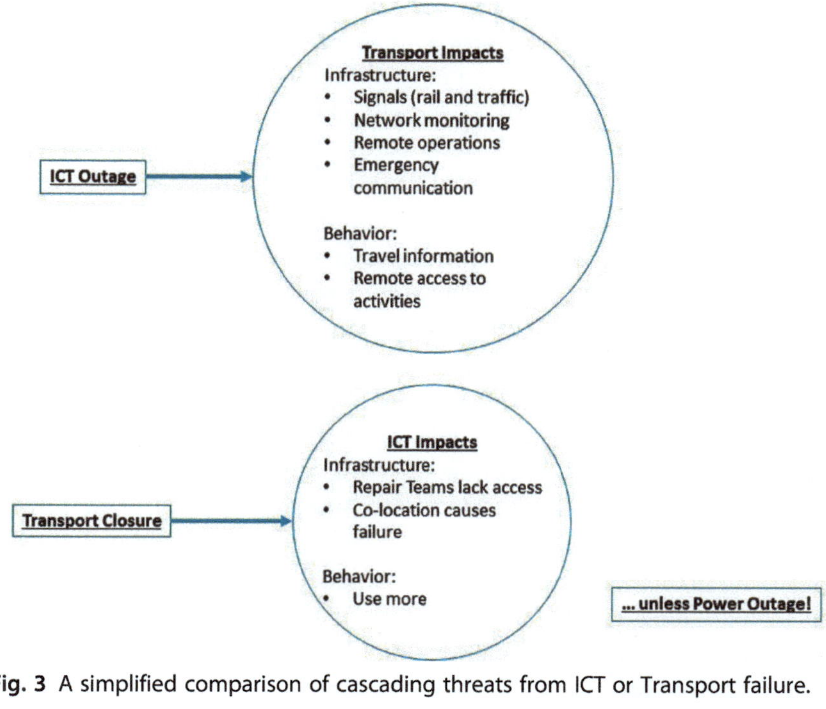

Fig. 3 A simplified comparison of cascading threats from ICT or Transport failure.

level, and risk assessments by Internet service providers focus more on customer service, maintenance and standards, rather than resilience and the potential for a national emergency (Lazarus, 2013, 2014; OfCom, 2014; Schulman and Spring, 2011).

In comparison, transport infrastructure systems are often older, public or publically subsidized, with national railways and local bridges in particular lacking redundancy, all of which make transport less resilient to severe weather events, especially where there has been a lack of investment and maintenance back-logs (Brown et al., 2014). Railways, for example, are particularly at risk in high temperatures due to inadequately stressed rails and electrical failure or sagging overhead lines, whereas ICT lines are often designed to withstand temperature extremes (Dawson, 2016; Dobney et al., 2009; Ferranti et al., 2016). Transport networks are also dependent upon the availability of energy and ICT infrastructure for key elements of operation, while ICT infrastructure is only dependent upon transport where repairs are needed, and engineers struggle to access the relevant points in the network (Horrocks et al., 2010).

Various studies have reviewed the robustness of transport networks, from road and rail to air and inland waterways by using empirical data from past severe weather events to speculate on the likely impacts of extreme weather conditions which will be more prevalent as the global climate continues to change: storms, fluvial, pluvial and coastal flooding, heatwaves, heavy rain and high winds (Dawson, 2016; Jaroszweski et al., 2014; Koetse and Rietveld, 2009; Snelder and Calvert, 2016). Such events appear likely to replicate the risks of snow to "normal" dynamic accessibility by likely causing road closures, rail cancelations, and school closures, and thus similarly affecting travel behavior, even if snow events and freezing temperatures themselves occur less often under future climate change scenarios. Research and risk analysis suggests that transport infrastructure is more vulnerable to these severe weather events due to impacts such as storm surges in coastal areas, depth of floodwaters, landslips, sinkholes, coastal erosion, and trees falling in the heavy winds, than to the more gradual climate changes in temperature or precipitation (Brown et al., 2014; Dawson, 2016; Jaroszweski et al., 2010; Koetse and Rietveld, 2009). Energy and ICT infrastructure are also more vulnerable to severe weather events than to other climate changes, but in their case, high winds, gales, and lightening cause many more faults than flooding, and the speed of technology upgrades make it easier to augment the robust nature of ICT infrastructure by designing in resilience (Dawson, 2016; Horrocks et al., 2010; McColl et al., 2012).

For example, where ICT connections use historic copper wires originally installed for voice telephony, they may be unsuitable for high bandwidth applications and face reduced asset life and additional maintenance, compounded by increased temperatures and humidity (Lazarus, 2013, 2014; OfCom, 2014; Schulman and Spring, 2011). Fiber-copper hybrid networks are also vulnerable to extreme weather events such as the one described above in Lancaster, UK, whereas a network of robust optical fibers not only from hubs to street cabinets, but also between a hub and individual residences is much more resilient as was seen during the same weather event in nearby rural areas, which maintained their ICT connections (Brunnen, 2016). ICT infrastructure is also sometimes housed in historic industrial buildings located on floodplains, and is known to become inaccessible to repair teams if transport routes are blocked, especially if there are no clear lines of responsibility within the sector for emergency response or incorporating strategic planning for resilience as the technology is refreshed (Horrocks et al., 2010; Lazarus, 2014; Schulman and Spring, 2011; UKCIP, 2013). Therefore, the challenge becomes one of governance and policies to reinforce the robust nature of ICT infrastructure, which is why it is important that ICT is not viewed as a "critical" infrastructure in isolation, but one upon which many other infrastructures and behaviors are dependent (Horrocks et al., 2010). In the following sections, the importance and potential of ICT to improve travel behavioral resilience is explored and could add to the case for better governance and integration of ICT into adaptation and emergency planning.

3. The resilience potential of ICT

3.1 Information increases efficiency: The next best thing to reliability?

Severe weather events can cause substantial disruption to transport networks and services, including not only road closures and rail cancelations, but also delays due to road traffic incidents, congestion, diversions, and speed restrictions. Delays increase individuals' capability constraints as they cannot be physically present at an activity if they are stuck somewhere on the transport network, and the increased time in transit reduces the time available for the activity. However, ICT has a major role to play in reducing temporal inefficiencies through travel information. Surveys have indicated that travelers' greatest concern is not the cost or total journey time, but rather the reliability of journey time for different modes or routes when used regularly (Lyons, 2006; Wang et al., 2009). Thus, it is not surprising that even when there is no adverse weather or other disruption, the demand for real-time, mobile journey planning is increasing and those who use such services are more likely to change their travel plans or have more flexible travel patterns (Wang et al., 2009; Wockatz and Schartau, 2015). Combined with location-based services, travel information enables users to be notified of the quickest route to access goods, participate in activities, or to find others in their social network, all based on where they are at a given time (Arribas-Bel, 2014; Ratti et al., 2006). This can result in an increase in short, multi-purpose, linked trips to "other" locations, for example, if leisure opportunities are available near the workplace, and is one reason that direct home-work commuting is in decline (Astroza et al., 2017; Le Vine et al., 2017; Phithakkitnukoon et al., 2010; Wang and Law, 2007). Yet it also can have a substantial impact upon the ability to change timing, route, or mode of transport during a severe weather event or other disruption.

Information is often sought in response to the expectation of disruption, with an improved perception of the reliability of alternative services if trustworthy information on delays, diversions and other options is available (Chorus et al., 2006; Lyons, 2006; Pender et al., 2014). The transport authorities in New York recorded large increases in the number of Twitter "followers" before major storms and hurricanes, with few then "unfollowing" after the event, suggesting that the overall level of engagement, and the rapidity and flexibility of future response increases through use of ICT (Chan and Schofer, 2014). Another study that used Twitter's geotagged data from natural disasters occurring around the world in 2013 and 2014 concluded that human mobility patterns in the most general sense of an individual's spatial area of travel and activity are highly resilient, and remain predictable in all but the most extreme scenarios (Wang and Taylor, 2016). As this study was informed by big data from an ICT source, one additional conclusion might be that ICT itself through geotagged social media was assisting users in maintaining their activity spaces. At a more local level, knowledge of alternatives during a major storm enabled commuters to switch from delayed or canceled train services to more resilient if occasionally diverted bus services, including a Park and Ride bus in the outbound direction to access an edge-of-town business park (Budnitz et al., 2018). In Hong Kong during the Occupy Central Movement, the metro rail system was more resilient, and had enough spare and added capacity to cope with well-informed travelers shifting from disrupted road-based transport (Loo and Leung, 2017).

Meanwhile, data and records of the use of ICT by travelers can enable transport authorities and operators to make their services and information more efficient and relevant, providing real-time information to the right people in the right places during disruption, and creating a feedback loop that results in yet more efficient, sustainable, and resilient alternatives (Cats and Jenelius, 2014; Haworth et al., 2014; Nair et al., 2013). Weather data are important too, although false warnings could actually reduce the level of response, so coordination between weather authorities, transport authorities or operators, and others who have a clear understanding of the timing, location, and extent of any potential impacts is essential (Lee et al., 2009). Yet the fewer the choices of modes and the longer the distance, the more likely not only that the available transport infrastructure or services will be disrupted by severe weather, but also that, if disruption is lengthy or recurrent, travelers will be forced to make decisions about rescheduling and relocating activities (Marsden et al., 2013). There is evidence that when faced with such decisions, people prefer advance planning, known routines, and space-time flexibilities with which they are already familiar, e.g., telecommuting (De Palma and Rochat, 1999; Marsden et al., 2016).

3.2 Telecommuting and spatial redundancy

Multi-modal studies in three different European countries indicate adverse weather results in the postponement or cancelation of many leisure journeys, but that commuters rarely cancel their trips, but may change mode, route, and timing of travel, with the latter being most common (Cools and Creemers, 2013; De Palma and Rochat, 1999; Khattak and De Palma, 1997; Sabir et al., 2010). This is because regularly employed commuters tend to prefer routine, organize their day around work obligations, and have less discretion to choose not to travel (De Palma and Rochat, 1999; Le Vine et al., 2017). Indeed, on a daily basis, people's activities are least affected by changes in the weather during the normally compact morning rush hour between 8 and 9 AM (Horanont et al., 2013), more variable in the evening peak, partly because people appear to choose to leave work earlier or later during bad weather (Singhal et al., 2014), and most affected on the weekend when not just the travel, but also the activity itself may be canceled due to bad weather (Arana et al., 2014; Sabir et al., 2008). This "fixed" nature of work in time and place is largely due to coupling and authority constraints, such as the need for joint or team working, meetings, delivery of services to clients and customers, and management oversight. Yet that is changing as various spatially and temporally flexible working patterns including telecommuting or using ICT to replace all or some of the journey to and from work, are increasing, even if a lag in employer support has resulted in a slower trajectory than researchers might have expected (Cairns et al., 2004; Felstead, 2012; Siha and Monroe, 2006). Furthermore, the stated desire for telecommuting and the flexibility to work from home once or twice a week suggests considerable suppressed demand, particularly among women and part-time workers, fewer of whom telecommute regularly, but who are more likely to say they want to, perhaps due to additional care-giving responsibilities (Headicar and Stokes, 2016; Lavieri et al., 2018; Singh et al., 2013).

The level of telecommuting can be difficult to measure, as it is counted in different ways by different surveys, and depends upon the type of employment: directly employed, indirectly employed, self-employed, full-time, part-time; the definition of place: home, on transport, in alternative locations; the definition of time: full-days, part-days, overtime; and the work tasks (Allen et al., 2015; Bailey and Kurland, 2002; Felstead, 2012; Haddad et al., 2009). However, in all these definitions, telecommuting is reducing coupling constraints. For example, one of the material benefits of ICT is to reduce production costs through remote oversight, so early telecommuting practices often took the form of low-paid clerical work under contract or agency employment as firms used ICT to manage remote workers (Bailey and Kurland, 2002; Karlsson et al., 2010). Subsequently, the development of ICT and the knowledge economy with its autonomous, task-based work culture has been a fundamental component in changing patterns of work (Felstead and Henseke, 2017). Studies from the United States, the Netherlands, and the United Kingdom indicate that telecommuters are now most likely to be found among the professional, better educated, more internet-savvy sectors of the population, and many firms feel that to attract such people, flexibility needs to at least be available even if it is not chosen (Ellen and Hempstead, 2002; Headicar and Stokes, 2016; Peters et al., 2004; Singh et al., 2013; Walls et al., 2006).

As the popularity of telecommuting increases, it offers greater opportunities for increasing resilient travel behaviors, especially if employers are proactive. For example, the United States Federal Government's Telework Enhancement Act of 2010 required remote working be included in emergency planning strategies for its employees, and it was reported that a third of government employees telecommuted during Hurricane Sandy (Allen et al., 2015). Even without this strategic planning, a UK study surveying people in areas affected by the 2013–14 floods, a snow event in 2013, and the closure of a major road bridge in Scotland found evidence that some commuters adapted by working from home and from alternative destinations, or by temporally flexible working such as delayed starts and compressed work weeks (Marsden et al., 2016). Similar evidence was found in American studies of other major road/bridge closures and of commuters who were not employees of the Federal Government during Hurricane Sandy, the latter indicating that people also used ICT to "crowdsource" shared transport and flexible office space with electricity (Kaufman et al., 2012; van Herick et al., 2012; Zhu et al., 2010). Commuters can also use ICT to coordinate non-work coupling constraints, such as arranging a trusted surrogate to pick up children when the parent, usually the mother, who may dedicate substantial time and effort to building networks of such surrogates, is delayed by disruption (Schwanen and Kwan, 2008).

Indeed, as developments in ICT, particularly cloud computing and 3–5 G mobile internet enables access to information anywhere at any time, even when stranded on transport services, ever more people can participate in activities, including work, from unspecified locations (Lyons, 2018; Messenger and Gschwind, 2016). This may be beneficial during disruptions in the short-term, but the debate over its longer-term sustainability and adaptive capacity continues. The potential for avoiding congestion in real-time or connecting and multi-tasking in a traffic jam influences the marginal costs of time spent traveling, which is a concern for those attempting to forecast the potential use, benefits and impacts of both ICT and new transport technologies (Kwan et al., 2007; Le Vine et al., 2015; van Wee et al., 2013). A Canadian study suggested that mobile ICT increases the number of trips, distance traveled and therefore emissions, while a study from the United Kingdom correlates virtual accessibility, measured by variables such as possession of an ICT device and subscription to/coverage of a network, to more discretionary trips and longer distance tours (Lavieri et al., 2018; Miranda-Moreno et al., 2012). One international study questions whether the reduction in transport spend due to use of ICT for access implies less travel or enables more efficient travel over more dispersed networks (Bris et al., 2017). Researchers question whether the long-term effects of ICT on travel demand will be more population dispersal and sprawl, as those who telecommute often live further from their workplace, but not only is the direction of this effect unclear, but also it is dependent upon geographic and economic characteristics, and whether the study includes only telecommuters, or their households, colleagues or the wider population

(Choo et al., 2005; De Abreu e Silva and Melo, 2018; De Vos et al., 2018; Ellen and Hempstead, 2002; Gubins et al., 2017; Hu and He, 2016; Qin et al., 2016; Zhu, 2013). A possible future scenario is one where telecommuting does result in more travel and more sprawl long-term, potentially reducing travel modes and options available, and resulting in less dynamic accessibility and resilience. However, the flexibility telecommuting offers to coordinate with others, especially for work activities, and to avoid disruption, potentially by staying home and reducing the pressure on key routes needed by emergency responders, indicates there is substantial scope for ICT to increase overall resilience and for a scenario where appropriate steps are taken to offer redundancy of access through both transport, ICT, and land use planning.

3.3 Recovery and long-term change

ICT can relax the fixed nature of work travel for some categories of workers, but not for all, and not for an indefinite period of time. Telecommuting from home or alternative spaces may increase over a period of extended disruption perhaps because there are additional opportunities for communication between employers and employees using ICT after a weather event (Kaufman et al., 2012; Marsden et al., 2016). Yet, for those whose work is fixed in time and space because a manual task cannot be done elsewhere or a face-to-face interaction is required, then ICT enables the relaxation of other constraints on the spatial and temporal availability of services. ICT can direct people to local facilities of which they may not be aware, or help them continue to travel through ride-sourcing and reinforcing messages from the authorities about replacement options as networks recover (Loo and Leung, 2017). Online shopping and personal services such as banking and health offer more access outside business hours, and reduce the risks of traveling in severe weather, even if goods must be delivered at some point (Andreev et al., 2010; Chatterjee et al., 2018; Headicar and Stokes, 2016; Rohr et al., 2016). Personal business, food shopping, and other necessary if flexible trips may be undertaken on route to or from work as linked trips to increase travel efficiency and dynamic accessibility, although telecommuters cannot make such trips when they work from home and shift workers are limited by service opening hours (Allen et al., 2015; De Abreu e Silva and Melo, 2018; Järv et al., 2018; Susilo and Kitamura, 2005; Zhu, 2012). Likewise, many more commuters are limited by more time-consuming travel between work and home during disruption, such that, along with postponement and cancelation of non-work trips, reduced opportunity for linked trips is another response to adverse weather.

However, if work is available over the internet, perhaps other activities and services can be made available within walking distance, as adverse weather like extreme cold and flooding was associated in two studies with less disruption of active travel trips and increased walking distance (Marsden et al., 2016; Sabir et al., 2010). Positive integration of urban planning and form can enable communities to make sustainable and resilient travel choices (Headicar, 2015; Hickman et al., 2013), and with the rise of telecommuting and other forms of flexible working, the push to increase sustainable travel choices must include non-work trips. If jobs and populations are unlikely to be distributed evenly, particularly if viewed in terms of employment sectors and labor skills, so flows are also unlikely to be even (Reggiani et al., 2011; Ubøe, 2004). This uneven-ness can be exacerbated by ICT, as it undermines the traditional assumption that the main trade-off in residential location choice is between house prices and commuting costs (Clark et al., 2003; Ma and Banister, 2006). Telecommuters tend to live further from their regular workplace than those who don't telecommute, and although they may choose suburban or metropolitan areas with a diversity of jobs, employment and residential areas in the 21st century are often dispersed (Chowdhury et al., 2013; De Abreu e Silva and Melo, 2018; Ellen and Hempstead, 2002). Yet there is evidence that telecommuters travel more for activities like shopping and personal business, particularly those who live in mixed use neighborhoods or areas of higher density (Asgari and Jin, 2017; Loo and Wang, 2018; Singh et al., 2013). Furthermore, even though trip chaining is associated with traveling further, perhaps because it often accompanies longer-distance commuting trips, people who live in high density areas are also more likely to undertake complex trip chains yet travel shorter distances (Chen and Akar, 2017).

Thus, planning for services, shopping, and facilities in suburban areas can enable residents to make these trips by foot or bicycle if they so choose, and maintain access when more distant centers are made inaccessible by weather. About 20% of any given population are estimated to change jobs or move home each year, and while many of these individuals also change their mode and pattern of commuting, the choice to move home or job is influenced not only by commuting costs, but are also by socio-demographics, urban form, and the cost of moving itself (Clark et al., 2016; Dargay and Hanly, 2007; Van Acker et al., 2010; van Ommeren et al., 1999). If ICT is reducing the importance of commuting costs to these decisions, then other factors like urban form or the presence of children in the household become more relevant, and planning neighborhoods with key facilities has greater potential to increase the number of sustainable and resilient neighborhoods over sprawling, car-dependent suburbs.

4. A look to the future: Vision and validate

Along with proposals for less forecasting and more scenario planning comes the term "vision and validate" (Marsden et al., 2018). The previous sections discussed ways in which ICT might overcome additional space-time constraints created by severe weather, other unforeseen incidents and situations, and planned events and disruptions. Yet only a few of the studies investigating the impact of weather on travel behavior validated this with evidence that telecommuting or other ICT had been employed to overcome transport disruption, and none reviewed whether these had an influence on long-term behavior (Marsden and Docherty, 2013). Furthermore, those few case studies, while enlightening, are neither spatially nor temporally extensive. ICT infrastructure, operation, and use is as full of overlapping and uneven networks as are transport systems, with levels of accessibility and capacity dependent upon the end users' own capabilities, their placement in time and space, the Internet Service Provider involved, the type of connection, and the technology used to manage the connection (Blank et al., 2018; Graham, 2013; Nardotto et al., 2015; Tranos et al., 2013). For example, the quality or download speeds of fixed broadband services are affected by increased ICT activity and data flows, which is commonly tracked by time of day to estimate peak demand, but is also likely to occur during extreme weather events (Fu et al., 2016; Nardotto et al., 2015; Riddlesden and Singleton, 2014). Likewise, studies have recorded less mobile phone use and fewer social interactions in the morning peak (Aledavood et al., 2015; Louail et al., 2014), but this may not be the case during a severe weather event, if people are using their ICT devices to track disruption (Lee et al., 2009). Thus, severe weather adds further layers of temporal and spatial variation in internet activity across ICT networks that have yet to be researched in parallel with transport accessibility.

Similarly, as shown in Fig. 4, transport accessibility is dependent not only on the time, cost, or distance parameters of the transport systems and networks available, but also the gravitational pulls of land use, distribution of population and jobs, and the form of the built environment (Banister, 2008; Halás et al., 2014; Martinez and Viegas, 2013; Reggiani et al., 2011). A variety of socio-demographic characteristics are relevant to both ICT

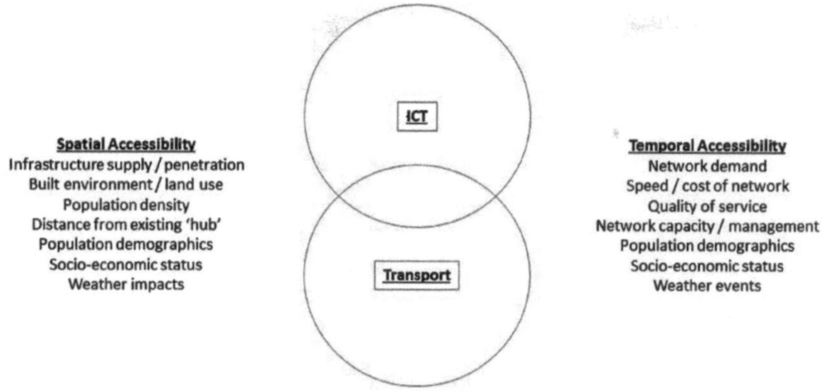

Fig. 4 Variables influencing dynamic accessibility/level of constraints on transport/ICT networks.

penetration and use and to travel behavior; including wealth, education, deprivation, age, presence of children, and urban living, each of which can be aligned to neighborhood classifications and household features (Blank et al., 2018; Clark et al., 2016; Hauge et al., 2010; Hincks et al., 2018; Longley et al., 2008; Lovelace et al., 2014; Riddlesden and Singleton, 2014). An exception might be more deprived groups who live near prime markets for fast broadband benefitting from offers of better quality service sooner than places which are at a distance from such markets (Nardotto et al., 2015). However, those who live near transport hubs similarly benefit, no matter their socio-economic status. Therefore, validation of changes in both travel behavior and internet activity during times of disruption must include spatial, demographic, and geographic analysis.

Validation and modeling must also be able to assess how ICT use, as well as travel behavior can vary during times of disruption. Researchers have seized the opportunities offered by big data sources, especially from mobile phone network data and GPS-based location services to capture large samples of space-time paths with minimal cost (Arribas-Bel, 2014; Lovelace et al., 2016; Miller, 2005). Robust models have been developed that confirm that individual mobility follows certain patterns and is largely predictable, ranking important places in people's lives, particularly work and home, and validating this against national surveys and revealed travel (Gonzalez et al., 2008; Isaacman et al., 2011; Noulas et al., 2012; Song et al., 2010). Yet direct commuting trips are decreasing as a percentage of total trips taken, partly due to previously discussed trends of increased telecommuting and trip chaining, and partly due to other economic restructuring toward more self-employment, contract working, and jobs where there is no fixed workplace, all resulting in observed increases in intra-personal, daily travel variability that do not fit the narrow definition of commuting (Crawford et al., 2018; Haddad et al., 2009; Le Vine et al., 2017; Messenger and Gschwind, 2016). Thus, data from ICT sources are well-placed to research patterns of regular, but less frequent activity, such as secondary places of work, irregular trips for tourism or business travel, and atypical days when there are planned or unplanned events, including severe weather (Becker et al., 2013; Calabrese et al., 2010; Steenbruggen et al., 2015; Wang et al., 2017).

In conclusion, ICT has a myriad of effects on travel behavior, from providing an alternative means of dynamic accessibility which may complement or substitute for physical travel to increasing the efficiency of use and operation of transport services. The increased flexibility of work and travel patterns and of dynamic accessibility for a growing proportion of the population likewise increases the potential for increased resilience through the familiar flexibility and online accessibility that ICT provides. However, the size and direction of these effects varies from study to study and place to place, and is changing as rapidly as ICT itself is developing and expanding over time. Not only does future research into case studies of weather events need data from both transport and ICT to jointly assess the simultaneous changes in access and disruption, but also the detailed granular data and data science methodologies used to determine that human mobility is broadly predictable (Gonzalez et al., 2008; Song et al., 2010) could be usefully applied to gaining a better understanding of the ways in which it is also variable. Substantial work has been and is being done to give time geography methodological foundations (Arribas-Bel and Tranos, 2018; Miller, 2005; van Wee et al., 2013; Wang et al., 2018), and there is some recognition of how ICT is not only a useful data source to track dynamic accessibility, but can also change it (Cats and Jenelius, 2014). However, this area of study is relatively young and much more could be done, particularly in different cultures and contexts, such as cities of the Global South, where the balance of access options and the importance of socio-economic factors are different, and also where there are more vulnerabilities to the impacts of climate change and the risks of extreme weather. Thus, while this review highlights the potential of ICT as a resilient travel behavioral alternative, and includes examples where it has been used as one, much more work is required in many different geographies to translate potential into policy, and validate the different scenarios that may occur under the combined influences of ICT, weather, and travel behavior.

References

Adler, M.W., van Ommeren, J.N., 2016. Does public transit reduce car travel externalities? Quasi-natural experiments' evidence from transit strikes. J. Urban Econ. 92, 106–119. https://doi.org/10.1016/j.jue.2016.01.001.

Aledavood, T., López, E., Roberts, S.G.B., Reed-Tsochas, F., Moro, E., Dunbar, R.I.M., Saramäki, J., 2015. Daily rhythms in mobile telephone communication. PLoS One 10, e0138098. https://doi.org/10.1371/journal.pone.0138098.

Allen, T.D., Golden, T.D., Shockley, K.M., 2015. How effective is telecommuting? Assessing the status of our scientific findings. Psychol. Sci. Public Interest 16, 40–68. https://doi.org/10.1177/1529100615593273.

Andreev, P., Salomon, I., Pliskin, N., 2010. Review: state of teleactivities. Transp. Res. C: Emerg. Technol. 18, 3–20. https://doi.org/10.1016/j.trc.2009.04.017.

Arana, P., Cabezudo, S., Peñalba, M., 2014. Influence of weather conditions on transit ridership: a statistical study using data from smartcards. Transp. Res. A Policy Pract. 59, 1–12. https://doi.org/10.1016/j.tra.2013.10.019.

Arribas-Bel, D., 2014. Accidental, open and everywhere: emerging data sources for the understanding of cities. Appl. Geogr. 49, 45–53. https://doi.org/10.1016/j.apgeog.2013.09.012.

Arribas-Bel, D., Tranos, E., 2018. Characterizing the spatial structure(s) of cities "on the fly": the space-time calendar. Geogr. Anal. 50, 162–181. https://doi.org/10.1111/gean.12137.

Asgari, H., Jin, X., 2017. Impacts of telecommuting on nonmandatory activity participation: role of endogeneity. Transp. Res. Rec. J. Transp. Res. Board 2666, 47–57. https://doi.org/10.3141/2666-06.

Astroza, S., Garikapati, V.M., Bhat, C.R., Pendyala, R.M., Lavieri, P.S., Dias, F.F., 2017. Analysis of the impact of technology use on multimodality and activity travel characteristics. Transp. Res. Rec. J. Transp. Res. Board 2666, 19–28. https://doi.org/10.3141/2666-03.

Bailey, D.E., Kurland, N.B., 2002. A review of telework research: findings, new directions, and lessons for the study of modern work. J. Organ. Behav. 23, 383–400. https://doi.org/10.1002/job.144.

Banister, D., 2008. The sustainable mobility paradigm. Transp. Policy 15, 73–80. https://doi.org/10.1016/j.tranpol.2007.10.005.

Becker, R., Cáceres, R., Hanson, K., Isaacman, S., Loh, J.M., Martonosi, M., Rowland, J., Urbanek, S., Varshavsky, A., Volinsky, C., 2013. Human mobility characterization from cellular network data. Commun. ACM 56, 74–82. https://doi.org/10.1145/2398356.2398375.

Beiler, M.O., Marroquin, L., McNeil, S., 2016. State-of-the-practice assessment of climate change adaptation practices across metropolitan planning organizations pre- and post-Hurricane Sandy. Transp. Res. A Policy Pract. 88, 163–174. https://doi.org/10.1016/j.tra.2016.04.003.

Bell, M., Gault, A., Thompson, M., 2016. Meeting Carbon Budgets—2016 Progress Report to Parliament: Executive Summary. Committee on Climate Change. 1–17. Available from: https://www.theccc.org.uk/publications/.

Blank, G., Graham, M., Calvino, C., 2018. Local geographies of digital inequality. Soc. Sci. Comput. Rev. 36, 82–102. https://doi.org/10.1177/0894439317693332.

Böcker, L., Dijst, M., Prillwitz, J., 2013. Impact of everyday weather on individual daily travel behaviors in perspective: a literature review. Transp. Rev. 33, 71–91. https://doi.org/10.1080/01441647.2012.747114.

Bonsall, P., 2004. Traveller behavior: decision-making in an unpredictable world. J. Intell. Transp. Syst. Technol. Plann. Oper. 8, 45–60. https://doi.org/10.1080/15472450490437744.

Bris, M., Pawlak, J., Polak, J.W., 2017. How is ICT use linked to household transport expenditure? A cross-national macro analysis of the influence of home broadband access. J. Transp. Geogr. 60, 231–242. https://doi.org/10.1016/j.jtrangeo.2017.03.012.

Brown, R., Curley, J., Smith, B., 2014. Transport Resilience Review: A Review of the Resilience of the Transport Network to Extreme Weather Events. Department for Transport. Web ISBN 9781474106627.

Brunnen, D., 2016. Floods Reveal Weaknesses in the Resilience of UK Broadband. Computer Weekly.

Budnitz, H., Chapman, L., Tranos, E., 2018. Better by bus? Insights into public transport travel behavior during Storm *Doris* in Reading, UK. Weather 73 (2), 54–60. https://doi.org/10.1002/wea.3058.

Cairns, S., Sloman, L., Newson, C., Anable, J., Kirkbride, A., Goodwin, P., 2004. Smarter Choices—Changing the Way We Travel London. Department for Transport.

Calabrese, F., Colonna, M., Lovisolo, P., Parata, D., Ratti, C., 2010. Real-time urban monitoring using cell phones: a case study in Rome. IEEE Trans. Intell. Transp. Syst. 12, 141–151. https://doi.org/10.1109/TITS.2010.2074196.

Cats, O., Jenelius, E., 2014. Dynamic vulnerability analysis of public transport networks: mitigation effects of real-time information. Netw. Spat. Econ. 14, 435–463. https://doi.org/10.1007/s11067-014-9237-7.

Chan, R., Schofer, J., 2014. Role of social media in communicating transit disruptions. Transp. Res. Rec. J. Transp. Res. Board 2415, 145–151. https://doi.org/10.3141/2415-16.

Chapman, L., Azevedo, J.A., Prieto-Lopez, T., 2013. Urban heat & critical infrastructure networks: a viewpoint. Urban Climate 3, 7–12. https://doi.org/10.1016/j.uclim.2013.04.001.

Chatterjee, K., Goodwin, P., Schwanen, T., Clark, B., Jain, J., Melia, S., Middleton, J., Plyushteva, A., Ricci, M., Santos, G., Stokes, G., 2018. Young People's Travel—What's Changed and Why? Review and Analysis. Report to Department for Transport. UWE Bristol, UK. https://www.gov.uk/government/publications/young-peoples-travel-whats-changed-and-why.

Chatterton, J., Clarke, C., Daly, E., Dawks, S., Elding, C., Fenn, T., Hick, E., Miller, J., Morris, J., Ogunyoye, F., Salado, R., 2016. The costs and impacts of the winter 2013 to 2014 floods. In: Delivering Benefits Through Evidence. Environment Agency, Bristol, pp. 1–266. ISBN: 978-1-84911-372-4.

Chen, Y.-J., Akar, G., 2017. Using trip chaining and joint travel as mediating variables to explore the relationships among travel behavior, socio-demographics, and urban form. J. Transp. Land Use 10, 573–588. https://doi.org/10.5198/jtlu.2017.882.

Choo, S., Mokhtarian, P.L., Salomon, I., 2005. Does telecommuting reduce vehicle-miles traveled? An aggregate time series analysis for the US. Transportation 32, 37–64. https://doi.org/10.1007/s11116-004-3046-7.

Chorus, C.G., Molin, E.J.E., Van Wee, B., 2006. Use and effects of advanced traveller information services (ATIS): a review of the literature. Transp. Rev. 26, 127–149. https://doi.org/10.1080/01441640500333677.

Chowdhury, T.A., Scott, D.M., Kanaroglou, P.S., 2013. Urban form and commuting efficiency: a comparative analysis across time and space. Urban Stud. 50, 191–207. https://doi.org/10.1177/0042098012452324.

Circella, G., Mokhtarian, P., 2017. Impacts of information and communication technology. In: Giuliano, G., Hanson, S. (Eds.), The Geography of Urban Transportation, fourth ed The Guildford Press, New York, London, pp. 86–109.

Clark, W., Huang, Y., Withers, S., 2003. Does commuting distance matter? Commuting tolerance and residential change. Reg. Sci. Urban Econ. 33, 199–221. https://doi.org/10.1016/SO166-0462(02)00012-1.

Clark, B., Chatterjee, K., Melia, S., 2016. Changes to commute mode: the role of life events, spatial context and environmental attitude. Transp. Res. A Policy Pract. 89–105. https://doi.org/10.1016/j.tra.2016.05.005.

Cools, M., Creemers, L., 2013. The dual role of weather forecasts on changes in activity-travel behavior. J. Transp. Geogr. 28, 167–175. https://doi.org/10.1016/j.jtrangeo.2012.11.002.

Cools, M., Moons, E., Wets, G., 2009. Assessing the impact of weather on traffic intensity. Weather, Climate, Soc. 2, 60–68. https://doi.org/10.1175/2009WCAS1014.1.

Cools, M., Moons, E., Creemers, L., Wets, G., 2010. Changes in travel behavior in response to weather conditions: do type of weather and trip purpose matter? Transp. Res. Rec. J. Transp. Res. Board 2157, 22–28. https://doi.org/10.3141/2157-03.

Cox, A., Prager, F., Rose, A., 2011. Transportation security and the role of resilience: a foundation for operational metrics. Transp. Policy 18, 307–317. https://doi.org/10.1016/j.tranpol.2010.09.004.

Crawford, F., Watling, D.P., Connors, R.D., 2018. Identifying road user classes based on repeated trip behaviour using bluetooth data. Transp. Res. A Policy Pract. 113, 55–74. https://doi.org/10.1016/j.tra.2018.03.027.

Dargay, J., Hanly, M., 2007. Volatility of car ownership, commuting mode and time in the UK. Transp. Res. A Policy Pract. 41, 934–948. https://doi.org/10.1016/j.tra.2007.05.003.

Dawson, R., 2016. Infrastructure. In: UK Climate Change Risk Assessment 2017. Committee on Climate Change, pp. 1–111. Evidence Report, Chapter 4. www.theccc.org.uk.

De Abreu e Silva, J., Melo, P.C., 2018. Does home-based telework reduce household total travel? A path analysis using single and two worker British households. J. Transp. Geogr. 73, 148–162. https://doi.org/10.1016/j.jtrangeo.2018.10.009.

De Palma, A., Rochat, D., 1999. Understanding individual travel decisions: results from a commuters survey in Geneva. Transportation 26, 263–281. https://doi.org/10.1023/A:1005121605832.

De Vos, D., Meijers, E., van Ham, M., 2018. Working from home and the willingness to accept a longer commute. Ann. Reg. Sci. 61, 375–398. https://doi.org/10.1007/s00168-018-0873-6.

Dobney, K., Baker, C.J., Chapman, L., Quinn, A.D., 2009. The future cost to the United Kingdom's railway network of heat-related delays and buckles caused by the predicted increase in high summer temperatures owing to climate change. Proc. IMechE Part F: J. Rail and Rapid Transit 224, 25–34. https://doi.org/10.1243/09544097JRRT292.

Ellen, I., Hempstead, K., 2002. Telecommuting and the demand for urban living: a preliminary look at white-collar workers. Urban Stud. 39, 749–766. https://doi.org/10.1080/00420980220119552.

Felstead, A., 2012. Rapid change or slow evolution? Changing places of work and their consequences in the UK. J. Transp. Geogr. 21, 31–38. https://doi.org/10.1016/j.jtrangeo.2011.10.002.

Felstead, A., Henseke, G., 2017. Assessing the growth of remote working and its consequences for effort, well-being and work-life balance. N. Technol. Work. Employ. 32, 195–212. https://doi.org/10.1111/ntwe.12097.

Ferranti, E., Chapman, L., Lowe, C., et al., 2016. Heat-related failures on Southeast England's railway network: insights and implications for heat risk management. Weather, Climate, Soc. 8, 177–191. https://doi.org/10.1175/WCAS-D-15-0068.1.

Ferranti, E., Chapman, L., Whyatt, D., 2017. A Perfect Storm? The collapse of Lancaster's critical infrastructure networks following intense rainfall on 4/5 December 2015. Weather 72, 3–7. https://doi.org/10.1002/wea.2907.

Fu, G., Horrocks, L., Winne, S., 2016. Exploring impacts of climate change on UK's ICT infrastructure. Infrastruct. Asset Manag. 3, 42–52. https://doi.org/10.1680/jinam.15.00002.
Gonzalez, M.C., Hidalgo, C.A., Barabasi, A.-L., 2008. Understanding individual human mobility patterns. Nature 453, 779–782. https://doi.org/10.1038/nature06958779.
Goodwin, P., 2012. Peak Travel, Peak Car and the Future of Mobility: Evidence, Unresolved Issues, Policy Implications, and a Research Agenda. International Transport Forum Discussion Paper. Paris. https://doi.org/10.1787/5k4c1s3l876d-en.
Graham, M., 2013. Geography/internet: ethereal alternate dimensions of cyberspace or grounded augmented realities? Geogr. J. 179, 177–182. https://doi.org/10.1111/geoj.12009.
Gubins, S., de Graaff, T., van Ommeren, J., 2017. Does New Information Technology Change Commuting Behavior? Working Paper. http://thomasdegraaff.nl/publications/newinformationtechnology/.
Guo, Z., Wilson, N.H.M., Rahbee, A., 2007. The impact of weather on transit ridership in Chicago, Illinois. Transp. Res. Rec. J. Transp. Res. Board 2034, 3–10. https://doi.org/10.3141/2034-01.
Haddad, H., Lyons, G., Chatterjee, K., 2009. An examination of determinants influencing the desire for and frequency of part-day and whole-day homeworking. J. Transp. Geogr. 17, 124–133. https://doi.org/10.1016/j.jtrangeo.2008.11.008.
Hagerstrand, T., 1970. What about people in regional science. In: Ninth European Congress of the Regional Science Association, pp. 7–21.
Halás, M., Klapka, P., Kladivo, P., 2014. Distance-decay functions for daily travel-to-work flows. J. Transp. Geogr. 35, 107–119. https://doi.org/10.1016/j.jtrangeo.2014.02.001.
Hauge, J.A., Jamison, M.A., Marcu, M.I., 2010. Consumer usage of broadband internet services: an analysis of the case of Portugal. In: Dwivedi, Y.K. (Ed.), Adoption, Usage, and Global Impact of Broadband Technologies. IGI Global, Pennsylvania, pp. 198–214. ISBN: 978-1-60960-013-6.
Haworth, J., Shawe-Taylor, J., Cheng, T., Wang, J., 2014. Local online kernel ridge regression for forecasting of urban travel times. Transp. Res. C: Emerg. Technol. 46, 151–178. https://doi.org/10.1016/j.trc.2014.05.015.
Headicar, P., 2015. Settlement patterns, urban form and travel. In: Barton, H.T.S., Burgess, S., Grant, M. (Eds.), The Routledge Handbook of Planning for Health and Well-being. Routledge, Abingdon.
Headicar, P., Stokes, G., 2016. On the Move 2: Making sense of travel trends in England 1995–2014. Technical Report. Independent Transport Commission. http://www.theitc.org.uk/wp-content/uploads/2016/11/OTM2-Technical-Report-FINAL.pdf.
Hickman, R., Hall, P., Banister, D., 2013. Planning more for sustainable mobility. J. Transp. Geogr. 33, 210–219. https://doi.org/10.1016/j.jtrangeo.2013.07.004.
Hincks, S., Kingston, R., Webb, B., Wong, C., 2018. A new geodemographic classification of commuting flows for England and Wales. Int. J. Geogr. Inf. Sci. 32, 663–684. https://doi.org/10.1080/13658816.2017.1407416.
Hofmann, M., O'Mahony, M., 2005. The Impact of adverse weather conditions on urban bus performance measures. In: IEEE Conference on Intelligent Transportation Systems. Vienna, Austria, pp. 431–436.
Hooper, E., Chapman, L., Quinn, A., 2014. Investigating the impact of precipitation on vehicle speeds on UK motorways. Meteorol. Appl. 21, 194–201. https://doi.org/10.1002/met.1348.
Horanont, T., Phithakkitnukoon, S., Leong, T.W., Sekimoto, Y., Shibasaki, R., 2013. Weather effects on the patterns of people's everyday activities: a study using GPS traces of mobile phone users. PLoS One 8, 1–14. https://doi.org/10.1371/journal.pone.0081153.

Horrocks, L., Beckford, J., Hodgson, N., Downing, C., Davey, R., O'Sullivan, A., 2010. Adapting the ICT Sector to the Impacts of Climate Change. Final Report. Issue 5. Department for Environment, Food and Rural Affairs.

Hu, L., He, S.Y., 2016. Association between telecommuting and household travel in the Chicago metropolitan area. J. Urban Plann. Dev. 142 (3), 04016005, 1–8. https://doi.org/10.1061/(ASCE)UP.1943-5444.0000326.

Isaacman, S., Becker, R., Caceres, R., Kobourov, S.G., Martonosi, M., Rowland, J., Varshavsky, A., 2011. Identifying important places in people's lives from cellular network data. In: 9th International Conference on Pervasive Computing (Pervasive).

Jaroszweski, D., Chapman, L., Petts, J., 2010. Assessing the potential impact of climate change on transportation: the need for an interdisciplinary approach. J. Transp. Geogr. 18, 331–335. https://doi.org/10.1016/j.jtrangeo.2009.07.005.

Jaroszweski, D., Hooper, E., Chapman, L., 2014. The impact of climate change on urban transport resilience in a changing world. Prog. Phys. Geogr. 38, 448–463. https://doi.org/10.1177/0309133314538741.

Jaroszweski, D., Hooper, E., Baker, C., Chapman, L., Quinn, A., 2015. The impacts of the 28 June 2012 storms on UK road and rail transport. Meteorol. Appl. 22, 470–476. https://doi.org/10.1002/met.1477.

Järv, O., Tenkanena, H., Salonena, M., Ahas, R., Toivonena, T., 2018. Dynamic cities: location-based accessibility modelling as a function of time. Appl. Geogr. 95, 101–110. https://doi.org/10.1016/j.apgeog.2018.04.009.

Kalkstein, A.J., Kuby, M., Gerrity, D., Clancy, J.J., 2009. An analysis of air mass effects on rail ridership in three U.S. cities. J. Transp. Geogr. 17, 198–207. https://doi.org/10.1016/j.jtrangeo.2008.07.003.

Karlsson, C., Maier, G., Trippl, M., Siedschlag, I., Owen, R., Murphy, G., 2010. ICT and regional economic dynamics: a literature review. In: de Panizza, A., Bogdanowicz, M. (Eds.), EUR—Scientific and Technical Research Series. 102. Institute for Prospective Technological Studies, Spain. ISSN 1018-5593. https://doi.org/10.2791/46419.

Kaufman, S., Qing, C., Levenson, N., Hanson, M., 2012. Transportation During and After Hurricane Sandy. Rudin Center for Transportation, NYU Wagner Graduate School of Public Service.

Khattak, A.J., De Palma, A., 1997. The impact of adverse weather conditions on the propensity to change travel decisions: a survey of Brussels commuters. Transp. Res. A Policy Pract. 31, 181–203. https://doi.org/10.1016/S0965-8564(96)00025-0.

Kilpelainen, M., Summala, H., 2007. Effects of weather and weather forecasts on driver behavior. Transport. Res. F: Traffic Psychol. Behav. 10, 288–299. https://doi.org/10.1016/j.trf.2006.11.002.

Kim, J., Mahmassani, H.S., Alfelor, R., Chen, Y., Hou, T., Jiang, L., Saberi, M., Verbas, Ö., Zockaie, A., 2013. Implementation and evaluation of weather-responsive traffic management strategies: insight from different networks. Transp. Res. Rec. J. Transp. Res. Board 2396, 93–106. https://doi.org/10.3141/2396-11.

Koetse, M.J., Rietveld, P., 2009. The impact of climate change and weather on transport: an overview of empirical findings. Transp. Res. Part D: Transp. Environ. 14, 205–221. https://doi.org/10.1016/j.trd.2008.12.004.

Kwan, M., Dijst, M., Schwanen, T., 2007. The interaction between ICT and human activity-travel behavior. Transp. Res. A Policy Pract. 41, 121–124. https://doi.org/10.1016/j.tra.2006.02.002.

Lavieri, P., Dai, Q., Bhat, C.R., 2018. Using virtual accessibility and physical accessibility as joint predictors of activity-travel behavior. Transp. Res. A Policy Pract. 118, 527–544. https://doi.org/10.1016/j.tra.2018.08.042.

Lazarus, A., 2013. Openreach Response to Service-Related Questions in Ofcom's Consultation Documents. Openreach.

Lazarus, A., 2014. Openreach Response to Ofcom's Fixed Access Market Reviews: Openreach Quality of service and Approach to Setting LLU and WLR. Charge Controls: Non-Confidential Version. Openreach.

Le Vine, S., Zolfaghari, Z., Polak, J., 2015. Autonomous cars: the tension between occupant experience and intersection capacity. Transp. Res. C Emerg. Technol. 52, 1–14. https://doi.org/10.1016/j.trc.2015.01.002.

Le Vine, S., Polak, J., Humphrey, A., 2017. Commuting Trends in England 1988–2015. Department for Transport.

Lee, K., Meyer, R.J., Bradlow, E.T., 2009. Analyzing risk response dynamics on the web: the case of hurricane Katrina. Risk Anal. 29, 1779–1792. https://doi.org/10.1111/j.1539-6924.2009.01304.x.

Longley, P.A., Webber, R., Li, C., 2008. The UK geography of the e-society: a national classification. Environ. Plan. A 40, 362–382. https://doi.org/10.1068/a3912.

Loo, B., Leung, K.Y.K., 2017. Transport resilience: the occupy central movement in Hong Kong from another perspective. Transp. Res. A Policy Pract. 106, 100–115. https://doi.org/10.1016/j.tra.2017.09.003.

Loo, B., Wang, B., 2018. Factors associated with home-based e-working and e-shopping in Nanjing, China. Transportation 45, 365–384. https://doi.org/10.1007/s11116-017-9792-0.

Louail, T., Lenormand, M., García Cantú, O., Picornell, M., Herranz, R., Frias-Martinez, E., Ramasco, J.J., Barthelemy, M., 2014. From mobile phone data to the spatial structure of cities. Sci. Rep. 4, 5276, 1–12. https://doi.org/10.1038/srep05276.

Lovelace, R., Ballas, D., Watson, M., 2014. A spatial microsimulation approach for the analysis of commuter patterns: from individual to regional levels. J. Transp. Geogr. 34, 282–296. https://doi.org/10.1016/j.jtrangeo.2013.07.008.

Lovelace, R., Birkin, M., Cross, P., Clarke, M., 2016. From big noise to big data: toward the verification of large data sets for understanding regional retail flows. Geogr. Anal. 48, 59–81. https://doi.org/10.1111/gean.12081.

Lyons, G., 2006. The role of information in decision-making with regard to travel. Intell. Transp. Syst. 153, 199–212. https://doi.org/10.1049/ip-its:20060001.

Lyons, G., 2015. Transport's digital age transition. J. Transp. Land Use 8, 1–19. https://doi.org/10.5198/jtlu.2014.751.

Lyons, G., 2018. Getting smart about urban mobility—aligning the paradigms of smart and sustainable. Transp. Res. A Policy Pract. 115, 4–14. https://doi.org/10.1016/j.tra.2016.12.001.

Ma, K.-R., Banister, D., 2006. Excess commuting: a critical review. Transp. Rev. 26, 749–767. https://doi.org/10.1080/01441640600782609.

Marsden, G., Docherty, I., 2013. Insights on disruptions as opportunities for transport policy change. Transp. Res. A Policy Pract. 51, 46–55. https://doi.org/10.1016/j.tra.2013.03.004.

Marsden, G., Shires, J., Ferreira, A., Anable, J., 2013. Understanding and modelling decision-making for intra-regional demand management policies. In: World Conference on Transport Research. Rio De Janeiro, pp. 1–17.

Marsden, G., Anable, J., Shires, J., Docherty, I., 2016. Travel behavior response to major transport system disruptions: implications for smarter resilience planning. In: Preparing for Major Disruptions to Transport Systems. OECD, Leipzig, pp. 5–27.

Marsden, G., Dales, J., Jones, P., Seagriff, E., Spurling, N., 2018. All Change? The Future of Travel Demand and the Implications for Policy and Planning. The First Report of the Commission on Travel Demand. ISBN: 978-1-899650-83-5. http://www.demand.ac.uk/wp-content/uploads/2018/04/FutureTravel_report_final.pdf.

Martinez, L., Viegas, J.M., 2013. A new approach to modelling distance-decay functions for accessibility assessment in transport studies. J. Transp. Geogr. 26, 87–96. https://doi.org/10.1016/j.jtrangeo.2012.08.018.

Mattson, L.-G., Jenelius, E., 2015. Vulnerability and resilience of transport systems: a discussion of recent research. Transp. Res. A Policy Pract. 81, 16–34. https://doi.org/10.1016/j.tra.2015.06.002.
McColl, L., Pali, E.J., Thornton, H.E., Sexton, D.M.H., Betts, R., Mylne, K., 2012. Assessing the potential impact of climate change on the UK's electricity network. Clim. Chang. 115, 821–835. https://doi.org/10.1007/s10584-012-0469-6.
Meng, M., Zhang, J., Wong, Y.D., Au, P.H., 2016. Effect of weather conditions and weather forecast on cycling travel behavior in Singapore. Int. J. Sustain. Trans. 10, 773–780. https://doi.org/10.1080/15568318.2016.1149646.
Messenger, J.C., Gschwind, L., 2016. Three generations of telework: new ICTs and the (R) evolution from home office to virtual office. N. Technol. Work. Employ. 31, 195–208.
Miller, H.J., 2005. A measurement theory for time geography. Geogr. Anal. 37, 17–45.
Miranda-Moreno, L.F., Eluru, N., Lee-Gosselin, M., Kreider, T., 2012. Impact of ICT access on personal activity space and greenhouse gas production: evidence from Quebec City, Canada. Transportation 39, 895–918. https://doi.org/10.1007/s11116-012-9428-3.
Mitsakis, E., Papanikolaou, A., Ayfadopoulou, G., Salanova, J., Doll, C., Giannopoulos, G., Zerefos, C., 2014. An integrated framework for linking climate change impacts to emergency adaptation strategies for transport networks. Eur. Transp. Res. Rev. 6, 103–111. https://doi.org/10.1007/s12544-013-0114-0.
Mokhtarian, P., Salomon, I., 2001. How derived is the demand for travel? Some conceptual and measurement considerations. Transp. Res. A Policy Pract. 35, 695–719. https://doi.org/10.1016/S0965-8564(00)00013-6.
Nair, R., Coffey, C., Pinelli, F., Calabrese, F., 2013. Large-scale transit schedule coordination based on journey planner requests. Transp. Res. Rec. 2351, 65–75. https://doi.org/10.3141/2351-08.
Nardotto, M., Valletti, T., Verboven, F., 2015. Unbundling the incumbent: evidence from UK broadband. J. Eur. Econ. Assoc. 13, 330–362. https://doi.org/10.1111/jeea.12127.
Noulas, A., Scellato, S., Lambiotte, R., Pontil, M., Mascolo, C., 2012. A tale of many cities: universal patterns in human urban mobility. PLoS One 7, 1–10. https://doi.org/10.1371/journal.pone.0037027.
OfCom, 2014. Infrastructure Report 2014. OfCom, pp. 1–188.
Pender, B., Currie, G., Delbosc, A., Shiwakoti, N., 2014. Social media use during unplanned transit network disruptions: a review of literature. Transp. Rev. 34, 501–521. https://doi.org/10.1080/01441647.2014.915442.
Peters, P., Tijdens, K.G., Wetzels, C., 2004. Employees' opportunities, preferences, and practices in telecommuting adoption. Inf. Manag. 41, 469–482. https://doi.org/10.1016/S0378-7206(03)00085-5.
Phithakkitnukoon, S., Horanont, T., DiLorenzo, G., Shibasaki, R., Ratti, C., 2010. Activity-aware map: identifying human daily activity pattern using mobile phone data. In: Salah, A.A. et al., (Eds.), Human Behavior Understanding. Springer-Verlag, Istanbul, Turkey, pp. 14–25. https://doi.org/10.1007/978-3-642-14715-9_3.
Pregnolato, M., Ford, A., Robson, C., Glenis, V., Barr, S., Dawson, R., 2016. Assessing urban strategies for reducing the impacts of extreme weather on infrastructure networks. R. Soc. Open Sci. 3, 1–15. https://doi.org/10.1098/rsos.160023.
Qin, X., Zhen, F., Zhuc, S.-J., 2016. Centralisation or decentralisation? Impacts of information channels on residential mobility in the information era. Habitat Int. 53, 360–368.
Quarmby, D., Smith, B., Green, C., 2010. The Resilience of England's Transport Systems in Winter: An Independent Review. Final Report. Department for Transport, London.
Ratti, C., Pulselli, R.M., Williams, S., Frenchman, D., 2006. Mobile landscapes: using location data from cell phones for urban analysis. Environ. Plann. B. Plann. Des. 33, 727–748. https://doi.org/10.1068/b32047.

Reggiani, A., Bucci, P., Russo, G., 2011. Accessibility and impedance forms: empirical applications to the German commuting network. Int. Reg. Sci. Rev. 34, 230–252. https://doi.org/10.1177/0160017610387296.

Riddlesden, D., Singleton, A.D., 2014. Broadband speed equity: a new digital divide? Appl. Geogr. 52, 25–33. https://doi.org/10.1016/j.apgeog.2014.04.008.

Rogers, C., Bouch, C., Williams, S., Barber, A., Baker, C., Bryson, J., Chapman, D., Chapman, L., Coaffee, J., Jefferson, I., Quinn, A., 2012. Resistance and resilience—paradigms for critical local infrastructure. In: Proceedings of the Institution of Civil Engineers. ICE Publishing, pp. 73–84. https://doi.org/10.1680/muen.11.00030Paper.

Rohr, C., Ecola, L., Zmud, J., Dunkerley, F., Black, J., Baker, E., 2016. Travel in Britain in 2035: Future Scenarios and Their Implications for Technology Innovation. RAND Europe.

Sabir, M., Van Ommeren, J., Koetse, M.J., Rietveld, P., 2008. Welfare effects of adverse weather through speed changes in car commuting trips. In: Institute T, (Ed.), Discussion Paper. VU University, Amsterdam, pp. 1–21. TI 2008-087/3.

Sabir, M., van Ommeren, J., Koetse, M.J., Rietveld, P., 2010. Impact of weather on daily travel demand. In: Proceedings of the Tinbergen Institute discussion paper. VU University, Amsterdam.

Saneinejad, S., Roorda, M.J., Kennedy, C., 2012. Modelling the impact of weather conditions on active transportation travel behavior. Transp. Res. Part D: Transp. Environ. 17, 129–137. https://doi.org/10.1016/j.trd.2011.09.005.

Schulman, A., Spring, N., 2011. Pingin' in the rain. In: Internet measurement conference 2011. Berlin: Association for Computing Machinery, pp. 19–28. https://doi.org/10.1145/2068816.2068819.

Schwanen, T., Kwan, M.-P., 2008. The Internet, mobile phone and space-time constraints. Geoforum 39, 1362–1377. https://doi.org/10.1016/j.geoforum.2007.11.005.

Siha, S.M., Monroe, R.W., 2006. Telecommuting's past and future: a literature review and research agenda. Bus. Process. Manag. J. 12, 27https://doi.org/10.1108/14637150610678078.

Sims, R., Schaeffer, R., Creutzig, F., Cruz-Núñez, X., D'Agosto, M., Dimitriu, D., Figueroa Meza, M.J., Fulton, L., Kobayashi, S., Lah, O., McKinnon, A., Newman, P., Ouyang, M., Schauer, J.J., Sperling, D., Tiwari, G., 2014. Transport. In: Edenhofer, O., Pichs-Madruga, R., Sokona, Y., Farahani, E., Kadner, S., Seyboth, K., Adler, A., Baum, I., Brunner, S., Eickemeier, P., Kriemann, B., Savolainen, J., Schlömer, S., von Stechow, C., Zwickel, T., Minx, J.C. (Eds.), Climate Change 2014: Mitigation of Climate Change. Contribution of Working Group III to the Fifth Assessment Report of the Intergovernmental Panel on Climate Change. Cambridge University Press, Cambridge, United Kingdom and New York, NY, USA.

Singh, P., Paleti, R., Jenkins, S., Bhat, C.R., 2013. On modeling telecommuting behavior: option, choice, and frequency. Transportation 40, 23. https://doi.org/10.1007/s11116-012-9429-2.

Singhal, A., Kamga, C., Yazici, A., 2014. Impact of weather on urban transit ridership. Transp. Res. A Policy Pract. 69, 379–391. https://doi.org/10.1016/j.tra.2014.09.008.

Snelder, M., Calvert, S., 2016. Quantifying the impact of adverse weather conditions on road network performance. EJTIR 16, 128–149. ISSN: 1567-7141.

Song, C., Qu, Z.Q., Blumm, N., Barabási, A.-L., 2010. Limits of predictability in human mobility. Science 327, 1018–1021. https://doi.org/10.1126/science.1177170.

Steenbruggen, J., Tranos, E., Nijkamp, P., 2015. Data from mobile phone operators: a tool for smarter cities. J. Telecommunications Policy 39, 335–346. https://doi.org/10.1016/j.telpol.2014.04.001.

Stover, V.W., McCormack, E.D., 2012. The impact of weather on bus ridership in pierce county, Washington. J. Public Transport. 15, 95–110. https://doi.org/10.5038/2375-0901.15.1.6.

Suarez, P., Anderson, W., Mahal, V., Lakshmanan, T.R., 2005. Impacts of flooding and climate change on urban transportation: a systemwide performance assessment of the Boston metro area. Transp. Res. Part D: Transp. Environ. 10, 231–244. https://doi.org/10.1016/j.trd.2005.04.007.

Susilo, Y.O., Kitamura, R., 2005. Analysis of day-to-day variability in an individual's action space: exploration of 6-week mobidrive travel diary data. Transp. Res. Rec. 1902, 124–133. https://doi.org/10.1177/0361198105190200115.

Tranos, E., Ioannides, Y., 2015. Ubiquitous digital technologies and spatial structure: a preliminary analysis. In: *55th Congress of the European Regional Science Association: "World Renaissance: Changing Roles for People and Places"*, Lisbon, Portugal. European Regional Science Association (ERSA), Louvain-la-Neuve.

Tranos, E., Reggiani, A., Nijkamp, P., 2013. Accessibility of cities in the digital economy. Cities 30, 59–67. https://doi.org/10.1016/j.cities.2012.03.001.

Tsapakis, I., Cheng, T., Bolbol, A., 2013. Impact of weather conditions on macroscopic urban travel times. J. Transp. Geogr. 28, 204–211. https://doi.org/10.1016/j.jtrangeo.2012.11.003.

Ubøe, J., 2004. Aggregation of gravity models for journeys to work. Environ. Plan. A 36, 715–729. https://doi.org/10.1068/a3635.

UKCIP, 2013. Ofcom's Fixed Asset Market Review—Overview of Climate Change Impacts. UKCIP, School of Geography and the Environment, OUCE, Oxford.

United Nations, 2015. Sustainable development goals. In: Goal 11 target. United Nations. http://www.un.org/sustainabledevelopment/sustainable-development-goals/. (Accessed 12 June 2017).

Van Acker, V., Van Wee, B., Witlox, F., 2010. When transport geography meets social psychology: toward a conceptual model of travel behaviour. Transp. Rev. 30, 219–240. https://doi.org/10.1080/01441640902943453.

van Herick, D., Mokhtarian, P.L., He, X., 2012. Calculation of changes in vehicle miles traveled for drive-alone commuting during a temporary freeway closure: The fix I-5 project in Sacramento, California. Transp. Res. Rec. J. Transp. Res. Board 67–76. https://doi.org/10.3141/2319-08.

van Ommeren, J., Rietveld, P., Nijkamp, P., 1999. Job Moving, residential moving, and commuting: a search perspective. J. Urban Econ. 46, 230–253. https://doi.org/10.1006/juec.1998.2120.

van Wee, B., Geurs, K., Chorus, C., 2013. Information, communication, travel behavior and accessibility. J. Transp. Land Use 6, 1–16. https://doi.org/10.5198/jtlu.v6i3.282.

Walls, M., Safirova, E., Jiang, Y., 2006. What Drives Telecommuting? The Relative Impact of Worker Demographics, Employer Characteristics, and Job Types. Resources for the Future, Washington DC.

Wang, J.Y.T., 2015. 'Resilience thinking' in transport planning. Civ. Eng. Environ. Syst. 32, 180–191. https://doi.org/10.1080/10286608.2015.1014810.

Wang, D., Law, F.Y.T., 2007. Impacts of information and communication technologies (ICT) on time use and travel behavior: a structural equations analysis. Transportation 34, 513–527. https://doi.org/10.1007/s11116-007-9113-0.

Wang, Q., Taylor, J.E., 2016. Patterns and limitations of urban human mobility resilience under the influence of multiple types of natural disaster. PLoS One 11, 1–14. https://doi.org/10.1371/journal.pone.0147299.

Wang, X., Khattak, A., Fan, Y., 2009. Role of dynamic information in supporting changes in travel behavior: two-stage process of travel decision. Transp. Res. Rec. J. Transp. Res. Board 2138, 85–93. https://doi.org/10.3141/2138-12.

Wang, Z., He, S., Leung, Y., 2017. Applying mobile phone data to travel behaviour research: a literature review. Travel Behav. Soc. https://doi.org/10.1016/j.tbs.2017.02.005.

Wang, Y., Chen, B.Y., Yuan, H., Wang, D., Lam, W.H.K., Li, Q., 2018. Measuring temporal variation of location-based accessibility using space-time utility perspective. J. Transp. Geogr. 73, 13–24. https://doi.org/10.1016/j.jtrangeo.2018.10.002.

Wockatz, P., Schartau, P., 2015. IM Traveller Needs and UK Capability Study: Supporting the realisation of Intelligent Mobility in the UK. Transport Systems Catapult. TSC-TN-OCT15-V01.

Zhu, P., 2012. Are telecommuting and personal travel complements or substitutes? Ann. Reg. Sci. 2012, 619–639. https://doi.org/10.1007/s00168-011-0460-6.

Zhu, P., 2013. Telecommuting, household commute and location choice. Urban Stud. 50, 2441–2459. https://doi.org/10.1177/0042098012474520.

Zhu, S., Levinson, D., Liu, H.X., Harder, K., 2010. The traffic and behavioral effects of the I-35W Mississippi River bridge collapse. Transp. Res. A Policy Pract. 44, 771–784. https://doi.org/10.1016/j.tra.2010.07.001.

CHAPTER FOUR

Relationships between mobile phone usage and activity-travel behavior: A review of the literature and an example

Yihong Wang[a,*], Gonçalo Homem de Almeida Correia[a,b], Bart van Arem[a]
[a]Department of Transport and Planning, Delft University of Technology, Delft, The Netherlands
[b]Department of Civil Engineering, University of Coimbra, Coimbra, Portugal
*Corresponding author: e-mail address: y.wang-14@tudelft.nl

Contents

Advances in Transport Policy and Planning, Volume 3
ISSN 2543-0009
https://doi.org/10.1016/bs.atpp.2019.08.001

Abstract

Almost everyone has a mobile phone today. In addition to calls and text messages, people are utilizing mobile apps and websites to connect to the world and explore different content anytime and anywhere. The use of smart phones generates billions of records, including spatiotemporal trajectories, and various mobile phone usage details, such as call duration, and frequency of visiting a certain type of website. Most transportation researchers have only focused on spatiotemporal traces, which represent activity-travel behavior of users. However, it is worth making full use of smart phone data to study how mobile phone usage is related to activity-travel behavior. This chapter first reviews the existing literature on the relevant topics to demonstrate the lack of research on the relationship between mobile internet usage and activity-travel behavior. Based on an 11-day dataset from Shanghai that includes not only spatiotemporal traces but also the frequencies of browsing different categories of mobile internet content (e.g., tourism and finance), we examine several relationships between mobile internet usage and activity-travel behavior.

Keywords: Mobile phone usage, Mobile internet usage, Mobile phone data, Spatio-temporal traces, Travel behavior, Activity patterns, Location choice, Variety seeking, Commuting behavior

1. Introduction

With the rapid development of Information and Communication Technologies (ICT), people have started using mobile devices in their daily lives. Most mobile devices do not only provide services to users, but also record information about the use of the device and sometimes also spatio-temporal traces (Li et al., 2011; Zhang and Sawchuk, 2012). Relative to other mobile devices such as wearable devices, mobile phones are most commonly used. People have traditionally used mobile phones to communicate with friends and families by making calls and using SMS (short message service). More recently, smart phones in addition allow visiting websites, subscribing to news, and playing online games, thanks to fast-growing mobile internet technologies. Consequently, every day, billions of data records are generated by mobile phones. Such mobile phone data often include spatiotemporal traces of users, which represent their actual movements (Ahas et al., 2010; Calabrese et al., 2014; Ratti et al., 2006). Many studies have explored how to measure activity-travel behavior from mobile phone traces, in terms of activity patterns (Diao et al., 2016; Järv et al., 2014; Yin et al., 2017), trip generation (Bwambale et al., 2017; Çolak et al., 2015), location choice (Chen et al., 2014; Molloy et al., 2017;

Y. Wang et al., 2017), mode choice (Phithakkitnukoon et al., 2017; Wang et al., 2010), departure time choice (Alexander et al., 2015), route choice (Bierlaire et al., 2013; Chen, 2013). Moreover, mobile phone data also include information about how users communicate with other people, such as call duration (Z.-Q. Jiang et al., 2013b; Wang et al., 2018a), as well as how they connect to internet services, such as frequency of visiting a website (Wang et al., 2018b; Z. Wang et al., 2017), both of which are generally called as mobile phone usage in this chapter.

Apparently, the two types of information in mobile phone data motivate two seemingly separate research directions: studying activity-travel patterns and studying mobile phone usage patterns. However, it is also worth combining these two types of information together and studying the relationships between mobile phone usage and activity-travel behavior (Ben-Elia et al., 2018; Ben-Elia and Zhen, 2018; van den Berg et al., 2013). The earliest research on travel and telecommunication originates from the 1980s when ICT were emerging and people were wondering if ICT, especially telecommuting, would reshape travel behavior (Mokhtarian, 1990; Salomon, 1986). Since then, it has been extensively debated whether telecommunication usage substitutes for travel (Salomon, 1998) or complements it (Mokhtarian, 2003). Nevertheless, the context of this debate is mostly outdated, and few studies have examined this relationship by considering mobile internet usage as a dominant usage of telecommunication today.

Based on the identified relationships (no matter if it is substitution or complementary), researchers attempted to characterize travelers by their mobile phone usage and further explain or predict their travel behavior (Bwambale et al., 2017; Wang et al., 2018a; Wang et al., 2018b) and even provide visiting location recommendations (Husain and Dih, 2012; Lian et al., 2015). This is regarded as a solution to travel behavior modeling using mobile phone traces, where personal attributes (e.g., socio-demographics) are absent due to privacy concerns, since increasingly more urban decision makers intend to prevent expensive traditional travel survey data. Researchers have also done the other way around: providing location-based services such as recommending internet content based on the places that a user has visited (Ahas and Mark, 2005; Lee et al., 2005).

In this study, we first present a review of the existing literature related to (1) mobile phone technology, (2) mobile phone usage, (3) activity-travel behavior that can be derived from mobile phone traces, and most importantly, (4) the relationships between mobile phone usage and activity-travel behavior. Since it is found that such relationships have not been studied adequately in the context of mobile internet usage, we continue our work with a case study in the city of Shanghai, China, to add recent empirical evidence to this research area. Using Shanghai Unicom WO+ Open Data Application Contest,[a] this is one of the first studies that use mobile internet usage data and mobile phone traces to address the following questions: (1) it addresses the question about the relationship between activity-travel and mobile phone usage in the mobile internet era by providing empirical evidence; and (2) it presents a possibility of accounting for the heterogeneity of activity-travel behavior revealed in mobile phone traces by using mobile internet usage data. At the end of this chapter, conclusions are drawn and future research directions are pointed out.

2. Literature review

This section consists of four parts. Part 1 and 2, respectively, present a review of the literature on mobile phone technology and the literature on mobile phone usage. The third part reviews the approaches that derive activity-travel behavior from mobile phone traces. Finally, the fourth part provides the results of a literature review on the relationships between mobile phone usage and activity-travel behavior, and based on this review develops a conceptual framework to understand this relationship.

2.1 Mobile phone technology

Mobile phones have played an important role in people's lives. They have not only been used as a communication device but also served as a sensing device to collect information from its users (Lane et al., 2010). This study mainly focuses on two types of user information: (1) mobile phone usage, and (2) spatiotemporal traces. In this subsection, we discuss the mobile phone technologies that enable the generation of spatiotemporal traces of users. There are mainly four location systems that can record mobile phone users' spatiotemporal traces: (1) cellular-network-based positioning system (Demissie et al., 2013), (2) GPS positioning system (Wolf et al., 2004), (3) Wi-Fi positioning system (Danalet et al., 2016), and (4) Bluetooth positioning system (Delafontaine et al., 2012). In this chapter, we limit our scope to cellular-network-based positioning system, which generates the most widely applied type of mobile phone data in travel behavior research (Wang et al., 2017).

[a] https://www.kesci.com/woplus/ (retrieved date: 5th January 2017).

Mobile phones are able to communicate with each other and connect to the mobile internet, based on cellular networks composed of transceivers that cover their respective land areas. With the movement of a mobile phone, it searches and connects to the nearest transceiver. This process is known as mobile phone positioning (Chen et al., 2016). Positioning data about such connections between users and transceivers are recorded mostly for cellular network operators' own purposes (e.g., billing), which are often not related to transportation, whilst as a by-product, they have been utilized by urban decision makers and researchers to estimate and understand mobility patterns (Wang and Chen, 2018). Because such data are in terms of spatiotemporal traces, researchers named them as mobile phone traces (Jiang et al., 2013a).

Mobile phone traces can be categorized into event-driven traces and network-driven traces (Pinelli et al., 2015). Call detail records and records of internet connections belong to the former one since the production of these data is triggered by user events, including usage of calls, SMS, and internet (Pinelli et al., 2015). Network-driven data are generated regardless whether people are using phones, but either in a periodic way or when a phone moves between two areas. Due to the nature of event-driven traces, their sampling is usually infrequent and could be biased to specific locations, e.g., home locations, and times, e.g., during the evenings; on the other hand, the sampling rate of network-driven traces is relatively higher and stable over time (Calabrese et al., 2014).

Spatial inaccuracy has always been an issue if mobile phone traces are used to estimate locations and represent individual mobility (Ahas et al., 2007). There are mainly two causes: (1) the difference between the actual location of a user and the location of the transceiver that the user is connecting to, and (2) the possibility of a user switching the connection between towers due to signal jumps even if the user is not moving (Alexander et al., 2015; Wang and Chen, 2018). To solve the first problem, the simplest way is to regard the transceiver's location or its Voronoi cell as a proxy for the user's location (Montjoye and Smoreda, 2014). Some telecom providers can estimate locations with a higher accuracy based on triangulation with several factors including the number of surrounding cells and received signal strength. The accuracy can reach about 100–500 m in urban areas and 400–10,000 m in rural areas, reported in a Chinese study (Wang et al., 2017b). Qi et al. (2016) named the second problem as the oscillation problem, to which Wang and Chen (2018) have presented an in-depth review on the solutions, including heuristic rules, spatiotemporal clustering, etc. Those algorithms can be used to preprocess mobile phone traces before conducting activity-travel behavior analysis.

2.2 Mobile phone usage

While in the past mobile phone usage referred to making calls and sending SMS text, nowadays it also includes using mobile internet services such as browsing the internet. All these kinds of mobile phone usage can be measured to quantify user preferences, such as the preference for longer calls or the preference for a certain type of content on the internet. Researchers have observed that different people use mobile phones in different ways (Sey, 2011), and they have further investigated whether personal characteristics, such as socio-demographic attributes (Blumenstock et al., 2010) and socio-economic attributes (Rahmati et al., 2012), would influence how people use mobile phones.

In the early stage of mobile technology when mobile penetration rate was not as high as it is today, researchers noticed that mobile phone usage and access actually differed by socio-economic profile, better known as the "mobile divide" or "digital divide" (Blumenstock and Eagle, 2010; Compaine and Kimmelman, 2001; Rice and Katz, 2003). For example, only wealthy people could afford mobile phones or mobile services during that period. Nevertheless, we have now entered an age where mobile phones have penetrated almost everywhere (Asongu, 2015; Thulin and Vilhelmson, 2007). While people across different societal segments all own mobile phones, the ways in which they use mobile phones still vary considerably.

Using the interview data of 1481 children and 1505 adolescents, Thomas et al. (2009) found that people in Germany with a lower socio-economic status used mobile phones relatively longer per day. In the empirical study by Blumenstock et al. (2010) using call detail records with complementary survey data from Rwanda, men were found to make more outgoing calls and receive less incoming calls than women. Moreover, the users owning televisions and the ones owning refrigerators (both indicating a higher economic status in Rwanda at that time) had longer daily call duration, compared to the others.

However, such research results have gradually become irrelevant and even invalid because fewer people are making calls, and very few people are still sending SMS text in the mobile internet era (Ofcom, 2013). Instead, people are using apps for countless functions, including, but not limited to, browsing the internet, sending emails, playing online games and instant messaging. Researchers have shifted their focus to mobile internet usage and started figuring out that mobile internet usage also differs among people from different population segments. Rahmati et al. (2012) carefully selected three groups of 34 mobile users from Houston, the United States, with high, low and very low socio-economic status, respectively, mainly based on household income. In their sample, users with a lower socio-economic status accessed mobile internet services more frequently. In addition, people with different socio-economic status were found to prefer different categories of websites. Pearce and Rice (2013) conducted a survey in Armenia and collected the data from 1420 voluntary and anonymous adults. They found that not only socio-economic (i.e., income) but also socio-demographic (e.g., gender, age and education) differences significantly influence mobile internet access as well as mobile internet activities. In the Netherlands, a survey was conducted from 2010 to 2013 to create a panel that consists of over 108,000 people representative of the Dutch population, and their demographics and internet usage (including mobile internet usage) were collected (van Deursen et al., 2015). The results showed that different people used internet for different purposes. For example, men, younger people, higher educated people and people with higher than average incomes significantly had more internet activities especially for personal development. Overall, while personal attributes are always an important factor influencing mobile phone usage, the mobile phone usage patterns of people from different socioeconomic or sociodemographic strata vary between different countries, for different purposes, and could even change over time.

In addition to using socio-economic strata to explain the differences in mobile phone usage, researchers have done the other way around: using mobile phone usage to predict socio-economic information (Frias-Martinez et al., 2013; Soto et al., 2011). This kind of research is necessary as well because it is too expensive to carry out traditional census surveys nationwide, and at the same time, survey results are very likely to be soon outdated (Calabrese et al., 2013). Comparably, mobile phone data are cheaper to obtain and faster updated, thus being able to help the government monitor socio-economic dynamics in a certain area.

2.3 Deriving activity-travel behavior from mobile phone traces

2.3.1 Stay extraction

Algorithms have been designed to extract trips and derive origin-destination (OD) information from mobile phone traces (Chen et al., 2014). Among all the spatiotemporal traces, they distinguish where users stay from where users pass by, and all the detected stay points can further be used to calculate stay areas, finally regarded as trip origins and destinations (Alexander et al., 2015). In general, the extraction of a stay point depends on two scale parameters, a time threshold and a distance threshold. A stay point is regarded as a sequence of traced positions where the distance between any pair of positions is less than a distance threshold, and the time spent at these positions is greater than a time threshold. A stay area is defined as a set of stay points which are close in space but far away in time. In addition, such methods are able to solve the problems of false movements, caused by mobile signal jumps between the towers (Alexander et al., 2015). After these procedures, activity locations can be determined, but activity purposes still need to be inferred with the use of complementary information (Jiang et al., 2017).

2.3.2 Activity purpose detection

To detect activity purposes, researchers reference the ground-truth spatial information, such as the information of POIs (points of interest) around activity locations (Demissie et al., 2015; Phithakkitnukoon et al., 2010). A more advanced approach is to calibrate a machine learning model (e.g., a decision tree) using travel survey data or other ground-truth mobility data, which associates activity purposes with several explanatory variables (Liu et al., 2013). Such a model can further be applied to mobile phone traces to label trip destinations with activity purposes. Without the availability of complementary information, arbitrary parameters can be set to infer home and work locations of mobile users based on general knowledge (e.g., most people stay home at night), and activity purpose can then be labeled as either home, work or other activity (Ahas et al., 2010).

2.3.3 Estimating other mobility information

Time-of-day information (i.e., start and end times of a trip or an activity) can also be estimated, which can help estimate the daily activity schedule of a traveler (Alexander, 2015). The accuracy level of time-of-day information is largely dependent on the temporal sampling rate of mobile phone traces. Observing the daily schedules of an individual across several days can help understand the rhythms of activity-travel behavior and better determine meaningful locations for this person (e.g., home and work locations). It is also possible to estimate mode and route choices, only given the mobile phone traces of a high temporal sampling rate as well as a high spatial resolution (Chen, 2013; Wang et al., 2010).

2.3.4 *From sample to population*

Notwithstanding the high mobile penetration rate everywhere, most of the times, researchers can only get access to a sample of limited size. Sometimes it is because that mobile network companies who provide mobile phone data do not dominate the market (Calabrese et al., 2013). It is also very likely that they do not want to expose the data of all of their users for commercial and privacy reasons (e.g., Laurila et al., 2012; Montjoye and Smoreda, 2014). Due to the sampling process, problems may arise if researchers aim to estimate not only individual travel behavior but also travel demand of a given population (Wesolowski et al., 2013). The sampled users might not be distributed geographically in the way as the population is (Kang et al., 2012). To solve this issue, Calabrese et al. (2011) compared the spatial distribution of the users' detected home locations and the one of the population revealed in the census data, and they calculated an expansion factor for each zone to upscale users to population. Another approach is to validate the movements derived from mobile phone traces by using the traffic ground truth data. Iqbal et al. (2014) scaled up the estimated OD matrix by using the scaling factors which would lead to better matches with the observed traffic counts.

2.4 Relationships between mobile phone usage and activity-travel behavior

The relationship between telecommunication and travel is a long-time debatable topic. This issue has been extensively discussed because researchers have observed two opposing possible effects of ICT on travel: either a substitute relationship or a complementary relationship. (Kamargianni and Polydoropoulou, 2013; Nobis and Lenz, 2009; Salomon, 1986). In recent years, researchers have especially focused on the relationship between mobile phone usage and travel, and they found that the actual relationships are more complex (Aguiléra et al., 2012; Mokhtarian, 2009), as there are many linkages between different dimensions of activity participation, travel patterns and mobile phone usage (Ben-Elia et al., 2014; Srinivasan and Raghavender, 2006).

In Section 2.2, we have already explained how mobile phone usage is dependent on personal attributes including socio-economic and socio-demographic ones. In fact, in most travel behavior models, such personal attributes are also assumed to be one of the major factors influencing behavioral heterogeneity among a given population (Rasouli and Timmermans, 2014). Extensive research has found that travel preferences are significantly different between older and younger people (Bernhoft and Carstensen, 2008;

Moschis and Ünal, 2008), between people with higher and lower household income (Lu and Pas, 1999), between people owning cars and not owning cars (van Wee et al., 2002), etc. In summary, both mobile phone usage and activity-travel behavior are influenced by personal attributes.

Based on this conceptual framework, it is not difficult to deduce that mobile phone usage and activity-travel behavior are somehow related to each other. For example, younger people tend to make more trips and use mobile phones more frequently (Yuan et al., 2012). This kind of deduction is quite useful not only for understanding the relationship between mobile phone usage and travel, but also for modeling heterogeneity in travel behavior using mobile phone data since traditional personal attributes are missing there in most cases for privacy reasons (Blondel et al., 2015).

It is also reasonable to add direct interactions between activity-travel behavior and mobile phone usage in our conceptual framework. For example, it can be hypothesized that those who travel more would also make more use of mobile phones while on the move. Also, driving calls are quite frequent but less on public transit, where internet usage is more pervasive. Despite the microscopic mechanisms of such interactions, the main idea of our conceptual framework still holds: mobile phone usage can be used to model heterogeneity in travel behavior.

Yuan et al. (2012) found the correlation between mobile phone usage, in terms of call frequency, and travel behavior, in terms of activity space, across different age groups. Bwambale et al. (2017) suggested utilizing call behavior, such as call frequency and duration, to explain the heterogeneity in trip generation behavior, since this information, supplementary to mobile phone traces, is less privacy-sensitive but still related to some characteristics of a person. However, mobile phones are less used for calls today (Ofcom, 2013), making call behavior a less useful indicator; in contrast, people spend more time on mobile internet services. Moreover, mobile internet usage may reflect more detailed information about one's specific interests and lifestyles. Therefore, mobile internet usage data, if available, should encompass a better reflection of individuals' traits (Wang et al., 2018b), whilst not much research has been done in this regard possibly due to the lack of such data. The following part of this chapter attempts to fill this gap by carrying out a case study on the relationships between mobile internet usage and activity-travel behavior.

3. Case study

The case study is conducted in Shanghai, China, one of the most populated and fastest growing cities all over the world. We are allowed to access a sample dataset of Unicom mobile users. As one of the three mobile carriers in China, Unicom was reported to have had about 270 million users, more than 20% of the population in China, by the beginning of 2017. In the provided dataset, each anonymous user ID corresponds to not only their mobile internet usage but also their spatiotemporal traces from 27th of December 2015, to 6th of January 2016. The study period includes a new year's holiday from 1st of January to 3rd January.

In the data collection process, every trace of a user would be recorded once the user had any mobile phone activity, in terms of a call, SMS text, a voice mail, or an internet connection. However, for privacy reasons, the data provider aggregated the traces hour by hour for each user. Thus, the provided dataset only includes the location where a user stayed for the longest time within an hour. If a user did not have any mobile phone activity within that hour, we are not able to know where the user was, and it is called a missing trace.

To prevent the impact of missing traces on our further analysis, we only target the 46,007 users who had spatial records for at least 80% of the total hours during the study period. According to the data provider, due to the inherent detection inaccuracy, the actual position of a trace is estimated to lie within the 200×200 m square of which the center is the detected point. This spatial error is reasonably small and acceptable for our further analysis.

The mobile internet usage data were also aggregated by the data provider, who classified a select number of apps and websites into different categories. As a result, there are 13 categories of mobile internet content in total, including "finance," "food," "news," "housing," "car," "entertainment," "education," "job," health," "game," "shopping," "tourism," and "sports." Finally, the page view counts of each user are provided, respectively, for the 13 categories. According to the data provider, different apps may have different ways to count such "page views." For example, in some cases, they count the times an app has been opened; in some other cases, they count the times an app has been interacted with users. Therefore, such page views should only be compared across categories after being normalized.

4. Methodology

Fig. 1 presents the flowchart of the research methods for the case study. First, the indicators of mobile internet usage, namely preferred category of mobile internet content and total usage intensity, can be calculated

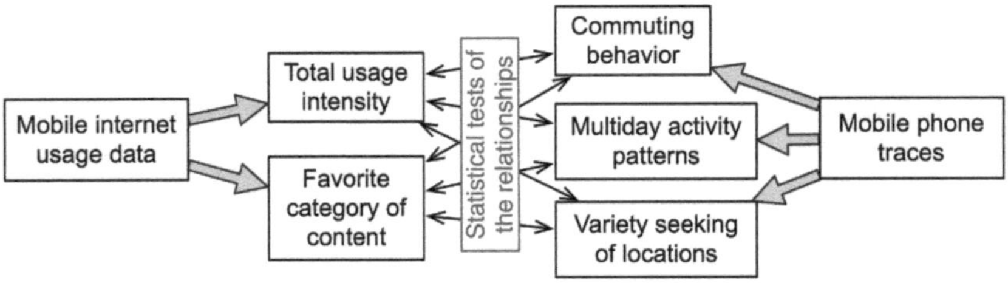

Fig. 1 The flowchart of the research methods for the case study.

for each user using mobile internet usage data. Second, the indicators of activity-travel behavior, including commuting behavior, variety seeking of locations, and multiday activity patterns, can also be calculated for each user using mobile phone traces. Finally, the relationships can be statistically tested between the indicators of mobile internet usage and the indicators of activity-travel behavior.

4.1 Indicators of mobile internet usage

This study considers an individual's mobile internet usage, in terms of the frequencies of browsing different categories of websites and apps via mobile internet over several days. More specifically, this information is provided in two indicators: (1) the frequency of browsing all contents, which reflects an individual's general mobile internet usage intensity, and (2) one's favorite category of mobile internet content, which reflects an individual's lifestyle and interest.

Let f_{un} indicate the frequency of browsing a category of mobile internet content n (e.g., finance or shopping) through mobile apps and/or websites by an individual u across several days. Given this, the two indicators of one's mobile internet usage during a period can be derived: (1) one's favorite category of mobile internet content N_u, and (2) the frequency of browsing all mobile internet contents F_u, which is further classified into two levels: high usage (higher than the median), and low usage (lower than the median), designated by a dummy variable F_u'.

4.2 Stay extraction from mobile phone traces

Stay points need to be distinguished from pass-by points among all mobile phone traces, and signal jumps should be reduced. An extensive literature has discussed these problems as well as their case-by-case solutions. In this study, we adopt the approach and parameter settings suggested by Alexander et al. (2015). Consider T_{ui} as the *i*-th spatiotemporal trace of an individual *u*, including three elements lon_{ui}, lat_{ui}, and $time_{ui}$ which represent longitude, latitude and timestamp, respectively.

First, for each user, the traces that are spatially close (within 300 m) to their subsequent observations need to be distinguished and sets of geographically close traces are obtained. Second, the medoid of the coordinates within each set is calculated. Third, the hierarchical clustering algorithm is applied to consolidate the sets that are close in space but far apart in time, using 500 m as the threshold. As a result, if the distance between two sets is shorter than 500 m, they are combined as a cluster. Fourth, the medoid of the coordinates within each cluster is calculated. Fifth, a duration threshold is assumed to identify whether a user stayed or passed by, and finally we can know where a user stayed for an activity and whether it is a location where the user had visited before. In our case study, it is stipulated that at least two consecutive traces close in space can determine a stay point, which will necessarily lead to overlooking some short activities; however, this is the best that can be done to extract stay points with these data.

4.3 Indicators of activity-travel behavior

In this study, we specifically focus on three aspects of activity-travel behavior: (1) commuting behavior, (2) variety seeking of locations, and (3) multiday activity patterns.

4.3.1 Commuting behavior

Home and work locations (if any) should be detected for each user at first. We apply the thresholds and rules mainly following the approach of Alexander et al. (2015). For each user, home location is defined as the location with the most stay traces from 7 to 8 a.m. on weekdays, on weekends, and on holidays. Work location is then defined to be the place to which one cumulatively traveled the maximum distance from home, max(vd), where v is the number of visits between 8 a.m. and 7 p.m. on weekdays, and d is the distance of a place from home. In addition, if a user visits the detected work location fewer than 2 days per week, it is not regarded as a work location. We further label the stay traces at the detected home location as home activity. The same applies to labeling work activity, and the remaining stay traces are labeled as secondary activity. The drawback of this approach is that only stable home and work locations can be detected.

After the process described above, we can generate two indicators of one's commuting behavior: (1) a dummy variable C_u stating whether user

u is a commuter, and (2) the commuting distance CD_u of user u if $C_u = 1$, further classified into two levels: longer commuting distance (longer than the median) and shorter commuting distance (shorter than the median), designated by CD_u'.

4.3.2 Variety seeking of locations

Another aspect of behavior to investigate is variety seeking of locations. People have been shown to have significantly different preferences in variety seeking of locations (Leszczyc et al., 2000; Leszczyc and Timmermans, 1997). Some people tend to explore new locations as much as possible, whilst the others tend to visit the places that they are familiar with (Pappalardo et al., 2015). We indicate one's variety seeking of locations by calculating the number of distinct locations L_u that user u has visited during the study period, and L_u is further classified into two levels: high variety seeking of locations (higher than the median) and low variety seeking (lower than the median) of locations, designated by L_u'.

4.3.3 Multiday activity patterns

Activity patterns are related to one's choices of activity type, frequency, sequence, start time and duration (Arentze and Timmermans, 2004). In our study, we especially focus on activity type and duration. For each individual, we calculate the share of time used for out-of-home activity within each day, represented by AP_{ud}, which means the proportion of out-of-home activities of user u on day d. Using the longitudinal mobile phone traces, we can observe multiday activity patterns of each user, which can further be clustered using the k-means clustering algorithm. The number of clusters can be determined by using the DB-index, which can indicate the compactness of a clustering solution (Davies and Bouldin, 1979). CL_u is used to designate which cluster user u belongs to.

4.4 Relating mobile internet usage to activity-travel behavior

We have two categorical indicators of mobile internet usage, N_u and F_u', and we have four categorical indicators of activity-travel behavior, C_u, CD_u', L_u' and CL_u. Pearson's chi-squared test is used to examine the statistical dependence between these variables (McHugh, 2013).

5. Results and discussion

5.1 Activity-travel behavior

Based on the detection algorithms, around 30% of mobile users are identified as commuters, and the distribution of their commuting distances is shown in Fig. 2. While the shape of the distribution looks similar to the ones found in Boston, Milan, etc. (Kung et al., 2014), the median and the mean of commuting distance are significantly higher in Shanghai, which are about 7.7 and 10 km, respectively. This is reasonable because of the large scale of the city, and also the figures are very close to the ones reported by the urban authority (Lu and Gu, 2011).

Fig. 3 shows the distribution of unique number of visited locations across the users during the 11 days. The median and the mean of the distribution are 3 and 3.125, respectively, indicating that people only visited three different places on average. It should be noted again that the detection algorithms used in this study tend to overlook short activities, as a side effect of stay extraction; therefore, it is likely that we have underestimated the unique numbers of visited locations. However, the impact of this underestimation is not huge because we do not focus on abstract values and we only group people into those with high variety seeking of locations and those with low variety seeking of locations.

The proportion of out-of-home hours is calculated for each user on each day, and each user can further be described by a vector of such proportions across 11 days. Based on these vectors, the users are clustered by applying the

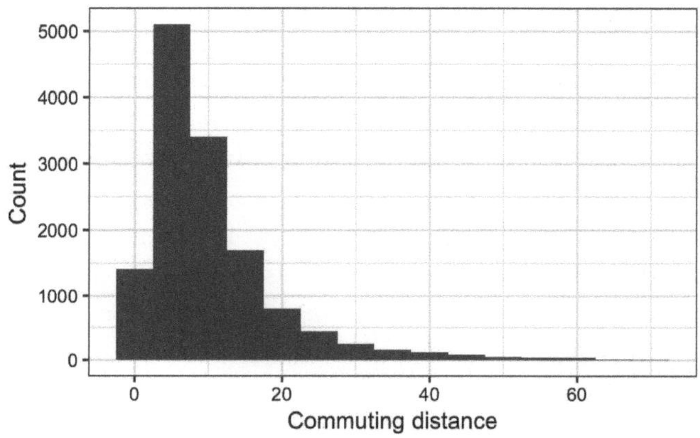

Fig. 2 The histogram of commuting distance (km).

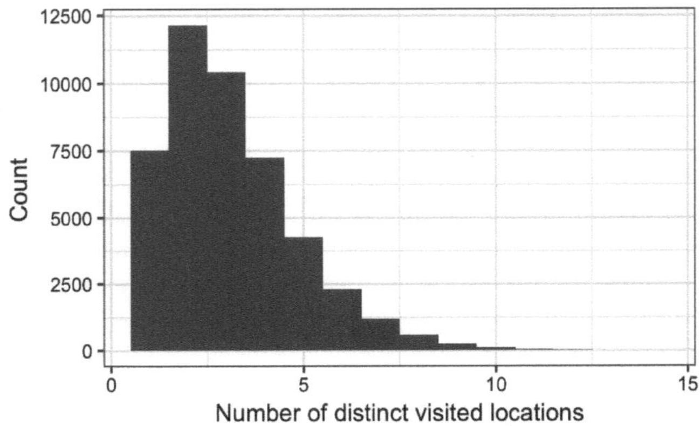

Fig. 3 The histogram of unique number of visited locations.

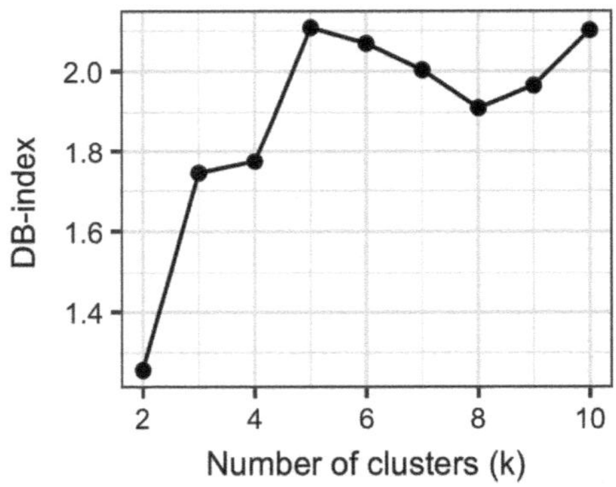

Fig. 4 The DB-index of clustering multiday activity patterns.

k-means algorithm. We consider the range of k from 2 to 10, and DB-index is calculated in each case to indicate the compactness of clusters, as shown in Fig. 4. A lower DB-index indicates more compact clusters.

While it can be observed that the clusters are most compact when $k=2$, we also investigate the clusters when $k=3$ and $k=4$, as shown in Fig. 5, for the sake of interpretation. Note that day 1 is Sunday; day 6, 7 and 8 are new year's holiday; the other days are weekdays. It is not difficult to figure out that cluster 1 in the first case ($k=2$) can somehow be decomposed into cluster 1 and cluster 2 in the second case ($k=3$). Cluster 2 in the second case ($k=3$) seems to represent the pattern of a typical commuter with 30% of time being not at home on weekdays on average. Cluster 1 in the second case ($k=3$) is relatively difficult to interpret, but it seems to further be decomposed into cluster 3 and 4 in the third case ($k=4$), which,

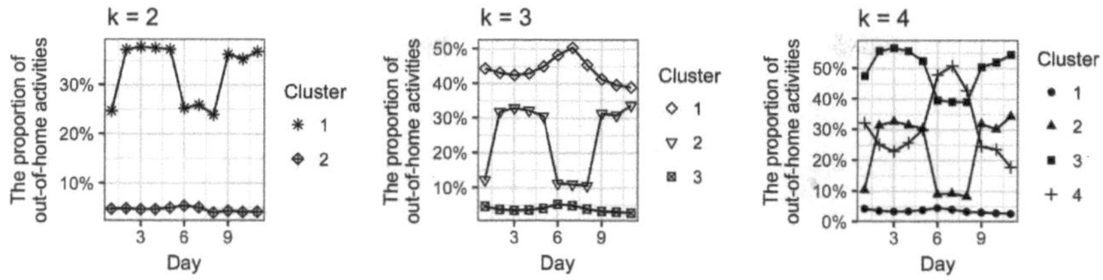

Fig. 5 The clusters of multiday activity patterns.

respectively, represent the commuters who stayed less time at home and the people who were more active on weekend and holiday. Considering both cluster compactness and interpretability, we use four clusters to distinguish multiday activity patterns, and cluster 1, 2, 3, and 4 are named as "inactive traveler," "typical commuter," "active commuter," and "weekend traveler," respectively.

5.2 The relationships between activity-travel behavior and mobile internet usage intensity

According to the results of our statistical tests, people with different intensity levels of total mobile internet usage seem to have significantly different activity-travel behavior, as shown in Fig. 6. First, people using more often mobile internet are more likely to be a commuter and have longer commutes. Second, people with higher usage intensity level also visited more distinct locations than the others during the 11 days. Third, those who frequently used mobile internet spent more time away from home in general. Especially, a clear difference in total usage intensity can be observed between inactive users and typical commuters. On the other hand, the difference between the other two clusters is not very significant.

A common pattern behind these observations is that people who travel more and longer tend to be active mobile internet users as well. A similar finding was reported by Yuan et al. (2012), who observed the positive correlation between high call frequency and larger activity space. We substantiate such a complementary relationship in the context of mobile internet.

5.3 The relationships between activity-travel behavior and favorite category of mobile internet content

Fig. 7 shows the statistical test results of the relationships between activity-travel behavior and favorite category of mobile internet content. In general, dependence can be found between each pair of variables as indicated by the

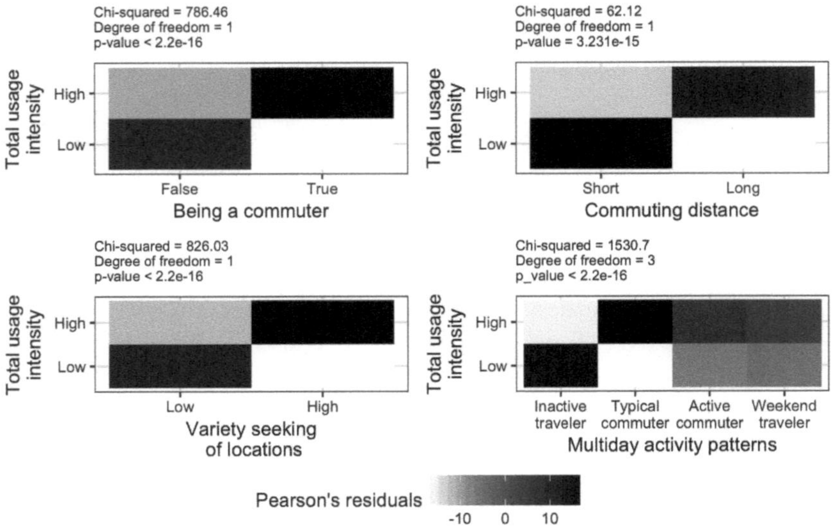

Fig. 6 Associations between activity-travel behavior and mobile internet usage intensity.

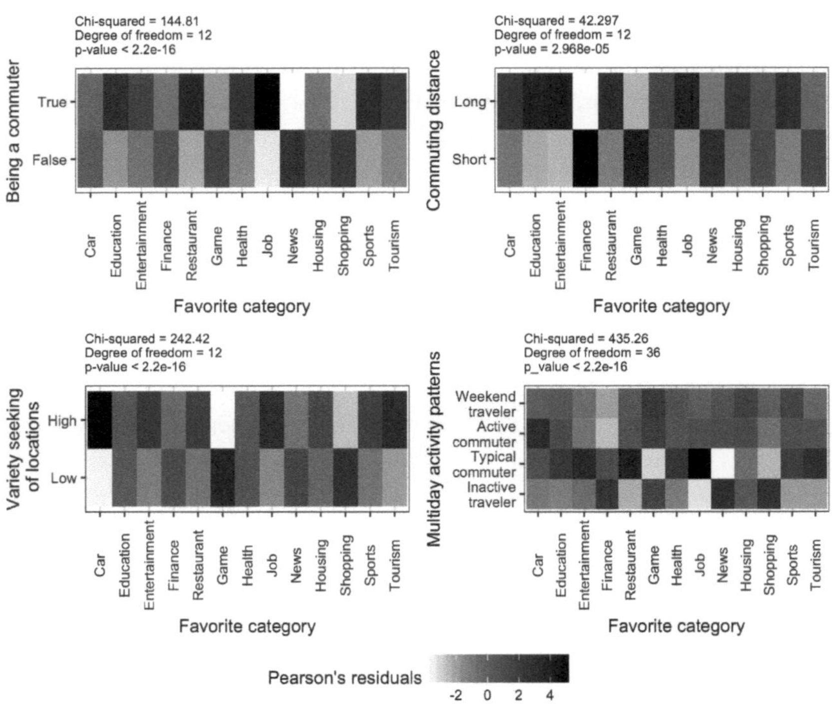

Fig. 7 Associations between activity-travel behavior and favorite category of mobile internet content.

low *P*-values. Especially, some associations between specific categories stand out. First, a commuter significantly preferred job-related content compared to a non-commuter. The other categories of content that interested commuters include restaurant and sports. On the other hand, a non-commuter was more likely to be attracted to the content related to online shopping and news. Second, a user with a shorter commute was significantly attracted to the content related to finance and game; in contrast, a user with a longer commute was more interested in the content related to education and entertainment. Third, those who visited more distinct locations seem to be the ones who were interested in the content related to car and tourism, whilst those who visited fewer distinct locations preferred the content related to game and online shopping. Fourth, it is hard to distinguish the preference of weekend travelers and active commuters, except that active commuters are significantly more interested in car-related content, compared to the others.

It is difficult to reason the significant associations merely based on such observations. However, some of them are quite consistent with common sense. For example, typical commuters were interested in job-related content; inactive travelers spent more time on games and online shopping; those who visited more distinct locations preferred the content related to car and tourism.

6. Conclusions and recommendations

This chapter has presented a literature review on the relationships between mobile phone usage and activity-travel behavior, and performed a case study, as a complementary example, to empirically investigate the relationships in the context of mobile internet. In Section 2, we built a simple conceptual framework to help understand the relationships between mobile phone usage and activity-travel behavior through literature review: they are related to each other because they are both dependent on personal attributes such as socio-economic and socio-demographic attributes. In Section 3–5, we used a mobile phone dataset from Shanghai, China, to inspect the relationships between activity-travel behavior of the users, revealed in spatiotemporal traces, and their mobile internet usage, including the frequencies of browsing different categories of content through mobile apps and websites. Some significant and interpretable relationships that we found are highlighted as follows:

- Those who traveled more and longer were likely to use mobile internet more often.
- Commuters were more interested in job-related content.
- Inactive travelers spent more time on games and online shopping.
- Those who visited more distinct locations preferred the content related to car and tourism.

Based on our study, a couple of research directions can be further investigated. First, more aspects of activity-travel behavior can be included in this kind of analysis. In our study, we only considered activity pattern and location choice mainly due to the relatively lower sampling rate of our data (i.e., one trace per hour); however, it is possible to detect travel mode choice, departure time choice and even route choice with higher-resolution data, and the relationships between mobile internet usage and these choices can then be examined. Second, although we only explored the statistical dependence between some indicators of mobile internet usage and activity-travel behavior, attempts could be made to build explanatory travel behavior models based on our findings, by using both mobile phone traces and mobile internet usage data. Such models can incorporate mobile internet usage as an element to distinguish different population segments and further explain behavioral heterogeneity.

Acknowledgments

We would like to express our gratitude to the Shanghai Unicom WO+ Open Data Application Contest for making the mobile phone data available for this research. Thanks go also to the TRAIL research school and the Dutch Organization for Scientific Research (NWO) for sponsoring the first author for his PhD study. The assigned grant code is 022.005.030.

References

Aguiléra, A., Guillot, C., Rallet, A., 2012. Mobile ICTs and physical mobility: review and research agenda. Transp. Res. A Policy Pract. 46, 664–672. https://doi.org/10.1016/J.TRA.2012.01.005.

Ahas, R., Mark, Ü., 2005. Location based services—new challenges for planning and public administration? Futures 37, 547–561. https://doi.org/10.1016/J.FUTURES.2004.10.012.

Ahas, R., Laineste, J., Aasa, A., Mark, Ü., 2007. The Spatial Accuracy of Mobile Positioning: Some Experiences with Geographical Studies in Estonia, in: Location Based Services and TeleCartography. Springer, Berlin Heidelberg, Berlin, Heidelberg, pp. 445–460. https://doi.org/10.1007/978-3-540-36728-4_32.

Ahas, R., Silm, S., Järv, O., Saluveer, E., Tiru, M., 2010. Using Mobile positioning data to model locations meaningful to users of Mobile phones. J. Urban Technol. 17, 3–27. https://doi.org/10.1080/10630731003597306.

Alexander, L.P., 2015. Cell Phone Location Data for Travel Behavior.

Alexander, L., Jiang, S., Murga, M., González, M.C., 2015. Origin–destination trips by purpose and time of day inferred from mobile phone data. Transp. Res. C 58, 240–250. https://doi.org/10.1016/j.trc.2015.02.018.

Arentze, T.A., Timmermans, H.J., 2004. A learning-based transportation oriented simulation system. Transp. Res. B Methodol. 38, 613–633. https://doi.org/10.1016/j.trb.2002.10.001.

Asongu, S., 2015. The impact of mobile phone penetration on African inequality. Int. J. Soc. Econ. 42, 706–716. https://doi.org/10.1108/IJSE-11-2012-0228.

Ben-Elia, E., Zhen, F., 2018. ICT, activity space–time and mobility: new insights, new models, new methodologies. Transportation 45, 267–272. https://doi.org/10.1007/s11116-018-9870-y.

Ben-Elia, E., Alexander, B., Hubers, C., Ettema, D., 2014. Activity fragmentation, ICT and travel: An exploratory Path Analysis of spatiotemporal interrelationships. Transp. Res. A Policy Pract. 68, 56–74. https://doi.org/10.1016/J.TRA.2014.03.016.

Ben-Elia, E., Lyons, G., Mokhtarian, P.L., 2018. Epilogue: the new frontiers of behavioral research on the interrelationships between ICT, activities, time use and mobility. Transportation 45, 479–497. https://doi.org/10.1007/s11116-018-9871-x.

Bernhoft, I.M., Carstensen, G., 2008. Preferences and behaviour of pedestrians and cyclists by age and gender. Transport. Res. F: Traffic Psychol. Behav. 11, 83–95. https://doi.org/10.1016/J.TRF.2007.08.004.

Bierlaire, M., Chen, J., Newman, J., 2013. A probabilistic map matching method for smartphone GPS data. Transp. Res. C Emerg. Technol. 26, 78–98. https://doi.org/10.1016/J.TRC.2012.08.001.

Blondel, V.D., Decuyper, A., Krings, G., 2015. A survey of results on mobile phone datasets analysis. EPJ Data Sci. 4, 10. https://doi.org/10.1140/epjds/s13688-015-0046-0.

Blumenstock, J., Eagle, N., 2010. Mobile Divides: Gender, Socioeconomic Status, and Mobile Phone Use in Rwanda. In: Proceedings of the 4th ACM/IEEE International Conference on Information and Communication Technologies and Development - ICTD '10. ACM Press, New York, New York, USA, pp. 1–10. https://doi.org/10.1145/2369220.2369225.

Blumenstock, J.E., Gillick, D., Eagle, N., 2010. In: Who's Calling? Demographics of Mobile Phone Use in Rwanda. 2010 AAAI Spring Symp. Ser. AAAI Press.

Bwambale, A., Choudhury, C., Hess, S., 2017. Modelling trip generation using mobile phone data: A latent demographics approach. J. Transp. Geogr. https://doi.org/10.1016/j.jtrangeo.2017.08.020.

Calabrese, F., Di Lorenzo, G., Liu, L., Ratti, C., 2011. Estimating origin-destination flows using Mobile phone location data. IEEE Pervasive Comput. 10, 36–44. https://doi.org/10.1109/MPRV.2011.41.

Calabrese, F., Diao, M., Di Lorenzo, G., Ferreira, J., Ratti, C., 2013. Understanding individual mobility patterns from urban sensing data: a mobile phone trace example. Transp. Res. C Emerg. Technol. 26, 301–313. https://doi.org/10.1016/j.trc.2012.09.009.

Calabrese, F., Ferrari, L., Blondel, V.D., 2014. Urban sensing using Mobile phone network data: a survey of research. ACM Comput. Surv. 47, 1–20. https://doi.org/10.1145/2655691.

Chen, J., 2013. Modeling Route Choice Behavior Using Smartphone Data. Rep. TRANSP-OR.

Chen, C., Bian, L., Ma, J., 2014. From traces to trajectories: how well can we guess activity locations from mobile phone traces? Transp. Res. C Emerg. Technol. 46, 326–337. https://doi.org/10.1016/J.TRC.2014.07.001.

Chen, C., Ma, J., Susilo, Y., Liu, Y., Wang, M., 2016. The promises of big data and small data for travel behavior (aka human mobility) analysis. Transp. Res. C Emerg. Technol. 68, 285–299. https://doi.org/10.1016/j.trc.2016.04.005.

Çolak, S., Alexander, L.P., Alvim, B.G., Mehndiratta, S.R., González, M.C., 2015. Analyzing cell phone location data for urban travel. Transp. Res. Rec. J. Transp. Res. Board 2526, 126–135. https://doi.org/10.3141/2526-14.

Compaine, B.M., Kimmelman, G., 2001. The Digital Divide Confronts the Telecommunication Act of 1996, the Digital Divide: Facing a Crisis or Creating a Myth? MIT Press.

Danalet, A., Tinguely, L., Lapparent, M.d., Bierlaire, M., 2016. Location choice with longitudinal WiFi data. J. Choice Model. 18, 1–17. https://doi.org/10.1016/j.jocm.2016.04.003.

Davies, D.L., Bouldin, D.W., 1979. A cluster separation measure. IEEE Trans. Pattern Anal. Mach. Intell. PAMI-1, 224–227. https://doi.org/10.1109/TPAMI.1979.4766909.

Montjoye, Y.D., Smoreda, Z., 2014. D4D-Senegal: the second Mobile phone data for development challenge. arXiv Prepr.arXiv.

Delafontaine, M., Versichele, M., Neutens, T., Van de Weghe, N., 2012. Analysing spatiotemporal sequences in Bluetooth tracking data. Appl. Geogr. 34, 659–668. https://doi.org/10.1016/J.APGEOG.2012.04.003.

Demissie, M.G., Correia, G., Bento, C., 2013. Intelligent road traffic status detection system through cellular networks handover information: an exploratory study. Transp. Res. C Emerg. Technol. 32, 76–88. https://doi.org/10.1016/j.trc.2013.03.010.

Demissie, M.G., Correia, G., Bento, C., 2015. Analysis of the pattern and intensity of urban activities through aggregate cellphone usage. Transportmetrica A Transp. Sci. 11, 502–524. https://doi.org/10.1080/23249935.2015.1019591.

Diao, M., Zhu, Y., Ferreira, J., Ratti, C., 2016. Inferring individual daily activities from mobile phone traces: a Boston example. Environ. Plan. B Plan. Des. 43, 920–940. https://doi.org/10.1177/0265813515600896.

Frias-Martinez, V., Soguero-Ruiz, C., Frias-Martinez, E., Josephidou, M., 2013. Forecasting socioeconomic trends with cell phone records. In: Proceedings of the 3rd ACM Symposium on Computing for Development–ACM DEV '13. ACM Press, New York, New York, USA, p. 1. https://doi.org/10.1145/2442882.2442902.

Husain, W., Dih, L.Y., 2012. A framework of a personalized location-based traveler recommendation system in mobile application. Int. J. Multimed. Ubiquitous Eng. 7 (3), 11–18.

Iqbal, M.S., Choudhury, C.F., Wang, P., González, M.C., 2014. Development of origin–destination matrices using mobile phone call data. Transp. Res. C Emerg. Technol. 40, 63–74. https://doi.org/10.1016/j.trc.2014.01.002.

Järv, O., Ahas, R., Witlox, F., 2014. Understanding monthly variability in human activity spaces: a twelve-month study using mobile phone call detail records. Transp. Res. C Emerg. Technol. 38, 122–135. https://doi.org/10.1016/J.TRC.2013.11.003.

Jiang, S., Fiore, G. a, Yang, Y., Ferreira, J., Frazzoli, E., González, M.C., 2013a. A review of urban computing for mobile phone traces. Proc. 2nd ACM SIGKDD Int. Work. Urban Comput. - UrbComp '13 1. doi:https://doi.org/10.1145/2505821.2505828

Jiang, Z.-Q., Xie, W.-J., Li, M.-X., Podobnik, B., Zhou, W.-X., Stanley, H.E., 2013b. Calling patterns in human communication dynamics. Proc. Natl. Acad. Sci. U. S. A. 110, 1600–1605. https://doi.org/10.1073/pnas.1220433110.

Jiang, S., Ferreira, J., González, M.C., 2017. Activity-Based Human Mobility Patterns Inferred from Mobile Phone Data: A Case Study of Singapore. IEEE trans. BIG DATA 208–219.

Kamargianni, M., Polydoropoulou, A., 2013. In: Does Social Networking Substitute for or Stimulate Teenagers ' Travel ? Findings from a Latent Class Model. Int. Choice Model. Conf.

Kang, C., Liu, Y., Ma, X., Wu, L., 2012. Towards estimating urban population distributions from Mobile call data. J. Urban Technol. 19, 3–21. https://doi.org/10.1080/10630732.2012.715479.

Kung, K.S., Greco, K., Sobolevsky, S., Ratti, C., 2014. Exploring universal patterns in human home-work commuting from mobile phone data. PLoS One 9, e96180. https://doi.org/10.1371/journal.pone.0096180.
Lane, N., Miluzzo, E., Lu, H., Peebles, D., Choudhury, T., Campbell, A., 2010. A survey of mobile phone sensing. IEEE Commun. Mag. 48, 140–150. https://doi.org/10.1109/MCOM.2010.5560598.
Laurila, J.K., Gatica-Perez, D., Aad, I., J., B., Bornet, O., Do, T.-M.-T., Dousse, O., Eberle, J., Miettinen, M., 2012. The Mobile Data Challenge: Big Data for Mobile Computing Research, EPFL scientific publications.
Lee, H.J., Choi, J.Y., Park, S.J., 2005. Context-Aware Recommendations on the Mobile Web. Springer, Berlin, Heidelberg, pp. 142–151. https://doi.org/10.1007/11575863_30.
Leszczyc, P.P., Timmermans, H., 1997. Store-switching behavior. Mark. Lett. 8, 193–204. https://doi.org/10.1023/A:1007910503617.
Leszczyc, P.T.L.P., Sinha, A., Timmermans, H.J., 2000. Consumer store choice dynamics: an analysis of the competitive market structure for grocery stores. J. Retail. 76, 323–345. https://doi.org/10.1016/S0022-4359(00)00033-6.
Li, Z., Li, M., Wang, J., Cao, Z., 2011. Ubiquitous data collection for mobile users in wireless sensor networks. In: 2011 Proceedings IEEE INFOCOM. IEEE, pp. 2246–2254. https://doi.org/10.1109/INFCOM.2011.5935040.
Lian, D., Ge, Y., Zhang, F., Yuan, N.J., Xie, X., Zhou, T., Rui, Y., 2015. Content-aware collaborative filtering for location recommendation based on human mobility data. In: 2015 IEEE international conference on data mining. IEEE, pp. 261–270. https://doi.org/10.1109/ICDM.2015.69.
Liu, F., Janssens, D., Wets, G., Cools, M., 2013. Annotating mobile phone location data with activity purposes using machine learning algorithms. Expert Syst. Appl. 40, 3299–3311. https://doi.org/10.1016/j.eswa.2012.12.100.
Lu, X., Gu, X., 2011. The fifth travel survey of residents in Shanghai and characteristics analysis. Urban Transp. China 9, 1–7.
Lu, X., Pas, E.I., 1999. Socio-demographics, activity participation and travel behavior. Transp. Res. A Policy Pract. 33, 1–18. https://doi.org/10.1016/S0965-8564(98)00020-2.
McHugh, M.L., 2013. The chi-square test of independence. Biochem. Medica 23, 143–149. https://doi.org/10.11613/BM.2013.018.
Mokhtarian, P.L., 1990. A typology of relationships between telecommunications and transportation. Transp. Res. A Gen. 24, 231–242. https://doi.org/10.1016/0191-2607(90)90060-J.
Mokhtarian, P.L., 2003. Telecommunications and travel. The case for complementarity. J. Ind. Ecol. https://doi.org/10.1162/108819802763471771.
Mokhtarian, P., 2009. If telecommunication is such a good substitute for travel, why does congestion continue to get worse? Transport. Lett. 1, 1–17. https://doi.org/10.3328/TL.2009.01.01.1-17.
Molloy, J., Moeckel, R., Molloy, J., Moeckel, R., 2017. Improving destination choice modeling using location-based big data. ISPRS Int. J. Geo Inf. 6, 291. https://doi.org/10.3390/ijgi6090291.
Moschis, G.P., Ünal, B., 2008. Travel and leisure services preferences and patronage motives of older consumers. J. Travel Tour. Mark. 24, 259–269. https://doi.org/10.1080/10548400802156711.
Nobis, C., Lenz, B., 2009. Communication and mobility behaviour–a trend and panel analysis of the correlation between mobile phone use and mobility. J. Transp. Geogr. https://doi.org/10.1016/j.jtrangeo.2008.11.013
Ofcom, 2013. Communications Market Report. Ofcom.

Pappalardo, L., Simini, F., Rinzivillo, S., Pedreschi, D., Giannotti, F., Barabási, A.-L., 2015. Returners and explorers dichotomy in human mobility. Nat. Commun. 6, 8166. https://doi.org/10.1038/ncomms9166.

Pearce, K.E., Rice, R.E., 2013. Digital divides from access to activities: comparing mobile and personal computer internet users. J. Commun. 63, 721–744. https://doi.org/10.1111/jcom.12045.

Phithakkitnukoon, S., Horanont, T., Lorenzo, G.D., Shibasaki, R., Ratti, C., 2010. Activity-aware map : identifying human daily activity pattern using mobile phone data. In: Human Behavior Understanding. Springer, pp. 14–25. https://doi.org/10.1007/978-3-642-14715-9_3.

Phithakkitnukoon, S., Sukhvibul, T., Demissie, M., Smoreda, Z., Natwichai, J., Bento, C., 2017. Inferring social influence in transport mode choice using mobile phone data. EPJ Data Sci. 6, 11. https://doi.org/10.1140/epjds/s13688-017-0108-6.

Pinelli, F., Lorenzo, G.D., Calabrese, F., 2015. In: Comparing Urban Sensing Applications Using Event and Network-Driven Mobile Phone Location Data. Mob. Data Manag. (MDM), 2015 16th IEEE Int. Conf.

Qi, L., Qiao, Y., Abdesslem, F.B., Ma, Z., Yang, J., 2016. Oscillation Resolution for Massive Cell Phone Traffic Data. In: Proceedings of the First Workshop on Mobile Data - MobiData '16. ACM Press, New York, New York, USA, pp. 25–30. https://doi.org/10.1145/2935755.2935759.

Rahmati, A., Tossell, C., Shepard, C., Kortum, P., Zhong, L., 2012. Exploring iPhone usage: the influence of socioeconomic differences on smartphone adoption, usage and usability. In: Proceedings of the 14th International Conference on Human-Computer Interaction with Mobile Devices and Services - MobileHCI '12. ACM Press, New York, New York, USA, p. 11. https://doi.org/10.1145/2371574.2371577.

Rasouli, S., Timmermans, H., 2014. Activity-based models of travel demand: promises, progress and prospects. Int. J. Urban Sci. 18, 31–60. https://doi.org/10.1080/12265934.2013.835118.

Ratti, C., Pulselli, R.M., Williams, S., Frenchman, D., 2006. Mobile landscapes: using location data from cell phones for urban analysis. Environ. Plan. B Plan. Des. 33 (5), 727–748. https://doi.org/10.1068/b32047.

Rice, R.E., Katz, J.E., 2003. Comparing internet and mobile phone usage: digital divides of usage, adoption, and dropouts. Telecommun. Policy 27, 597–623. https://doi.org/10.1016/S0308-5961(03)00068-5.

Salomon, I., 1986. Telecommunications and travel relationships: a review. Transp. Res. A Gen. 20, 223–238. https://doi.org/10.1016/0191-2607(86)90096-8.

Salomon, I., 1998. Technological change and social forecasting: the case of telecommuting as a travel substitute. Transp. Res. C Emerg. Technol. 6, 17–45. https://doi.org/10.1016/S0968-090X(98)00006-0.

Sey, A., 2011. 'We use it different, different': making sense of trends in mobile phone use in Ghana. New Media Soc. 13, 375–390. https://doi.org/10.1177/1461444810393907.

Soto, V., Frias-Martinez, V., Virseda, J., Frias-Martinez, E., 2011. Prediction of Socioeconomic Levels Using Cell Phone Records. Springer, Berlin, Heidelberg, pp. 377–388. https://doi.org/10.1007/978-3-642-22362-4_35.

Srinivasan, K.K., Raghavender, P.N., 2006. Impact of mobile phones on travel. Transp. Res. Rec. J. Transp. Res. Board 1977, 258–267. https://doi.org/10.1177/0361198106197700130.

Thomas, S., Heinrich, S., Kühnlein, A., Radon, K., 2009. The association between socioeconomic status and exposure to mobile telecommunication networks in children and adolescents. Bioelectromagnetics 31, 20–27. https://doi.org/10.1002/bem.20522.

Thulin, E., Vilhelmson, B., 2007. Mobiles everywhere. Young 15, 235–253. https://doi.org/10.1177/110330880701500302.

van den Berg, P., Arentze, T., Timmermans, H., 2013. A path analysis of social networks, telecommunication and social activity–travel patterns. Transp. Res. C Emerg. Technol. 26, 256–268. https://doi.org/10.1016/J.TRC.2012.10.002.

van Deursen, A.J.A.M., van Dijk, J.A.G.M., ten Klooster, P.M., 2015. Increasing inequalities in what we do online: a longitudinal cross sectional analysis of internet activities among the Dutch population (2010 to 2013) over gender, age, education, and income. Telematics Inform. 32, 259–272. https://doi.org/10.1016/J.TELE.2014.09.003.

van Wee, B., Holwerda, H., van Baren, R., 2002. Preferences for modes, residential location and travel behaviour: the relevance for land-use impacts on mobility. Eur. J. Transp. Infrastruct. Res. 2, 305–316.

Wang, F., Chen, C., 2018. On data processing required to derive mobility patterns from passively-generated mobile phone data. Transp. Res. C Emerg. Technol. 87, 58–74. https://doi.org/10.1016/J.TRC.2017.12.003.

Wang, H., Calabrese, F., Di Lorenzo, G., Ratti, C., 2010. In: Transportation Mode Inference from Anonymized and Aggregated Mobile Phone Call Detail Records. IEEE Conf. Intell. Transp. Syst. Proceedings, ITSC. https://doi.org/10.1109/ITSC.2010.5625188.

Wang, Y., Correia, G., de Romph, E., Timmermans, H.J.P., 2017a. Using metro smart card data to model location choice of after-work activities: an application to Shanghai. J. Transp. Geogr. 63, 40–47. https://doi.org/10.1016/j.jtrangeo.2017.06.010.

Wang, Z., He, S.Y., Leung, Y., 2017b. Applying mobile phone data to travel behaviour research: a literature review. Travel Behav. Soc. 11, 141–155. https://doi.org/10.1016/J.TBS.2017.02.005.

Wang, Y., Correia, G., de Romph, E., Santos, B.F., 2018a. Road network design in a developing country using mobile phone data: an application to senegal. IEEE Intell. Transp. Syst. Mag. https://doi.org/10.1109/MITS.2018.2879168.

Wang, Y., Correia, G., van Arem, B., Timmermans, H.J.P.(.H.)., 2018b. Understanding travellers' preferences for different types of trip destination based on mobile internet usage data. Transp. Res. C Emerg. Technol. 90, 247–259. https://doi.org/10.1016/j.trc.2018.03.009.

Wesolowski, A., Eagle, N., Noor, A.M., Snow, R.W., Buckee, C.O., 2013. The impact of biases in mobile phone ownership on estimates of human mobility. J. R. Soc. Interface 10, 20120986. https://doi.org/10.1098/rsif.2012.0986.

Wolf, J., SchöUnfelder, S., Samaga, U., Oliveira, M., Axhausen, K., 2004. Eighty weeks of global positioning system traces: approaches to enriching trip information. Transp. Res. Rec. J. Transp. Res. Board 1870, 46–54. https://doi.org/10.3141/1870-06.

Yin, M., Sheehan, M., Feygin, S., Paiement, J.-F., Pozdnoukhov, A., 2017. A generative model of urban activities from cellular data. IEEE Trans. Intell. Transp. Syst. 1–15. https://doi.org/10.1109/TITS.2017.2695438.

Yuan, Y., Raubal, M., Liu, Y., 2012. Correlating mobile phone usage and travel behavior–a case study of Harbin. China. Comput. Environ. Urban Syst. 36, 118–130. https://doi.org/10.1016/J.COMPENVURBSYS.2011.07.003.

Zhang, M., Sawchuk, A.A., 2012. USC-HAD: a daily activity dataset for ubiquitous activity recognition using wearable sensors. In: Proceedings of the 2012 ACM Conference on Ubiquitous Computing–UbiComp '12. ACM Press, New York, New York, USA, p. 1036. https://doi.org/10.1145/2370216.2370438.

CHAPTER FIVE

ICT, millennials' lifestyles and travel choices

Yongsung Lee[a], Giovanni Circella[a,b,*]
[a]School of Civil and Environmental Engineering, Georgia Institute of Technology, Atlanta, GA, United States
[b]Institute of Transportation Studies, University of California at Davis, Davis, CA, United States
*Corresponding author e-mail addresses: giovanni.circella@ce.gatech.edu; gcircella@ucdavis.edu

Contents

Abstract

Millennials are often called "digital natives" because they grew up during the era of rapid development and widespread adoption of information and communication technology (ICT) in various aspects of everyday life. On average, millennials hold more positive attitudes toward the adoption of new technologies, and even in the transportation field they include a large portion of early adopters and frequent users of shared mobility services such as carsharing, ridehailing, and micromobility. In this chapter, we summarize the findings from the literature regarding the adoption of ICT solutions, in particular among millennials, and their relationships with travel choices. Further, we explore various patterns with which millennials and members of the previous generations use ICT applications in key domains of everyday life, and their relationships with travel choices, focusing in particular on travel mode choice. To do that, we analyze a rich transportation survey dataset collected in 2018 in California ($N = 3631$). We apply latent-class cluster analysis (LCCA) and identify three rather distinctive groups: *intense users, moderate users*, and *light users* of ICT. Interestingly, many intense ICT users are young educated adults

Advances in Transport Policy and Planning, Volume 3
ISSN 2543-0009
https://doi.org/10.1016/bs.atpp.2019.08.002

living in cities with limited access to vehicles, while many light users are less-educated seniors from low-income households living in small towns or rural areas. Many millennials and members of Generation Z are found in the intense user class, while many Baby Boomers and members of the Silent Generation are in the light user class. On average, intense ICT users are more often found to be multimodal travelers who use public transportation, ridehailing, carsharing, and active travel modes, while moderate/light ICT users are more auto-oriented individuals. Consistent with expectations, the rather mobile and ICT-oriented lifestyles of millennials are associated with less car-dependent travel choices. Still, it is not clear the extent to which this reflects a true preference toward technological solutions over traditional ways of living and moving around vs. it is the result of lower access to private vehicles, temporary conditions and a transient stage in life.

Keywords: Millennials, Information and communication technology, Lifestyle, Travel choices, Shared mobility

1. Introduction

Millennials (and, similarly, the members of the younger "Generation Z") are often considered "digital natives," who grew up during the era of rapid development and widespread adoption of information and communication technology (ICT) in various aspects of everyday life. Today's young adults are reported to hold more positive attitudes toward new technologies and are inclined towards replacing low-tech solutions with their technological counterparts. Millennials lead the adoption of new ICT devices and services (e.g., smartphones, tablets, and online Social Network Services, or SNS), and they view the internet, personal mobile ICT devices, and online SNS as positive inventions for society, more so than the members of the preceding generations (Deloitte, 2019; Jiang, 2018; Nielsen, 2014). Millennials are also early adopters and frequent users of shared mobility services such as carsharing, ridehailing, and micromobility (e.g., dockless bikesharing or electric scooter sharing)—the familiarity with ICT is essential for the use of these services (Alemi et al., 2019; Wang et al., 2018). Several studies also suggest that millennials may be more motivated to ride public transportation than members of the preceding generations because real-time transportation apps help anticipate delays and plan accordingly, and internet connectivity helps riders better tolerate (and make good use of) travel time through multitasking (Malokin et al., 2019; Watkins et al., 2011). Millennials are currently the largest birth cohort: thus, even small effects of ICT use on their daily life add up to huge consequences on society.

Transportation scholars, planners, and policymakers have attempted to understand the relationships of ICT use and travel outcomes in the general population and, especially, among millennials. In this chapter, we summarize some of the findings from the literature exploring in particular the relationships between ICT use and transportation-related choices among young adults. Further, we analyze recent survey data from California (N=3631 adults, 18 years old or older, living in the state) and apply latent-class cluster analysis (LCCA) on indicators of ICT use in various settings for e-shopping, online SNS, and transportation-related services. With LCCA, we identify unobserved groups of individuals with unique patterns of ICT use. The model includes individuals' socioeconomic and demographic characteristics and their residential neighborhoods as active covariates. As a post-processing analysis, we compute average monthly frequencies for various travel mode-purpose combinations for the members of each class. The analysis helps identify three rather distinguished groups of individuals, with very peculiar characteristics in terms of ICT use and related travel choices: *intense users*, *moderate users*, and *light users*. Several differences are observed in these groups in terms of household income, educational attainment, worker/student status, access to vehicles, and residential neighborhood type. Intense ICT users, who include many millennials and Gen Zers living in denser urban areas, make a higher number of trips, on average, than those belonging to the other classes. Interestingly, however, the average vehicle miles driven of intense ICT users are lower than for moderate users, who include many Gen Xers and Baby Boomers residing in suburban areas with better access to privately-owned vehicles. That is, intense ICT users choose lifestyles that are highly mobile but that are also, on average, less reliant on the use of a private vehicle. Whether their intense ICT use stimulates/discourages their choice of certain travel modes, or is an effect of other personal choices and/or stage in life, is unclear, though, as our methodological approach does not allow to ascertain causality between ICT adoption and travel-related choices.

This chapter is organized as follows. Section 2 presents a summary of previous studies that have focused on the relationships between the adoption of ICT and travel-related choices, focusing in particular on the relevance of this topic to understand millennials' behaviors. Section 3 provides details on research design. It presents a conceptual framework for the analysis of the complex relationships between ICT and travel behavior, and it introduces the method of analysis, as well as the data and key variables used in the study. Section 4 presents the results of the analysis. In Section 5, we discuss the analyzed ICT use and travel patterns, and their implications. Finally, Section 6 concludes with future research directions and calls for alternative data collection efforts.

2. Literature review

For the last few decades, transportation scholars have investigated the relationships between the adoption of ICT and travel behavior through a variety of research approaches. While earlier work focused more on the net effects of ICT on demand for physical travel, in terms of substitution vs. complementarity (Mokhtarian, 2002, 2009), recent work provides conceptual frameworks that cover much broader scopes, whose components directly or indirectly affect travel demand. Circella and Mokhtarian (2017) present a comprehensive summary of the ICT and transportation literature, which covers the impacts of ICT on various components of human behaviors, and of society. Their review ranges from the impacts of ICT on the spatial form of cities (including the conflicting trends towards eventual decentralization vs. recentralization), to the organization of work (e.g., including telecommuting and distributed offices), business practices of retail and logistics industries, and individual-level choices (e.g., residential location, vehicle ownership and travel mode choices, to name some of the most relevant). Dal Fiore et al. (2014) examine human needs at various levels including physiological, safety, belonging, esteem, and self-actualization, for which physical travel can be an important means. The authors then explore the ways in which ICT affect the fulfillment of such needs by playing as a facilitator of or a constraint on existing demand, or as motivator of latent, unrealized demand. One such example is the spatial reconfiguration of trip destinations, facilitated by real-time location-based information via ICT (e.g., online reviews on new stores, sales promotion available on the internet, and restaurant suggestions from navigation systems).

Although the literature includes a number of effective conceptual frameworks, it presents limited empirical evidence in terms of the identification of specific (causal) links. A recent discussion article lists a few challenges in the empirical investigation of ICT and travel behavior. These challenges included the need for complex modeling structures (e.g., those that include bidirectional links of causality), the inclusion of unobserved but critical variables in the data (e.g., attitudes and preferences), the rapid obsolescence of previous conceptualizations (e.g., due to the rapid development and evolution of ICT devices and applications), and the omission of societal trends/factors in microanalysis (Ben-Elia et al., 2018). Regarding the conceptualization, Schwanen (2015) asserts to respond to the increasing adoption of mobile internet-enabled devices (e.g., smartphones) and a fast-expanding (and evolving) array of applications on them. In doing so, he suggests analyzing an environment surrounding a "mobile application" (i.e., a smartphone app) for a better understanding of ICT and travel behavior. Ettema (2018) answers his call and provides a qualitative examination of two such environments, one centered on *WhatsApp*, an instant messaging app, and the other around travel feedback apps, which are "aimed at reducing people's car use, by providing them feedback about their travel behavior" (p. 284). As for the operationalization of ICT use, some studies employ *binary* indicators of daily use of the internet or ownership of a smartphone as proxy variables that capture the exposure to/use of ICT (Blumenberg et al., 2016). In comparison, other studies find that the frequency of use of several applications or the type of use, and not just a binary indicator of the use, better relates to travel behavior and mobility choices (Astroza et al., 2017). Another recent approach is taken by Lachapelle and Jean-Germain (2019), in which the authors analyzed a one-day time use diary in Canada. The authors modeled the travel time and trip frequency on the survey day by the individuals' intensity of internet use for several purposes: communication, shopping, and the consumption of online media. Although better than a simplistic approach based on binary indicators, summing qualitatively different types of activities under generic categories may not help reveal links between specific ICT use and its travel impacts.

Among the research gaps in the literature is a "loose" link between lifestyles vis-à-vis ICT and the use of ICT-enabled transportation services, such as shared mobility. That is, when modeling the adoption and frequency of using carsharing, ridehailing, micromobility (e.g., bikesharing and electric scooter sharing), or other emerging transportation services, most studies lack measurements of lifestyle choices related to the adoption of ICT devices/services. Previous studies employed *generic* attitudinal factors that measure the extent to which individuals are technologically savvy, early adopters of ICT, or embracing technological solutions for everyday life; however, the ways in which individuals adopt ICT in various domains of life (e.g., for communication, shopping, and media consumption (Lachapelle and Jean-Germain, 2019)) are not well incorporated into modeling. This practice in the literature may lead to wrong evaluation of the effects, and/or eventual omitted variable biases. After all, ICT lifestyle choices affect "domain-specific" travel behaviors and mobility choices directly (e.g., the use of online SNS directly generates/removes physical trips) or indirectly (e.g., ICT-oriented lifestyles help individuals try new mobility services). Unfortunately, many datasets (e.g., collected with the U.S. National Household Travel Survey, or NHTS) lack good information on the use of ICT devices/services, which prevents researchers from developing more realistic behavioral models and deriving policy implications. In brief, a focus on ICT lifestyles and its association with "mobility styles" in general (and use of shared mobility services in particular) allows us to explore the relationships between ICT and travel behavior beyond the limit of conventional discussions in the field, which was to determine ICT substitution of or complementarity with travel behavior.

Recent studies find that millennials (young adults who were born in the last two decades of the twentieth century) have travel patterns and mobility choices that differ from those of the preceding generations at the same age and stage in life. McDonald (2015) investigated longitudinal changes in key travel outcomes (e.g., trip rates and vehicle miles traveled, or VMT) of millennials and members of the preceding generations in the United States from 1995 to 2009. Her study shows that, after lifecycle and period effects are controlled for, millennials made fewer trips and drove fewer miles than their counterparts at the same age. She suggests those remaining differences may come from attitudes and preferences, which are specific to millennials: e.g., better awareness of environmental/health impacts of auto-oriented lifestyles, more practical approaches toward car ownership and driving, and adoption and frequent use of ICT apps. Blumenberg et al. (2016) attempted to explicitly test the effects of ICT use on travel behavior with similar longitudinal data but with a longer time span from 1990 to 2009. They found that one's use of the internet was *positively* correlated with VMT. Since their survey data recorded internet use until the late 2000s (i.e., before smartphones were widely adopted for internet access, beyond business people), the internet use variable may have captured lifestyles that educated or relatively wealthier segments in the population could choose (i.e., those who are more mobile on average). Delbosc and Currie (2013) examined trends in driver's license holding in developed countries in the West, and they listed ICT use among the factors behind the declining trend of millennial drivers (i.e., pointing to a dominant substitution effect). Other scholars focused on multimodal travel behaviors—the use of various travel modes instead of a single mode—and showed that millennials are more multimodal compared to older adults (Astroza et al., 2017; Ralph, 2017; Vij et al., 2017). As for the use of public transportation, the literature presents a mixed picture. Using nationwide transportation survey data from the

United States, Brown et al. (2016) confirmed that young adults rode more transit trips in the 2000s, but many factors behind their transit use would not last long as these young individuals become older (e.g., lifecycle factors common to young adults who live in cities). Shaheen and Cohen (2018) noted that several factors would play a critical role in transit ridership in coming years: e.g., public-private partnerships for first/last mile access and vehicle automation technologies.

In brief, existing studies find generational differences in travel behavior and mobility choices, but they do not confirm the extent to which these differences are attributable to ICT use of millennials.

Direct links among millennials' lifestyle, ICT use, and travel behaviors are found in their adoption and frequent use of ICT-enabled shared mobility services. ICT is central to the use of such services because without mobile ICT devices and apps, in most cases users cannot check the availability, make online transactions, access and return (or exit from) requested transportation means, or contact the service providers if needs arise (e.g., for safety reasons). Thus, it is obvious that millennials as digital natives are more motivated/better suited to use those means frequently than older adults (even after stage in life, demographic and socioeconomic traits are controlled for). As for shared mobility use by millennials, recent studies have largely focused on emerging transportation services including ridehailing and micromobility. Alemi et al. (2018a) show that millennials in California are more likely to use ridehailing, and ICT use (use of Facebook and online social media) and ICT-related attitudes also account for the adoption of such services. Their findings are consistent with other studies showing that college-educated, single or childless young adults living in cities account for a large portion of the early adopters and frequent users of these services (Rayle et al., 2016). Similar, when looking at micromobility services, e.g., docked/dockless bike and electric scooter sharing, many users are college graduates or have post-graduate degrees, are young adults between 21 and 45, members of households without children, live in cities with limited access to personal vehicles, and make trips by a combination of various travel modes (Shaheen & Cohen, 2019).

Recent studies find that millennials are not a monolithic group regarding socioeconomic traits, residential preferences, travel behavior, and mobility choices, though. Statistics show that about half of them (44% of ages 21–36 as of 2017) are racial/ethnic minorities, their share of either foreign-born or those who have foreign-born immigrant parents (23% of the individuals of age 6–21 as of 2002) is higher than for the preceding generations, and they live in a society where income inequality has grown considerably in the last decades, especially among minority groups (Cilluffo & Cohn, 2019; Fry et al., 2018; Fry and Parker, 2018). Also, while millennials are presumably an "urbanite" generation, they are so in varying degrees. Studies show that the recent trends of relocation to cities are more pronounced among educated whites (Baum-Snow and Hartley, 2016; Couture and Handbury, 2017), and in selected "superstar" cities (Kolko, 2016, 2017). Regarding travel behavior, studies find heterogeneous groups in the population in general, and among millennials in particular, with a "carless, but relying on new mobility services" group that is certainly present but does not include the majority of individuals—not even in California where the share of new-mobility users is likely to be larger than in other states (Lee et al., 2019; Ralph, 2017). In the context of the adoption and frequency of use of ridehailing services, millennials are found to form a few distinctive groups in terms of their preferences (Alemi et al., 2018b). In brief, for various reasons, the relationships between ICT and travel behavior may also take multiple forms in the population, and the approach of modeling and estimating *average effects in the population* may fail to identify important target groups, whose members present more responsiveness to transportation planning and policy.

3. Research design

3.1 Conceptual framework

In this chapter, we analyze ICT use patterns and their relationships with travel outcomes, in a sample of adults, 18 years old or older in the State of California in 2018. Our main research questions are:

1. How do millennials and the members of preceding/following generations use various ICT applications in the various domains of everyday life?
2. Are there differences in ICT use patterns within millennials, and between them and the members of the other generations?
3. What socioeconomic, demographic, built environment, and attitudinal factors explain such differences?
4. How are travel behavior choices *associated* with their ICT use patterns, when other confounding factors are controlled for?

Fig. 1 presents a conceptual framework that specifies the relationships among several sets of variables in the study. ICT use patterns are measured by a set of indicators that record the frequencies with which individuals use various ICT applications. A latent (i.e., not observable) categorical variable is assumed to account for individuals choosing certain ICT use patterns.

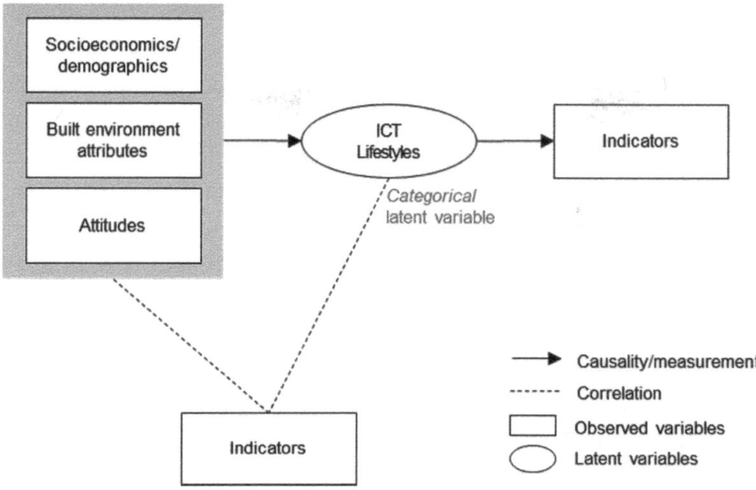

Fig. 1 Conceptual framework of factors affecting ICT lifestyles and travel outcomes.

That is, we assume that individuals choose how often to use various ICT applications in connected ways, not independently for each application (e.g., frequent e-shoppers might be also more likely to use SNS frequently, on average). Although researchers cannot observe the latent variable, they can estimate probabilities of individuals belonging to one category or another by individuals' characteristics. In other words, socioeconomic and demographic (SED), built-environment (BE), attitudinal (AT), and other characteristics account for individuals choosing certain ICT-related lifestyles (e.g., frequent/intense vs. occasional/light use). For instance, those who do not own a car may use ICT applications more for checking transit schedules and wait times, and those living in urban neighborhoods may order more online deliveries for various items in part because high density in cities allows fast deliveries or convenient returns. In Fig. 1, the travel mode choice refers to the travel frequency for various mode-purpose combinations. We examine them by computing their correlations with individual characteristics and their chosen ICT lifestyles.

3.2 Data and variables

In this chapter, we analyze survey data collected from a sample of adults (18 years old or older, $N=3631$) across the State of California in 2018 (for more information on survey design and data collection efforts, refer to the project report from Circella et al., 2019). The survey collected information on individuals' attitudes, use of ICT applications in several domains of everyday life, use of shared mobility services such as ridehailing and carsharing, and perceptions, willingness to adopt, and envisioned use patterns of autonomous vehicles (AV) in the future, among other groups of variables. In fact, this data set is the results of the second wave of data collection in a study with a rotating panel approach, with the first survey that was administered in 2015 (Circella et al., 2016, 2017). For the second wave of data collection, the research team expanded cases to all adults, and not just the two generations of millennials and members of Generation X as in 2015, and introduced a rotating panel structure to refresh the panel and replace members of the panel that drop out. Although the interval between two waves is not very long, as following waves are continuously collected, the entire panel study will be a great source of information, for example, to help assess the impact of generation, lifestyle and period effects, as well as the impacts of the evolving landscapes of ICT applications to daily life in general and to transportation in particular.

The research team employed a quota sampling approach based on the type of neighborhoods (e.g., urban, suburban, towns, and rural communities) and the six regions of California (Los Angeles region, San Francisco region, Sacramento region, San Diego region, Central Valley region, and the remaining areas) where the respondents live to collect a sufficient number of cases from various segments of the population, especially from groups that are less studied or challenging to recruit. The research team recruited respondents through multiple channels including by mailing out a paper copy of a questionnaire to a group of randomly selected individuals at their mailing address (who could return the fill-in questionnaire by mail, or complete the survey online) and sampling members from online opinion panels. At the time of writing this book chapter, the research team is in the process of examining individual cases and computing weights, to correct for non-representativeness of the adult population in California. Thus, in this book chapter, we analyze data and present outcomes from the unweighted sample.

Using these data, we examine the frequency of use of ICT applications that support different types of activities, including e-shopping for various categories of products, socializing via online SNS, and searching for transportation-related information. We choose these ICT applications as they have implications on travel demand for maintenance and discretionary activities, as well as travel experience (e.g., get updates on real-time traffic conditions via smartphone apps). We exclude the frequency of telecommuting, which may have implications on subsistence trips, because not all individuals in the dataset work or study out of home. We use four to five variables for each domain as "indicators" that measure the intensity of individuals using certain ICT applications. For e-shopping, respondents reported their frequencies of online purchases for physical books/DVDs, e-books/streaming services, clothing/shoes, grocery items/fresh products/flowers, and electronics in a four-point Likert-type scale with the following levels: *Never*, *Less than once a month*, *1–3 times a month*, and *>4 times a month*. For SNS use, they reported their frequency of using Facebook, Twitter, Instagram/Snapchat, and WhatsApp/WeChat in a six-point Likert-type scale with levels: *Never*, *Less than once a month*, *At least once a month*, *At least once a week*, *Everyday*, and *Multiple times per day*. For transportation-related ICT use, respondents reported the frequencies of using the internet to check traffic to plan their route or departure time, check when a bus or train will arrive, decide which means of travel to use, identify trip destinations/places of interest (e.g., restaurants and cafés), and navigate in real time (e.g., Google Maps and in-vehicle GPS) on a five-point Likert-type scale with options: *Seldom or never*, *At least once a year*, *At least once a month*, *At least once a week*, and *Daily*. The survey had additional questions on e-shopping regarding the chosen delivery/return options, which were not included in this analysis, as we believe the chosen questions are better proxies for e-shopping intensities in general, and we do not want a single domain (in this case, e-shopping) to dominate the classification of individuals in the latent classes, because of too many indicators that are related to that domain.

As travel-behavior measures, we compute trip frequencies for mode-purpose combinations in multiple steps. The data include answers to two sets of questions, related to the frequencies of using travel modes for commute trips and for non-commute trips. For each set, respondents reported their use of 11 travel modes on an ordinal scale with categories *Not available* (only for commuting trips), *Available but I never use it* (*Never use*, for non-commuting trips), (Use) *less than once a month*, *1–3 times a month*, *1–2 times a week*, *3–4 times a week*, and *5 or more times a week*. The travel modes include, for commute trips, *Car alone*, *Car with others* (e.g., *carpooling)*, *Work/school-provided bus or shuttle*, *Public bus*, *Light rail/train/subway* (e.g., *BART, LA Metro)*, *Commuter train* (e.g., *Amtrak, Caltrain)*, *Taxi* (e.g., *Yellow Cab)*, *Ridehailing* (e.g., *Uber, Lyft)*, *Shared ridehailing* (e.g., *UberPOOL, Lyft Line)*, *Bicycle or e-bike*, *Walk or skateboard*. For non-commute trips, the shuttle option is not available and it is replaced by *Carsharing* (e.g., *Zipcar, Car2Go)*. For the computation of the travel mode use frequencies, we first convert the respondents' answers from the ordinal scale to monthly frequencies measured on a *continuous* scale. That is, we recode Less than once a month as 0.5/month, 1–3 times a month as 2/month, 1–2 times a week as 6/month, 3–4 times a week as 14/month, and 5 or more times a week as 20/week. Then, we group the 11 travel modes into five groups based on their similarity and implications on sustainable transportation. These five groups are *car alone*, *car with others*, *public transit*, *new shared mobility services*, and *active travel* modes. Note that the first two original modes are not grouped with the other modes because of their different contributions to traffic congestion, energy consumption, and greenhouse gas (GHG) emission. Finally, we sum monthly frequencies separately for each of the five travel-mode groups. That is, for each individual, we compute 10 continuous frequencies (five for commutes and five for non-commute trips) out of 22 ordinal input variables. Although not without measurement errors, this approach helps us depict travel-mode use profiles of individuals in a comprehensive manner.

3.3 Methods

For the examination of ICT use among individuals in the California data, we employ a latent-class cluster analysis (LCCA) approach, which helps identify unobserved groups with homogeneous ICT use patterns in the data (for applications of LCCA to travel behavior, see Lee et al., 2019; Molin et al., 2016; Ralph, 2017). LCCA consists of a few components.

First, *indicators* are measurements for underlying perceptions/behaviors of interest, and in our case, they refer to the 14 categorical variables capturing the frequency levels of individuals using ICT applications for e-shopping, online SNS, and transportation-related services. Obviously, these indicators are highly correlated with one another (e.g., frequent e-shoppers are often intense SNS users). To model these correlations, LCCA assumes a latent categorical variable, which affects individuals' frequency levels of using various ICT applications. We may interpret this latent discrete variable as ICT lifestyles that individuals chose. That is, once the latent variable is controlled for (e.g., among cases belonging to the same latent class), there remains no correlation among these indicators (i.e., local independence). For a given number of latent classes, which researchers find the most reasonable, LCCA computes *mean* values for those indicators for each latent class and the probability of individuals belonging to each latent class. We identify several unobserved groups in the sample—groups with distinctive ICT lifestyles—whose members present ICT use patterns that are rather homogeneous within each class, but heterogeneous across classes. Unlike deterministic classification schemes including K-means clustering,

LCCA *probabilistically* assigns individuals to classes. After all, researchers (and often individuals themselves) cannot observe class membership, and LCCA estimates the likelihood of individuals belonging to one class or another, but it does not identify their classes with 100% certainty.

Second, *active covariates* also affect the class probabilities of individuals. In fact, class membership is a latent categorical variable, for which LCCA computes the probabilities of individuals having each value of the variable. Active covariates work as explanatory variables in the class membership model, accounting for the reasons individuals belong to one class or another. In our case, we use socioeconomic and demographic characteristics, the type of one's residential neighborhood, and commuting-related attributes as active covariates. That is, individuals with various backgrounds are assumed to choose certain ICT lifestyles that best serve their needs and lifestyles.

Third, *inactive covariates* do not affect the class membership, and we use them to explore any correlation with specific classes in a post-processing stage. In our case, we treat the frequencies of using various travel modes for commute and non-commute trips (henceforth *leisure* trips) as inactive covariates. Since inactive covariates are *not* modeled to affect/be affected by indicators or active covariates, we interpret that a group of individuals with certain socioeconomics/demographics (i.e., members of a latent class) choose *both* ICT lifestyles *and* travel mono/multimodality. To estimate separate "effects" of those factors (e.g., tease out the effect of ICT use on mode choice), we would need to employ more complex analytical methods such as integrated choice and latent variable (ICLV) and structural equations modeling (SEM). With those methods, individuals' characteristics and their ICT use are modeled to account for the chosen travel mode use patterns. We leave complex modeling for future research.

4. Results

After the removal of individuals with missing values for key variables, the final sample contains 3631 individuals who live across California and were recruited via multiple channels. We first examine the way and the extent to which the final sample deviates from the socioeconomic and demographic statistics of the entire population in California. We extract these statistics from the 2013 to 2017 U.S. Census American Community Survey (ACS) 5-year estimates, which is the latest release at the time of writing. Since ACS is limited regarding cross tabulations, we compare sample and population statistics for each variable separately. Table 1 presents summary statistics for gender, race and ethnicity, household incomes,

Table 1 Summary statistics of socioeconomic/demographic characteristics.

Class	Light ICT users	Moderate ICT users	Intense ICT users	Total sample	CA[a]	ACS category[b]
(Share in the sample)	32.4%	47.2%	20.4%	N=3631		
Gender						
Male	45.3%	43.8%	46.7%	44.9%	49.7%	
Female	54.2%	55.1%	52.6%	54.3%	50.3%	
Annual household income						
0–25,000	18.7%	9.6%	10.9%	12.8%	18.7%	
25,001–50,000	23.6%	15.6%	17.3%	18.5%	19.7%	
50,001–75,000	19.4%	16.4%	15.0%	17.1%	16.3%	
75,001–100,000	14.5%	14.9%	16.6%	15.1%	12.2%	
100,001–150,000	12.8%	22.2%	19.0%	18.5%	15.7%	
>150,000	10.9%	21.3%	21.2%	17.9%	17.5%	
Educational attainment						
Less than high school	2.5%	1.1%	1.8%	1.7%	16.8%	
High school	13.5%	6.2%	9.7%	9.3%	21.8%	
Some college	39.2%	32.0%	22.4%	32.4%	31.8%	
Bachelor's	27.1%	36.4%	40.4%	34.2%	19.0%	
Graduate	14.6%	19.0%	20.4%	17.9%	}10.6%	
Professional	3.1%	5.2%	5.3%	4.6%		
Race/ethnicity						
Caucasian	79.2%	74.6%	61.4%	73.4%	60.6%	
African American	3.2%	3.7%	8.5%	4.5%	5.8%	
Asian	8.8%	14.1%	20.3%	13.6%	14.1%	
Native American	3.7%	4.5%	4.8%	4.3%	0.4%	
Hispanic	17.6%	19.9%	32.4%	21.7%	38.8%	
Living arrangement						
Living with the partner	52.9%	66.3%	61.8%	61.0%	46.7%	
Living with a child	27.5%	39.5%	46.1%	37.0%		

Table 1 Summary statistics of socioeconomic/demographic characteristics.—cont'd

Class	Light ICT users	Moderate ICT users	Intense ICT users	Total sample	CA[a]	ACS category[b]
Living with parent(s)	8.0%	11.1%	15.1%	10.9%		
Living with relative(s)	6.4%	9.0%	12.1%	8.8%		
Living with roommate(s)	4.5%	5.5%	7.7%	5.6%		
Living alone	26.7%	13.3%	13.1%	17.6%		
Household characteristics						
Household size	2.28	2.76	3.03	2.66	2.96	
# of driver's license holders	1.77	2.03	1.97	1.93		
# of vehicles	1.89	2.21	1.88	2.04	1.78[c]	
Work/study status						
Student	3.8%	10.1%	25.3%	11.2%	10.8%	
Worker	45.9%	66.0%	81.2%	62.6%	58.2%	
Housing type						
Single-family house	68.2%	68.2%	59.5%	66.4%	65.1%	
Multi-family house	24.5%	28.3%	38.5%	29.1%	31.1%	
Housing tenure						
Own	67.3%	61.7%	51.6%	61.4%	54.5%	
Reported neighborhood type						
Urban	25.1%	28.8%	54.1%	32.8%		
Suburban	41.9%	50.9%	38.3%	45.4%		
Small town	19.9%	13.3%	5.1%	13.8%		
Rural	13.0%	7.0%	2.5%	8.0%		
Age/generation[d]						
Age (mean)	58.08	48.59	38.43	49.59		
Generation Z (18–21)	1.0%	2.5%	5.8%	2.7%	6.6%	15~18[e]

Continued

Table 1 Summary statistics of socioeconomic/demographic characteristics.—cont'd

Class	Light ICT users	Moderate ICT users	Intense ICT users	Total sample	CA[a]	ACS category[b]
Millennials (22–37)	12.0%	25.2%	49.1%	25.8%	29.3%	19∼34[e]
Generation X (38–53)	25.4%	34.2%	32.0%	30.9%	26.4%	35∼50[e]
Baby Boomer (54–72)	42.9%	32.1%	11.9%	31.5%	26.8%	51∼69[e]
Silent generation and older (73 and older)	18.7%	6.1%	1.2%	9.2%	10.9%	70 or older[e]
# of days to commute[d]						
Commuting to work	3.99	3.85	4.17	3.97		
Commuting to school	0.19	0.34	0.95	0.47		
Telecommuting	0.72	0.89	1.34	0.97		

[a]These statewide statistics for California come from the U.S. Census American Community Survey (ACS) 2013–2017 5-year estimates, which is the latest release (and the closest to the time of the survey administration) at the time of writing this manuscript.
[b]For some variables, the U.S. Census ACS has different categories from those in our dataset.
[c]ACS records the shares of households with zero, one, two, and three or more vehicles. We computed this average by assuming that households with three or more vehicles own three vehicles.
[d]Ages in parentheses indicate those as of 2018. Generation Zers were born in 1997 or later, millennials from 1981 to 1996, Generation Xers from 1965 to 2000, Baby Boomers from 1946 to 1964, and the members of the silent generation from 1928 to 1945 (Dimock, 2019).
[e]These are the ages of individuals in 2015 (for the ACS data) that correspond to those age groups in 2018.

educational attainment, household size, household characteristics (e.g., family or non-family, living with children), household vehicles, worker/student status, housing type, housing tenure, neighborhood types, share of generations, and the like.

Compared to the ACS estimates, the sample contains more female respondents and fewer male respondents. More cases in the sample reported annual household incomes greater than $50,000. On average, those in the sample are better educated than the population in California. Especially the share of those with less than or equal to high-school education is smaller in the sample, while the share of those with Bachelor's and graduate/professional degrees is almost double. Note that the ACS estimates present educational attainment for those who are 15 or older, while our sample for this study contains only adults, those who are 18 or older. That is, the share of those with less than high school education among adults in California will be certainly lower than 16.8%; however, the gap is huge with the ratio of 1–10 (1.7% vs. 16.8%), suggesting that on average, the final sample contains better educated individuals than the entire population in California. After all, many survey studies reported over representation of the more educated in the samples than the less educated. Given that ICT use is highly correlated with educational attainment, this likely means that the share of intense ICT users in the sample will be *larger* than in the entire population in California.

As for race and ethnicity, Caucasians and Native Americans are overrepresented in the sample, while those of Hispanic origin are less so. A further investigation for each recruitment channel will shed light on any systematic difference between cases recruited by several methods, such as mailing to random addresses, inviting through online opinion panels, and re-recruiting the same individuals who participated in the 1st wave survey in fall 2015 through an online opinion panel. As for household composition, the share of those who live with their partner are larger in the sample than in California, while the mean household size is smaller in the sample than in California. One's student/worker status in the sample is similar to that in California, and so is housing type. Interestingly, homeowners are overrepresented in the sample, which may be related to the chosen quota sampling strategy that oversampled individuals in less-populated regions such as small town and rural areas in California where houses are more affordable. The members of Generation Z are less represented in the sample, which is consistent with findings in the survey literature that report that young adults are more difficult to be recruited in surveys.

For the estimation of latent classes, we employ *M*plus, which computes a few goodness-of-fit measures for solutions with varying numbers of latent classes. Since these solutions are not nested to one another, we use three information criteria—Akaike Information Criterion (AIC), Bayesian Information Criterion (BIC), and sample-size adjusted BIC. The lower their values are, the better a given solution fits the data. Table 2 shows that their values keep decreasing as the number of latent classes increases. However, instead of choosing the best solution based only on those goodness-of-fit measures, we also take into account the interpretability of solutions: e.g., whether the profiles of ICT indicators differ in meaningful ways among classes, whether given ICT use patterns align well with the socioeconomic and demographic profiles of class members based on previous studies, whether the smallest class is large enough to capture a sizeable

Table 2 Goodness of fit measures for latent class analysis solutions.

	One class	Two classes	Three classes	Four classes
# of free parameters	113	140	225	310
Log likelihood				
H0 value	−132,063.822	−60,675.171	−59,591.812	−58,821.309
H0 scaling correction factor for MLR	1.5934	1.0633	1.1463	1.1438
Information criteria				
Akaike Information Criteria (AIC)	264,354	121,630	119,634	118,263
Bayesian Information Criteria (BIC)	265,054	122,498	121,028	120,184
Sample-size adjusted BIC	264,695	122,053	120,313	119,199
Class size (from the largest to the smallest)				
	100.0%	53.8%	47.2%	32.0%
		46.2%	32.1%	27.2%
			20.7%	23.9%
				16.9%

subgroup with distinctive lifestyles or it mainly consists of rare outliers in the sample, and the like. At last, we choose a solution with three latent classes: *moderate ICT users* (47.2% of the sample), *light ICT users* (32.4%), and *intense ICT users* (20.4%). Below we discuss our main outcomes from ICT patterns of these classes (indicators), socioeconomic and demographic characteristics of the members of these classes (active covariates), and monthly trip rates for mode-purpose combinations (inactive covariates).

Figs. 2–5 present the distribution of several frequency categories for using selected ICT applications for the final sample as a whole and for each class separately. Note that Fig. 2 displays average behaviors in the sample regarding their use of ICT applications, unweighted (i.e., not representative of the population of California). For e-shopping, about a quarter of respondents reported that they purchased given items online at least one to three times a week. Respondents chose to buy grocery items online more often than other items in part because these items (e.g., processed food such as

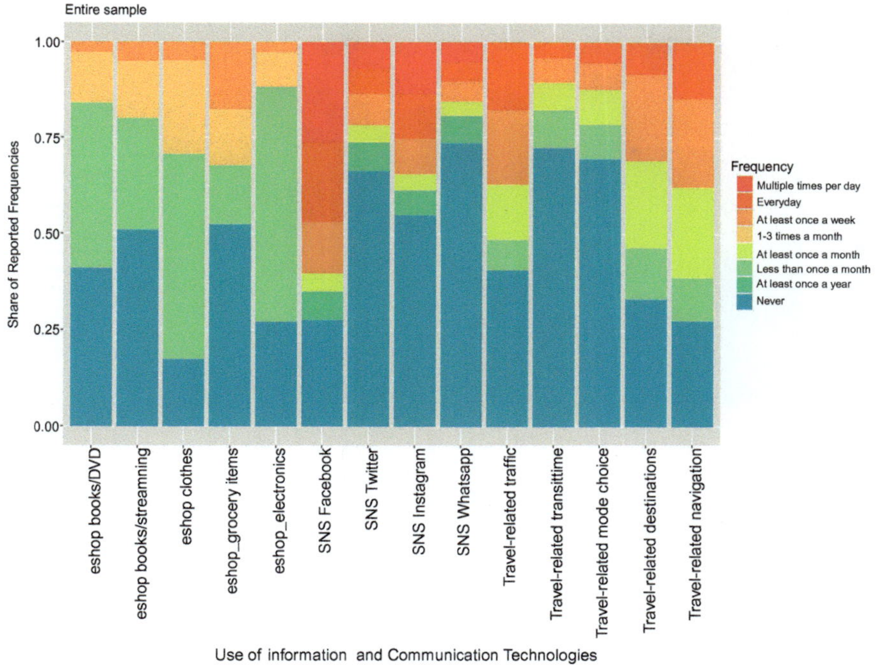

Fig. 2 Patterns of ICT use in the full sample.

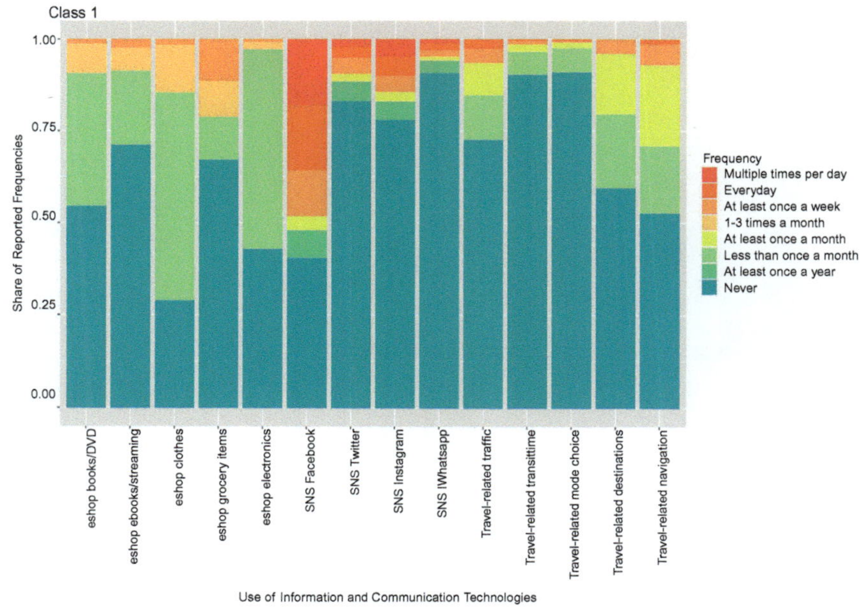

Fig. 3 Patterns of ICT use for *light users*.

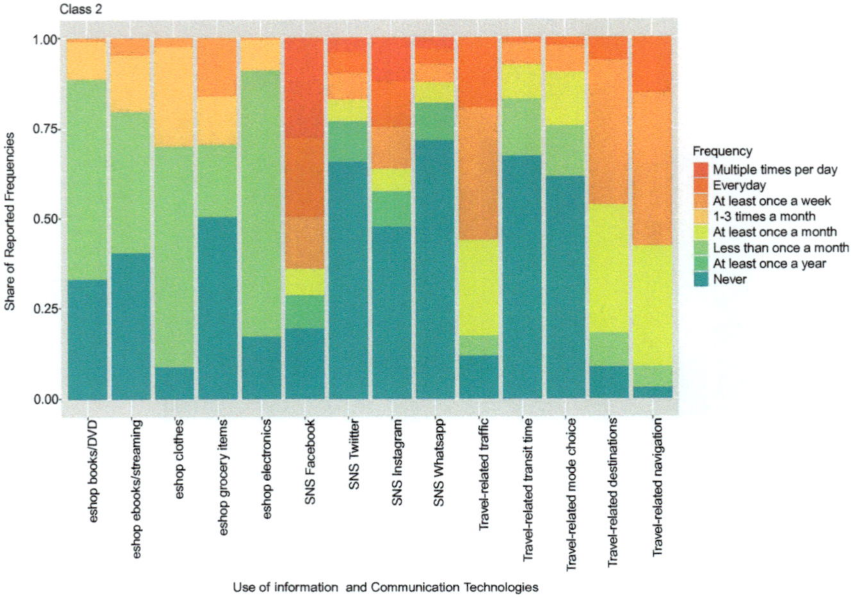

Fig. 4 Patterns of ICT use for *moderate users.*

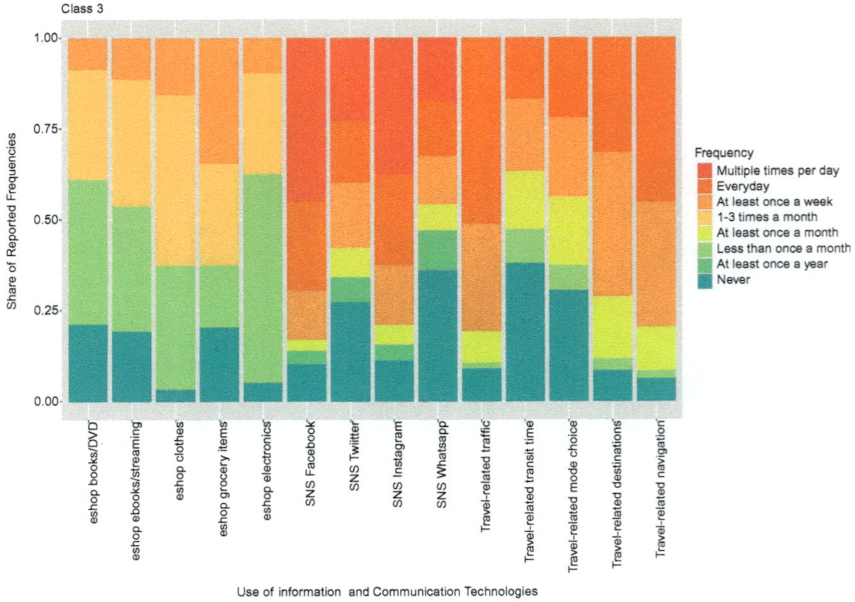

Fig. 5 Patterns of ICT use for *intense users.*

serials, snacks, and canned food) need more frequent purchases than others such as electronics (e.g., tablets, laptops, desktops, or other tech gadgets). Since different items have different purchasing cycles, an alternative question for future research could ask for the proportion of shopping for certain items that people do online vs. offline. This is a standardization scheme that allows to compare e-shopping behaviors across qualitatively different items.

Second, we find larger shares of online SNS users, compared to e-shoppers, with moderate frequencies, or at least once a week. About a half of respondents used Facebook, a quarter of respondents checked or posted on Twitter, a third of respondents used Instagram, Snapchat, or similar (photo- or emoticon-based short communication tools), and about a fifth of respondents WhatsApp, WeChat, or similar services. Third, for ICT use vis-à-vis transportation, about a third of respondents used ICT applications for checking traffic, identifying new destinations, and navigating paths in real time at least one a week, but respondents did less so for checking transit schedules and choosing travel modes. After all, alternative means of travel to personal vehicles are not very popular in the United States. For example, the *commute* mode share by transit in California is 5.2% in the 2013–2017 ACS estimates. Still, the share of those who used ICT at least once a week for transit schedules and mode choices appears larger than expected in part because people also use transit for *leisure* trips, or they ride transit not every day but on a weekly basis. Alternatively, the final sample may have oversampled multimodal travelers such as transit riders.

Now, let us examine the ICT use patterns for the three latent classes in comparison to the sample averages. *Moderate users* present frequencies of ICT use that are very close to the sample average, except for three indicators—checking traffic to plan my route or departure time, identifying trip destinations/places of interest, and navigating in real time. Among *light users*, about half of the members reported "Never" for most ICT applications. An additional 30% of the members reported that they do it "less than once a month." Interestingly, light users use Facebook relatively more often than other ICT applications. Also, among transportation-related ICT applications, some of their members use ICT to check traffic, new destinations, and real-time navigation. Not surprisingly, *intense users* adopt all 14 ICT applications more frequently than the other classes. Especially for online SNS, the majority of the members use them at least once a week, and for Facebook and Instagram, close to a half of the members in this class check/post on them multiple times a day. As for online purchases, many members of this class do e-shopping for all listed items at least one to three times a month. In relation to transportation, intense ICT users use ICT applications to do the same activities as the other two classes do, but they check transit schedules and chose travel modes with ICT more frequently, suggesting that this class may contain more multimodal travelers than the others.

Next, we investigate the characteristics of the members belonging to three latent classes regarding their socioeconomics, demographics, residential neighborhood types, and commute attributes. Please note, Table 1 presents summary statistics for three classes separately (one column for each class), which we computed by applying latent-class probabilities as weights (e.g., the probabilities of individual cases belonging to the moderate user class are used for the creation of summary statistics for that class). In comparison, Table 3 displays the membership model outcomes with the largest class, moderate users, omitted as the reference category. These two tables help us understand the characteristics of the members of the three classes.

The members belonging to the *light ICT user* class present the following distinctive characteristics. Compared to those belonging to the other classes, more members of this class make household incomes below $75,000/year, or fewer members make incomes in the high bracket, over $100,000/year. More members received education less than or equal to high school, and fewer members were educated more than or equal to a Bachelor's degree. More members are found as Caucasians, and fewer as minorities. More members live alone, and fewer members live with the partner, a child, parents, relatives, or roommates. As a result, on average their households are the smallest among the three classes. Obviously, this class has fewer driver license holders and fewer private vehicles per household. Their shares of workers or students are also lower than in the other classes. Interestingly, their homeownership rate is higher than the other classes in part because many of them are in later stages in life with the silent generation composing 18.7% of the class, and live in small towns and rural areas, where houses are more affordable for those in low- and moderate-income brackets. In brief, light users appear less familiar with ICT applications and their lifestyles are less associated with, or dependent on, ICT solutions.

The *moderate ICT user* class shows an income distribution that is similar to that of the entire sample, except the slightly fewer cases in the low household income bracket under $75,000/year and slightly more cases in the high bracket over $100,000/year. As for educational attainment, fewer members of the class received less than or equal to high school education, while more members earned equal to or more than a Bachelor's degree. Their racial and

Table 3 Membership model results ($N=3631$, Moderate ICT users is the reference category).

Explanatory variable	Heavy ICT users		Light ICT users	
Female	−0.171		−0.221	**
Household income (reference: 0–25,000)				
25,001–50,000	−0.027		−0.155	
50,001–75,000	−0.183		−0.438	**
75,001–100,000	0.112		−0.610	***
100,001–150,000	−0.065		−1.126	***
>150,000	0.003		−1.127	***
Educational attainment (reference: Bachelor's)				
Less than high school	−0.127		0.836	**
High school	0.010		0.807	***
Some college	−0.693	***	0.298	**
Graduate degree	0.020		−0.014	
Professional degree	−0.206		−0.147	
Race (reference: Caucasian)				
African American	−0.864	***	0.295	
Asian	−0.443	**	0.232	
Native American	0.135		0.344	
Hispanic origin	0.621	***	−0.081	
Living arrangement				
Live with the partner	0.055		−0.342	***
Live with a child	0.046		−0.118	
Household size	0.154	***	−0.135	**
Study/work status				
Study	0.555	***	−0.999	***
Work	−0.103		−0.341	*
Single-family house	0.018		0.172	
Homeowner	−0.214		0.672	***
# of vehicles	−0.274	***	−0.079	

Continued

Table 3 Membership model results ($N=3631$, Moderate ICT users is the reference category).—cont'd

Explanatory variable	Heavy ICT users		Light ICT users	
Commute frequency				
Commute to work	0.174	***	0.010	
Commute to school	0.193	***	−0.055	
Telecommute	0.137	***	−0.100	**
Reported neighborhood type (reference: rural)				
Urban	1.177	***	−0.642	***
Suburban	0.500		−0.694	***
Small town	−0.054		−0.320	

Notes: *** $P<0.01$, ** $P<0.05$, and * $P<0.1$.

ethnic composition does not differ much from that of the entire sample. Its household composition is also similar to that of the sample, except the share of individuals living alone noticeably lower. On average, this class shows average household size and number of drivers similar to the sample, but its members have better access to vehicles, which is consistent with their chosen neighborhood types, with a half of them living in suburbs.

The *intense ICT user* class presents an income distribution similar to that of the sample and that of the moderate user class. As for educational attainment, noticeably higher shares of the members of this class obtained Bachelor's, graduate, or professional degrees. Interestingly, fewer Caucasians but more minorities belong to this class compared to the entire sample, especially with the share of Hispanics larger by more than 10 percentage points (than that of the sample). Compared to the other classes, more members live with a child, parent, relative, or roommate, but fewer live alone. As a result, this class presents the largest household size on average among the three classes. Given that many young adults belong to this class (e.g., 49.1% of the class being millennials), this may be associated with lower access to vehicles. That is, living in larger households with about the same number of drivers, but slightly fewer vehicles than the sample imply that intense ICT users somehow need to have their travel needs met by alternative travel modes, not by driving or being driven in private vehicles. In this sense, use of ICT may be an effective strategy to overcome limited access to cars. Fewer members live in single-family houses, but more live in multi-family houses, which are consistent with their lowest homeownership rate and highest share of urban residence (e.g., 54.1% among them reported living in urban neighborhoods). Commuters in this class have more days per week for commuting, both for work and school, and this class also telecommutes more on average than the others. In sum, the intense user class consists of many educated young adults with lower access to personal vehicles, and more than half of the class live in cities, where traveling by alternative modes is more feasible than in suburbs or rural areas.

We now turn to discussing inactive covariates, i.e., travel mode use frequencies, for the three latent classes. Note that the computation of average monthly frequencies for selected mode-purpose combinations are done after the estimation of LCCA. Thus, readers are advised to interpret the frequencies as summary statistics for individual latent classes, for which the effects of various factors are not separately identified. For example, while we cannot determine whether higher frequencies of one class are caused by certain covariates of their members, we can clearly see correlation patterns among covariates, ICT use patterns, and mode use frequencies. Also, note that commute trips (from home to one's work/school) are computed only for commuters (either workers or students) of each latent class, but leisure trips are computed for all members of each latent class.

Fig. 6 displays a bar chart in which the colors of individual bars indicate the monthly frequencies for mode-purpose combinations, for each latent class separately and for the entire sample. In many cases, moderate users' frequencies are similar to those of the entire sample, while the other two latent classes present distinctive patterns. Intense ICT users make the highest number of trips for all mode-purpose combinations, while light ICT users make the lowest number of trips for all mode-purpose combinations. Interestingly, intense users also make more drive-alone and carpool trips than the others, both for commute and leisure trips. This pattern is at odds with a popular notion that ICT substitutes for physical trips, or replaces vehicle trips with those by alternative modes. After all, ICT may support drivers by providing real-time, integrated, and rich (e.g., cloud-sourced) information on when, where, and how to get there. Note that Fig. 6 informs us of travel outcomes of latent classes, not separately identified effects of ICT on trip generation. Thus, it is not clear to what extent ICT increases/decreases the number of trips by various travel modes. Instead, we interpret that compared to the other classes, intense users choose *more mobile* lifestyles, which are a function of both ICT use and various individual characteristics

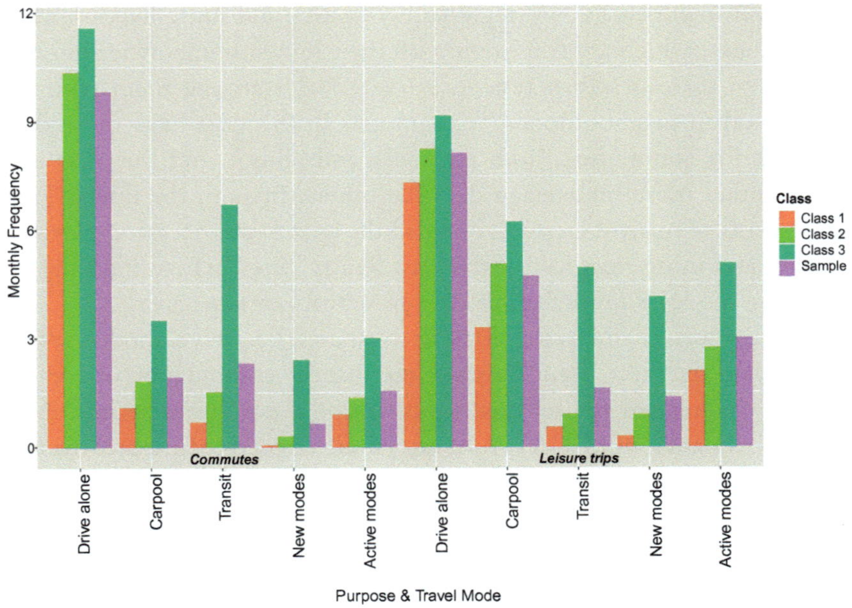

Fig. 6 Monthly frequency of using travel modes by latent class of ICT users.

including income, educational attainment, worker/student status, household composition, residential neighborhood types, and the like. That is, the *net* effects of all those confounding factors are larger for intense users than for the other classes.

While intense ICT users are more mobile than the members of the other classes, they make higher proportions of trips by alternative modes including public transit and emerging transportation services. In other words, on average they are more multimodal. Transit-trip frequencies by intense users are very much pronounced, consistent with their more frequent use of ICT for checking transit schedules and making mode choices. Moreover, on average, intense users reported to drive *fewer* miles than moderate users: intense users drive 118.0 miles, moderate users 134.0 miles, light users 94.4 miles, and the entire sample 117.9 miles per week. This may suggest that intense users drive shorter distances per trip, on average, or use carpool as a passenger more than as a driver compared to moderate users. This also relates to their urban residential neighborhoods (54.1% among intense users vs. 28.8% among moderate users). In contrast, moderate users reside more in suburbs (50.9% among moderate users vs. 38.3% among intense users), where the organization of carpool trips is more challenging compared to that in urban neighborhoods because of sparsely placed destinations. Given that light users are the oldest among the three latent classes and fewer than half of their members work or study, it is obvious that they have lower trip rates than those belonging to the other two classes. They rarely use public transit and shared mobility services, for which the use of ICT applications is either required or greatly improving their travel experience.

5. Discussion

5.1 Measurement of ICT use

The survey data and analytical methods of this chapter have merits and also shortcomings in terms of understanding ICT use patterns and their impacts on travel behaviors. First, we are not aware of studies that explicitly model the associations of ICT use across multiple domains of everyday life. In this chapter, we do so by employing LCCA, which assumes a latent discrete variable to affect the use of ICT in various contexts, such as e-shopping, socializing with others online, and getting help vis-à-vis transportation. By doing so, we depict a *whole* picture of individuals' ICT-related lifestyles. In this sense, our approach differs from other studies that model travel outcomes as a function of ICT use in *specific* domains: for instance, studies that estimate the impacts of e-shopping on shopping trips. While legitimate and insightful, these studies implicitly assume no cross-domain effects from ICT use to travel demand (e.g., zero effects of online SNS use on shopping trips). Our approach also differs from studies that analyze data with coarse measures for ICT use: e.g., the number of hours spent on the Internet (Lachapelle and Jean-Germain, 2019). Instead, in this chapter we analyze the frequency levels for several different activities in several domains, which provide a *fine-grained* picture of ICT use in the entire sample (and for each latent class separately). In doing so, our analysis corroborates findings in the literature that the ownership of smartphones or mobile internet-enabled devices does not well predict the probability of individuals of being intense ICT users (Lavieri et al., 2017). For instance, our sample reveals that moderate and intense ICT users do not differ much in their smartphone ownership rates, 97.4% and 99.6%, respectively (with the remaining ownership rates being 77.3% for light users and 91.3% for the entire sample; One's smartphone ownership status is not included among active covariates).

Readers are advised to note the limitations of the ICT measures in this chapter, designed to capture individuals' form and intensity of ICT use across multiple domains of everyday life. First, these measures are self-reported, and likely less accurate than objective measures taken by the observation of actual behaviors: e.g., activity logs stored in internet browsers or smartphone apps. Second, the use of frequency categories, initially chosen for the reduction of response burdens, is not ideal, or less precise, although it was an effective compromise between the complexity/precision of survey questions and the reliability of their answers. Third, asking frequencies may not be enough to analyze potentials of ICT in affecting travel demand. For example, as for SNS, the main data contain no information on the type/nature of user activities, e.g., whether users make new friends online or merely invite old friends into online environments, whether they use SNS for personal or professional purposes, whether they check promotions or attend events of which they would have not learned without those apps, and the like. Although collecting such detailed/nuanced data and identifying effective analytical methods is challenging, those questions help identify several causal channels whose net effects we analyze (and discuss) in this chapter.

5.2 Generational effects

The nature of the data, a cross-sectional dataset collected in 2018, does not allow us to estimate "true" cohort effects. In fact, such effects are difficult to even define, let alone to estimate. After all, the landscape of ICT devices and applications have dramatically and rapidly changed in the last couple of decades since the widespread adoption of the Internet in the late 1990s. Also, ICT applications related to mobile devices have transformed the ways we use ICT for daily life (e.g., desktops connected to the Internet vs. smartphones on 4G LTE networks). Thus, it is not obvious what to choose as equivalent devices and services in the past, as counterparts to the current ICT applications, when Gen Xers and Baby Boomers were at the same age as millennials are now. Conventional approaches for the estimation of generation effects may not be effective for the study of ICT use and their effects on activities, travel, and lifestyle choices. Moreover, we see the introduction of new ICT applications in emerging forms, e.g., Internet of Things, augmented reality (AR), smart cities, automated driving, and Mobility as a Service. That is, as available/popular ICT applications evolve, new mobility services become feasible and affordable, or the current services lose customer bases and go out of business, undergo transformative changes, and the like. Analyzing longitudinal data with measurements of ICT applications, use, and impacts in consistent analytical frameworks would help understand the evolving nature of ICT use and their impacts on other parts of daily life.

Fig. 7 presents the shares of the three latent classes for each generation in the sample. While millennials and members of Gen Z more often belong to

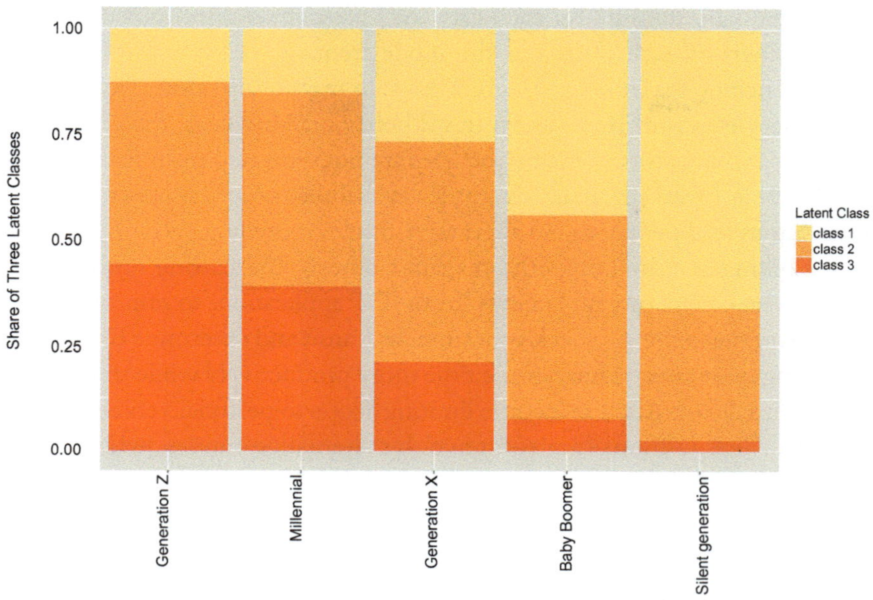

Fig. 7 Composition of latent classes by generation.

the intense ICT user class, the larger shares of preceding generations are among light or moderate users. Note that differences in class composition across generations are captured by their differences in socioeconomic/ demographic characteristics, residential neighborhood types, and commute attributes. That is, the membership model does not control for attitudes and perceptions. Thus, once attitudes such as tech-embracing or tech-savviness are also accounted for, the differences across generations would change, likely in ways that among younger adults even more intense users are present, and among older adults fewer intense users are found. As discussed, the larger share of intense users among Gen Z and millennials, compared to older generations, are not entirely attributable to cohort effects. However, given that these young adults grew up in the era in which the adoption and use of new ICT applications have become part of everyday life, it is safe to say that these digital natives use ICT applications in various life domains more than preceding generations to organize activities, trips, and everyday life.

5.3 ICT substitution of, complementarity with, or modification of travel demand

This chapter does not identify the effects of ICT applications on the choice of travel modes. Travel outcomes are treated as inactive covariates, and they do not affect the identification of individuals' latent class membership. That is, mode frequencies are computed separately at the post-estimation stage, and as summary statistics for each class they present *net* travel outcomes for the members of each class. For the mode frequencies by each class, one might conclude that more use of ICT leads to higher trip rates, or the complementary effects of ICT use on travel behavior. However, the contributions of various factors to the frequencies are not separated from that of ICT use. Possible causal mechanisms are: (1) availability of and support by ICT applications lead people to use alternative modes more (e.g., STRAVA that makes biking as a fun competition against others), (2) existing multimodal travelers seek help, or gain benefits, from ICT applications to improve their travel experiences (e.g., check wait time for transit and determine best route for biking or scooter-riding, or use time more productively while traveling), or (3) third factors (such as income limiting access to personal vehicles) have people to live without cars and travel by alternative modes, which then combined with ICT applications (e.g., ridehailing, bike/scooter sharing program). What we observe here are their *net* effects present among a sample of California adults as of 2018 fall. That is, to divide effects in multiple groups, more research needs be followed. Below are suggestions of effective analytical frameworks for doing so.

5.4 Alternative causal structures

The analytical framework and methods employed in this chapter have a limitation in identifying separate effects of ICT use on travel behaviors, and here are suggestions for future studies that attempt to do such identification. First, LCCA with mode frequencies as *inactive* covariates does not estimate effects of various factors on mode choices, but instead produces summary statistics for individual classes, which readers can interpret as *net* travel outcomes. The chosen LCCA structure assumes that individuals' socioeconomic/demographic, built environment, and commute characteristics lead them to choose both ICT and travel lifestyles. Although this assumption is not incorrect, its limitation is also clear. Instead, structural equations modeling (SEM) allows researchers to model complex causal relationships via the inclusion of multiple endogenous variables in a modeling system. In our case, an SEM alternative will estimate separate effects of various factors (including individual characteristics and their ICT use patterns) on mode choices.

Endogeneity appears to be present in the relationships between the use of ICT applications and travel outcomes. Here are reasons for such endogeneity. First, we see simultaneity between them, e.g., the use of certain

ICT applications affect mode choices (e.g., online shopping causes a reduction in leisure trips, which otherwise would have been higher), and certain mode choices require use of specific ICT applications (a person first considers taking public transit, and then checks apps for transit schedules and waiting time). Moreover, attitudes are not included in the chosen LCCA (i.e., key variables are omitted in the model). Such attitudes include, but are not limited to, those related to technology adoption, perceptions of various travel modes, and waiting in general and vis-a-vis transit/ridehailing services. Last but not least, the California survey includes more questions on e-shopping, especially those on use of various delivery/return options. Given that ICT indicators chosen in the analysis are limited in terms of capturing their connections to travel demand, a less complete set of indicators may lead to measurement errors, which is another source of endogeneity.

As for effective handling of endogeneity in the chosen LCCA, a couple of approaches are feasible. First, one straightforward solution is to allow bidirectional relationships between ICT use and mode choices in an SEM specification. Second, instead of allowing such bivariate relationships for all individuals in the sample, a latent-class SEM estimates a membership model and a structural model simultaneously. That is, for the members of a certain latent class, ICT use affects mode choices, while for those of another class, the opposite is true. By doing this, researchers can avoid the limitations for bivariate links in SEM, while also identifying characteristics for the members of each latent class via the membership model. Third, as an alternative modeling approach, propensity-score matching can be incorporated into SEM with simple structures. For example, first identify two groups of individuals in the sample –one consists of intense ICT users, and the other consists of comparable cases, i.e., those who are as likely to be intense ICT users but happen not to use ICT applications that much. Only for these two groups of "experiment" and "control" cases, a following SEM estimates the effects of ICT use on mode choices. Since the two groups are equivalent in the first place except their use of ICT, any systematic differences in travel outcomes between them are attributable to their use or non-use of ICT.

6. Conclusion

In this chapter, we discuss the relationships among millennials' lifestyles, the use of ICT and travel choices, through a review of the relevant literature and the analysis of a sample collected from 3631 adults in various parts of California in 2018. We classify the use of ICT in three domains, i.e., e-shopping, SNS, and use of transportation services, with three classes of users, identifying *light*, *moderate*, and *intense ICT users*. For the members of each latent class, we discuss their socioeconomic, demographic, built environment, and commute characteristics. Consistent with previous studies, many intense ICT users are found to be young educated adults living in cities with lower access to private vehicles, while many light users are less-educated seniors from lower-income households who live in small towns or rural areas. Many millennials and Gen Zers are found to belong to the intense user class, while many Baby Boomers and members of the silent generation are in the light ICT user class. The analysis of the travel frequencies for various mode-purpose combinations for the each latent class reveals that, on average, intense users more often travel with various modes including transit, ridehailing/carsharing, and active modes, while moderate/light users are more auto-oriented.

The analysis reported in this chapter has several limitations, for which we provide suggestions for future research, both in terms of methods and data collection. First, attitudes are omitted in the analysis, but they are expected to account for individuals' choice of ICT and mobility lifestyles. Further, our travel outcome measures are the number of trips, not that of out-of-home activities, which has limitations in distinguishing multimodality (i.e., use of multiple modes for a given time period) and intermodality (i.e., use of multiple modes for a single trip). Since this analysis is unweighted, its results are not representative of the population in California. The main model examines correlation patterns of the characteristics of the members of individual latent classes and their ICT use and mode choice but did not estimate separate effects of various factors including ICT use on travel outcomes. Since the LCCA specification does not explicitly estimate the effects of ICT on travel outcomes, we recommend alternative modeling approaches to estimate the ICT impacts or identify members of certain subgroups whose ICT use and mode-choice patterns differ from the others.

Acknowledgments

This chapter builds on the results from a study funded by the National Center for Sustainable Transportation (NCST), which receives funding from the USDOT and Caltrans through the University Transportation Centers program. The authors would like to thank Caltrans, the NCST and USDOT, for their support of university-based research in transportation. The authors also would like to thank Patricia L. Mokhtarian, Susan Handy, Dan Sperling, Grant Matson, Farzad Alemi, Jai Malik, and Ali Etezady for their contributions to the survey design, data collection and data analyses in the project.

References

Alemi, F., Circella, G., Handy, S., Mokhtarian, P., 2018a. What influences travelers to use Uber? Exploring the factors affecting the adoption of on-demand ride services in California. Travel Behav. Soc. 13, 88–104. https://doi.org/10.1016/j.tbs.2018.06.002.
Alemi, F., Circella, G., Mokhtarian, P., Handy, S., 2018b. Exploring the latent constructs behind the use of ridehailing in California. J. Choice Model. 29, 47–62.
Alemi, F., Circella, G., Mokhtarian, P., Handy, S., 2019. What drives the use of ridehailing in California? Ordered probit models of the usage frequency of Uber and Lyft. Transp. Res. C Emerg. Technologies 102, 233–248.
Astroza, S., Garikapati, V.M., Bhat, C.R., Pendyala, R.M., Lavieri, P.S., Dias, F.F., 2017. Analysis of the impact of technology use on multimodality and activity travel characteristics. Transp. Res. Rec. 2666 (1), 19–28.
Baum-Snow, N., Hartley, D.A., 2016. Accounting for Central Neighborhood Change, 1980–2010. Working Paper 2016–09, Federal Reserve Bank of Chicago, Chicago, IL. Retrieved from http://hdl.handle.net/10419/172925. (Last Access on August 6, 2019).
Ben-Elia, E., Lyons, G., Mokhtarian, P.L., 2018. Epilogue: the new frontiers of behavioral research on the interrelationships between ICT, activities, time use and mobility. Transportation 45 (2), 479–497.
Blumenberg, E., Ralph, K., Smart, M., Taylor, B.D., 2016. Who knows about kids these days? Analyzing the determinants of youth and adult mobility in the US between 1990 and 2009. Transp. Res. A Policy Pract. 93, 39–54.
Brown, A.E., Blumenberg, E., Taylor, B.D., Ralph, K., Voulgaris, C.T., 2016. A taste for transit? Analyzing public transit use trends among youth. J. Public Transp. 19 (1), 49–67.
Cilluffo, A., Cohn, D.V., 2019. 6 Demographic Trends Shaping the U.S. and the World in 2019. Retrieved from https://www.pewresearch.org/fact-tank/2019/04/11/6-demographic-trends-shaping-the-u-s-and-the-world-in-2019/. (Last Access on August 6, 2019).
Circella, G., Mokhtarian, P.L., 2017. Impacts of information and communication technology. In: Giuliano, G., Hanson, S. (Eds.), The Geography of Urban Transportation, 4th ed. Guilford Press, New York, NY, pp. 86–109.
Circella, G., Fulton, L., Alemi, F., Berliner, R.M., Tiedeman, K., Mokhtarian, P.L., Handy, S., 2016. What Affects Millennials' Mobility? PART I: Investigating the Environmental Concerns, Lifestyles, Mobility-Related. A Research Report from the National Center for Sustainable Transportation. Retrieved from https://escholarship.org/uc/item/6wm51523. (Last Access on August 6, 2019).
Circella, G., Alemi, F., Tiedeman, K., Berliner, R.M., Lee, Y., Fulton, L., Mokhtarian, P.L., Handy, S., 2017. What affects millennials' mobility? Part II: the impact of residential location, individual preferences and lifestyles on young adults' travel behavior in California. A Research Report from the National Center for Sustainable Transportation, Retrieved from https://escholarship.org/uc/item/5kc117kj. (Last Access on August 6, 2019).
Circella, G., Matson, G., Alemi, F., Handy, S., 2019. Panel Study of Emerging Transportation Technologies and Trends in California: Phase 2 Data Collection. A Research Report from the National Center for Sustainable Transportation. Retrieved from https://escholarship.org/uc/item/35x894mg. (Last Access on August 6, 2019).
Couture, V., Handbury, J., 2017. Urban Revival in America, 2000 to 2010. National Bureau of Economic Research https://doi.org/10.3386/w24084. Working Paper Series, No. 24084.
Dal Fiore, F., Mokhtarian, P.L., Salomon, I., Singer, M.E., 2014. "Nomads at last"? A set of perspectives on how mobile technology may affect travel. J. Transp. Geogr. 41, 97–106.
Delbosc, A., Currie, G., 2013. Causes of youth licensing decline: a synthesis of evidence. Transp. Rev. 33 (3), 271–290.

Deloitte, 2019. The Deloitte Global Millennial Survey 2019 Societal Discord and Technological Transformation Create a "Generation Disrupted" Retrieved from https://www2.deloitte.com/global/en/pages/about-deloitte/articles/millennialsurvey.html. (Last Access on August 6, 2019).

Dimock, M., 2019. Defining Generations: Where Millennials end and Generation Z begins. Pew Research Center. Retrieved from https://www.pewresearch.org/fact-tank/2019/01/17/where-millennials-end-and-generation-z-begins/. (Last Access on August 6, 2019).

Ettema, D., 2018. Apps, activities and travel: a conceptual exploration based on activity theory. Transportation 45 (2), 273–290.

Fry, R., Parker, K., 2018, November 15. Early Benchmarks Show 'Post-Millennials' on Track to Be Most Diverse, Best-Educated Generation Yet. Pew Research Center. Retrieved from https://www.pewsocialtrends.org/2018/11/15/early-benchmarks-show-post-millennials-on-track-to-be-most-diverse-best-educated-generation-yet/. (Last Access on August 6, 2019).

Fry, R., Igielnik, R., Patten, E., 2018. How millennials today compare with their grandparents 50 years ago. March 16, Pew Research Center, Retrieved from http://www.pewresearch.org/fact-tank/2018/03/16/how-millennials-compare-with-their-grandparents/#!0. (Last Access on August 6, 2019).

Jiang, J., 2018, May 2. Millennials Stand Out for Their Technology Use, But Older Generations also Embrace Digital Life. Pew Research Center. Retrieved from https://www.pewresearch.org/fact-tank/2018/05/02/millennials-stand-out-for-their-technology-use-but-older-generations-also-embrace-digital-life/. (Last Access on August 6, 2019).

Kolko, J., 2016, March 30. Urban Revival? Not for Most Americans. Retrieved from http://jedkolko.com/2016/03/30/urban-revival-not-for-most-americans/. (Last Access on August 6, 2019).

Kolko, J., 2017, May 24. Return to Cities an Urban Legend, Mostly. The New York Times. p. A18. Retrieved from https://www.nytimes.com/2017/05/22/upshot/seattle-climbs-but-austin-sprawls-the-myth-of-the-return-to-cities.html. (Last Access on August 6, 2019).

Lachapelle, U., Jean-Germain, F., 2019. Personal use of the internet and travel: evidence from the Canadian general social Survey's 2010 time use module. Travel Behav. Soc. 14, 81–91.

Lavieri, P.S., Garikapati, V.M., Bhat, C.R., Pendyala, R.M., Astroza, S., Dias, F.F., 2017. Modeling individual preferences for ownership and sharing of autonomous vehicle technologies. Transp. Res. Rec. 2665 (1), 1–10.

Lee, Y., Circella, G., Mokhtarian, P.L., Guhathakurta, S., 2019. Are millennials more multimodal? A latent-class cluster analysis with attitudes and preferences among millennial and generation X commuters in California. Transportation. https://doi.org/10.1007/s11116-019-10026-6.

Malokin, A., Circella, G., Mokhtarian, P.L., 2019. How do activities conducted while commuting influence mode choice? Using revealed preference models to inform public transportation advantage and autonomous vehicle scenarios. Transp. Res. A Policy Pract. 124, 82–114.

McDonald, N.C., 2015. Are millennials really the "go-nowhere" generation? J. Am. Plann. Assoc. 81 (2), 90–103.

Mokhtarian, P.L., 2002. Telecommunications and travel: the case for complementarity. J. Ind. Ecol. 6 (2), 43–57.

Mokhtarian, P., 2009. If telecommunication is such a good substitute for travel, why does congestion continue to get worse? Transp. Lett. 1 (1), 1–17.

Molin, E., Mokhtarian, P., Kroesen, M., 2016. Multimodal travel groups and attitudes: a latent class cluster analysis of Dutch travelers. Transp. Res. A Policy Practice 83, 14–29.

Nielsen, 2014. Millennials–Breaking the Myths. Retrieved from https://www.nielsen.com/us/en/insights/report/2014/millennials-breaking-the-myths/. (last access on August 6, 2019).
Ralph, K.M., 2017. Multimodal millennials? The four traveler types of young people in the United States in 2009. J. Plan. Educ. Res. 37 (2), 150–163.
Rayle, L., Dai, D., Chan, N., Cervero, R., Shaheen, S., 2016. Just a better taxi? A survey-based comparison of taxis, transit, and ridesourcing services in San Francisco. Transp. Policy 45, 168–178. https://doi.org/10.1016/j.tranpol.2015.10.004.
Schwanen, T., 2015. Beyond instrument: smartphone app and sustainable mobility. Eur. J. Transp. Infrastruct. Res. 15 (4), 675–690.
Shaheen, S., Cohen, A., 2018. Is it time for a public transit renaissance? Navigating travel behavior, technology, and business model shifts in a Brave New World. J. Public Transp. 21 (1), 67–81. https://doi.org/10.5038/2375-0901.21.1.8.
Shaheen, S., Cohen, A., 2019. Shared Micromobility Policy Toolkit: Docked and Dockless Bike and Scooter Sharing. Retrieved from https://escholarship.org/uc/item/00k897b5. (Last Access on August 6, 2019).
Vij, A., Gorripaty, S., Walker, J.L., 2017. From trend spotting to trend 'splaining: understanding modal preference shifts in the San Francisco Bay Area. Transp. Res. A Policy Pract. 95, 238–258. https://doi.org/10.1016/j.tra.2016.11.014.
Wang, K., Akar, G., Chen, Y.-J., 2018. Bike sharing differences among millennials, Gen Xers, and baby boomers: lessons learnt from New York City's bike share. Transp. Res. A Policy Pract. 116 (1–14).
Watkins, K.E., Ferris, B., Borning, A., Rutherford, G.S., Layton, D., 2011. Where Is My Bus? Impact of mobile real-time information on the perceived and actual wait time of transit riders. Transp. Res. A Policy Pract. 45 (8), 839–848.

PART II

Evolution of travel time use

CHAPTER SIX

The wicked problem of travel time use and the effects of ICTs

Glenn Lyons*
Mott MacDonald Professor of Future Mobility, Faculty of Environment and Technology, University of the West of England, Frenchay Campus, Bristol, United Kingdom
*Corresponding author: e-mail address: glenn.lyons@uwe.ac.uk

Contents

Abstract

Travel time matters. It is part of many people's everyday lives. Saving of travel time and the value attributed to it remain a principal justification for investment in the transport system which in turn shapes that system, its use and in turn influences people's everyday lives. Travel time has been the subject of increasing attention in the digital age with a growing realization that how people are using their travel time could have implications for their travel choices and wider behavior as well as for how worthwhile travel

Advances in Transport Policy and Planning, Volume 3
ISSN 2543-0009
https://doi.org/10.1016/bs.atpp.2019.04.001

time is and for the values of travel time savings that apply in transport appraisal. This chapter offers insights into the treatment of travel time in transport appraisal over time. It explores a number of considerations regarding travel time use in a world that is increasingly connected, with potential flexibility in how, where and when activities are undertaken. The proposition that travel time use and how it is valued is a wicked problem is addressed with the conclusion that greater interdisciplinary collaboration is called for in further examining this important topic.

Keywords: Travel time, Travel time use, Value of travel time, VTTS, Wicked problem

1. Introduction

This chapter considers travel time use and how it is valued—a topic of considerable significance for both travel behavior and transport investment decisions, and one for which Information and Communications Technologies (ICTs) are now intrinsic. The amount of literature on the topic continues to grow. This reflects, in part, the changing nature of people's travel and time use as the digital age unfolds. However, the enduring, if not increasing, attention the topic is receiving also concerns its complexity and indeed, I suggest, the prospect that—at least in terms of *valuing* travel time—that it may reach beyond being complex to being a wicked problem. The chapter gives attention to how travel time—in particular saved travel time—is treated in economic appraisal of transport investment options, specifically in the UK and with a focus on rail travel. Following from this, a series of issues are identified which I consider contribute to the topic's potentially wicked nature and which are of importance in the topic's ongoing examination and in turn for transport policy and practice.

1.1 Travel time matters

On average, each person spends around an hour a day traveling (DfT, 2018a). The working age population of the UK (aged 16–64) is 41.3 M (ONS, 2018)—the potential for the equivalent of 5.5 M working days (assuming a 7.5 h working day) of travel time each day in the UK. This in turn equates to being over four times the size of the UK's National Health Service workforce (standing at 1.3 M[a]—one of the biggest employers in the world). A lot of time collectively is involved. Travel time matters. It is integral to our daily lives. It affects what we do, what we experience and how we

[a] https://digital.nhs.uk/data-and-information/areas-of-interest/workforce#summary

feel. It affects our travel choices. It substantially affects the economic case for investment in transport aimed at saving travel time. This in turn shapes the transport system itself, how we use it and how society overall evolves.

From a personal point of view, I first became interested in travel time—and more particularly travel time use and its value—in 2002. I was sitting on a train and it struck me, as I looked around, that people were doing things with their time and yet transport economics was *apparently* assuming that travel time was unproductive, wasted time. My curiosity was aroused. Was transport economics guilty of a major oversight? I've been on a journey of discovery ever since. This journey has involved examination of the (changing) uses of travel time, its meaning and value and the transport system and appraisal implications.

1.2 The march of the digital age

The timing of the start of my own journey corresponded with the emergence of the Web and the beginning of what would become a mainstreaming of digital connectivity in society. Fig. 1 illustrates a selection of landmarks in the "march of the digital age" dating back to the registration of Google.com as a domain name in 1997. In 2002, I was sat on the train with a mobile phone not a smartphone. I did not have mobile internet. I was not sending emails on the move. Apps were not yet heard of and the popularity of social media lay in the future, as did the developments and hype (promulgated by such social media) concerning technological

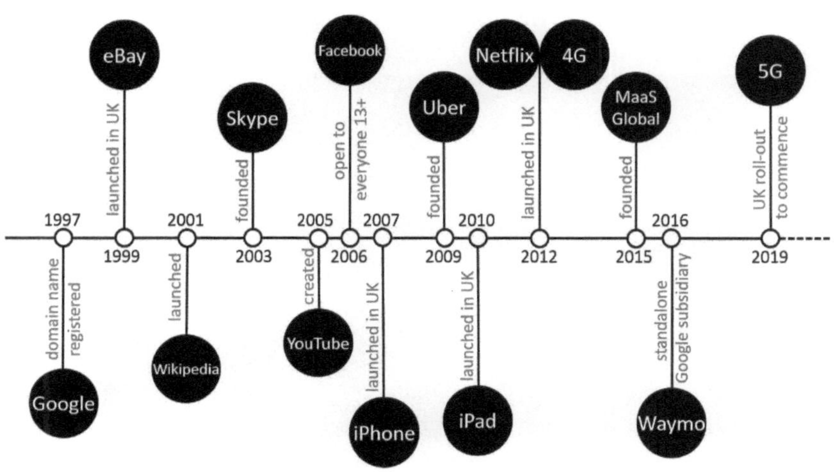

Fig. 1 The march of the digital age.

innovations such as mobility-as-a-service and driverless cars. Indeed, there was not even a national website in the UK for planning train journeys—the National Rail Enquiries website was to be launched the following year (focused upon pre-trip use from computers with wired internet connections).

It can be easy to lose sight of the stealthy but powerfully cumulative way in which the digital age is permeating many people's lives, and facilitating and influencing their consumption of time in their social and business practices, including time on the move. Fig. 2, taken in 2018, is emblematic of the interplay between transport and telecommunications that now exists. Connectivity in our lives can be as much about our use of mobile devices as it is about our use of the transport system. As such, examination of how people use their travel time in the digital age has given rise to an ever-growing body of literature spanning different disciplines.

1.3 A topic of enduring interest

It was apparent early on in my own journey of discovery that interest in the topic from others preceded my own. Patricia Mokhtarian in particular had written a paper with Ilan Salomon in 2001 which introduced the notion of the *positive utility* of travel—potential benefit gained from travel itself and from the use of travel time; as distinct from travel only being a disutility—a "cost" incurred in order to realize benefits from what takes place upon completion of the journey (Mokhtarian and Salomon, 2001). When considering the treatment of travel time in terms of the economic appraisal of investment in transport schemes, interest in the topic reaches much further back. The International Transport Forum of the OECD

Fig. 2 Advertisement for the new iPhoneX in the London Underground. *Image taken by author.*

held its first roundtable on valuing travel time (or more particularly travel time *savings*) half a century ago (ECMT, 1969).[b] Productive use of journey time was considered but dismissed as a concern facing how savings in travel time during the course of the working day were being valued—not least because at that time investment in roads was the order of the day and it was suggested there was little opportunity for productive use of travel time in road vehicles. This early roundtable nevertheless reminds us that travel time use is not something that has only arrived with the digital age.

Interest in the topic continues to be strong, reflective in part of a changing world, and also of the complex (if not "wicked") nature of the topic itself. Patricia Mokhtarian at the end of 2018 shared her reflections on the title question of her distinguished address—"what do the expanding uses of travel time portend for policy, planning, and life?" (Mokhtarian, 2018). The OECD in September 2018 held a roundtable entitled "Zero value of time" with the title being a prompt for exploring whether or not the value of travel time savings is being eroded over time as prospects for uses of travel time change (with as much, if not more, interest in rail than road, unlike the case in 1969).[c] Both of these pieces of work (see also Ben-Elia et al., 2018) point to unresolved and emerging questions in the face of ongoing change and uncertainty over the future.

Travel time use is set to remain an important topic for academic study and as something affecting, and affected by, the ongoing shaping and use of the transport system.

The purpose of this chapter is to provide the reader with a sense of how the topic has evolved and what issues may lie ahead. Section 2 provides an account of developments in interpreting and valuing travel time (centered upon UK experience, including my own) with a particular focus upon rail travel. Section 3 then highlights a series of issues that I suggest, among others, deserve new or ongoing attention. The chapter ends with a concluding discussion.

1.4 A wicked problem?

The reader is encouraged to reflect, as they read on, upon the proposition that valuing travel time use is a wicked problem. Many problems in transport analysis are complex and challenging to solve; but they are soluble—for instance the traveling salesman problem or system optimization of traffic

[b] https://doi.org/10.1787/9789282104811-en

[c] https://www.itf-oecd.org/zero-value-time-roundtable

assignment in relation to travel time for a fixed O-D matrix of trips. However, another class of problems are those known as "wicked." "A wicked problem is a problem that is difficult or impossible to solve because of incomplete, contradictory, and changing requirements that are often difficult to recognize."[d] Head considers such problems to be "marked by value divergence, knowledge gaps and uncertainties, and complex relationships to other problems" (Head, 2010: 21). Wicked problems are resistant to resolution. In our transport analysis, we must be more mindful of the distinction between complex and wicked problems if we are to better appreciate how to deal with problems of the latter sort. Is value of travel time a wicked problem? This is returned to in the final section.

2. Treatment of travel time and its value in economic appraisal of transport

2.1 The orthodox approach to economic appraisal of transport investment

When transport investment is being considered, a central (if not necessarily overriding) consideration is the economic benefit likely to accrue from the investment compared with the costs involved. The major source of benefit (DETR, 1999) derives from speeding up journeys, in other words achieving savings in travel time. Such saved time is assumed to have a monetary value. Journey purpose is treated as a key factor. Journeys that take place during the course of work have values of travel time savings that are based on what is known as the "cost savings approach" (or wage rate approach). In essence, the average wage rate (monetary value per unit of time) of users of a given mode is taken to reflect value of time and in turn value of travel time *savings*. Notably, until October 2013, the UK Department for Transport's guidance on transport appraisal stated the following:

> *"Time spent travelling during the working day is a cost to the employer's business. It is assumed that* ***savings in travel time convert non-productive time to productive use*** *and that, in a free labour market, the value of an individual's working time to the economy is reflected in the wage rate paid"* (DfT, 2011a: 2 – emphasis added).

Meanwhile, for travel outside the course of work, a *willingness to pay* approach is assumed. Empirical work is periodically undertaken to establish how much transport users are prepared to pay to save travel time. Willingness to pay will vary between individuals, affected in part by means to pay,

[d] https://en.wikipedia.org/wiki/Wicked_problem

so it is assumed that an equity value applies to all non-work travel, thereby avoiding investment that might favor those with greater means to pay. See Lyons and Urry (2005) and Wardman and Lyons (2016) for an extended explanation of the orthodox approach.

A key point of clarification—particularly in relation to travel during the working day—is the distinction between travel time and *saved* travel time. It is the latter that is valued in economic appraisal. The quote above may *appear* to suggest that *all* travel time is assumed unproductive (or wasted). Strictly speaking, the assumption is that the portion of journey time that is saved is time that would have otherwise been unproductive, leaving the prospect for *some* time within a journey to have been productively used without affecting the assumption. On this basis, it has been argued (Fowkes, 2001; Fowkes et al., 1986) that the orthodox approach need not be undermined by the fact that people clearly can make some use of their time while they travel. This is illustrated in Fig. 3—which depicts the case of a 60-min journey being reduced in duration (as a result of transport investment) by 20 min—as the assumed position (situation 1).

I use Fig. 3 to illustrate a number of ways in which this assumed position could be challenged (particularly, but not exclusively, for travel where the individual is not in charge of controlling the vehicle):

Situation 2—What if within the 60-min work journey (being reduced to 40 min) I was being productive for more than 40 min? In this case, only some of the time being saved is that which would have been unproductive.

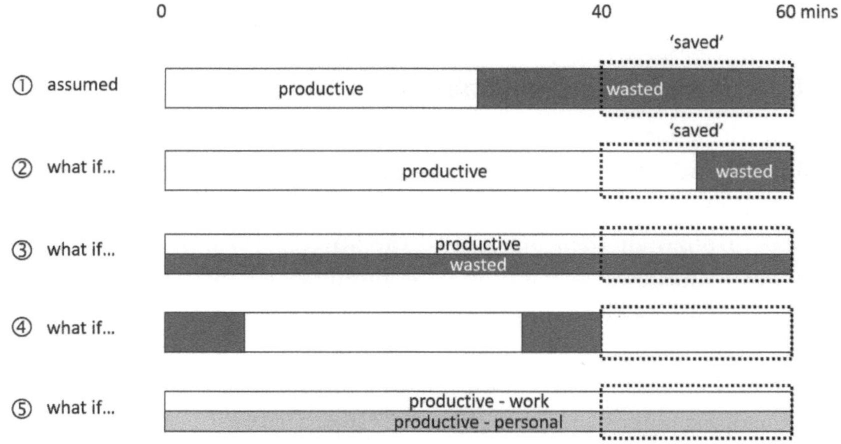

Fig. 3 The implications for the value of travel time savings of reducing a 60-min work journey by 20 min.

Situation 3—What if, during my 60-min work journey, my time is used throughout but in a way that suggests it is not as productive as work time I spend outside of travel—i.e., it is partly productive and partly wasted? In this case again, only some of the time being saved is that which would have been unproductive.

Situation 4—What if I am "fully" productive within the journey with the exception of needing time at the beginning and end of my productive activity to set up and pack up respectively (perhaps as I might also do, incidentally, in the conventional workplace)? In this case, shortening the journey by 20 min is saving time in which I would already have been productive. A shorter journey does not do away with the time needed for setting up and in turn packing up.

Situation 5—What if for some of the time during my journey I am doing activities relating to my paid employment and for the other time I am doing activities that do *not* relate to my paid employment? This leaves the question of whether the saved 20 min should be valued based on the cost-savings approach or the willingness to pay approach.

In all of situations 2–5, the robustness of the orthodox approach is brought into question (notwithstanding that the approach concerns the *aggregate* time savings of *all* travelers not only me). Back in 1977 David Hensher had articulated the idea that some time in a journey during the course of work could be productive and that account might be taken of *how* productive such time use was when compared to equivalent time use outside of travel (Hensher, 1977). Empirically addressing this idea has been attempted but proves challenging (see Wardman and Lyons, 2016 for further details on the "Hensher equation").

2.2 Use of travel time on trains

Potential challenge to the orthodoxy has become most apparent in relation to rail travel. Indeed a meta-analysis of empirical evidence regarding the proportion of travel time spent working suggests a modal hierarchy from train (highest) through air then bus and to car (lowest) (Wardman and Lyons, 2016). Fig. 4 illustrates what is now a commonly seen behavior, namely people using mobile technologies to engage in similar activities on the train to those in "the office."

Unique longitudinal data has been able to capture how rail travel time use is changing over time in the case of Great Britain between 2004 and 2014 (Lyons et al., 2007, 2013, 2016). Over that period, the number of rail journeys increased by 50%. The proportion of households with internet

Fig. 4 The familiar sight of technology-enabled time use during rail travel. *Images taken by author.*

access increased from around 50% to over 80%. By 2014, nearly 60% of individuals had mobile internet access (Lyons et al., 2016). 35% of business travelers in 2014 made "very worthwhile" use of their time on the train compared to 28% in 2004 (Lyons et al., 2016: Table 3). In 2004, 18% of business travelers indicated that having electronic devices with them had made their time spent on the train a lot better. In 2014, this figure had increased to 39% (Lyons et al., 2016: Table 7). In 2014, 11% of business travelers indicated that how they could use their travel time was the main reason for choosing to travel by train, with a further 23% indicating it was an important factor (Lyons et al., 2016: Table 5). Examination over the 10-year period revealed a decline in paper-based technologies accompanying travelers as they were replaced by mobile ICTs. Such ICTs themselves in some cases were then superseded by newly emerging technologies (for example the Personal Digital Assistant and MP3 player giving way to the Smartphone). With demand for rail travel growing faster than rail capacity, crowding had become an issue by 2014. Considering all rail travelers, Lyons et al. (2016) suggested that crowding may explain in part why the increase in the proportion of *all* travelers making very worthwhile use of their time seen between 2004 and 2010 did not continue to 2014.

2.3 Investing in rail and a fresh look at values of travel time

Over a similar period, the UK Government has been considering the case, and justifying its decision, to invest in high-speed rail (an investment estimated at £56 billion and billed as the largest infrastructure project in Europe).

An early assessment of part of the scheme using the standard economic appraisal approach put the costs at £8.4bn and the benefits at £11.8bn. Of these benefits, £8.8bn was attributed to travel time savings (Atkins, 2004). One of the frequently asked questions set out by the Government on its website during its 2011 High Speed 2 consultation was as follows: "*I've heard that the business case is based on the idea that all the time passengers spend on trains is wasted. Isn't that stupid?*". This is addressed in the economic appraisal report for high-speed rail (DfT, 2011b). The report acknowledges that "[i]f a business passenger spends half of the time on a train working fully productively, then saving half an hour in travel time may only save 15 minutes of 'lost' productive time" (DfT, 2011b: 51). However, it is assumed in the report that if productive travel time use is taken into account in this way then so too must: (i) the adverse effects of crowding on productive time use (with more capacity being provided by HS2 thus adding value); and (ii) the benefits from those travelers switching from car to HS2 both in terms of reduced journey times and more productive use of their time on the move. Skepticism has nevertheless remained regarding such a major investment, justified on the basis of speeding up journeys. A later economic assessment of the investment used an alternative methodology focused instead upon the impact on regional economies. Reportedly, this was strongly criticized by a leading economic geographer, Professor Henry Overman, with the implication that the approach applied was made up and the results unreliable.[e]

More recently the Department for Transport commissioned a study "to investigate the feasibility of differing approaches to valuing business travel time savings" (Wardman et al., 2013: 6) with recognition of recent interest in rail travel time use that has stimulated debate (Lyons et al., 2007; Mott MacDonald et al., 2009). As a result of this study, some important caveats were introduced into the updated (draft) online appraisal guidance for values of time. In this it was noted that "[d]ue to the uncertainties and inconsistencies in the existing evidence, the Department believes that fresh empirical evidence on business travellers' willingness-to-pay for travel time savings is required" (DfT, 2013: 6). This led in turn to a major study involving new revealed and stated preference surveys, with analysis to establish values of time both for travel during and outside the course of work on the basis of willingness to pay (thereby superseding the cost savings approach for

[e] https://www.telegraph.co.uk/news/uknews/road-and-rail-transport/10427468/HS2-benefits-essentially-made-up-economists-tell-MPs.html

travel during the course of work). Perhaps remarkably, this was the first major revision to values of travel time based on new survey evidence for some 20 years (since 1994). The study's aim included taking account, within the methodology, of travel time use and its effect on willingness to pay. It might have been supposed that this would have highlighted a downward pressure on value of saving travel time as a result of travel time use. However, it was found that, all else being equal, travel time use had no effect on the values of travel time. The report noted that "[t]he result relating to time use is of particular interest. One of the criticisms of the Department's current values for business travel is that they fail to reflect the increasing opportunities for people to work while travelling. By contrast, WTP-based values should reflect how travel time is used, given current travelling conditions and opportunities to use that time" (Arup et al., 2015).[f] The latest guidance from the Department for Transport for economic appraisal of transport schemes uses the values derived from this study (DfT, 2017).

In presenting the work at the International Transport Forum "Zero Value of Time" roundtable in September 2018, the study's lead author Professor Richard Batley did note the following qualifications on this apparent lack of effect of travel time use on the value of travel time[g]: possible confounding with other factors, such as time and distance; perhaps insufficient variation in (opportunities to use) travel time productively across the surveyed trips; the importance of time use may not have been fully captured by the SP exercise; and also possible that travelers, when completing hypothetical choice tasks, did not relate these back to the real-world journey which these choice tasks related to (simple time-cost trade-offs). Notwithstanding the overall rigor of the study in addressing what is a complex territory, it would seem that the matter has not yet been laid to rest.

2.4 Summary

Valuing travel time savings has a long history, replete with empirical evidence, economic theory and analysis, and wider examination of time use, meaning and its consequences in social and behavioral terms. The fact that it continues to be a topic of research and debate underlines that it is something which is subject to changing conditions over time but also subject to unresolved differences of expert interpretation across commentators and

[f] Strictly speaking willingness to pay here should reflect *perceived* use of travel time since it refers to an ex ante decision and not the experienced travel time.

[g] Points reproduced from Professor Batley's presentation slide with his knowledge and agreement.

disciplines as well as perennial challenges of empirical measurement. At the ITF roundtable in 2018, I put it to those of us gathered that the topic may be wicked rather than only complex. Before returning to this in the concluding discussion, the next section explores a series of travel time considerations that, I hope, illustrates why the topic is so fascinating but also so challenging.

3. Six considerations of travel time use

The chapter thus far has centered upon the valuation of travel time savings in transport appraisal. This is clearly important. However, there are also broader interests in the study of travel time use, including its implications for travel behavior as well as its sociological significance in terms of its place in people's individual and collective lives. In this section of the chapter, the following six considerations are addressed:

1. measuring productivity in the knowledge economy;
2. the changing nature of activities and how they are undertaken;
3. the changing appeal of virtual mobility;
4. the relative prospects of travel time use between different modes and how these are changing;
5. the effect of travel time use on travel choices; and
6. the ownership of time.

3.1 Measuring productivity in the knowledge economy

The wish to be able to judge the absolute and relative productivity of travel time use in qualitative and subjective, if not quantitative and objective, terms has an obvious appeal—particularly if "productive" is interpreted as worthwhile in the sense that it may be good use of time for social as well as economic reasons. This can inform attempts to value travel time and travel time savings. It can also help inform design of travel environments and of artifacts to accompany the traveler. Moreover, it can inform an understanding of what matters to travelers that in turn affects their travel behavior. However, measuring productivity is complicated and, in some respects, it can be argued, impossible.

How much are people getting out of their time on the move beyond realizing benefits from reaching their destination? Being worthwhile, as judged by the individual, concerns meeting a need or desire. Do I value an opportunity to relax (and perhaps even sleep) on the move, to indulge in "time out" or to have some physical exertion? Is it an opportunity to invest in my social network? Are there work tasks that I can achieve that need doing and that might at least ease the pressure on me at other times? Just because people are observed to be using their time on the move in certain ways does not mean it is particularly productive or worthwhile—or to the extent that having the opportunity to reinvest the time elsewhere might be if the travel time could be saved. It could simply amount to killing time (Clayton et al., 2016; Zerubavel, 1981).

It may be possible to offer a subjective and qualitative view on how worthwhile a given journey has been. I can relay an account of how I spent my ourney time, how it made me feel and to what extent and why I had a sense of it being worthwhile (in absolute terms or in relation to my wider agenda and to time use outside of the travel environment). However, is seems much more problematic to be able to judge in quantitative terms *how productive* I may have been (or for my employer to judge on behalf of myself and other employees). This is especially so regarding knowledge work. I can measure how many envelopes I can fill and seal per unit time but how do I measure the progress that I have made on the train in being productive in writing part of an academic article or while driving in the car thinking about the structure of that article—versus drafting the conclusions on my couch at home? Indeed it is suggested that it is not possible to measure an individual's productivity in the knowledge economy (particularly at the level of a given episode of activity) (Ramírez and Nembhard, 2004).

Is it possible to compare the relative benefit of my time use on the move to using time outside of travel for the same purpose? Would I have written a document with more positive impact in the office, at home or in a hotel room than on the train or plane? Is the quality of my output independent of the environment in which it was generated? How variable might different environments be across different episodes of time use activity? For instance, one train journey might be very crowded, another noisy; perhaps another journey finds me tired or distracted. The same could be true of my office environment. If, because of a view on which environment best suits each task, I favor undertaking certain tasks while I travel and undertaking others when I am not traveling, is it appropriate to be asked to judge the productivity of doing a task on the move with doing that same task outside of travel in order to inform the valuing of travel time?

Are there complex second order effects and feedback loops from undertaking activities while traveling? For example, I may have determined that the best time to keep up to date with emails is while I travel. I devote travel time to this and feel productive and on top of things. Perhaps many other people are doing the same. Some would argue that growth in the use of email and social media exchanges may be generating a greater *quantity* of knowledge work rather than a greater quality. Unintended consequences of certain travel time uses may be that we do more of certain things while neglecting other things and yet get less benefit overall. For instance if I work on clearing my emails on the move am I party to increasing the overall volume of communication everyone is facing without necessarily increasing the overall benefits from that communication to the same degree?

3.2 The changing nature of activities and how they are undertaken

Activities are undertaken to realize an outcome benefit for the participant—for example earning money, maintaining social ties, staying fit and healthy, creating a sense of purpose, fostering a feeling of relaxation (or stimulation), and so on. Activities can be undertaken in different ways but different activities can emerge that achieve the outcome benefits. For example reading a newspaper has traditionally been paper-based. I can read a newspaper on the train. With a tablet PC, I can now choose to read an electronic version of the newspaper. However, I may not wish to as a passenger in a car due to travel sickness or as the driver since it would be unsafe to do so. Reading a newspaper is a means of keeping up to date with current affairs. There are other means of doing so. I may listen to the radio in the car or I could listen to podcasts. While on the train, I may use social media as an alternative.

There is an important distinction between form and function when it comes to travel time use. It seems very likely that forms of travel time use (just as with forms of time use outside of travel) will continue to evolve. We may, for example, find ourselves in immersive virtual reality environments or make use of augmented reality. Yet while forms may change, the function or outcome benefit sought may be more enduring. If I want some down time to relax then this is my goal. I could achieve it by reading a book, by having a book read to me, by watching a film, by watching people around me.

The state of flux in activity form makes the prospect of benefitting from observing and understanding it of potentially limited value in terms of the future of mobility. For this reason, it may be particularly beneficial to give more attention not to what we are doing or how we are doing it but to *why* we are doing it and what we believe we are getting out of it. This might provide important insights for transport planning including comparative insights over time and between different locations and contexts.

Nevertheless, as form changes this may also change functional effectiveness—am I able to achieve certain goals more easily than I was before in a mobile environment that in turn affects what I may choose, or need, to do with my time and how effective that time use proves to be?

3.3 The changing appeal of virtual mobility

Typically, travel is undertaken in order to access people, goods, services or opportunities. It is a form of connectivity provided by the transport system to realize access. However, connectivity (as noted earlier) is increasingly made possible by the telecommunications system. For some people, for some of the time, the opportunity exists not to travel in order to reach what they need: I can reach people through audio or videoconferencing or through entering online (gaming) worlds; I can reach goods by searching and purchasing online and they are delivered to me; I can similarly access some services such as insurance, banking, healthcare advice from my armchair; and I can network online or post promotional information about myself in search of employment or in creating employment for myself by doing business with others online. Chatterjee et al. (2018) point to time series data for England that reveals young men (aged 17–29) are spending on average 80 min *longer* per day at home than 20 years ago (and young women 40 min longer). Increasing use of ICTs is considered a likely explanatory factor.

Such virtual mobility may be expanding our overall capacity to engage or it may be substituting for alternative forms of engagement, or both (Mokhtarian, 2003). It points toward a growing spatio-temporal flexibility of activities (depending upon the resources at my disposal). If I can do my grocery shopping online, then *when* I choose to do this becomes more flexible and, indeed, I may not need to do it in a single sitting—the activity could become fragmented over time and space (Couclelis, 2004; Hubers et al., 2008). Depending upon the form of technology and connectivity on offer (and its capability and reliability) I may choose to do my grocery shopping partly at work, partly on the bus and finish off in the evening at home. In some cases activities have now become "on demand"—released from the shackles of where and when they can be performed. The rise of on-demand consumption of film and television is another case in point.

The changing appeal of virtual mobility is recognized to have a number of different consequences for transport (Mokhtarian, 1990; Salomon, 1986), not least in terms of whether it is contributing to a net increase or decrease in the amount of travel (and in turn time spent traveling) per person

(Lyons, 2015; Mokhtarian, 2009). The changing nature of the form of activities allied to spatio-temporal flexibility underlines the importance of not treating *travel* time use in isolation from time use *overall*—the latter provides key contextual insight for the former. The scope for flexibility in our use of time may have a bearing on how travelers cope with and tolerate the transport system when it faces reliability problems. I may be able to change the timing, mode or route of my journey before or after setting off if suitable information about disruption to my journey is available. Retiming may include choosing not to make or continue the journey. I may also be able to adjust my schedule of activity for the day such that delay in the journey I am on (with the resulting extended travel time) is addressed through travel time uses to lessen the impact of transport system shortcomings.

3.4 The relative prospects of travel time use between different modes and how these are changing

Building upon the issue of form and function of activities (considered above), it may be helpful to conceive of what might be termed the building blocks of activities as outlined in Table 1 below. The question then arises as to which building blocks are available for different modes and how this in turn dictates the repertoire of activities that are possible. Table 1 is illustrative but it acts as a provocation for examining *activity potential* across modes. Being able to think, for example, is possible across all modes. Nevertheless, the capacity for thinking in terms of quality and quantity will be variable. As a car driver, cognitive effort is required to control the vehicle. Such effort becomes freed up if the individual switches from being the driver to a

Table 1 The opportunity to engage in the building blocks of activities across modes.

	Car (driver)	Car (passenger)	Train	Bus	Walk	Cycle	Plane
Thinking	✓	✓	✓	✓	✓	✓	✓
Writing/typing	✗✗	?	✓	?	✗	✗	✓
Talking	✓	✓	✓	✓	✓	?	?
Listening	✓	✓	✓	✓	✓	?	?
Reading/watching	✗	?	✓	✓	?	✗	✓
Sleeping/resting	✗	✓	✓	?	✗	✗	✓
Exercising	✗	✗	✗	✗	✓	✓	✗
Eating/drinking	?	✓	✓	?	✓	?	?

passenger (or is part-way between thanks to assistive technologies). Thinking potential across other modes can likewise vary according to the cognitive effort required from the primary act of traveling. It will also vary according to external stimuli that enhance or detract from thinking. It may be possible to privatize public space to remove or suppress such stimuli—for example the use of noise-canceling headphones. Writing/typing is a key building block of documenting information and communicating it. For some modes (car driver, walk, cycle), this is impossible or at least difficult or dangerous (acknowledging for instance the pedestrians messaging on their smartphone as they walk). As such, activities that rely upon this building block are ruled out. Risk of travel sickness and/or "elbow room" may or may not inhibit writing/typing as a car or bus passenger. Indeed, for the train passenger a precondition may be the need to have a seat rather than be standing. Eating/drinking is rather more ambiguous in the tabulated interpretation. Is it safe to do so? Is there space and/or ride quality to do so (comfortably)? Is there the flexibility to have access to food within the journey?

This begins to illuminate the variability of activity potential across modes and some of the challenges and subtleties in interpreting the nature and extent of potential. It also points to ways and means that potential can be enhanced or compromised in terms of the travel time use setting. Within a given mode, design and technology enhancements could improve potential. Such enhancements could be to the extent that inaccessible building blocks become accessible—a case in point would be the prospect of self-driving cars whereby the driver effectively becomes a passenger. There are, of course, outlier examples such as the potential to have exercise equipment on planes and train although it hardly seems set to become accessible to the masses.

For many transport investments, transport appraisal considers a 60-year period ahead in terms of assessing the return on a major investment—including the value of travel time savings over this period (DfT, 2018b). In this context there is interest not only in making sense of today's activity potential across modes but in contemplating how this potential might change over the years and decades ahead as technological innovation continues. The availability of the building blocks could be enhanced but the different building blocks required to fulfill certain activities could change. Augmented reality might render physical keyboards redundant when we travel as we touch type on a holographic keyboard in front of us (to the initial bemusement of fellow travelers no doubt). Such redundancy might also arise if speech to text enhancements continue or even "thought to text" becomes a reality. This is of course wild speculation and yet should not be too quickly dismissed when we consider the developments that have taken place over the last 20 years (see Fig. 1). Imagine describing to someone in 1999 how people today would be swiping electronic screens with their fingers while on the move and with such screens being integral to multifunctional electronic devices that allowed you to reach out beyond the travel environment to other people and resources across the globe as well as having your entire office, music collection and even video library at your fingertips.

3.5 The effect of travel time use on travel choices

As noted earlier, in the case of rail travel, a significant minority of passengers have chosen to travel by rail *because* of the opportunities for travel time use. Indeed for some—particularly where travel is for business (someone else is paying) and is longer distance (reflecting a period of meaningful length to settle into productive tasks)—the idea of driving rather than catching the train can now appear rather old-fashioned and backward looking. Why would I travel by car and arrive at my meeting feeling tired from the driving task when I could have gone by train and focused on greater opportunity for doing something with my time before arriving at my destination (perhaps even preparing and then sending my slides for the meeting itself)? Of course, the appeal in this illustration presupposes that I have convenient access to suitable rail services, that those services offer a suitable (uncrowded) environment for me to use my time, and that the cost of rail travel is not prohibitive.

Given the prospect that time use could affect travel choices for some people for some journeys, the intriguing question emerges as to whether, assuming finite available funding, it would be better for investment in the transport system to focus upon making journey time better for travelers rather than making journey durations shorter (Bannister et al., 2019; Milakis et al., 2015). Resources permitting, a combination of both may appeal—indeed high-speed rail is typically also high-comfort rail. Making journey time better might include relatively simple innovations in the design of travel environments (including interchanges)—for example, a power socket seems increasingly a potential "life saver" for remaining active in the digital world (as well as the more challenging provision of reliable digital connectivity for mobile devices). Certain aspects of making journey time better without also making journeys more expensive may be challenging. For instance, most people would likely prefer more legroom or elbow room on a bus, train or plane but this would reduce the vehicle carrying capacity and increase fares. At the same time it is clear that individual travelers, thanks to innovations outside of, but related to, the transport sector (such as mobile technologies), are prepared to pay to equip themselves for travel in ways that improve the journey time experience.

Meanwhile, it is important to recognize that far from everyone views travel time use through the lens of a work-obsessed knowledge worker chasing productivity. As Jain and Lyons (2008) recognized, travel time can be a gift—a time to oneself to be off-stage and to unwind. In this context the prospect of listening to the radio (in all its low-tech splendor) on the commute home in the car might be a welcome reprieve, whereas if one were on a bus or train (or in a driverless car) the compulsion might be there to re-enter the rat race and do work. Allied to this, as found by Mokhtarian and Salomon through their "teleportation test" (Mokhtarian and Salomon, 2001; see also Jain and Lyons, 2008), when it comes to their commute, it seems people do not necessarily seek the ideal of zero travel time but rather signal in the region of 15–20 min—a period of time to adjust from one life role and set of activities to another.

As the boundaries between travel time and activity time blur and the nature of activities evolves with potentially more flexibility in where, when and how we engage in them, it seems plausible to contemplate a growing significant for travel time use, compared to journey duration, as a determinant of travel choice. However, our transport system's development has been rather locked into a paradigm of pursuit of faster journeys—perhaps with the ironic consequences that roads are often clogged by inefficiently used single occupant cars within which worthwhile use of time is limited. Future prospects then point to the possibility of mass transit becoming more appealing since it is more efficient at people movement and may face less need to compete with the car on speed if it can compete on time use potential (notwithstanding the issues raised by autonomous vehicles including cars and mass transit). Such considerations suggest that even if the value of travel time savings as currently addressed in appraisal is not affected, people's travel behavior may be. This raises important issues to be addressed in how transport investment is judged regarding the benefits it generates for society in the future.

There has also been recognition of the possibility that growing opportunities to use travel time in fruitful ways could create an upward pressure on how much time we are prepared to spend traveling as travel time becomes activity time. Such upward pressure may be compounded by effects on land use patterns as, notwithstanding monetary and environmental cost implications, it becomes more manageable to transcend longer distances (when the choice to travel is made rather than to engage virtually as a substitute for travel).

3.6 The ownership of time

Values of time in economic appraisal, as indicated in Section 2, vary according to the purpose of the journey—notably between when traveling during the course of work or outside the course of work. The logic of this follows from who is assumed to own the time in question—the former being one's employer and the latter being oneself. A businesswoman leaves the office and sets off in her car to visit a client. Time is money for her employer and time in the car is time that could otherwise be spent on other productive work activities. Of course, visiting the client is expected to be productive but there is a time cost in doing so due to the travel—and this is borne by the employer. This has a logic to it. However, consider an alternative scenario. The same businesswoman leaves the office and travels by train to visit a client. She is exhausted by the prior week's work and sleeps on the train. She arrives at the client's premises and, in her refreshed state, impresses the client to the point of winning new work. On the train back it's too late to return to the office—indeed she feels she is traveling outside her working day. She enjoys a read of her novel on the journey back—a treat for herself. Later that evening, enthused by the successful day, she returns to her laptop and writes up a record of the client meeting for her boss.

The example is contrived but deliberately so to highlight the ambiguity over who owns which time in the person's day, alongside the earlier discussed challenge of gauging productivity from time use. It further illustrates the spatio-temporal flexibility of work and the phenomenon of fragmentation referred to earlier. Research on rail travel in Norway (Gripsrud and Hjorthol, 2012) found that 27% of commuters had their travel time approved as working hours by their employers with the figure rising to 53% for business trips. Longitudinal studies would be helpful in revealing, within and between segments of the population and different geographic areas, how this is changing, or not, over time.

Looking further into the future, it seems plausible to suppose that determining ownership of time will become less clear—at least according to where and when time is being consumed. Especially in the knowledge economy, people *may* behave in an increasingly flexible and fluid way in terms of where and when they perform work and non-work activities. Indeed, employment structures themselves might change. In terms of valuing travel time savings when assessing the merits of transport investment decisions and their return on investment over decades ahead, this territory still requires further attention.

4. Concluding discussion

4.1 Travel time matters

This chapter has sought to provide a glimpse into the multifaceted topic that is travel time use and its value. It has been selective in its focus with particular (though not exclusive) emphasis given to rail travel and with an orientation towards considering knowledge workers. In practice, the coverage of the topic reaches much further but this is where particular attention and points of contention have applied in recent years. The chapter highlights developments regarding how travel time and in turn travel time savings are interpreted when valuing time in economic appraisal of transport investment options. Such appraisal also concerns modeling of how use of the transport system would be changed by the transport measure(s) being considered. Bringing the two together, appraisal aims to establish the total benefit that arises from the investment in terms of the monetary value of saved travel time across all travel using the transport system concerned, accumulated decades into the future after the scheme is introduced. Modeling the change in transport system use concerns how it is assumed transport system users behave in determining if, where, when, how and by which route they travel. This relates in part to accounting for how people's travel choices are affected by travel time and its use. The chapter has explored six considerations of travel time that serve to illustrate the nature and extent of issues that have a bearing on people's behavior and travel. It seems hard if not impossible to gauge the absolute or relative value of our travel time compared to the other time we consume. This is exacerbated by changes over time in the nature of activities themselves and the flexibility in time, space and means available to undertake them. There are consequences in turn for how a distinction is made between when our time is considered work time and when it is considered non-work time; and consequences for the relative appeal of different travel modes and the travel choices we make.

4.2 The escalator puzzle

Travel time clearly matters and questions persist over whether more value may be gained by investing in travel environments that enable people to get more from their travel time as opposed to investing in making journeys quicker to save travel time—or indeed from some combination of the two. A simple example concerning the saving versus using of travel time, which has intrigued me for some time, is the escalator and people's use of it. The escalator is a people mover—compared to a static staircase it allows you to get from one level to another more quickly.[h] So why do some people stand still when they have stepped onto an escalator and others continue walking on it (see Fig. 5)? I clearly would not make progress with my journey if I stood still on a static staircase. The escalator allows me to speed up my journey *if* I continue walking as well (assuming the escalator moves at walking speed). If I stand still, I am trading that chance to speed up my journey for something else. Is it the ability to rest? Is it because it replaces waiting at a later interchange for my next connection with waiting on a moving device (that still gives me a sense of journey progress)? Is it because I am really not so bothered about small savings in travel time because I'm talking with a traveling companion, or people watching, listening to music, watching a film on my smartphone or deep in thought? Making sense of how time is managed and consumed is not straightforward.

Fig. 5 If saving travel time is important, why do so many people stand still when on escalators? *Image taken by author.*

[h] In 2016/17 London Underground undertook a trial where people were expected to stand on both sides of the escalator (rather than the usual convention of standing on the right and walking on the left). By applying this new approach at busy times it was reported that congestion was cut by 30%. In other words, by standing still, people movement was greater than had they been walking.

4.3 A wicked problem

In reflecting upon the insights from this chapter, *is* the examination of travel time a complex undertaking or a wicked problem? In one sense, the distinction may seem academic. In any case, the topic has many dimensions that make it far from straightforward to make sense of. My own assessment is that valuing travel time (and perhaps accounting for travel time use in travel behavior modeling) has been treated as complex rather than as a wicked problem. This infers that those addressing the problem are of the view that it is soluble—at least to the extent that theory and assumptions can be applied with related empirical evidence assembled that satisfies those concerned that the solution is sufficiently robust; it is defensible. From my own experience of seeking to make sense of how orthodox transport appraisal employs economic theory to treat savings in travel time, it is apparent that those experts charged with achieving solutions to valuing travel time are wrestling with intellectually challenging and analytically demanding issues. Indeed, it calls for a strong grasp of such issues even to be able to engage in debating or challenging how such issues should be addressed.

The valuing of travel time, and in turn the assumption that speeding up journeys is inherently of value, has continued to be questioned by others. This may suggest that those others are simply unable to grasp the complexity of issues that the experts referred to above are dealing with. However, some of those others are also experts in their own right but from different backgrounds and with different disciplinary and theoretical perspectives. If they are questioning how travel time is treated in transport economics and they are doing so from more than a point of misperception or misunderstanding then might this point to the problem being wicked rather than complex? There may be an important distinction to be made between "experts at" (those who are charged by the powers that be to tackle and resolve the problem of valuing travel time) and "experts on" (those who have a legitimate expert view to contribute but who are not called upon to do so). It can be suggested that if the problem is indeed wicked rather than complex then it becomes more important that contributions from *both* categories of experts are brought to bear on the matter. This is what Roberts (2000) refers to as a *collaborative* strategy. At present, it appears that different constituencies of experts have interpreted aspects of the topic in different ways perhaps with different agendas in mind. To the extent that these different interpretations challenge one another then this is what Roberts refers to as a *competitive* approach. Meanwhile with regard to economic appraisal, treatment of travel time has involved an *authoritative* strategy—vesting responsibility (predominantly) in the hands of the "experts at" rather than the wider pool of "experts on" travel time use, its meaning and value.

We exist at a time when the nature of future mobility has become uncertain with myriad possible influences in social, technological, economic, environmental and political terms. It seems clear that time use, meaning and value will be a highly significant determinant of shaping that future. It remains a fertile topic for research and it would be wise, in my view, to acknowledge its wicked nature and foster greater inter-disciplinary collaboration to help inform our interpretation of travel time.

References

Arup, ITS Leeds and Accent, 2015. Provision of market research for value of time savings and reliability: non-technical summary report. Report to the Department for Transport, 14 August.

Atkins, 2004. High Speed Line Study: Summary Report. Strategic Rail Authority.

Bannister, D., Cornet, Y., Givoni, M., Lyons, G., 2019. From minimum to reasonable travel time. In: Hickman, R., Mella Lira, B., Givoni, M., Geurs, K. (Eds.), Transport, Space and Equity. Edward Elgar.

Ben-Elia, E., Lyons, G., Mokhtarian, P., 2018. Epilogue: the new frontiers of behavioral research on the interrelationships between ICT, activities, time use and mobility. Transportation 45 (2), 479–497.

Chatterjee, K., Goodwin, P., Schwanen, T., Clark, B., Jain, J., Melia, S., Middleton, J., Plyushteva, A., Ricci, M., Santos, G., Stokes, G., 2018. Young people's travel—what's changed and why? Review and Analysis. Final Report to the Department for Transport. http://eprints.uwe.ac.uk/34640.

Clayton, W., Jain, J., Parkhurst, G., 2016. An ideal journey: making bus travel desirable. Mobilities 12 (5), 706–725.

Couclelis, H., 2004. Pizza over the internet: e-commerce, the fragmentation of activity and the tyranny of the region. Entrep. Reg. Dev. 16, 41–54.

DETR, 1999. Transport and the Economy. The Standing Advisory Committee on Trunk Road Assessment, October. TSO, London.

DfT, 2011a. Values of time and vehicle operating costs TAG Unit 3.5.6. In: Transport Analysis Guidance (TAG). Department for Transport. April.

DfT, 2011b. Economic Case for HS2: The Y Network and London—West Midlands. Department for Transport, London.

DfT, 2013. Values of time and vehicle operating costs TAG unit 3.5.6—IN DRAFT. In: Transport Analysis Guidance (TAG). Department for Transport. October.

DfT, 2017. TAG UNIT A1.3—user and provider impacts. In: Transport Analysis Guidance (TAG). Department for Transport. March, https://assets.publishing.service.gov.uk/government/uploads/system/uploads/attachment_data/file/603254/webtag-tag-unit-a1-3-user-and-provider-impacts-march-2017.pdf.

DfT, 2018a. National Travel Survey: England 2017. Statistical Release. Department for Transport. https://assets.publishing.service.gov.uk/government/uploads/system/uploads/attachment_data/file/729521/national-travel-survey-2017.pdf.

DfT, 2018b. TAG UNIT A1.1 cost-benefit analysis. In: Transport Analysis Guidance. Department for Transport. Available at https://assets.publishing.service.gov.uk/government/uploads/system/uploads/attachment_data/file/712699/tag-unit-a1.1-cost-benefit-analysis-may-18.pdf.

ECMT, 1969. Theoretical and Practical Research on an Exact Time Saving: Report of the Sixth Round Table on Transport Economics Held in Paris on 13–14 November 1969, ECMT Round Tables, No. 6. OECD Publishing, Paris. https://doi.org/10.1787/9789282104811-en.

Fowkes, A.S., 2001. Principles of Valuing Business Travel Time Savings. ITS WP 562, Institute for Transport Studies. University of Leeds.

Fowkes, A.S., Marks, P., Nash, C., 1986. The Value of Business Travel Time Savings. ITS WP 214, Institute for Transport Studies. University of Leeds.

Gripsrud, M., Hjorthol, R., 2012. Working on the train: from 'dead time' to productive and vital time. Transportation 39, 941–956.

Head, B., 2010. Evidence-based policy: principles and requirements. In: Strengthening evidence based policy in the Australian federation. Volume 1: Proceedings, Roundtable Proceedings. Productivity Commission, Canberra, pp. 13–26. https://www.pc.gov.au/research/supporting/strengthening-evidence/roundtable-proceedings-volume1.pdf.

Hensher, D.A., 1977. Value of Business Travel Time. Pergamon Press, Oxford.

Hubers, C., Schwanen, T., Dijst, M., 2008. ICT and temporal fragmentation of activities: an analytical framework and initial empirical findings. Tijdschr. Econ. Soc. Geogr. 99 (5), 528–546.

Jain, J., Lyons, G., 2008. The gift of travel time. J. Transp. Geogr. 16, 81–89.

Lyons, G., 2015. Transport's digital age transition. J. Transp. Land Use 8 (2), 1–19.

Lyons, G., Urry, J., 2005. Travel time use in the information age. Transp. Res. A Policy Pract. 39, 257–276.

Lyons, G., Jain, J., Holley, D., 2007. The use of travel time by rail passengers in Great Britain. Transp. Res. A Policy Pract. 41, 107–120.

Lyons, G., Jain, J., Susilo, Y., Atkins, S., 2013. Comparing rail passengers' travel time use in Great Britain between 2004 and 2010. Mobilities 8 (4), 560–579. https://doi.org/10.1080/17450101.2012.743221.

Lyons, G., Jain, J., Weir, I., 2016. Changing times—a decade of empirical insight into the experience of rail passengers in Great Britain. J. Transp. Geogr. 57, 94–104. https://doi.org/10.1016/j.jtrangeo.2016.10.003.

Milakis, D., Cervero, R., van Wee, B., Maat, K., 2015. Do people consider an acceptable travel time? Evidence from Berkeley, CA. J. Transp. Geogr. 44, 76–86.

Mokhtarian, P.L., 1990. A typology of relationships between telecommunications and transportation. Transp. Res. A Policy Pract. 24 (3), 231–242.

Mokhtarian, P.L., 2003. Telecommunications and travel—the case for complementarity. J. Ind. Ecol. 6 (2), 43–57. E-commerce, the Internet and the Environment.

Mokhtarian, P.L., 2009. If telecommunication is such a good substitute for travel, why does congestion continue to get worse? Transp. Lett. 1, 1–17.

Mokhtarian, P.L., 2018. The times they are A-Changin': what do the expanding uses of travel time portend for policy, planning, and life? Transp. Res. Rec. https://doi.org/10.1177/0361198118798602.

Mokhtarian, P.L., Salomon, I., 2001. How derived is the demand for travel? Some conceptual and measurement considerations. Transp. Res. A Policy Pract. 35 (8), 695–719.

Mott MacDonald, Hugh Gunn Associates, TRI Napier University, Accent and Mark Bradley Research and Consulting, 2009. Productive use of rail travel time and the valuation of travel time savings for rail business travellers. Final Report to the Department for Transport.

ONS, 2018. UK Labour Market: December 2018. Statistical Bulletin. Office for National Statistics. December. https://www.ons.gov.uk/employmentandlabourmarket/peopleinwork/employmentandemployeetypes/bulletins/uklabourmarket/december2018/pdf.

Ramírez, Y.W., Nembhard, D.A., 2004. Measuring knowledge worker productivity—a taxonomy. J. Intellect. Cap. 5 (4), 602–628.

Roberts, N.C., 2000. Wicked problems and network approaches to resolution. Int. Public. Manag. Rev. 1 (1), 1–19.

Salomon, I., 1986. Telecommunications and travel relationships: a review. Transp. Res. A Policy Pract. 20 (3), 223–238.

Wardman, M., Lyons, G., 2016. The digital revolution and worthwhile use of travel time: implications for appraisal and forecasting. Transportation 43 (3), 507–530.

Wardman, M., Batley, R., Laird, J., Mackie, P., Fowkes, T., Lyons, G., Bates, J., Eliasson, J., 2013. Valuation of travel time savings for business travellers. Prepared for the Department for Transport, April, https://assets.publishing.service.gov.uk/government/uploads/system/uploads/attachment_data/file/251997/vtts_for_business_main_report-dft-005.pdf.

Zerubavel, E., 1981. Hidden Rhythms Schedules and Calendars in Social Life. University of California Press.

CHAPTER SEVEN

Activities while travelling? Travel time perception and travel time use in an era of automated driving

Viktoriya Kolarova[a], **Rita Cyganski**[a], **Barbara Lenz**[a,b,*]
[a]German Aerospace Center, Institute of Transport Research, Berlin, Germany
[b]Geography Department, Humboldt-Universität zu Berlin, Berlin, Germany
*Corresponding author: e-mail address: Barbara.Lenz@dlr.de

Contents

Abstract

Digitalization and automation of road vehicles will potentially change the way people spend and perceive travel time in the future. Automated driving opens up new opportunities to spend the travel time on other activities while traveling in a presumably more comfortable way. Considering the high uncertainty regarding the future impact of vehicle automation on mobility behavior and its importance for future transport planning and policy, analyzing the potential changes in travel time perception and time use from a user perspective becomes increasingly important. Leading questions include how, by whom, and in which context "additional" time—as active driving is no longer necessary—can be used and which are other important determinants of changes in travel time valuation in an autonomous vehicle. This chapter investigates risks and opportunities of potential changes in the value that people attribute to travel time.

Advances in Transport Policy and Planning, Volume 3
ISSN 2543-0009
https://doi.org/10.1016/bs.atpp.2019.07.002

It provides a comprehensive review of relevant literature. Based on state-of-knowledge on the topic and results from own empirical works, the authors conceptualize the role of the context as an important determinant of alternative travel time perception and time use. Finally, policy implications and future research needs are discussed.

Keywords: Time use, Automated driving, Value of travel time savings, Travel activities, Utility of travel

1. Introduction

1.1 Automated driving and its potential impact on travel behavior

The ever increasing automation and digitalization of road vehicles are expected to enable completely new options to use travel time; this trend seems to be one of the big "game changers" for future mobility. The likely impact, though, will be highly dependent on the level of automation assumed.

Following an existing classification, vehicle automation is defined by five levels—from no automation (level 0), through low or partly automation (level 1 and 2), conditional automation (level 3) and high (level 4) to full automation, i.e., driverless (level 5) (SAE, 2014). The highest level of automation does not only relieve the driver from the task of driving, thus providing the option of alternative travel time use. It also enables additional new mobility services, such as "vehicle-on-demand" (VoD) or "shared automated vehicles" (SAV), which will be similar to current carsharing or taxi services, but operating without a driver (Lenz and Fraedrich, 2016). Such services can be used individually or trips can be shared with other users with similar destination; the benefit for the users will be lower cost, but include some waiting times (Kröger and Kickhöfer, 2017). Also, these services can facilitate multimodal trips when the SAVs are implemented as first or last mile solution in areas where public transport is deficient today (Mosquet et al., 2015; Ohnemus and Perl, 2016; Yap et al., 2016). Digitalization, on the other hand, is related to the digital distribution and processing of information. Digitalization has substantially eased on-demand information retrieval in all areas of daily life, thus being a key element for the flexible and easy use and combination of different mobility offers. At the same time, it has led to increased connectivity of road vehicles. "Connected vehicles" can be defined as vehicles with on-board equipment that allows for the communication with other vehicles as well as with the infrastructure or roadside sensors (Zmud et al., 2015). Additionally, connectivity enables the use of platform-based carsharing services or vehicle-based infotainment applications likewise. The latter ones are in-vehicle systems that provide information and entertainment context to automobile users, such as audio or video entertainment for passengers, internet access or navigation and route-related information services. Vehicle automation and vehicle connectivity can evolve independently from each other. However, some experts believe that the convergence of both will provide benefits to mobility, safety, and environment (Zmud et al., 2015).

While automated and connected driving bear chances for improvements in both individual mobility and the traffic system, there is also the risk that new transport issues emerge as "driving in a car" becomes more comfortable and accessible for new user groups: (i) At higher levels of automation car users will no longer have to drive or pay attention to the traffic, so that they can switch their attention to other activities while traveling (Anderson et al., 2014; Trommer et al., 2016). (ii) Automated vehicles, private or in kind of new mobility options such as vehicle-on-demand, provide new or additional access to motorized transport for people who are currently not able or not allowed to drive, like disabled persons, elderly or adolescents. Improvements in travel quality and new travel options are likely to change mode choices, but also trip destinations and trip length. From a transport management point of view, automated driving can improve traffic safety and capacity of the transport network as vehicles can operate in a more efficient way than human drivers (Anderson et al., 2014). The effect of automation on capacity depends, however, on the diffusion rate of AVs (Friedrich, 2016). At the same time, given the expected increase in attractiveness of individual motorized transport, automated driving may lead to an increase in overall vehicle-kilometers traveled and therefore to more emissions (unless we consider AVs to be also electric vehicles) and higher congestion levels, mainly in case of a primarily individual use of such vehicles (Bahamonde-Birke et al., 2018; Childress et al., 2014; Trommer et al., 2016).

1.2 Expectations about travel time use in an era of automated driving

Automated driving will allow spending travel time on other activities, while increased connectivity of cars does not only support automation but also provides connection to infotainment services and internet in the car, thus opening up new opportunities for time use while traveling. There is an increasing body of literature that addresses this issue from both a conceptual and empirical perspective. On the conceptual side, main topics are the applicability of alternative time use while driving in an automated vehicle (Can the "additional" time be used—How? By whom? In which context?) and the potential re-scheduling of entire daily (or even multi-day) activity plans (e.g., Pudāne et al., 2018a). On the empirical side, most studies investigate the attitudes and expectations of car users toward the option to use the time in a vehicle alternatively and how this affects travel time perception. Connected to this is the question about people's willingness to spend an increasing amount of time for travel, in particular from home to work, which could have—in the medium run—considerable impact on housing choice and settlement structures. Productivity gains and time efficiency are expected notably for the use of private automated vehicles (e.g., Anderson et al., 2014; KPMG, 2015; Pakusch et al., 2018; Wadud et al., 2016). However, the productive time use assumption is postulated mainly in theoretical works and still needs to be validated by empirical data. Moreover, the range of activities that can be performed en-route depends not only on the concrete context, but also on the considered vehicle automation level. It can be expected that higher levels of automation (level 4 and 5) will be most beneficial to the users as on these levels the driver does not have to pay attention to the traffic or intervene in case of emergency (required, for instance, by level 3 automation).

In the following, we examine the risks and opportunities of potential changes in the value that people allocate to travel time. In doing so, we put the context-specific influence on alternative travel time perception and time use in the foreground. The remainder of this contribution is structured as follows: First, we will give a comprehensive overview of theoretical concepts and empirical findings from the literature that are relevant for analyzing changes in travel time perception and time use in the context of automated driving. In the next section, we conceptualize the role of the context on potential travel time perception and time use and underpin our concept with empirical insights that we obtained from own studies. We discuss the topic with view on the empirical insights presented in the previous section. Finally, we summarize what we know so far about how automation will affect travel time perception and time use, and elaborate on questions yet unanswered. In the same vein, we discuss the implications of the results for transport planning and policy as well as for future research needs.

2. State of the art

2.1 Concepts to address changes in travel time perception and time use

In theoretical and empirical works on automated driving, changes in travel time use are postulated as one of the most important advantages of vehicle automation for the users. However, depending on the study focus, time use is considered from different perspectives.

Studies with focus on user acceptance of automated vehicles explore the factors which influence the willingness to use automated driving, including the opportunity for alternative time use and increased comfort (Cyganski et al., 2015; Fraedrich et al., 2016; Zmud et al., 2016). User acceptance models often used in such studies (e.g., TAM, Davis, 1985, 1989; the further development UTAUT, Venkatesh et al., 2003; or integrated acceptance models, Lucke, 1995, Lüthje, 2007) are usually based on psychological and innovation adoption theories describing individual behavior, such as the Theory of Planned Behavior (Ajzen, 1991) and the Diffusion of Innovation Theory (Rogers, 1995). Common determinants of user acceptance of new technologies include individual characteristics, such as socio-demographic factors and attitudes, as well as technology attributes, such as perceived advantage and ease of use, and—in addition—context-specific factors. Context-specific factors can be either related to the social, cultural, regulative, geographical and economic context (Langert, 2008; Litfin, 2000; Lucke, 1995) or to the usage context, i.e., the compatibility of the new technology with user needs and experience (Lüthje, 2007). When interpreting the role of travel time use and perception from a user acceptance perspective, researchers are interested in exploring the relative advantage, i.e., perceived usefulness, of driving in an automated vehicle, including desirable activities while traveling. Main purpose is exploring how new alternatives for activities (and related time use) are perceived by road users and which characteristics of these new alternatives influence user acceptance of automation technologies in transport. Based on a more explorative methodology and on innovation research concepts, they are an essential research step when exploring a new mobility alternative, not yet available in the market, and its perceived advantages and potential diffusion in the socio-technical system. Theoretical approaches used in these surveys are therefore more likely to come from innovation research, psychology, travel behavior research, or some from consumer behavior research. The implications derived from the results help exploring the field of behavioral change, once automated vehicles become a desirable mode of travel. On the one hand mode choice depends on users' needs and preferences, on the other it depends on the travel context. In the longer run, acceptance studies may not only inform transport planning, but also support anticipating the take-up and market penetration of new mobility options, such as automated vehicles or vehicle-on-demand services (Woisetschläger, 2015).

While in modeling-based travel behavior research, the focus is similar to user acceptance studies (looking into determinants of mode choice, i.e., preference for an automated vehicle over other alternatives), the purpose of the travel behavior research is slightly different. Travel time is considered as a decisive determinant of mode choices, and the utility (or rather the disutility) of travel time is quantified in empirical studies in order to predict (future) choices of travelers (Knapp, 1997; Ortúzar and Willumsen, 2011). Modeling mode choices is an important part of modeling travel demand and aims at forecasting potential changes in travel patterns and their impact on the traffic system. The main purpose of the travel behavior research is to quantify the effect of determinants of travel demand and to forecast potential impact of changing attributes on the use of transportation alternatives. The results of the modeling exercises support policy decisions and transport planning. Similar to user acceptance surveys, the potential market share, i.e., market penetration of automated vehicles, can be analyzed with modeling methods. Both research on user acceptance of new mobility option and (modeling-based) travel behavior research are part of the transport research, however, the first one focus on exploring new mobility options and the second one on daily mobility patterns and their determinants.

The analysis of mode choices as it is used in modeling approaches is usually centered on estimating the value of travel time savings (VTTS)—a concept which reflects the assumption in microeconomic theory that people make transport decisions in the context of constrained time budgets. Time allocation theories that underline this assumption are known since the 1960s (Becker, 1965; De Serpa, 1971; Jara-Diaz, 2000; Johnson, 1966; Oort, 1969). According to the theoretical framework, people choose whether they spend their time on one activity or another, and also how much they are willing to pay to save time spent on a particular activity (Hensher, 2011). Therefore, the subjective VTTS is the willingness to pay for saving travel time, i.e., for one unit of travel time savings (Jara-Diaz, 2000). Travel time improvements are considered in transport planning and particularly in transport improvement projects as the most important benefit (Ortúzar and Willumsen, 2011) and hence, VTTS are an essential factor in transport research. For automated driving, it is reasonable to assume that the willingness to pay for travel time savings changes along with the perception of the time spent in a vehicle. Analyzing these changes is crucial, given the importance of VTTS in transport planning, crucial when preparing for a future with automated vehicles.

Although estimating, i.e., quantifying, the VTTS is a standard approach when addressing mode choices in transport research, *explaining* observed differences in VTTS is discussed in much less theoretical and empirical works. Yet this aspect becomes increasingly important considering the potential impact of automated driving on time perception. Exploring the cognitive process in mode choice decisions, i.e., how alternative characteristics, such as comfort or opportunity for alternative time use, influences those mode choices, can be seen as an overlapping area with user acceptance research.

Concepts in travel behavior research that deal with the positive utility of travel and explore the role of well-being in mode choice preferences are suitable for explaining potential changes in the VTTS for automated driving. In travel behavior research, the demand for transport is traditionally considered as derived (Ortúzar and Willumsen, 2011). As described above, the travel is—according to the concept—considered only as a means to reach the destination, and consequently an individual seeks to minimize travel time. Mokhtarian and Salomon (2001) stress, however, that travel is not always a derived demand, but can also be desired for its own sake. They suggest that the nature of affinity for travel has three elements: the activities conducted at the destination, the activities that can be conducted while traveling, and the activity of traveling itself (Mokhtarian and Salomon, 2001). The first element corresponds to the view of travel time as a derived demand whereas the other two consider cases where travel time per se provides certain utility to the traveler. In the context of automated driving, it is reasonable to assume that the utility of the activity conducted at the destination will most likely remain the same, while the possibility of conducting activities during the trip and the travel experience will be affected by automated driving. Along these lines, further relevant research explores in detail the role of (travel-based) multitasking (e.g., Circella et al., 2012; Singleton, 2017, 2019) and subjective well-being elements or travel experience on the valuation of travel time (e.g., Mokhtarian, 2018b; Singleton, 2017, 2019). Subjective well-being represents "a broad category of phenomena that includes people's emotional responses, domain satisfaction, and global judgments of life satisfaction" (Diener et al., 1999). In the context of travel behavior, there are different conceptual models which explore the relationship between subjective well-being and travel, one of which, developed by Ettema et al. (2010), considers activities while traveling, experiences while traveling, and travel itself as important factors which influence subjective well-being. Subjective well-being in the context of travel can be measured in the short term, e.g., considering commute stress, or on long term, e.g., general satisfaction with life (Mokhtarian, 2018a).

Even though conducting activities while traveling and travel experiences are strongly related to each other, theoretical and empirical work suggests considering both as separated aspects of travel time evaluation and travel satisfaction (e.g., Mokhtarian and Salomon, 2001; Pudāne et al., 2018b; Singleton, 2017). First, multitasking as the *behavior* for doing multiple activities at the same time (or "polychronicity" as the *degree of preference* for such behavior) is explored by several researchers, also in the context of traveling. Circella et al. (2012) conceptualize a general typology of multitasking behavior along the dimensions "share of time" and "share of resources" spent on each task providing a detailed definition of this phenomenon. A special attention is placed on conducting other activities while traveling as a form of multitasking since travel is often conceptualized as (unproductive) transition time and hence invites other activities to be overlaid on it (see the concept of travel as a derived demand above). According to Circella et al. (2012), travel can be an either active (e.g., driving) or passive (e.g., sitting in a vehicle as a passenger) activity depending on the resources in terms of "a quantified composite of the physical and mental *energy* required to conduct activities" (Circella et al., 2012). In transport research, the role of multitasking on time valuation has been explored mainly in the context of public transportation (e.g., Gamberini et al., 2013; Lyons and Urry, 2005), and the findings suggest that conducting activities while traveling indeed influences the travel time evaluation (e.g., Ettema et al., 2012; Frei et al., 2015). Studies on activities conducted while traveling in a car (e.g., listening to music) are rather rare (e.g., a very recent one from Malokin et al., 2019); the role of current and prospective multitasking in a car has received more attention in recent studies, also due to the issue of potential activities feasible while driving in an automated car (e.g., Fraedrich et al., 2016; Kyriakidis et al., 2015; Wadud and Huda, 2019).

Second, travel experiences or intrinsic utility of travel is conceptualized and explored in several research works considering, among others, the affective evaluation of traveling and the relationship between subjective well-being and travel behavior (an overview of relevant concepts related to travel experiences can be found in Singleton, 2017, 2019). Research in this area suggests that besides instrumental factors, also emotions or non-instrumental factors in traveling affect mode choices (e.g., Steg, 2005, see also Singleton, 2017, 2019). Subjective well-being as a psychological concept encompasses hedonic (experience of happiness and pleasure) and eudemonic (experience of meaning of life and personal growth) aspects, and it is recognized to be linked to travel behavior (De Vos et al., 2013). In the context of automated driving, especially travel experience (i.e., the hedonic aspect of subjective well-being) may play an important role considering that increase in convenience and comfort are among the most important advantages of AVs from a user perspective, besides the time utilization (e.g., Pakusch et al., 2018). The role of travel experiences on evaluation of travel time and travel time satisfaction as well as the role of individual and context characteristics has been explored in previous works mainly with focus on commuting trips. Travel experiences are found to be important for mode choices and travel satisfaction in the context of both public transport (e.g., Ettema et al., 2012; Jain and Lyons, 2008) and car use (e.g., Ettema et al., 2010; Steg, 2005). Commuting time, for instance, is discussed to be in some cases a "gift" or important transition time between home and work rather than a burden (e.g., Jain and Lyons, 2008). Also, long distance travel with young children is found to be a perceived as a quality time with the family (Price and Matthews, 2013). Considering the eudemonic aspects of traveling by car, the enjoyment of driving oneself can be discussed as a part of people's opportunities for development (this aspect is mentioned also in the official report of the German Ethics Commission Automated and Connected Driving, see BMVI, 2017). This aspect of subjective well-being might have the opposite effect on the willingness to use an AV or the perception of travel time in an AV than hedonic aspects of automated driving, such as stress relief.

Moving from a primary focus on travel time use to considering allocation of the daily time budget on different activities, further model developments in the context of automated driving consider the potential re-scheduling of daily activity plans due to automation. For instance, Pudāne et al. (2018b) adopt a time-geography approach and time use perspective for conceptualizing future time allocation. The authors use those theoretical approaches to better interpret the results of focus groups discussion with potential users of automated cars regarding potential time use and to create in a following work optimization models which capture the effect of the feasibility of on-board activities on time use (Pudāne et al., 2018a). Following the arguments also mentioned in the context of the positive utility of travel above, Pudāne et al. (2018b) stress the importance of separating satisfaction with travel and on-board activities as both have different sources and will potentially affect travel time perception and re-arrangements in daily activity patterns differently. Furthermore, the authors suggest a classification of on-board activities depending on their priority level and novelty. This classification allows understanding potential re-arrangements of activities. Along these lines, we propose that the concrete context of a travel or trip plays an important role and suggest taking this context additionally into account when considering feasibility, necessity and/or type of activities performed while traveling. For instance, certain activities require quiet environment, certain equipment, vehicle design or certain minimum time duration. In a follow-up work, Pudāne et al. (2018a) propose a broader modeling framework for capturing the effect of the ability to perform on-board activities in an automated vehicle on time use and travel behavior. The model considers not only the changed travel time utility, but also accounts for a possible shift of activities to the time spent while riding an automated car (i.e., to the AV as a location for specific activities) which in turn can change daily activity patterns (including travel). Their model is in line with time allocation theories and allows for exploring effects of multitasking behavior (such as potential daily activities re-scheduling) that are overlooked in other studies. Potential re-scheduling of daily activities in the era of AVs is also explored in a study conducted by Das et al. (2017). Here, time use survey data are used in order to analyze potential changes in time use of selected user groups of AVs. Although potential changes in daily time use patterns are not in focus of our review, these works are an important part of the discussion on the broader and long-term impact on travel behavior resulting from the possibility of conducting other activities while traveling in an AV.

Fig. 1 summarizes the introduced approaches and concepts and their relationship to travel time in the context of automated driving.

In summary, while altered time use and changes in travel time perception are considered in user acceptance studies on automated driving as well as in mode choice studies, the focus of these types of studies is slightly different. Consequentially, they use different approaches and methodologies to assess and explain the role of changes in travel time perception, once automated driving becomes available. However, the existing theoretical concepts

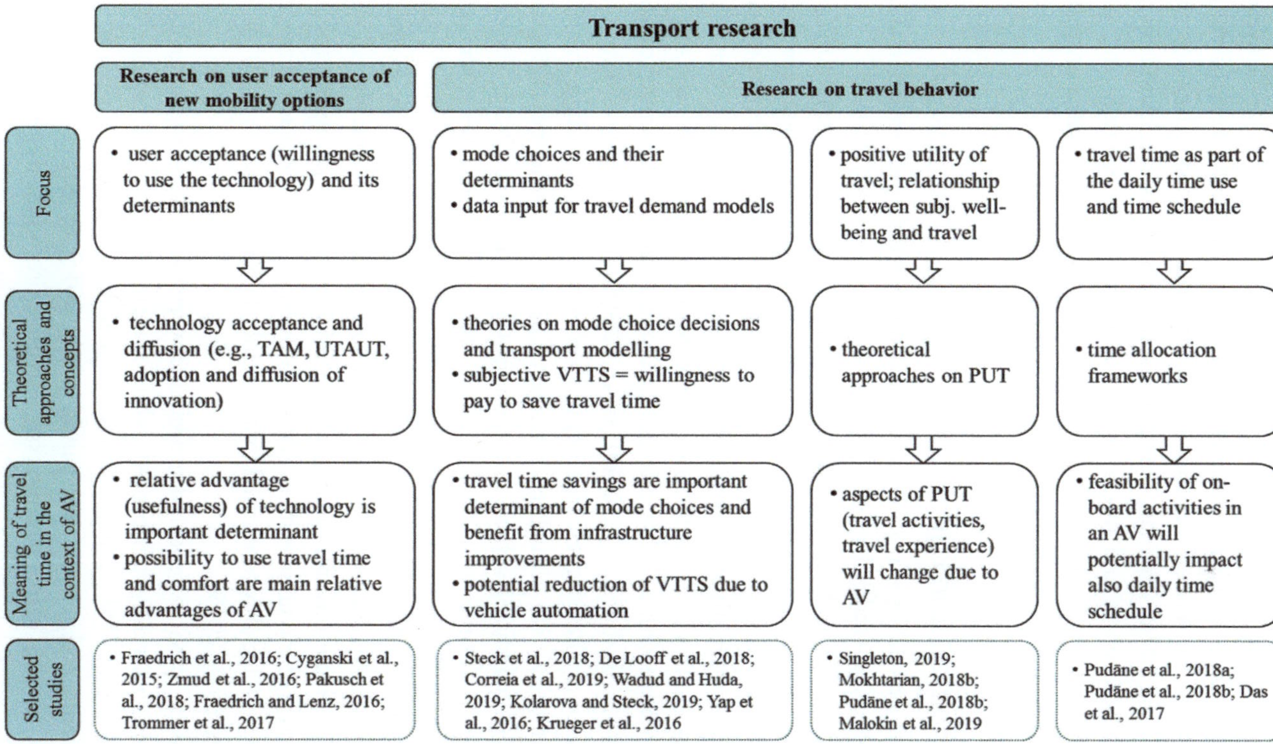

Fig. 1 Overview of research fields on travel time in the context of automated driving.

which address user acceptance of new technologies, time allocation and value of travel time savings, and the positive utility of travel all contribute to the development of a conceptual basis for *quantifying and explaining* changes in travel time perception and time use in the context of vehicle automation. Moreover, combining the theoretical approaches described above in an interdisciplinary research on the impact of automated driving on time perception and mode choices is a promising research path since there are many overlaps in the concepts, and hence they are compatible and comprehensive to each other to a certain degree.

2.2 Empirical findings

What do we know so far about time use and travel time perception in an AV from empirical studies on the topic?

First, studies looking into potential factors that influence travel time perception in automated vehicles, suggest that, different from the theoretically postulated increase in productive time use, potential users are not eager to spend their travel time working or getting other things done. Although an SP study found a lower willingness to pay for saving travel time for an automated vehicle with an office interior than for a vehicle with an interior offering 'leisure facilities' (De Looff et al., 2018), the results of early user acceptance studies suggest that being able to work while riding in an AV is reported by only a small percentage of people/respondents (12%) as an important benefit of vehicle automation (Cyganski et al., 2015; Fraedrich et al., 2016). Moreover, the results from explorative qualitative studies indicate that the idea of working in the automated car is seen by some potential users as a potentially rather negative aspect of vehicle automation. Concerns about trends toward increasingly efficient-oriented society and blurring lines between private, leisure, and work activities were arguments against the productive use of travel time in an AV mentioned in the same study (Fraedrich and Lenz, 2016; also confirmed by the results from Pudāne et al., 2018b, see also Singleton, 2019).

Indeed, activities reported as desirable were found to be to a large extent those also currently performed while traveling (Fraedrich et al., 2016; Pudāne et al., 2018b) and in particular rather passive activities, such as window gazing and relaxing (Cyganski et al., 2015, Fraedrich et al., 2016). A look at the categorization of activities proposed by Pudāne et al. (2018b) described in the previous section supports the assumption that the desirability of activities in an AV depends also on contextual and individual characteristics. High-priority activities, such as working or doing business, are desired often by people who experience time pressure; current optional activities, such as phone checking or reading the news, are more desirable by people with a short travel time that does not allow for more substantial activities (Cyganski et al., 2018; Pudāne et al., 2018b). Given the possibility to arrange the interior of road vehicles the way people want to, new optional activities, such as exercising or watching movies, are found to be desired predominantly by people currently having less time in their schedule for such activities (Pudāne et al., 2018b). In the same vein, the results of a study conducted by Wadud and Huda (2019) indicates that, besides the trip purpose, also the direction (driving to work vs. driving from work back home) influences desirable non-driving activities while riding in an AV. While preparing for work or business related engagements are preferred tasks during outbound trips, relaxing or sleeping/snoozing is more popular on return-to-home trips (Wadud and Huda, 2019). At the same time, one potentially negative effect of giving up the driving task and enabling other activities has to be mentioned – the potential loss of driving pleasure and potential boredom, mentioned as a disadvantage of automated driving in various studies (Fraedrich and Lenz, 2016; Pudāne et al., 2018b; Trommer et al., 2017). The loss of driving pleasure can be seen from both sides – as a desirable activity performed during traveling (a more instrumental view) and as having an own intrinsic utility including individual development, enjoyment, feeling of control. Additionally, previous studies on time perception in currently available modes of transport found that subjective time perception in public transport differs from time perception in the car. Among other factors, this difference is related to mode-specific characteristics – the time is perceived rather shorter in a car, where the driver is actively involved in the driving task compared to public transport due to the passive role of the passenger (Heggie, 1976; Wächter, 2002). This raises the question whether car driving can be seen as a desirable on-board activity and which elements of car driving make up its intrinsic utility (driving pleasure). In particular it seems worthwhile exploring which activities *en-route* compensate or outperform the utility of driving, when there is feasibility of new types of activities. This has to be explored considering also the potential role of the driver on the different automation levels and whether the AVs driving manoeuvers still have to be monitored similar to autopilot functions in a plane or not. Along these lines, lack of trust in the technology in the early phase of the introduction of automated driving will potentially make watching the roadway and overseeing the system the most popular activities while riding in an AV – evidences for this can be found for instance in Fraedrich et al. (2016) and Wadud and Huda (2019).

Second, considering further qualitative factors of travel, such as perceived comfort and satisfaction with travel as well as the relationship between travel and well-being, previous empirical studies reported a higher perceived stress level for commuters traveling by car than traveling by any other mode of transport – even though mode-specific stressors were taken into account for all modes of transport, such as walking time to the public transport (Legrain et al., 2015). Along these lines, Singleton (2017) found that travel experiences (in terms of travel subjective well-being) are, beside the travel activities performed on-board, an important determinant of the travel utility for commuting trips and that activities are rather performed to pass the time than being productive. Based on these insights and empirical evidences from the literature, Singleton (2019) suggests that increased comfort and stress-relief while traveling (elements of subjective well-being) will play a more important role than travel-based multitasking or productive time use in the context of automated driving. Overall, however, the relationship between time perception in an AV and satisfaction with travel or travel experience is postulated mostly only on a conceptual level (Mokhtarian, 2018b; Singleton, 2019). Early empirical insights on the role of intrinsic utility of traveling in an AV are provided in explorative studies (Fraedrich and Lenz, 2016; Pudāne et al., 2018b; Trommer et al., 2016) or in user acceptance and public opinion surveys where comfort and stress-free driving were found to be an important benefit of automation from a user perspective, beside the feasibility of altered time use (Continental, 2015, 2018; Fraedrich et al., 2016; Pakusch et al., 2018).

Third, as described above, one important part of quantifying the changes in time perception is estimating changes in the VTTS, once automated driving becomes available. In previous studies on VTTS, different values for currently available alternatives were estimated and their dependency on trip characteristics, such as trip purpose, trip length or perceived comfort level, was explored. The output of such studies, conducted usually to be representative for a particular country (e.g., Arup, ITS Leeds and Accent, 2015; Axhausen et al., 2015), is an important basis for transport infrastructure planning and policy. Generally speaking, VTTS are found to be higher for commuting trips than for leisure or shopping trips; driving under congestion has higher values attributed than driving in free-flowing traffic conditions; and VTTS for car passengers are found to be lower than for car drivers (Abrantes and Wardman, 2011; Ho et al., 2015; Mackie et al., 2003; Shires and De

Jong, 2009). The reasons behind the differences in the VTTS between car drivers and car passengers are, however, not explicitly analyzed in the literature. Putting these results in relation to automated driving suggests that automated driving might reduce VTTS since people will potentially travel as passengers. This may apply especially to certain trip types, such as commuting or to certain traffic situations, such as heavy traffic, as it provides the opportunity for switching attention to other activities and reduce negative effects of traveling by car (see discussion above on a conceptual level).

While assessing VTTS for currently available modes of transport is possible using revealed preferences methods (RP), the quantification of the VTTS for new alternatives, such as automated driving, must rely on stated preference (SP) approaches. Acknowledging that SP approaches might suffer from acute hypothetical bias that reduces their validity (Fifer et al., 2014), they are a useful tool for gaining first empirical insights on potential user preferences in the context of new mobility options which are currently not available in the market, such as AVs. First empirical studies that used SP methods found indeed a reduction in VTTS for automated driving on commuting and long-distance trips, but small or no changes for (short) leisure or shopping trips (e.g., Correia et al., 2019; Kolarova and Steck, 2019; Steck et al., 2018). Moreover, different VTTS were found for privately owned automated vehicles and shared automated vehicles (SAV) indicating that privately owned ones are perceived as a more attractive option than shared ones (e.g., Steck et al., 2018). Also, the results of SP studies indicate further that using an SAV alone and sharing it with strangers are perceived as two clearly distinct options (Krueger et al., 2016). At the same time, an SP survey considering an AV as an egress mode to the next train station found higher VTTS for this option (i.e., a more negative perception of the time spent in such vehicles) compared to driving manually which the authors presume to be attributed to lack of experience with the technology, trust issues or to the limited feasibility of performing other activities on this short stage of a multimodal trip (Yap et al., 2016). Overall, results suggest that there are still considerable uncertainties regarding the perception of on-demand services which are expected to be highly affected by the service characteristics, such as cost and travel time, but also for the case of ride-sharing systems and use or other business cases (e.g., first/last mile solution). In the context of travel time perception in such services, privacy issues (in case of sharing a vehicle with strangers) and trust in technology might sharply affect travel activities and perceived comfort level.

In summary, empirical evidences so far indicate that context-specific characteristics (e.g., trip purpose, trip length, subsequent activities or congestion levels) as well as vehicle characteristics (e.g., comfort level) will highly affect the evaluation of travel time. Desirable activities while riding automatically and the pleasure of traveling in an AV (or the intrinsic utility of automated driving) have to be considered as two distinct aspects of the utility of time spent in an AV. Regarding on-board activities, the empirical findings so far propose that being productive in the car might not be among the most desirable ways to spend the time in an AV. Indeed, time use patterns might remain the same as today. Regarding intrinsic utility of riding automatically, stress-relief, increased comfort and a more pleasant travel might prove as important determinants of the perception of time spent in an AV. Negative evaluation of time spent in an AV can, on the other hand, result from perceived pressure for being productive while traveling, loss of driving pleasure and potential boredom resulting from the now passive role of the former car driver.

3. Conceptualizing "context" as relevant factor influencing alternative travel time perception and time use

3.1 Conceptual considerations

Considering what we know so far about potential determinants of travel time evaluation in an AV, we propose that one of the most important determinants of alternative travel time use and perception is the context of the travel itself, because it affects the feasibility of desired activities and the need to perform certain activities or improve travel experience. Consequentially, as "context" we do not consider the macro-level context, including the social, regulative or economic context, where the technology is implemented, but rather the micro-level context in terms of a particular trip on which automation might or might not provide specific "new" benefits. In other words, travel time perception and time use today is determined by different context- and situation-related characteristics and these in turn influence the way how time in an AV will be spent and perceived in the future.

Fig. 2 gives an overview of the proposed conceptual model that acknowledges the influence of context-related factors on time perception and preferences for activities—both with respect to the current situation as well as in the context of automated driving.

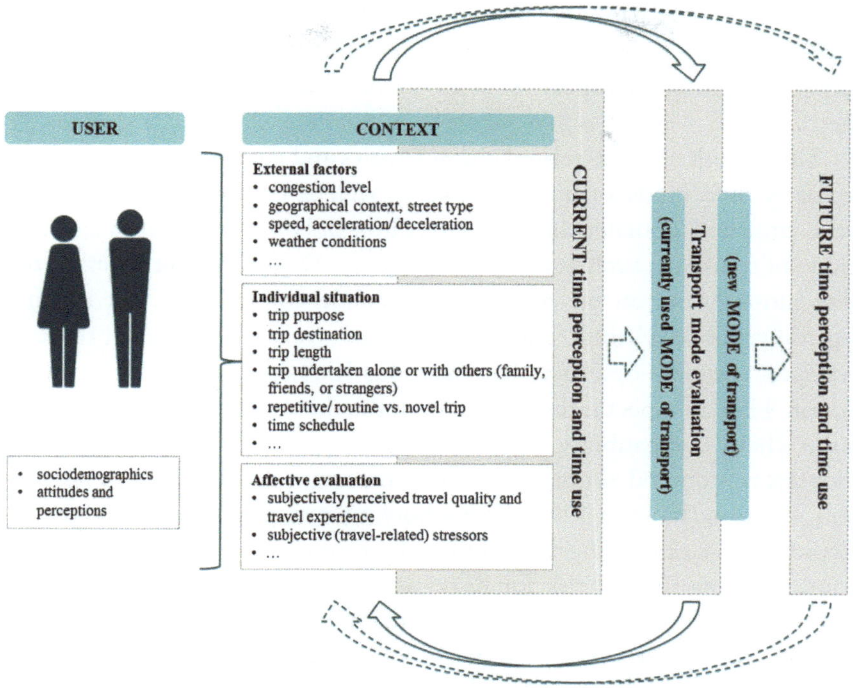

Fig. 2 Conceptual model on the role of context as influencing factor on current and future time perception and time use.

First, we propose that the relevant context-related characteristics can be divided in three categories—external factors, individual situation and affective evaluation of the travel or a current trip. *External factors* are context-related aspects that the user cannot influence, such as congestion level on the street, the geographical context where the trip takes place (e.g., in urban areas, on the highway, etc.) or weather conditions. The *individual situation* refers to the characteristics of the individual trips of the user which in turn are highly dependent on his/her activity patterns and/or sociodemographics (e.g., employment status, children, etc.). *Affective evaluation* refers to how the user perceives the current context and his/her trip and which are the main subjective travel-related stressors from the user point of view (e.g., congestion, crowded public transport, time pressure).

Second, all these context characteristics shape the current travel time perception and time use and influence the evaluation of the currently used mode of transport (e.g., how people evaluate car driving to work depending on trip length, congestion level, etc.). At the same time, also the chosen mode of transport shape the way people perceive the travel time (e.g., traveling as a passenger in a car or public transport vs. driving) and the feasibility of activities while traveling (e.g., being able to perform other activities in public transport vs. need to concentrate on the driving task in the car).

Third, both context-related characteristics and current evaluation of the regularly used mode of transportation as well as current characteristics of travel time will influence the time perception and time use in a new available mode of transport, such as automated vehicle. Depending on whether this new mobility option provides certain benefits for the user, for instance regarding the travel time, compared to the currently used mode, the user evaluates the new option as beneficial for his/her current usage context or not. This last aspect is discussed also in the theory of diffusion of innovation, where compatibility of an innovation with the needs of potential adopters is proposed as one of the most important determinants of innovation adoption (Rogers, 1995). The following examples aim to illustrate this relationship: Commuting trips are usually routine trips, take place in peak hours resulting in high risk for heavy traffic or crowded public transport, and are associated with high time pressure (being on time at work or having enough time for after work activities). People might therefore enjoy being able to be driven automatically on such trips avoiding driving stress in stop-and-go traffic and performing other activities, such as preparing for their work, writing with friends, or relaxing after work, especially when having a long commuting trip. Also long-distance drives, e.g., on holiday or weekend trips, are often perceived as an exhausting and tedious task. Being able to be driven automatically might improve long-distance travel by enabling traveling in a more comfortable way and spending the travel time with travel companions in a more qualitative way. Regular leisure trips, on the other hands, such as going to a sports studio or to meet friends or shopping trips are usually shorter than commuting ones and also less stressful. In this case, being driven automatically will be less beneficial as such trips are usually too short to perform any (meaningful) activities.

In this sense, the context can be seen as an overarching concept considering the facilitating conditions to perform other activities (or to relax) on the one hand and individual preferences for spending the travel time on the other. Moreover, we propose that the relationship between the context and travel activities can go in both directions—(i) the context can influence the feasibility and necessity for on-board activities; (ii) the desirable activities can in turn determine the requirements on equipment, vehicle interior design, need for private space, or certain minimal trip duration. Also, although productive time use might not be one of the most desirable activities while traveling, this might change under certain conditions, such as availability of tele-working or consideration of travel time as regular working hours by the employer (which is likely to apply to certain user groups only). Considering the relationship between travel experience and the context, we assume that the current context in terms of travel satisfaction with the trips currently made by car or other mode of transport will also be crucial for evaluating the benefits of automated driving by the users. For instance, high congestion level on commuting trips made by car today might cause stress for car drivers. The possibility to drive automatically can then be evaluated as a stress-relief and hence, time spent in an AV on these trips as a more positive experience than driving. Contrary to this, loss of driving pleasure, perceived pressure to be productive in the car and lack of trust in the technology might result in experiencing riding in an AV as uncomfortable, stressful or boring.

3.2 Empirical insights from own research

The empirical findings reported in this section are derived from four studies that we have conducted on the topic of time evaluation and mode choice in the context of automated driving. We have selected these studies as they provide empirical evidences for the role of the context on travel time perception and time use in an AV. These include explorative qualitative studies based on focus group discussions with potential users of the technology as well as quantitative studies relying on stated preference methods. The methodologies and main empirical results related to the effect of context-specific factors on travel time perception or desirable activities in an AV are briefly reported. Some of the studies were already mentioned in the literature review in chapter two. However, in this section we discuss the results from those studies in light of on the postulated role of context-related characteristics on the travel time perception and time use in an AV.

In the first study, focus group discussions with potential users of AVs were conducted in Germany, United States and China. In the following, however, we will focus on the results from the United States and Germany, where three focus groups discussions with 21 participants were conducted in each country. Focus of the discussions was current mobility behavior and potential use of AV (incl. Perceived benefits and potential usage scenarios). The transcribed recordings from the discussions were analyzed using context analysis. The results suggest that users would most likely use an AV on long-distance and on commuting trips. This supports the hypothesis of the importance of trip purpose on willingness to use an AV. The main expected benefits are time savings, comfort, and less stress while the main concerns are related to loss of driving pleasure, loss of control, and risk of malfunction (see Trommer et al., 2016, 2017 for more details on the methodology and the results). The following selected quotes from the focus groups discussions illustrate the role of the context for evaluating the perceived benefits from an AV related to time perception and time use:

"It gains more time. You can use the time for other activities—this is a benefit, it is a kind of luxury" (Christiane, 46 years old, Germany).

"For me I think it [automated driving] would change my trips, because of the present situation in our area—the traffic jam in the morning and the evening. That [automated driving] would definitely change it—I wouldn't care" (Richard, 61 years old, USA).

"I think it [automated driving] is fantastic, it is a relief. I had felt I would probably have less pressure, less stress. I would feel like I would be more alert with my kids if my kids were in the car [while driving automatically]… It's just because when I'm driving I can't pay attention to whether they are being good back there or not. "(Alexia, 35 years old, USA).

The examples from the discussion shed light on the fact that there are different reasons behind evaluating traveling in an AV as a positive experience—including travel activities and stress relief. For both, the individual context plays an important role—including congestion on the route or traveling with children. The explorative qualitative study provided important insights on potential perceived benefits and usage of automated driving; in order to explore on a broad statistical basis the relationship between the factors we carried out a follow-up quantitative study.

In the second study, changes in time perception and mode choices resulting from vehicle automation were quantified performing discrete choice experiments and advanced choice modeling (the study design and methodology description can be found in Steck et al., 2018 and Kolarova et al., 2018). The main goal of the study was to quantify the changes in VTTS for automated driving and to analyze the determinants of the changes. The study sample consisted of 485 respondents selected to be representative by age and gender for the German population between 18 and 65 years old. Different types of trips were considered—commuting trips ($n=172$) and leisure or shopping trips ($n=333$). In the discrete choice experiments, the respondents could choose between walking, cycling, using public transport, using a privately owned automated vehicle or using a shared automated vehicle. Using the estimated coefficients for time and cost, value of travel time savings (VTTS) for each mode of transport were estimated (including differentiation between automated and manually driving). The results show a reduction in VTTS by 31–36% for automated driving compared to manually driving, however, only for commuting trips. For leisure or shopping trips, there were no statistically significant differences between VTTS for automated driving compared to driving manually. Moreover, traveling in an AV on commuting trips was perceived similar to traveling in public transport.

Comparable results were found in the third study where we focused on long-distance travel (e.g., holiday or weekend trips). In this study, similar study design and modeling procedure as in the second study were used, while the choice set for travel modes included interurban bus, train, airplane, and a privately owned AV (see Kolarova and Steck, 2019 for detailed description of the methodology). The study sample consisted of 441 respondents selected using the same criteria as in the previously reported study. The results suggest a VTTS reduction by 22% for automated driving compared to driving manually on long distances. The results of both studies on VTTS for AV suggest that the trip purpose plays an important role on time evaluation in an AV. Also, they indicate a certain effect of the trip length as commuting trips are in general (and also in our sample) longer than shopping or leisure trips and there is perceived benefit of automated driving on long-distance trips.

The fourth selected study focuses on commuting trips and the role of context-related and user characteristics on the travel time perception and desirable activities in an AV. The study sample consisted of 487 participants recruited to be again representative by age and gender for the German population between 18 and 65 years old. The online questionnaire captured detailed information on the respondents' currently made regular trips to work as well as the expected characteristics of the same commuting trip, assuming having the option for automated driving.

First, different aspects of traveling in an AV were analyzed using descriptive statistics. Following the differentiation between the two elements of the positive utility of travel in an AV proposed in the literature, we have collected data on (i) desirable activities in an AV and (ii) time perception or affective evaluation of the travel time in an AV. Desirable activities in the AV were captured using the same activities categories on a five-point Likert scale also used in Cyganski et al. (2015) and Fraedrich et al. (2016). The evaluation of the trip in an AV was assessed using an adaptation of selected aspects from the satisfaction with travel scale (STS) developed by Ettema

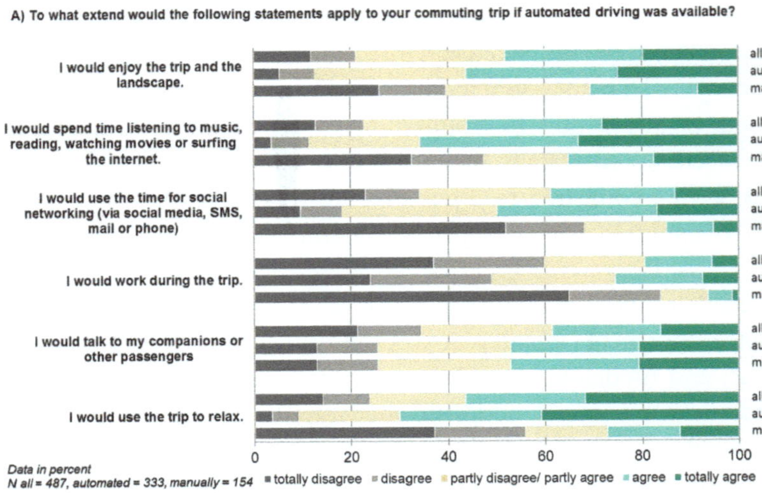

Fig. 3 Desirable activities while traveling depending on preferences for automated driving.

et al. (2011). Fig. 3 presents the descriptive analyses of desirable activities during commuting. Results are reported both for all respondents as well as differentiated depending on whether users would prefer automated driving or to drive manually.

The results show that working during the trip as well as using the time for social networking are the less preferred activities. Even with the option for automated driving, especially the willingness to work while commuting remains very low. In contrary to this, using the trip to relax, spending the time listening to music, reading, etc. as well as enjoying the trip and the landscape seem to be the most desirable activities on commuting trips, especially in the case of automated driving.

Fig. 4 shows the potential travel time evaluation for a commuting trip once automated driving becomes available. Again, both overall results as well results depending on whether the users would prefer driving automated or manually are presented. Comparing the two groups, users anticipating to be using the automated driving function expect an improved travel experience, especially in terms of having a more enjoyable trip and being more relaxed compared to those preferring to drive manually. The evaluation of the travel time is related to the desirable travel activities (most obviously in the case of using the trip to relax and evaluating the travel as relaxing). However, results from a factor analysis show that the evaluation of the travel time and the travel activities are two distinct factors (as suggested by

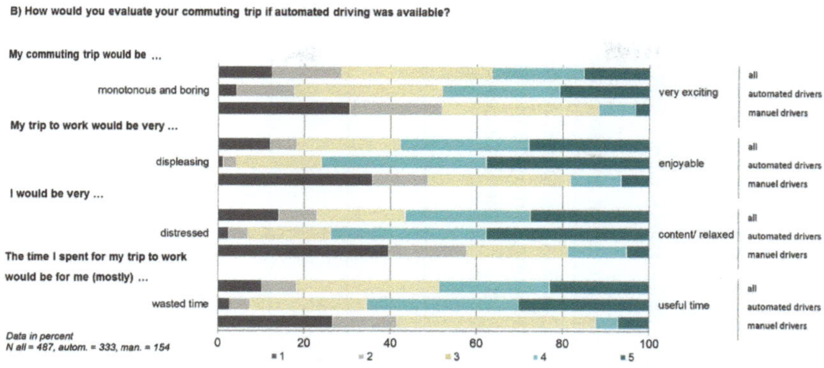

Fig. 4 Travel time evaluation/perception on commuting trips depending on preferences for automated driving.

Singleton, 2017, 2019; Mokhtarian, 2018b). Moreover, two types of activities in an AV could be differentiated—active travel time use (e.g., work, using the time for social networking) and more passive travel time use (e.g., relaxing, enjoying the trip and the landscape). The differences between these two types of activities are also reflected in the descriptive results presented in the figure.

The postulated relevance of context-related characteristics for travel time perception and time use in an AV was analyzed using structural equation modeling. First, the effect of context-related characteristics on current and future time perception was tested by adding the currently used mode of transport as an additional determinant at the same level as context in the model. As proposed in Fig. 2, there is a strong and complex relationship between the context-related characteristics, the time perception and use as well as the mode of transport used. Also, context-related stress factors are depending on the used mode of transport—congestion on the street can be a stressor for car drivers, crowded buses for public transport users. Considering car drivers and public transport user separately has led to better results in terms of plausible effects and model goodness of fit.

Results of the structural equation model presented in Table 1 are based on the sample of respondents presently using a car on their commuting trip and having stated that they would be willing to use automated driving on their current commuting trip ($n = 229$). Fig. 5 gives a simplified overview of the tested relationships—the direct effect of selected context-related characteristics on the travel activities in an AV and their indirect effect (where first order effects on current time use and time evaluation are analyzed). Obviously, not all elements addressed in the conceptual model presented

Table 1 Selected first results from structural equation model on the effect of the context on the current and future travel time perception and use (commuting trips; only car drivers, only people preferring automated driving, $n = 229$).

	CURRENT travel time perception and time use			**FUTURE travel time perception and time use**		
Variable	**Travel time evaluation: positive**	**Time use: work, social networking, making a call**	**Time use: relaxing, enjoying the trip and the landscape**	**Travel time evaluation: positive**	**Time use: work, social networking, making a call**	**Time use: relaxing, enjoying the trip and the landscape**
External factors						
Congestion level (only car users)	−0.893 ***	0.162	–	−0.192	0.386 *	–
Geogr. context: urban	–	–	–	–	−0.357 *	–
Geogr. context: trip between cities	–	–	–	–	−0.344 *	−0.260 *
Speed (faster than 50 km/h)	–	–	−0.205 *	–	–	–
Individual situation						
Trip duration (longer than 30 Min.)	−0.657 ***	–	−0.302 **	–	–	–

Affective evaluation[1]						
Positive connotation of car driving	0.576 ***	0.144 *	0.373 ***	–	–	–
User characteristics						
Male	−0.168	–	–	–	0.252 *	–
Age: 50+ years	–	−0.293 ***	–	–	–	–
Current time perc. and time use[1]						
Travel time evaluation: positive	na	na	na	–	–	−0.275 **
Time use: work, social networking, making a call	na	na	na	–	0.817 ***	0.485 **
Time use: relaxing, enjoying the trip and the landscape	na	na	na	–	−0.209	–

– "no sign. Effect found, removed from final model."
na "not applicable."
* $P<0.05$; ** $P<0.01$; *** $P<0.001$.
[1] 5-Point-likert scale.

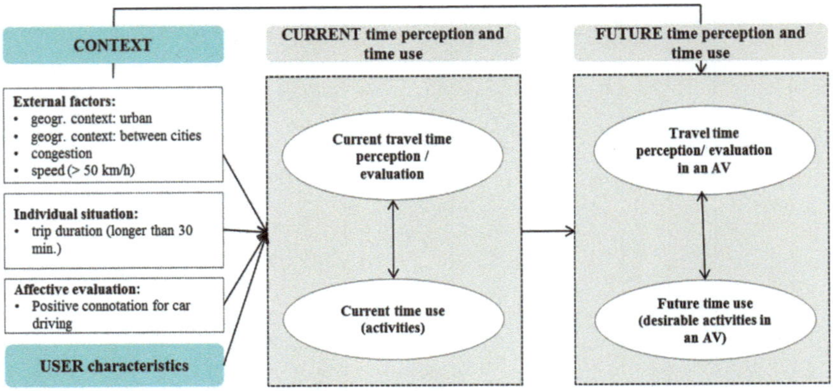

Fig. 5 Overview of direct and indirect effects of context-related characteristics on travel activities and time evaluation in an AV included in the structural equation model (only for car drivers).

were included in the structural equation modeling—partially due to attribute non-availability in the data set.

The external factors captured in the study were the geographical context where the commuting trip takes place, the congestion level and the speed. All were transformed for the analyses in dichotomous variables. For the geographical context, we differentiated between driving only in urban areas versus driving between different cities; the congestion level indicates whether there is in most of the cases a congestion on the commuting trip or not; the speed indicates whether the person is driving on average faster than 50 km/h or not (50 was chosen, because it is the speed limit in the city). Trip duration as an item describing the individual situation indicates whether the trip is longer than 30 min. Affective evaluation of the travel, in this concrete context by car, was captured on a five point Likert-scale using the following items: *"Driving a car means freedom to me."*; *"Driving a car primarily means relaxation for me."*; *"Car driving is enjoying for me."*. The items were used also by Cyganski et al. (2015) to capture attitudes toward car use. We used them in the analyses as indicators for a positive connotation of car driving.

The items used for capturing the future time perception are presented in Fig. 4; the same one were used to capture the current evaluation of the trip. The items used for capturing the time use can be found in Fig. 3. After a factor analysis, we divided the items into two categories: preferred active time use (incl. Working, social networking, making a call) and a passive time use (incl. Relaxing, enjoying the trip and the landscape).

Table 1 summarizes the results for the respondents currently using the car for their commuting trip as an example of the founded relationship between context, current time perception and time use and prospective time perception and use in an AV. The proposed research model shows overall a satisfying goodness of fit ($\chi 2 = 302.20$, df $= 210$, RMSEA $= 0.050$, GFI $= 0.839$, AGFI $= 0.771$, CFI $= 0.926$).

3.2.1 Effect of the context on the current travel time perception and time use

Congestion level, trip duration and positive connotation of car driving were found to affect the current perception of the time spend in the car. Longer trips and driving in congestion have a negative effect on the evaluation of the trip. When people evaluate driving positively, then they tend to evaluate also the commuting trip by car positively. A positive connotation of car driving affects also the time use on the commuting trip along with speed, trip duration, and the age of the user. A positive attitude to car driving has a strong positive impact on the preference for relaxing or enjoying the trip and the landscape. At the same it affects—to a significantly lesser extent—the preference for active time use, e.g., making a call, as working or social networking won't be a feasible activity when driving currently. One explanation for stating to use the time actively might be that people who do not experience car driving as a tedious task might be more likely to engage in multitasking during the trip. Regarding the context-related characteristics, trips which are longer than 30 min as well as trips with higher average speed (e.g., which takes place on highways) negatively affect the preferences (or perhaps also the ability) of relaxing while commuting or enjoying the trip. Also, the age of the driver affects the preferences toward current time use—people over 50 tend to spend travel time less actively.

3.2.2 Effect of the context on the future travel time perception and time use

None of the considered context factors has in the presented model an effect on the travel evaluation in an AV. Only congestion level was found to have a negative effect on time evaluation, but the effect was not statistically significant. Previous model estimations which considered also users of other modes of transport found only a tendency for the role of the trip duration—a trip length which is longer than 30 min affects the travel time evaluation negatively. For car users, however, we did not find a statistically significant effect. Results are different, though, with respect to the potential time use in an AV. People who drive currently in congestion were found to be more likely to prefer spending the time in an AV actively (e.g., working, social networking, making a call). Regarding the geographical context, some statistically significant effects on preferred time use in an AV were found, but not a clear tendency as both driving in the city and between cities were found to have similar negative effect on preferences for relaxing or enjoying the trip.

3.2.3 Effect of the current travel time perception and time use in the car on the time perception and time use in an AV

The results of the analyses clearly show that the way car drivers spend the commuting time today influences the way they anticipate using travel time in an AV—the preferred activities would most likely remain the same as today. These results confirm early empirical insights (for instance Cyganski et al., 2015) described in the previous part of the chapter.

In summary, the results of the presented own studies suggest that context characteristics, such as trip purpose and trip duration, play an important role—automated driving was found to be perceived less negative than driving manually on commuting and long-distance trips, but not on (shorter) leisure or shopping trips. Perceived benefits of vehicle automation include the feasibility of activities while traveling and a more relaxing and stress-free travel experience. These two elements of the utility of traveling in an AV, the travel experience and the anticipated time use, were confirmed to be closely related to each other, but still capturing distinct aspects. Moreover, we provided some empirical evidences that time use and time perception depends on the currently used mode of transport as well as the context in which commuting trips takes place and that time use patterns will potentially indeed remain the same (at least from the current user point of view).

4. Outlook

4.1 Transport planning and policy implications considering alternative travel time perception and time use

Currently, there are still high uncertainties how automated driving will change mode choice preferences and mobility patterns. At the same time, understanding and forecasting changes in travel behavior becomes increasingly important for transport planning and policy considering the chances and risks from the implementation of the technology. Qualitative explorative studies allow for important insights on the potential influencing factors on mode choices in the context of AVs as well as on the relationship between these factors. Modeling simulations provide a reliable tool to quantify the impact of potential future scenarios on travel behavior in which automated vehicles are considered. However, they neglect understanding decision making processes in the context of automated driving. Individual perception of future mobility options, though, will be essential as automated driving might completely change how people perceive and evaluate those options. Along these lines, empirical insights in changing perceptions of travel time for mode choice decisions might raise the need of rethinking or adjusting existing modeling frameworks.

Considering the results of the empirical studies presented above on the changes in travel time evaluation, a potential conflict between individual benefits from automated driving and societal goals, including the reduce of negative effects of individual motorized traffic, can be identified. On the one hand, the results suggest a more efficient or pleasurable travel time use for the users. On the other, considering the impact on travel behavior, there is a risk for an increase in car use and overall travel demand. The potential negative effect of the changes in the value of travel time is also intensively discussed in recent works, highlighting the need of early policy regulation when introducing the technology in the market and existing traffic system (e.g., Bahamonde-Birke et al., 2018; Gruel and Stanford, 2016; Wadud et al., 2016). In this context, considering the determinants of travel time perception changes, including context-specific factors, can support validating assumptions about how people make travel-related decisions which is—in the context of ever increasing automation and connectivity—important to assess.

Concretely, in the absence of policy interventions, an increase in the attractiveness of using a car, i.e., individual motorized transport, can lessen or even eliminate potential benefits from automated driving in terms of efficiency and emissions. Moreover, it can lead to an undesirable shift from public transport to private motorized transport. In order to unfold the potential of road vehicle automation, policy measures have to consider as one option facilitating and incentivizing the use of shared mobility, especially ride sharing concepts, and regulate, for instance by regulating the use individual automated vehicles. Additionally, the potential of using vehicle automation as a first/last mile solution as well as in the public transport sector and in this way facilitating multimodal trips should be explored as further option.

4.2 Further research needs

Several research topics can be drawn from the literature overview and first empirical insights on the travel time perception and time use in automated vehicles. The selected research fields below are in line with the discussion in other recently published position papers on travel time in the context of AVs (e.g., Milakis et al., 2017; Mokhtarian, 2018b; Pudāne et al., 2018b; Singleton, 2019) and complements the research needs in this area. The following areas of research connected to time perception and time use in an era of automated driving are discussed in the literature: the extent to which productive or hedonic (i.e., pleasurable) time use is a relevant factor in travel-related decision-making (Mokhtarian, 2018b, Singleton, 2019), the positive and negative effects of expanding uses of travel time (Mokhtarian, 2018b; Pudāne et al., 2018b), the role of time spent traveling as restorative and stress-relieving, i.e., the link between subjective well-being and travel time in an AV (Mokhtarian, 2018b; Singleton, 2019), and in general more research on first-order implications of AVs using both qualitative and quantitative methods for understanding, among others, the travel time implications of automated driving (Milakis et al., 2017, Mokhtarian, 2018b, Singleton, 2019). Based on the presented research in this chapter, we identify the further research needs:

First, the literature as well as early empirical insight suggests that the ′active′ travel time use (travel activities) and perceived travel time experience (perceived comfort and stress reduction) are two important determinants of travel time evaluation which have to be considered as two distinct aspects. Additionally, we propose that context-specific characteristics determine how travel activities and travel experience affect the travel time perception. While first steps toward providing empirical insights on the topic are already made, future research is needed for creating a holistic concept on the complex relationship between these factors. In this sense, looking on the topic from the other end, the utility of car driving itself as an activity and its intrinsic value for users, i.e., the disutility of potential loss of driving pleasure and boredom, has to be additionally explored. Moreover, besides considering the impact of different determinants of time evaluation, little is yet known about potential users groups characterized by their utility of automated driving (including time use and improved travel experience) rather than solely by their sociodemographic characteristics.

Second, most of the studies, including our research, focus heavily on the highest level of vehicle automation, i.e., on fully automated driving. However, it is likely that there will be a longer transition phase from the advanced assistance systems toward highly to fully automated vehicles. Thus, exploring travel time use and travel experience in the lower levels of automation becomes increasingly important when considering the impact of these automation levels on mobility. Whiles the range of feasible on-board activities may be limited, the perceived comfort and stress-relief potential might still be significant (e.g., in the case of stop-and-go pilot). Furthermore, there are still open questions regarding automated on-demand services—both regarding individually used SAVs and sharing the ride in an SAV where privacy issues, perceived comfort and waiting time or preorder of a vehicle will potentially influence the time use and evaluation of mobility services. First studies indicate also differences between privately owned AVs and SAVs; understanding this will be crucial for the analysis of the impact of automation on mode choices. Connected to this research area is the question of how travel time perception and time use in an AV may affect vehicle use or purchase decisions, i.e., vehicle ownership. Will the availability of vehicles on demand replace the need and preferences for owning a vehicle? Will motives for car use and ownership, including for instance status benefits associated with car ownership, change, and if they do, how will they do?

Third, conceptualizing the context as an important influencing factor, we put the focus more on daily and routinized trips, such as the commuting trips. Understanding the relevance of context-specific characteristics in the case of long-distance trips, however, is almost equally important considering the high share of kilometers traveled on such trips. Also other elements of the quality of travel on long distance trips, including recreation or time spent together with travel companions, might gain more importance.

Fourth, gaining additional insights on the determinants of travel time perception might lead to overthinking currently used transport modeling frameworks. The research on this topic should focus on whether the assumption made in current models regarding how people evaluate travel time and the role of travel time in general are still suitable when it comes to automated driving. At least, a better differentiation between the reasons behind, i.e., the determinants of, travel time evaluation is needed.

Along these lines, an interdisciplinary research on the impact of automated driving on travel time evaluation and mode choice decisions is a promising research path to go since, as shown above, there are many overlapping between concepts from the consumer or user acceptance research and transport research dealing with individual mode choice decisions. Moreover, many of the presented concepts are compatible and comprehensive to each other; for instance consumer decisions models in case of innovations or new technology and mode choice decisions in case of new mobility options, or the estimation of the value of travel time and the role of subjective well-being elements related to the travel time utility.

References

Abrantes, P.A.L., Wardman, M.R., 2011. Meta-analysis of UK values of travel time: an update. Transp. Res. A Policy Pract. 45, 1–17.

Ajzen, I., 1991. The theory of planned behavior. Organ. Hum. Decis. Process. 50, 179–211.

Anderson, J.M., Nidhi, K., Stanley, K.D., Sorensen, P., Samaras, C., Oluwatola, O.A., 2014. Autonomous Vehicle Technology: A Guide for Policymakers. Rand Corporation.

Arup, ITS Leeds, and Accent, 2015. Provision of Market Research for Value of Time Savings and Reliability. Phase 2 report to the Department for Transport. https://www.gov.uk/government/uploads/system/ uploads/attachment_data/file/470231/vtts-phase-2-report-issue-august-2015.pdf.

Axhausen, K., Ehreke, I., Glemser, A., Hess, S., Jödden, C., Nagel, K., Sauer, A., Weis, C., 2015. Ermittlung von Bewertungsansätzen für Reisezeiten und Zuverlässigkeit auf der Basis eines Modells für modale Verlagerungen im nicht-gewerblichen und gewerblichen Personenverkehr für die Bundesverkehrswegeplanung. FE-Projekt-Nr. 96.996/2011. BMVBS, Berlin.

Bahamonde-Birke, F.J., Kickhöfer, B., Kuhnimhof, T., 2018. A systemic view on autonomous vehicles: policy aspects for a sustainable transportation planning. DisP—Plan. Rev. 54 (3), 12–25.

Becker, G.S., 1965. A theory of the allocation of time. Econ. J. 76 (299), 493–513.

BMVI, 2017. Ethics comission. In: Automated and Connected Driving. Federal Ministry of Transport and Digital Infrastructure, Report, June 2017.

Childress, S., Nichols, B., Charlton, B., Coe, S., 2014. Using an activity-based model to explore possible impacts of automated vehicles. In: 94th Annual Meeting of the Transport Research Board, 11-15 January 2015, Washington, D.C.

Circella, G., Mokhtarian, P.L., Poff, L.K., 2012. A conceptual typology of multitasking behavior and polychronicity preferences. Int. J. Time Use Res. 9 (1), 59–107.

Continental, A.G., 2015. Continental Mobilitätsstudie 2015. Retrieved from: https://www.continental-corporation.com/resource/blob/12728/6259058bd7046da72638b19d8af4c112/mobilitaetsstudie-2015-data.pdf.

Continental, A.G., 2018. Continental Mobilitätsstudie 2018. Retrieved from: https://www.continental-corporation.com/resource/blob/155636/143035a4e9f11245f39d7583c70cde9e/die-studie-data.pdf.

Correia, G., Looff, E., Cranenburgh, S., Snelder, M., Arem, B., 2019. On the impact of vehicle automation on the Value of Travel Time while performing work and leisure activities in a car: theoretical insights and results from a stated preference survey. Transp. Res. A Policy Pract. 119, 359–382.

Cyganski, R., Fraedrich, E., Lenz, B., 2015. Travel-time valuation for automated driving: a use-case driven study. In: Proceedings of the 94th Annual Meeting of the TRB, 11.-15. January 2015, Washington, D.C, USA.

Cyganski, R., Heinrichs, M., von Schmidt, A., Krajzewicz, D., 2018. Simulation of automated transport offers for the city of Brunswick. Proc. Comput. Sci. 130, 872–879.

Das, S., Sekar, A., Chen, R., Kim, H.C., Wallington, T.J., Williams, E., 2017. Impacts of autonomous vehicles in consumers time-use pattern. Challenges 8 (2), 32.

Davis, F.D., 1985. A technology acceptance model for empirically testing new end-user information systems: theory and results. Doctoral dissertation, Massachusetts Institute of information technologiy, MIS Quarterly, pp. 319–340.

Davis, F.D., 1989. Perceived Usefulness, Perceived Ease of Use, and User Acceptance of Information Technology. MIS Q. 13 (3), 319–339.
De Looff, E., Correia, G.H.D.A., Van Cranenburgh, S., Snelder, M., Van Arem, B., 2018. Potential changes in value of travel time as a result of vehicle automation: a case study in the Netherlands. In: 97th Annual Meeting of the Transportation Research Board, 7-11 January 2018, Washington, D.C., USA.
De Serpa, A.C., 1971. A theory of the economics of time. Econ. J. 81 (324), 828–846.
De Vos, J., Schwanen, T., Van Acker, V., Witlox, F., 2013. Travel and subjective well-being: a focus on findings, methods and future research needs. Transp. Rev. 33 (4), 421–442.
Diener, E., Suh, E.M., Lucas, R.E., Smith, H., 1999. Subjective well-being: three decades of progress. Psychol. Bull. 125 (2), 276–302.
Ettema, D., Gärling, T., Olsson, L.E., Friman, M., Moerdijk, S., 2010. The road to happiness: measuring dutch car drivers´satisfaction with travel. Transp. Policy 27, 171–178.
Ettema, D., Gärling, T., Eriksson, L., Friman, M., Olsson, L.E., Fujii, S., 2011. Satisfaction with travel and subjective well-being: development and test of a measurement tool. Transport. Res. F: Traffic Psychol. Behav. 14, 167–175.
Ettema, D., Friman, M., Gärling, T., Olsson, L.E., Fujii, S., 2012. How in-vehicle activities affect work commuters´satisfaction with public transport. J. Transp. Geogr. 24, 215–222.
Fifer, S., Rose, J., Greaves, S., 2014. Hypothetical bias in stated choice esperiments: is it a problem? And if so, how do we deal with it? Transp. Res. A Policy Pract. 61, 164–177.
Fraedrich, E., Lenz, B., Maurer, M., Gerdes, J.C., Lenz, B., Winner, H., 2016. Taking a drive, hitching a ride: autonomous driving and car use. In: Autonomous Driving. Technical, Legal and Social Aspects. Springer, pp. 665–685.
Fraedrich, E., Cyganski, R., Wolf, I., Lenz, B., 2016. User Perspective on Autonomous Driving. A Use-Case-Driven Study in Germany. Working Paper, Geographisches Institut Humboldt-Universität zu Berlin, Berlin, p. 187.
Frei, C., Mahmassani, H.S., Frei, A., 2015. Making time count: traveler activity engagement on urban transit. Transp. Res. A Policy Pract. 76, 58–70.
Friedrich, B., 2016. The effect of autonomous vehicles on traffic. In: Maurer, M., Gerdes, J.C., Lenz, B., Winner, H. (Eds.), Autonomous driving. Technical, Legal and Social Aspects. Springer, pp. 317–334.
Gamberini, L., Spagnolli, A., Miotto, A., Ferrari, E., Corradi, N., Furlan, S., 2013. Passengers' activities during short trips on the London underground. Transportation 40 (2), 251–268.
Price, L., Matthews, B., 2013. Travel time as quality time: parental attitudes to long distance travel with young children. J. Transp. Geogr. 32 (528), 49–55.
Gruel, W., Stanford, J.M., 2016. Assessing the long-term effects of autonomous vehicles: a speculative approach. Transp. Res. Proc. 13, 18–29.
Heggie, I.G., 1976. Modal Choice and the Value of Travel Time. Oxford University Press.
Hensher, D.A., 2011. Valuation of travel time savings. In: Palma, A.D., Lindsey, R., Quinet, E., Vickerman, R. (Eds.), A Handbook of Transport Economics. Edward Elgar, pp. 135–159.
Ho, C.Q., Mulley, C., Shiftan, Y., Hensher, D.A., 2015. Value of travel time savings for multiple occupant car: evidence from a group-based modelling approach. In: 37th Australasian Transport Research Forum—ATRF 2015.
Jain, J., Lyons, G., 2008. The gift of travel time. J. Transp. Geogr. 16 (2), 81–89.
Jara-Diaz, S.R., 2000. Allocation and valuation of travel-time savings. In: Hensher, D.A., Button, K.J. (Eds.), Handbook of Transport Modelling. Elsevier Science Ltd, pp. 303–319.
Johnson, M.B., 1966. Travel time and price of leisure. Econ. Inq. 4 (2), 135–145.
Knapp, F.D., 1997. Determinanten der Verkehrsmittelwahl. In: Abhandlungen zur Nationalökonomie. vol. 10. Duncker & Humblot.

Kolarova, V., Steck, F., Cyganski, R., Trommer, S., 2018. Estimation of value of travel time savings for automated driving using revealed and stated preference method. Transp. Res. Proc. 31, 35–46.

Kolarova, V., Steck, F., 2019. Estimating impact of autonomous driving on value of travel time savings for long-distance trips using revealed and stated preference methods. In: Goulias, K., Davis, A. (Eds.), Mapping the Travel Behavior Genome. In: The Role of Disruptive Technologies, Automation, and Experimentation, Elsevier (in press).

KPMG, 2015. Connected and Autonomous Vehicles—The UK Economic Opportunity. KPMG LLP, London.

Kröger, L., Kickhöfer, B., 2017. Autonomous car-and ride-sharing systems: a simulation-based evaluation of various supply options for different regions. In: ITEA Annual Conference on Transportation Economics, Barcelona. ITF/OECD.

Krueger, R., Rashidi, T.H., Rose, J.M., 2016. Preferences for shared autonomous vehicles. Transp. Res. C: Emerg. Technol. 69, 343–355.

Kyriakidis, M., Happee, R., de Winter, J.C.F., 2015. Public opinion on automated driving: results of an international questionnaire among 500 respondents. Transport. Res. F: Traffic Psychol. Behav. 32, 127–140.

Langert, M., 2008. Der Anbau nachwachsender Rohstoffe in der Landwirtschaft Sachsen-Anhalts und Thüringens: eine innovations-und diffusionstheoretische Untersuchung. Dissertation, VDM-Verlag.

Legrain, A., Eluru, N., El-Geneidy, A.M., 2015. Am stressed, must travel: the relationship between mode choice and commuting stress. Transport. Res. F: Traffic Psychol. Behav. 34, 141–151.

Lenz, B., Fraedrich, E., 2016. New mobility concepts and autonomous driving: the potential for change. In: Maurer, M., Gerdes, J.C., Lenz, B., Winner, H. (Eds.), Autonomous driving. Technical, Legal and Social Aspects. Springer, pp. 173–191.

Litfin, T., 2000. Adoptionsfaktoren: Empirische Analyse am Beispiel eines Innovativen Telekommunikationsdienstes. Deutscher Universitäts-Verlag, Wiesbaden.

Lucke, D., 1995. Akzeptanz: Legitimität in der Abstimmungsgesellschaft. Leske + Budrich, Opladen.

Lüthje, C., 2007. Die Verbreitung von Innovationen. In: Birnbauer, N., Rosenstiehl, L.V. (Eds.), Marktpsychologie, Göttingen: Hogrefe. Verlag für Psychologie, pp. 291–341.

Lyons, G., Urry, J., 2005. Travel time use in the information age. Transp. Res. A Policy Pract. 39 (2–3), 257–276.

Mackie, P., Wardman, M., Fowkes, A., Whelan, G., Nellthorp, J., Bates, J., 2003. Values of Travel Time Savings in the UK. Full Report. ITS Working Papers, pp. 561–566.

Malokin, A., Circella, G., Mokhtarian, P., 2019. How do activities conducted while commuting influence mode choice? Using revealed preference models to inform public transportation advantage and autonomous vehicle scenaros. Transp. Res. A Policy Pract. 124, 82–114.

Milakis, D., Van Arem, B., Van Wee, B., 2017. Policy and society related implications of automated driving: a review of literature and directions for future research. J. Intell. Transp. Syst. 21 (4), 324–348.

Mokhtarian, P.L., Salomon, I., 2001. How derived is the demand for travel? Some conceptual and measurement considerations. Transp. Res. A Policy Pract. 35, 695–719.

Mokhtarian, P.L., 2018a. Subjective well-being and travel; restrospect and prospect. Transportation 46 (2), 493–513.

Mokhtarian, P.L., 2018b. The times they are a-changin′: what do the expanding uses of travel time portend for policy, planning, and life? Transp. Res. Rec. J. Transp. Res. Board 2672 (47), 1–11.

Mosquet, X., Dauner, T., Lang, N., Russmann, M., Mei-Pochtler, A., Agrawal, R., Schmieg, F., 2015. Revolution in the Driver's Seat: The Road to Autonomous Vehicles. Bcg. Perspectives, Boston Consulting Group.

Ohnemus, M., Perl, A., 2016. Shared autonomous vehicles: catalyst of new mobility for the last mile? Built Environ. 42 (4), 589–602.
Oort, C.J., 1969. The evaluation of travelling time. JTEP 3 (3), 279–286.
Ortúzar, J.D.D., Willumsen, L.G., 2011. Modelling Transport, fourth ed. JohnWiley & Sons, Ltd.
Pakusch, C., Weber, T., Stevens, G., Bossauer, P., 2018. Akzeptanz autonomer Verkehrsmittel: Eine Analyse relativer Mehrwerte selbstfahrender Autos im Vergleich zu heutigen Verkehrsmitteln. In: Proceedings of the Tagungsband Wirtschaftsinformatik, pp. 938–949.
Pudāne, B., Molin, E.J.E., Arentze, T.A., Maknoon, Y., Chorus, C.G., 2018a. A time-use model for the automated vehicle-era. Transp. Res. C: Emerg. Technol. 93, 102–114.
Pudāne, B., Rataj, M., Molin, E.J.E., Mouter, N., van Cranenburghm, S., Chorus, C.G., 2018b. How will automated vehicles shape users′ daily activities? Insights from focus groups with commuters in the Netherlands. Transp. Res. Part D: Transp. Environ. 71, 222–235.
Rogers, E.M., 1995. Diffusion of Innovations, fourth ed. Free Press, New York.
SAE, 2014. Taxonomy and Definition for Terms Related to on-Road Motor Vehicle Automated Driving Systems. SAE International Standard J3016.
Shires, J.D., De Jong, G.C.D., 2009. An international meta-analysis of values of travel time savings. Eval. Program Plann. 32, 315–325.
Singleton, P.A., 2017. Exploring the Postitive Utility of Travel and Mode Choice. Dissertation, Paper 3780. Portland State University.
Singleton, P.A., 2019. Discussing the "positive utilities" of autonomous vehicles: will travellers really use their time productively? Transp. Rev. 39 (1), 50–65.
Steck, F., Kolarova, V., Bahamonde-Birke, F.J., Trommer, S., Lenz, B., 2018. How autonomous driving may affect the value of travel time savings for commuting. Transp. Res. Rec. 2672 (46), 11–20.
Steg, L., 2005. Car use: lust and must. Instrumental, symbolic and affective motives for car use. Transp. Res. A Policy Pract. 39 (2), 147–162.
Trommer, S., Kolarova, V., Fraedrich, E., Kröger, L., Kickhöfer, B., Kuhnimhof, T., Lenz, B., Phleps, P., 2016. Autonomous Driving: The Impact of Vehicle Automation on Mobility Behaviour. Institute for Mobility Research.
Trommer, S., Fraedrich, E., Kolarova, V., Lenz, B., 2017. Exploring user expectations on autonomous driving. In: Automated Vehicle Symposium 2016, 19.-21. July 2016, San Francisco, USA.
Venkatesh, V., Morris, M.G., Davis, G.B., Davis, F.D., 2003. User acceptance of information technology: towards a unified view. MIS Q. 27 (3), 425–478.
Wächter, F., 2002. Determinanten der Verkehrsmittelwahl. Books on Demand GmbH, Norderstedt.
Wadud, Z., Huda, F.Y., 2019. Fully automated vehicles: the use of travel time and its association with intention to use. In: Proceedings of the Institution of Civil Engineers: Transport. Thomas Telford. ICE Publishing.
Wadud, Z., MacKenzie, D., Leiby, P., 2016. Help or hindrance? The travel, energy and carbon impacts of highly automated vehicles. Transp. Res. A Policy Pract. 86, 1–18.
Woisetschläger, D.M., 2015. Consumer perceptions of automated driving technologies: an examination of use cases and branding strategies. In: Maurer, M., Gerdes, J.C., Lenz, B., Winner, H. (Eds.), Autonomous Driving. Technical, Legal and Social Aspects. Springer, pp. 687–706.
Yap, M.D., Correia, G.H.D.A., Van Arem, B., 2016. Preferences of travellers for using automated vehicles as last mile public transport of multimodal train trips. Transp. Res. A Policy Pract. 94, 1–16.
Zmud, J., Tooley, M., Baker, T., Wagner, J., 2015. Path of Automated and Connected Vehicles Deployment: Strategic Roadmap for State and Local Transportation Agencies. Report No. TTI/SRP/15/161504-1, Texas A&M Transportation Institute.

Zmud, J., Sener, I.N., Wagner, J., 2016. Self-driving vehicles: determinants of adoption and conditions of usage. Transp. Res. Rec. J. Transp. Res. Board 2565, 57–64.

Further reading

Becker, F., Axhausen, K.W., 2016. Literature review on behavioral experiments for autonomous vehicles. Transportation 44 (6), 1293–1306.

Köhler, C., Sengenberger, W., 1983. Konjunktur und Personalanpassung. Personalanpassung in der deutschen und amerikanischen Automobilindustrie. Frankfurt A.M., New York: Campus

Kröger, L., Winkler, C., Kuhnimhof, T., 2018. Stepwise modelling of the impact of autonomous vehicles on the transport system in Germany for different scenarios. In: 46th European Transport Conference 2018, Dublin, 10.-12.10. 2018.

PART III

Socio-technical and methodological evolutions

CHAPTER EIGHT

Triggering behavior changes with information and incentives: An active traffic and demand management-oriented review

Qing Tang, Xianbiao Hu*
Department of Civil, Architectural and Environmental Engineering, Missouri University of Science and Technology, Rolla, MO, United States
*Corresponding author: e-mail address: xbhu@mst.edu

Contents

Abstract

Traditionally, methods to reduce traffic congestion have been focused on the capacity side. An increasingly popular approach is to look at issues from the demand side to trigger travel behavior changes, so as to achieve a better balance between the need to travel a particular route at a particular time and the capacity of available facilities which is defined by FHWA as active traffic and demand management strategy (ATDM). The provisions of dynamic traffic information and incentives are two most commonly seen methods to effectively influence people's travel behavior. This chapter aims to provide a comprehensive and in-depth review of the research work that focuses on triggering travel behavior changes with the provisions of dynamic traffic information and incentives via Information and Communication Technologies (ICT). Real-world system developments and current practices in adjusting travel behaviors will be summarized first,

Advances in Transport Policy and Planning, Volume 3
ISSN 2543-0009
https://doi.org/10.1016/bs.atpp.2019.05.002

followed by the review of various behavior change aspects, including departure time choice behavior, route choice behavior, mode choice behavior and destination choice behavior. Driving behavior, which is a densely populated topic is also reviewed and summarized. The reviewed studies are summarized and compared at the end of each corresponding section.

Keywords: Travel behavior change, Information and communication technologies (ICT), Active traffic and demand management (ATDM), Incentives, Behavior choices

1. Introduction

Traffic congestion happens due to demand-supply imbalance in the transportation network. Traffic flow slows down when the number of vehicles travel on the road increases or the roadway capacity decreases due to various reasons. It brings a series of issues including extra travel times for the drivers and passengers, increased fuel consumptions and greenhouse gas emissions, higher vehicular crash rates and so on. Traditionally, the focus has been on the capacity side such as building more roadway infrastructure to accommodate traffic demand with higher capacity, or applying Transportation System Management (TSM) strategies to increase capacity without adding physical infrastructure. Such strategy worked initially, but later on became increasingly expensive and unsustainable.

An increasingly popular approach is to look at issues from the demand side. For example, a strategy named Active Traffic and Demand Management (ATDM) aims at a better balance between the need to travel a particular route at a particular time and the capacity of available facilities to handle this demand efficiently. As defined by Federal Highway Administration (FHWA), ATDM is being considered as the market-ready technologies and innovative operational approaches that are becoming available for managing traffic congestion within the existing infrastructure (Luten et al., 2004). It refers to the wide-range and diversified characteristics of traffic management strategies deployed by transportation agencies that focus on using advanced technologies, available information, and valid methodologies, in order to monitor and manage the dynamic traffic conditions actively, and to influence people's need and intention to travel as well as their associated travel behavior, for the purpose of promoting efficient use of existing roadway systems and better handling of the vehicle demand (Hu, 2013). ATDM offers significant potential for reducing traffic congestion without the need to build additional lanes or infrastructure. The vision for ATDM research is to allow transportation agencies to increase traffic flow, improve travel time reliability, and optimize available capacity throughout the transportation network.

The emphasis of ATDM on travel behavior changes suggests a paradigm shift from the previous-popular term Advanced Traveler Information Systems (ATIS). Real-Time Traveler Information Systems or ATIS (such as Google, Waze, 511, etc.) provide pre-trip and/or enroute information allowing travelers to quickly assess and react to unfolding traffic conditions. The basic design concept is to present generic current information to travelers, leaving travelers to react to the information their own way. This "passive" way of managing traffic by providing generic traffic information makes it difficult to predict outcome and may even incur adverse effect, such as overreaction, which may lead to herding effects. Here, herding effects, or sometimes refers to "herd behavior," describes how individuals in a group can act collectively without centralized direction (Hu et al., 2017a, b). To be specific, if a particular road segment is identified to be free flowing, ATIS will recommend this route to every driver around. If they all follow the navigation device, after a while, this road segment will become congested, and drivers may find themselves stuck in traffic and sitting in the long queue again. On the contrary, ATDM aims to effectively influence people's travel demand by providing more travel options including departure time options, route choices and travel modes options, coordinating between travelers, improving people's driving behavior and smoothing traffic flow, and reducing the need for travel. Such behavioral adjustment approach has been receiving continual attention from both academic research and real-world practice, and this chapter aims to summarize the most important work to date.

There's also significant difference between ATDM and the traditionally defined Travel Demand Management (TDM). Most current TDM programs such as vanpooling, ridesharing, or transit focus on managing travel demand of specific groups of commuters but are limited in effectively managing demand for automobile drivers, who are unable or unwilling to participate in such programs. Another aspect of TDM worth noting are travel pricing strategies, such as congestion pricing, HOV to HOT conversion, and parking pricing, which aim to influence travelers' behavioral changes by imposing monetary penalties on commuters. Although some of these strategies have proven to be, to a certain extent, effective in changing travelers' behavior while increasing revenue generation, this "stick" approach remains controversial on issues like socio-economic equity and capacity utilization efficiency. Additionally, in practice, imposing road pricing is controversial and insight is lacking in key domains which could lead to different outcomes than those predicted by economic theory (Ben-Elia et al., 2011). ATDM goes beyond traditional TDM by not only not limiting itself to those non-auto travelers, but also including non-pricing strategies to effectively manage demand and subsequently the transportation system. As such, ATDM can be viewed as a conceptual merge between TDM, ATIS and TSM.

The provisions of dynamic traffic information and incentives are two most commonly seen methods to effectively influence people's travel behaviors in an ATDM system. With the use of Information and Communication Technologies (ICT) emerges among the population, more and more traffic information from various channels are collected and shared with public and social networks instantaneously. The real-time travel time and accidental information can help travelers plan ahead and adjust their departure times based on personal preferences and needs. For example, a commuter can leave later to avoid sitting in the queue caused by an accident, or a shopping trip can be canceled or rescheduled because of a foreseen delay. On the other hand, incentives, which could take forms of monetized lottery/rewards, free transit ticket, travel feedback (such as gas saved), or environmental contributions, is increasingly applied together with the state-of-art ICT in making a fundamental paradigm shift from the traditional passive travel information provision to an active traffic demand management tool, by influencing people's need and intention to travel as well as their associated travel pattern. With the impact of incentives, the information has more meaningful suggestions for the traveler and helps the decision-making process about what time to leave, what mode to use, which route to take, or even to travel or not (Hu et al., 2019).

This chapter aims to provide a comprehensive and in-depth review of the research work that focus on triggering travel behavior changes with the provisions of dynamic traffic information and incentives via ICT. Real-world system developments and current practices in adjusting travel behaviors will be summarized first in Section 2, followed by the review of various behavior change aspects, including departure time choice behavior (Section 3), route choice behavior (Section 4), mode choice behavior and destination choice behavior (Section 5). Driving behavior, which is a densely populated topic is also reviewed and summarized in Section 6. Section 7 concludes this chapter.

2. Systems development and current practices

Over the past few decades, before ICT was in place to support traveler's decision makings or collect data to enable research, some behavioral experiments were implemented to influence people's travel behavior decisions. For example, the University of Washington at Seattle engaged in the U-Pass program, which started in the 1990s and aimed to alleviate the traffic problem both around the campus and within the city. The program provided an array of transportation options, including transit service, preferential parking, consumer discounts, and rideshare matching. The benefits of this program had been significant: the building of 3600 new parking spaces had been avoided, 86% user satisfaction had been reported, and a reduction of 33% had been seen in parking permit purchases, plus 18% less in traffic counts during morning peak hour in 2002, compared with the data in 1983 (University of Washington, 2002). Lee County, FL used variable Bridge Tolls to manage the traffic congestion and was able to spread traffic away from the peak period. Over the peak hours, the tolls on two principal bridges were raised from 75 cents to one dollar, and for the off-peak time a 50-cent discount was provided. With the \$9.7 million grant from the Federal Highway Administration and another \$7 million "emergency revenue reserve," 5% of traffic was shifted from peak to off-peak time periods, although as many as half of respondents indicated they always or sometimes considered the discounts prior to making a trip across one of the bridges (Burris, 2001). Similar dynamic pricing strategy can also be found in Seattle, Los Angeles, San Diego, Atlanta, where dynamic pricing of High Occupancy/Toll (HOT) lanes and incentives for High Occupancy Vehicle (HOV) usage were provided.

The Neighborhood Eco (NECO) Pass program started in Denver, Colorado in 1997 to reduce single-occupancy vehicles (SOV) and had grown to include 45 neighborhoods and more than 6500 households. The NECO Pass was a yearly transit pass option that was primarily used by neighborhoods in the City of Boulder. The lower price and convenience of a NECO Pass were intended to incentivize residents to shift their mode of travel to transit. According to the report (National Research Center, 2016), SOV trips had declined by 7.7% since 1990. The transit-oriented development (TOD) in Hillsboro, in the Portland Metropolitan area in Oregon, had made it one of the most liveable communities. It featured a pedestrian friendly environment and mixed-use development in the station area which made it possible for the residents to walk to the light rail station. New tenants were offered a 1-year transit pass free of charge. Due to this program 83% of residents reported they used transit in May 1999, and transit usage for commuting had increased 22%. It was also reported that 85% of respondents stated they had reduced needs to drive because of the program (Podobnik, 2002). Zion National Park program started in 2000, and the propane-powered, shuttle system vehicles became the only vehicles permitted in the park during the peak season. Visitors were encouraged to park outside and used the shuttle free of charge to access the national park. Shuttle boarding reported for year 2002 was 2.35 million, and about 75% of the visitors rode the Zion Canyon shuttle. Besides the benefits from traffic and parking aspects, the local government benefited from this program as well, not only from the reduction in infrastructure cost but also from the economic growth (US National Park Service, 2003). In 2000, One Less Car program was launched in Seattle WA and continued through 2002. The program offered households information financial incentives to help them reduce their car use for all their trips. In total, 86 households participated in the study for a period of 6–9 weeks, ranging from households with children, to singles, to empty-nesters. Participating households received a weekly stipend of $85 to compensate them for the extensive data they recorded and the republic resource they saved. At the end of the study, participants reduced their drive-alone car miles by 27%, and the use of alternate modes of transportation increased more than 20% (Lee et al., 2013). In 2003, the NuRide (renamed as Agile Mile) program was established in the United States and offered through State and local governments and metropolitan planning organizations. NuRide program is a reward program for commuters who were encouraged to take non-motorized modes and car/vanpooling. Users who signed up received points for each green trip they record via an online portal. Points can be redeemed for coupons for restaurants and retail shops, services, movie tickets, etc. Since established, NuRide had built a presence in nine States. For example, in the Commonwealth of Massachusetts, NuRide indicated that participants in the State have saved more than 175 million miles of driving, more than 8 million gallons of gasoline, nearly $97 million in travel-related costs, and nearly 79,000 tons of emissions since its launch in 2010 (Bauer et al., 2018).

In 2001 in Japan, a survey of 335 drivers was carried out before and during an 8-day temporary freeway closure. The results illustrated that the frequency of switching to public transport during the closure was inversely related to the frequency of automobile commuting before the closure. Furthermore, habitual drivers tended to have negative beliefs about using public transport, and that the negative beliefs were corrected by actual experiences of using public transport (Fujii et al., 2001). In 2003, an experiment with respect to 43 drivers was carried out during an 8-day temporary freeway closure in Osaka, Japan, where 23 travelers were offered a 1-month free bus ticket, but the free ticket was not given to the other 20 drivers in a control group. The result showed that drivers who received a 1-month free bus ticket in the experiment used the bus more frequently after the intervention. The increase was 20% higher than the frequency of bus use before, although it turned out in this experiment that these behavior changes were not permanent (Fujii and Kitamura, 2003).

In Germany, 2003, a longitudinal study investigated the effects of an intervention on increased bus use among college students by offering the incentives of a pre-paid bus ticket. A two-wave panel design with a 1-year interval between waves was deployed. The intervention was found to influence attitudes toward bus use, subjective norms, and perceptions of behavioral control. The bus usage had increased by 35% and trips finished by car decreased by 13%, which indicated the incentive given to the travelers can influence their travel behavior as compared to their previous habitual behavior (Bamberg et al., 2002). In a different experiment, effects of an intervention (combination of information and a free public transport ticket) in changed decision context (moving to a new residence) on travel mode choice by car users was examined. The participants consisted of 241 people planning to move within the next 6 months to Stuttgart, Germany. A lottery ticket with attractive money prizes was used as an incentive to participate. The results showed that the intervention influenced attitude, subjective norm, and perceived behavioral control, and consistent with Ajzen's theory of planned behavior (Ajzen, 1991), these were the main causes of the change of travel mode (Bamberg et al., 2003).

Many other behavioral experiments have been implemented worldwide to adjust traveler's behavior decisions. For example, in Melbourne, Australia, an early bird ticket program was proposed to alleviate the rail overcrowding issue during peak hours. Free rail fares were provided for rail travelers completing their trips before 7:00 a.m. as incentives to shift demand from the peak to pre-peak trains in order to relieve the overcrowding problem. The cost of free rail program was nearly \$6M mainly in lost fares and around 8000–9000 passengers used the ticket on weekday. It ended up that 23% of ticket users (2000–2600 each week) had shifted from the peak hour by an average of 42 min; the ticket use was increased by 1.7% while overall rail usage was stable. After introduction of the early bird program, pre-7:00 a.m. loads increased 41%, reducing pressures for purchase/ operations of new peak trains saving 2.5–5.0 trains (2008) to a forecast saving of 8.05 trains in 2038. Financial analysis suggested the savings would substantially cover the financial costs of the free fares and that benefits would increase over time (Currie, 2011). Two fare policies, off-peak discounts and volume rebates, had been applied in South East Queensland attempting to alter passengers' travel behavior. The results showed that passengers' boarding times were not significantly altered under current off-peak discounts. However, volume rebates provided incentives to encourage more use of public transport (Yen et al., 2015).

In India, the INSTANT (for the Infosys-Stanford Traffic project) was conducted in Bangalore for 6 months from October 6, 2008, to April 10, 2009. There were about 14,000 commuters participating in the experiment, and bus data were collected from 9000 of them traveled in one of over 200 buses chartered by Infosys. The scheme awarded credits each day to employees based on their arrival times and each week the cumulative number of credits of each commuter was used by an algorithm to choose commuters who will win monetary rewards. The algorithm had three components: credit allocation, weekly reward draws and credit deduction. Every working day a commuter were awarded credits according to his/her swipe-in time: 1.5 credits for a swipe-in before 8 a.m., 1 credit for a swipe-in between 8 a.m. and 8:30 a.m. and no credit after 8:30 a.m. At the end of each week, the algorithm determined the level at which a commuter has qualified. After each reward draw, credits were deducted from both winners and non-winners. The results showed that the number of commuters arriving in each time segment had almost doubled over the period of the experiment and the number of buses that were over capacity had significantly reduced. The project attracted a large number of commuters to travel at off-peak hours, leading to an advancement of pickup times in the bus schedule (Merugu et al., 2009).

Such behavior experiments can also be found in Singapore. In June 2013, a "Travel Early, Travel Free," campaign was launched by Singapore's Land Transport Authority to alleviate subway crowding, which offered free trips to those who exited from 1 of the 16 (extended to 18 following the completion of a new subway line in 2014) city-center subway stations before 7:45 a.m. on weekdays. Commuters who exited within the next 15 min received a 50-cent discount. Preliminary data indicated a reduction of 7–8% in the number of commuters during the morning peak window

(Land Transport and Authority, 2014). Similarly, the randomized controlled trials on Singapore's subways were implemented in August 2014 and lasted for 10 weeks. Commuters who registered received a full rebate of their fares if they exited fare gates before the start of morning peak-travel time. A difference-in-differences analysis revealed that the effect of the free-trip offer was modest but robust during the promotional period: trips were 5.5% on average more likely to end before the morning peak time (Yang and Long Lim, 2018). The objective of both campaigns was to alleviate peak-time congestion commuters to travel pre-peak.

With the rapid advancements of ICT, systems have been developed to influence traveler's mode choice or departure time choice behaviors. Such systems could include smartphone apps, software, or frameworks that allow system operators to provide means such as dynamic traffic information or monetary incentives to travelers, with the goal of influencing their trip-making decisions. For example, as early as 2 decades ago, Georgia Power developed a software tool named "SmartRide" to track carpool, vanpool and transit use information and direct the information to its employees, with the goal of getting as many cars off the roads as possible during the 1996 Olympic Games in Atlanta. The company also provided fleet vehicles to its employees to run errands or go to meetings during the day, so those who used alternative transportation to commute to and from work would not feel trapped in the office during the day. This program successfully reduced 1.2 million Vehicle Miles Traveled (VMT) each month, with 13% of employees carpooling or vanpooling, 15% working compressed or flextime schedules, 5% using transit and another 5% doing telework (Luten et al., 2006). Over the last decade, carpool apps, including ad hoc causal carpooling, commercial ridesharing and other forms became very popular. Examples include Carma Share, Zimride, Waze Carpool, Rideamigos, BlaBlaCar, Uber, Lyft, iCarpool, GoKid and many others with varying penetration rates which is one of the key elements determining their effectiveness. However, due to page limitation they cannot be reviewed in-depth individually.

In 2006, the Spitsmijden project was launched in the Netherlands, which involved rewarding of commuters for avoiding traveling by car during the peak hours using automated vehicle identification technology. The test area was the Dutch A12 motorway corridor from Zoetermeer toward the Hague. Upon registration, one of two types of reward was chosen by the recruited 500 participants. The first type of reward was an amount of money ranging from 3 to 7 EURO for each morning rush hour that the participant avoided.

The second type comprised savings toward keeping a "Yeti" smartphone at the end of the trial (AENEAS, 2010). The results reported of the study indicated that positive incentives were able to reduce the amount of peak traffic of the participants by about 60% and travelers mainly responded to the incentives by shifting their car trips to the periods before and after the peak period (Ettema et al., 2010). It was also reported that travelers returned to the peak period when the incentives ended. Knockaert et al. (2012) also confirmed that a reward can be used as an effective policy instrument, and that the participant's behavior implied that the shadow prices of schedule delay were close to constant over time which was in line with the classic assumptions in the literature. Shifting departure time was found to be a more important behavioral response to policies for congestion relief than a modal shift or teleworking. Ben-Elia and Ettema (2011) further found out that although the reward influence the magnitude of change, choosing how to avoid the rush hour, which includes driving at other times, switching to another mode of transport or working from home, was not determined by the reward, but rather by different factors relating to the participants and their particular situations. More research work based on Spitsmijden will be discussed later in the corresponding behavior analysis sections.

The information- and reward-based travel demand management strategies started to be implemented on the smartphones. In 2013, Metropia (www.metropia.com), for example, used traffic prediction and coordinating technologies combined with user rewards to incentivize drivers so as to balance the traffic load on the network, and reduce traffic congestion. Screenshots from the app are presented in Fig. 1 to describe how the app works. Drivers use the app to plan a trip, and the system provides travel time

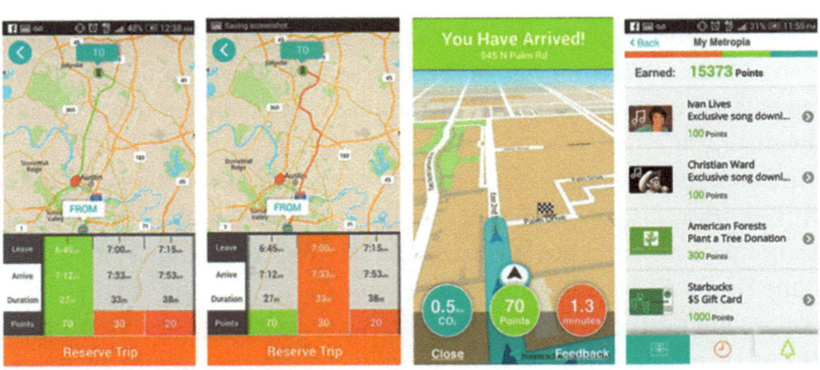

Fig. 1 Metropia smartphone app workflow.

prediction for every 15 min and varying levels of incentives which are based on the traffic condition with the goal of attracting users to the less congested departure times. The reward points are determined based on the departure time and congestion levels of the road. If the departure time and route selected by user is heavily congested, the points will be lower, and if the users are willing to leave during the non-peak hours, they can get more points. Once the user decides on the time and route to travel, the system will verify if the user indeed leaves at the time promised and follows the desired route, and if yes, the trip is validated and the points will be added to the user's account. The user can keep using the app to accumulate the points. The points carry monetary value, and can be used to redeem freebies such as Amazon and Starbucks gift cards (Hu et al., 2019). The goal of the app and its backend algorithms is to influence its users to reduce demand during peak hours for congested routes (Arian et al., 2018). Under the hood is a set of transportation system models and machine learning algorithms to estimate the dynamic traffic conditions in real time and further perform traffic predictions (An et al., 2016; Hu et al., 2017a, b), with the goal of improving real-world traffic conditions from user equilibrium (UE) or non-UE toward system optimum (SO) (Hu et al., 2017a, b; Hu and Chiu, 2015). A small-scale pilot field study was carried out in Los Angeles, CA together with Los Angeles Department of Transportation (LADOT) since April 2013 for a total of 10 weeks, the results showed that travel behavior changes were observed and 20% travel time could be saved for people who changed their travel behavior (Hu et al., 2015a, b). The system is currently available in a number of cities in the United States and is expected to expand to a few new cities in the near future.

In 2017, The Bella Mossa program was launched in Bologna, Italy and used a system of gamification and rewards to encourage people to choose environmentally friendly transportation modes such as walking, bicycling, or transit. They used a GPS-based smartphone application to track users' sustainable trips and then provide various rewards and incentives for their choices. During the initial 6-month launch of Bella Mossa program, 15,000 people actively participated in the incentive program, which resulted in an estimated 3.7 million km (2.3 million miles) of sustainable travel and 900,000 sustainable trips (Bauer et al., 2018).

Another smartphone-based application "incenTrip" was developed by researchers from the University of Maryland to study how to show the right travelers the right incentives delivered at the right time, with the goal of maximizing energy and travel time savings. The app aims to make commuting easier, faster and cheaper by encouraging commuters to make smart choices and reward them when they do. incenTrip app uses real-time data to predict travel times on multiple modes of transportation, offering commuters options for getting where they want to go and offering users points that can be redeemed for prizes. The app had 35,000 registered users (accounts for approximately 0.4% of the total 9 million population in the region) as of April 2018 per the Washington Post and is designed for use in the Washington and Baltimore regions (The Washington Post, 2018). The project was initially funded by the Traveler Response Architecture using Novel Signaling for Network Efficiency in Transportation (TRANSNET) program by U.S. Department of Energy's Advanced Research Projects Agency (ARPA-E) in 2018 (ARPA-E, 2018). The key goals of the app are through the development of integrated, personalized and real-time traveler information and incentive technologies, employ behaviorally sound and computationally efficient agent-based modeling (ABM) system to simulate the entire transportation system in real time, and ultimately incentivize more energy-efficient travel and mobility decisions. Fig. 2 illustrates the system architecture and workflow of the app. Through a demonstrative case study for a large-scale transportation system of the DC–Baltimore region, the capability of the proposed technology is highlighted with significant system-level energy savings, reasonable insights on individual travel behavior responses, as well as superior computational efficiency (Xiong et al., 2018). Under the hood is a new model that integrates an activity-based travel demand model (ABM) with a dynamic traffic assignment (DTA) model. Specifically, the integrated model includes InSITE, an ABM developed for the Baltimore Metropolitan Council, and DTALite, a mesoscopic DTA model. The integrated model simulates the complete daily activity choices of individuals residing in the model region, including long-term choices, such as workplace location; daily activity patterns, including joint household activities and school escorting; activity location choices; time-of-day choices; mode choices; and route choices (Zhang et al., 2018a, b).

Parking is another populous area for researchers and practitioners to offer real-time information and provide cost comparison with the goal of influencing driver's parking decisions. In April 2012, an incentive program named Congestion and Parking Relief Incentives (CAPRI) was launched in Stanford University in Palo Alto, California. Credits for avoiding peak parking hours were awarded to the travelers who enter and exit the main Stanford University campus by car at designated off-peak hours Monday

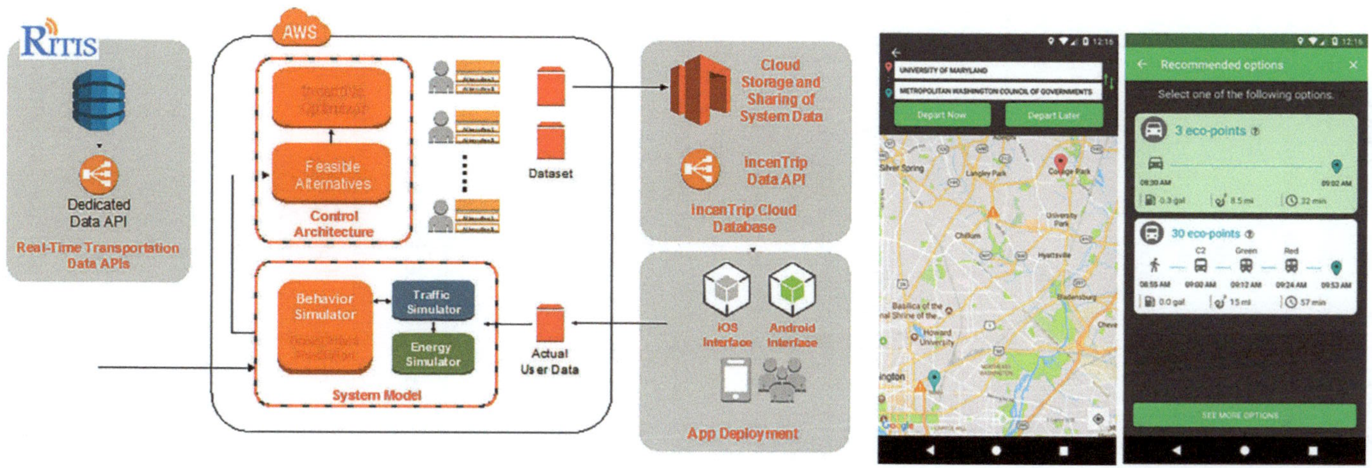

Fig. 2 (A) incenTrip architecture and (B) incenTrip workflow.

through Friday. The goal of the program was to manage the parking problem through dynamic parking pricing strategies to reduce peak-hour traffic. The credits can be used to win random cash rewards from $2 to $50 and the rewards can be accumulated and disbursed monthly via Stanford's payroll or through bank deposits (Stanford University, 2012). 3082 commuters registered for the automobile program and 975 registered for the working and biking incentives using the smartphone. A total of 10,200 permit-holding car commuters at Stanford were invited. The results showed that the rewards in CAPRI were effective in encouraging commuters to drive during off-peak hours, and to walk and bike (Yue, 2014; Yue et al., 2015). Aside from this kind of academic researches, commercial apps also emerged quickly in the market, such as Parking Panda, Parkmobile, Parker, ParkWhiz, and many others. The design principal of these type of apps is to offer drivers with the available parking information (and some with pricing information) on the smartphone, so as to assist drivers with their travel and reduce the time wasted in cruising to find a parking space, and the associated fuel consumption and negative environmental impacts.

A comparison of the reviewed system development and current practices is summarized in Table 1, in chronological order. The comparison is based on whether a real system/product had been developed and released (system development), if dynamic traffic information is provided (information), are incentives or pricing strategies (carrot versus sticks) used, the scale of experiment such as number of users and area of implementation, and what behavior choice(s) does it target at.

3. Departure time choice behavior

As one of the fundamental travel behavior dimensions, departure time choice is a densely populated area that has received lots of research attentions in the past. As reviewed in Section 2, majority of system development and behavior experiments efforts also focused on triggering department time change. Due to the high volume in literature, this section tries to review the most relevant and significant ones, specifically, those focused on answering the question of what it takes to trigger departure time changes. These literatures will be summarized according to different type of trips investigated, i.e. home-based trips, work and shopping trips, peak-hour trips and 24-h trips. Research on departure time evolution and learning is also summarized in this section. The reviewed studies are summarized and

Table 1 Comparison of systems development and behavior experiments.

Research	Date	System/Product development	Scale	ICT	Carrot or sticks	Behavior choices
U-Pass Program, UW	1991	No	Small	No	Incentives	Departure time, parking choice
Variable bridge toll, Lee County	1994	No	Midsize	No	Pricing	Departure time
SmartRide	1996	Yes	Midsize	Yes	N/A	Mode choice
NECO Pass Program	1997	No	Large	No	Incentives	Mode choice
Transit Pass Program, Portland	1999	No	Large	No	Incentives	Mode choice
Zion National Park	2000	No	Small	No	Incentives	Mode choice
One Less Cae Program	2000	No	Small	No	Incentives	Mode Choice
Pre-paid bus ticket, Germany	2003	No	Large	No	Incentives	Mode choice
Free bus ticket experiment, Japan	2003	No	Small	No	Incentives	Mode choice
NuRide	2003	Yes	Large	Yes	Incentives	Mode choice
Spitsmijden	2006	No	Large	Yes	Incentives	Departure time, mode choice, teleworking
INSTANT	2008	No	Large	No	Incentives	Departure time
Rail program, Melbourne	2008	No	Large	No	Incentives	Departure time
CAPRI	2012	No	Midsize	No	Incentives	Departure time, mode choice
Metropia	2013	Yes	Large	Yes	Incentives	Departure time, route choice, mode choice

Continued

Table 1 Comparison of systems development and behavior experiments.—cont'd

Research	Date	System/Product development	Scale	ICT	Carrot or sticks	Behavior choices
Subway program, Singapore	2013	No	Large	No	Incentives	Departure time
Bella Mossa program, Italy	2017	Yes	Large	Yes	Incentives	Departure time
incenTrip	2018	Yes	Large	Yes	Incentives	Departure time, route choice, mode choice

compared at the end of this section. It is generally agreed that a number of factors such as work schedule flexibility, mode, occupation, income, age, transportation level of service and others all influence departure time choice.

3.1 Home-based trips

The effect of Advanced Traveler Information Systems (AITS) on travelers' route and departure time changes of home-based trips was evaluated in Khattak et al. (1995). Survey data were collected from downtown Chicago automobile commuters, as when this early study was conducted, the data collection was challenging without real ICT in place. The survey mainly investigated the home-to-work trips and more than 60% of the respondents had used traffic information to modify their travel decisions. Analysis showed that respondents were more likely to change their departure times if they perceived traffic reports to be accurate and relevant, and frequently listened to traffic reports. The implication for Advanced Traveler Information Systems was that they may be designed to support both enroute and pre-trip decisions. ATIS performance, measured in terms of accuracy, relevance and timeliness would be critical in the success of such systems. Further, near-term prediction of traffic conditions on congested and unreliable routes (where conditions change rapidly) and incident durations was desirable.

The joint decisions of trip timing and mode choice for Home-Work-Home trips and the correlation between discrete and continuous decisions were investigated in the Greater Toronto Area. The joint model, with a multinomial logit model for mode choice and a continuous time hazard model for trip timing, allowed for unrestricted correlation between the unobserved factors influencing these two decisions. Strong correlations between unobserved factors influencing mode choice and trip timing were found across all occupation groups, and it proved that it sufficiently captured the peak spreading phenomenon (Nurul Habib, 2013; Nurul Habib et al., 2009).

The effect of constraints in work and in other daily trips/activities on the willingness to shift departure time and the willingness to pay for reducing travel time and travel delay was investigated in Thorhauge et al. (2016a, b). Detailed data on the full 24-h out-of-home activities and on the constraints for each of these activities were collected in a survey. A stated preference experiment to infer preferences on departure time choice was built, and a mixed logit model was estimated, based on the scheduling model, to account for the effects of daily activity schedules and their constraints. The results showed that measuring flexibility in terms of work start time or constraints at work did not provide exactly the same information, and if the presence of constraints were neglected, it would generally lead to biased value-of-time estimates. The shift in the departure time, especially toward a late departure time, was strongly overestimated (the predicted shift was more than double) when the effect of non-work activities and their constraints was not accounted for.

A group of researchers from the University of Maryland inferred travel decision with a mixed Bayesian network (BN) in Zhu et al. (2017a, b). A real-world case study was conducted by using the regional travel survey data (including 24-h out-of-home trips) for a two-dimensional decision modeling of both departure time choice and travel mode choice. The results demonstrated that mode and departure time were not independent of each other, and the variance of departure time choice across different social demographical variables was not as significant as the variance of mode choice. The proposed two-dimensional mixed BN provided better accuracy than decision tree models and nested logit models.

Heterogeneous travelers' behavior toward trip mode and departure time choices was investigated by considering those choices as a joint decision in Shabanpour et al. (2017). The survey data contained 210,000 home-based trip observations and detailed information for the travelers. First, a two-step clustering algorithm was applied to classify travelers into six distinct clusters to account for the heterogeneity in their decision-making behavior. Then, a joint discrete-continuous model was proposed for each cluster, in which the travel mode and departure time were estimated by a multinomial logit and a log-linear regression model, respectively. The results highlighted that travel time and household size significantly affect departure time decision. The increase in travel time resulted in earlier departure times and more vehicles in the household leaded to later departure time.

3.2 Work and shopping trips

Using data collected as part of a larger survey on the consequences of congestion charging on travel choices in the city of Edinburgh, multinomial logit models were calibrated to investigate the influence of non-work activities and socio-economic characteristics on scheduling flexible for work trips. The results showed that non-work activities and work schedule flexibility had an impact on departure time choice for the journey to work, which meant that even for those with flexible work schedules, but with other non-work commitments, the timing of their work trip may not be so flexible (Saleh and Farrell, 2005). In another research, in order to test the effect of flextime in reducing morning peak-hour traffic, a multinomial logit model was built which divided morning departure times as pre-peak (0:00 a.m. to 6:30 a.m.), peak (6:30 a.m. to 8:30 a.m.) and post peak (8:30 a.m. to 12:00 a.m.). The results demonstrated a correlation between having flextime and traveling in post-peak hours, and also proved that commuters with different characteristics may react diversely to flextime (Yang et al., 2016).

Bhat and Steed proposed a continuous-time hazard duration model for urban shopping trip departure time choice. Shopping trip data from the activity survey collected in the Dallas-Fort Worth metropolitan area was used. The effects of individual and household socio-demographics, employment attributes, and trip-related characteristics on departure time choice were presented and discussed. Application of the continuous-time model to forecast temporal shifts in shopping trip making due to changes in socio-demographic characteristics and trip-chaining behavior was demonstrated (Bhat and Steed, 2002). Yang et al. also studied the joint choice of residential location, travel mode, and departure time based on random utility maximization theory with Cross-Nested Logit model and traditional NL models. A number of exogenous variables including house price, travel time, travel cost, and factors depicting the individual socio-economic characteristics were defined, and the model choice sets were the combination of residential location subset, departure time subset, and travel mode choice subset. The model parameters were estimated using Beijing traffic survey data, and the direct and cross elasticity were calculated to analyze the change of alternatives probability brought by factors variation. Estimation results showed the Cross-Nested Logit model outperformed the three kinds of NL model, and decision makers would change first their departure times, then their travel modes, and finally their residential locations, when exogenous variables alter (Yang et al., 2013).

3.3 Peak-hour and 24-h trips

Departure time choice models were proposed based on the notion of a latent preferred arrival time using the peak-avoidance data of the Dutch "Spitsmijden" experiment, which involved the use of rewards (money or Smartphone credits) for encouraging drivers to avoid commuting during the morning peak hours. Three models were estimated to identify car drivers' choice of departure time when rewards were provided: a logit model, a mixture model and a latent class model regarding arrival time preference. The results indicated that the rewards, both monetary and in-kind (a Yeti smartphone) had a substantial effect on decreasing peak travel. Furthermore, in the latent-class specification, women were more likely to have a preferred arrival time compared to men (Ben-Elia et al., 2010).

Psychological factors were derived to build departure time hybrid choice model based on the theory of Planned Behavior, estimated them based on structural equation modeling, and included them into a discrete choice model. The psychological factors were measured based on an online questionnaire addressed to car commuters to the city center of Copenhagen in the peak hour. The effects of the psychological factors were different depending on framework conditions: for people with fixed starting times at work, the intention to arrive at work on time (as estimated by subjective norm, attitude, perceived behavioral control) had the strongest effect; for people with flexible working hours, the attitude toward short travel time was most relevant (Thorhauge et al., 2016a, b).

The direct effect of the intention on the actual behavior was explored in Thorhauge et al. (2017), which used data from Danish commuters in the morning rush hours in the Greater Copenhagen area. The role of intention as mediator between several latent effects and the behavior was studied. Attitude, social norms, and perceived behavioral control were found to affect the intention to behave in a given way. A hybrid choice model was applied to study the departure time choice. The results showed a significant effect of the intention to arrive at work on time on the departing time choice, and also a significant effect of the lower level mediators (such as attitude, intention, attitude, etc.) on intention. Furthermore, the attitude toward short travel time was also significant in explaining the departure time choice. Individuals who had a strong intention to be at work on time were forecasted to be less likely to reschedule their departure time.

How travelers changed their daily travel decisions based on accumulated experience was explored in Wang (1996), in which a two-stage simulation model was established to estimate people's timing choices and timing utility over all major activities. The hazard-rate duration was used to estimate the revealed preferences of Canadians on their major daily activities. With the results of this simulation, the tradeoff between travel time and the scheduling choices was examined and a commuter equilibrium was established on a basis of activity timing utility, work start time, and travel time. In a different research, a micro-simulation approach was applied to explore how travelers base their daily travel decisions on the accumulated experience gathered from repetitively traveling through the transport network. Individuals based their consecutive departure time decisions on a mental model, which was the outcome of a continuous process of perception updating according to principles of reinforcement learning. Individuals' daily travel decisions were linked to the traffic simulator SIAS-PARAMICS to create a simulation system in which both individual decision-making and system performance (and interactions between these two levels) were adequately represented. The simulation results suggested that the outcomes of the learning and adaptation process may not be straightforward, but was a powerful tool in modeling the dynamics in responses over time (Ettema et al., 2005).

3.4 Departure time learning and evolution

With the provision of dynamic traffic information and incentives, the day-to-day departure time choice evolution of the travelers was explored in Hu et al. (2019), using real observation data collected from a smartphone app "Metropia." Influenced by the current information and incentives provided in the app and the comparison with the experience gained from the last trip, a transformation process of traveler's day-to-day experience on departure time from an existing habit to a new one was analyzed. A binary choice model was proposed for the shift of departure time for each repeated morning commute trip comparing with the last one, which proved that users' experience in app engagement, previous travel time saving, habitual travel time, incentives, and commute flexibility were able to trigger day-to-day behavioral change for their morning home-to-work commutes.

In a relevant research, the impact of incentives on departure time for seven main trip purposes was analyzed to further provide a personalized incentive scheme to achieve an optimal manner at the system wide level. Two consecutive incentive schemes were compared, each lasting for over a 1-year period, to understand how effectively these incentive scenarios influence the departure time of seven trip purposes. Four accelerated failure time models were conducted to explain the time to observe a departure event and the acceleration factors for various trip purposes under two incentive scenarios. The results suggested that peak-hour travelers might be open to behavioral incentives that promote non-peak-hour departure time and incentives might need to be tailored based on time of the day and the purpose of the trip. Traveling for recreation, errands, and work was the most sensitive trip purposes to the incentives in the morning peak hour. However, in the evening peak hour, traveling for other trips, errands, and school became the most sensitive trip purposes (Arian et al., 2018).

The learning process of travelers' departure time choice behavior was modeled based on the Bayesian learning theory, using the information received from social media and location-aware mobile devices as inputs. A general framework was introduced for departure time choice with information sharing via social networks. The parameters in the learning model were estimated based on an experimental dataset. The agent-based approach, which was proposed to simulate travelers' choices, was applied to validate the model and examine the effect of different social network structures, in terms of both travel choices and transportation system performance (Xiao and Lo, 2016). Liu et al. validated that travelers can learn from their past travel experiences as well as the traffic forecasts offered by the transport information provider/agency in adjusting their departure time and mode choices, while the information agency learns from historical data in updating traffic forecast from day-to-day at the same time. When exploring the convergence of the proposed model to the dynamic bi-modal commuting equilibrium, the authors found that appropriate traffic forecast can help the system converge to the user equilibrium and user inertia might slow down the convergence speed of the day-to-day evolution model (Liu et al., 2018).

Relationship between commuters' departure time choices and the evolution of enroute traffic and a data linkage method was studied via a dynamic modeling framework in Dong and Cirillo (2018). A regional household travel survey data were linked to travel information obtained from the Google Map application program interface (API), creating a synthetic longitudinal dataset. Two decision rules, named perfect knowledge and stochastic changes, were applied to model the evolution of traffic. The results indicated that travel time, trip distance of commute trips, and commuters' socio-demographic influenced departure time choices.

A comparison of the reviewed departure time choice behavior research is summarized in Table 2, in chronological order. The comparison is based on the model developed, source of data (field data versus survey), size of data used (high, medium or low), provision of information or incentives, contributing factors it focused on, and the type of trips it investigated.

4. Route choice behavior

The design principals of most popular Advanced Travel Information Systems (ATISs) such as Google Maps, Waze or other navigation apps are to assist travelers in making better route choices by providing dynamic traffic information. As such, lots of research attention has been paid on studying the impact of traffic information and other factors on traveler's route choice behavior, and various methodologies frameworks and experiments have been designed in previous research. For example, five models were built in Abdel-Aty and FathyAbdalla (2006) to address drivers' diversion, compliance, and route choice under the effect of advanced traveler information systems. Dynamic data were collected by a travel simulator providing five different levels of traffic information/advice and collecting pre-trip and enroute route choices. The binomial and multinomial generalized extreme equations were used and the modeling results showed that expressway users were shown as the most travel time savers who would divert if they were guided to a less-travel time alternative.

The effects of pre-trip information on route-choice decisions when travel conditions were congested and stochastic were studied in Lindsey et al. (2014). A model based on the classical two route network was adopted, in which free-flow travel times and/or capacities on each route varied unpredictably due to such shocks as bad weather, accidents, and special events. The results showed that the benefits of information depend on differences between routes in free-flow costs, the shape of the travel cost functions, the severity of congestion and capacity shocks, and the degree of correlation between routes in travel conditions. The developed model was tested in Rapoport et al. (2014) in which an experiment was conducted. They reformulated the model for finite populations, and then tested and found support for its predictions in the experiment where under different

Table 2 Comparison of departure time choice behavior research.

Research	Date	Data source	Size of data	Type of trips	Provision of information, incentives	Major contributing factors	Model developed
Khattak et al. (1995)	1995	Survey	Medium	Home-to-work trips	Traffic reports	Personal characteristics	Probit model
Bhat and Steed (2002)	2002	Survey	Medium	24-h shopping trips	N/A	Socio-demographics, employment-related attributes and trip-related characteristics	Continuous-time hazard duration model
Saleh and Farrell (2005)	2005	Survey	Medium	24-h work trips	N/A	Non-work activities and socio-economic characteristics	Multinomial logit model
Gadda et al. (2009)	2009	Field	High	24-h trips	N/A	Demographic and trip-related variables	Lognormal and Weibull model
Nurul Habib et al. (2009)	2009	Survey	High	24-h H-W-H trips	N/A	Socio-demographic variables and trip attributes	Joint multinomial logit mode choice and continuous time hazard model
Ben-Elia et al. (2010)	2010	Field data	High	Peak-hour trips	Incentives	Incentives, social demographics	Logit, mixture, latent class model
Lemp et al. (2010)	2010	Survey	Medium	24-h trips	N/A	Transport-related variables	Continuous cross-nested logit model
Lemp and Kockelman (2010)	2010	Survey	High	24-h trips	Travel time	Individual-specific variables	Continuous logit model

Continued

Table 2 Comparison of departure time choice behavior research.—cont'd

Research	Date	Data source	Size of data	Type of trips	Provision of information, incentives	Major contributing factors	Model developed
Yang et al. (2013)	2013	Survey	Medium	24-h shopping trips	Travel time	Socio-economic variables and individuals' preference	Continuous cross-nested logit model
Thorhauge et al. (2016a, b)	2016	Survey	Medium	24-h out-of-home trips	Pricing	Work constraints, non-work activities	Mixed logit
Thorhauge et al. (2016a, b)	2016	Survey	Medium	Peak-hour work trips	Experienced congestion	Psychological factors	Hybrid choice model
Yang et al. (2016)	2016	Survey	Medium	24 h work trips	N/A	Individual characteristics	Multinomial logit model
Thorhauge et al. (2017)	2017	Survey	Medium	Peak-hour trips	Toll	Attitude, social norms, and perceived behavioral control	Hybrid choice model
Zhu et al. (2017a, b)	2017	Survey	High	24-h home-based trips	Travel cost	Social demographical variables	Mixed Bayesian network
Shabanpour et al. (2017)	2017	Survey	High		N/A	Individuals' and households' demographic	Multinomial logit and log-linear regression model

capacity scenarios, and with and without pre-trip information, subjects were asked to choose routes with payoff contingent on their performance.

The impact of enroute real-time information about the occurrence of an incident (prevailing) and ex post information on forgone payoffs on traveler's route choice behavior was studied in Lu et al. (2011). Data were collected from an interactive experiment in which participants made multiple rounds of route choices on a hypothetical network, and travel times were determined by performance functions of route flows from the previous round. Enroute real-time information increased the network's travel time savings and reliability under the experimental setting, yet FP information had the opposite effect. Real-time information at downstream nodes encouraged participants' strategic behavior at the origin. FP information appeared to increase risk-seeking behavior; it encouraged route switching without real-time information and suppressed it with real-time information. The sensitivity of travelers' response to information, especially in the case of accepting route suggestions depended on their perceptions of the provided information's accuracy.

Drivers' behavioral responses to social navigation route guidance under different information and incentive strategies was empirically evaluated in Djavadian et al. (2014). A traffic navigation application was developed and used in a pilot multiuser laboratory experiment, in which participants were asked to make route choices in a virtual travel environment under various information and incentive strategies. The results showed that drivers were more willing to comply with the social advice when they were well informed or rewarded, and female/novice drivers were more willing to comply with the social advice than were male drivers and experienced drivers. Zhang et al. (2018a, b) investigated the effects of social interaction information from friends on commuters' daily route choice decisions. The authors developed a day-to-day route-choice learning model with friends' travel information based on the Cumulative Prospect Theory (CPT), and then designed and conducted a laboratory behavioral experiment to collect the statistical data associated with subjects' actual route choice decisions. The results showed that a larger rate of social interactions in an online travel community does not necessarily lead to a better route-choice outcome for individuals or the whole system.

Several surveys and experiments were conducted to obtain the revealed preferences (RP) and stated preferences (SP) on route choice. Shiftan et al. (2011) conducted a field study and an in-laboratory experiment to obtain revealed preferences and stated preferences on route choice, and used a combined RP-SP route-choice model. The results suggested that when experience seeking increases, individuals tended to prefer a route characterized by lower average but greater variance of travel time. Other results confirmed that information had an impact on route-choice behavior although compliance with received information decreases with recent experience. Kusakabe et al. (2012) conducted a stated preference survey to describe drivers' route choice behaviors when traffic incident information was provided on a Variable Message Sign (VMS) in urban expressway networks. The results showed that travelers can assume travel time of their alternative routes according to the congestion information of the road section provided by VMS. Razo and Gao (2013) took a stated preference survey conducted with interactive maps in order to analyze strategic route choice, where a traveler was able to plan ahead for traffic information that s/he will receive in the future. The analysis suggested that a traveler's risk attitude was probability dependent, which was explained by a rank-dependent expected utility (RDEU) model. A latent-class mixed logit model for panel data was specified with a RDEU component and two latent classes, strategic and non-strategic route choice. The estimated results suggested that a route choice model under real-time information should consider both types of behavior.

With the continuous improvements of the computation, communication, sensor technologies and the era of big data coming, the connected vehicle environment was born at the century and experienced a rapid development period since 2010. Drivers can move with the real-time traffic information under the connected vehicle environment. Meanwhile, individual driving behavior (e.g., route choice) can influence the traffic state of the connected vehicle. Dai et al. (2018) investigated the relationship between the performance of traffic system and the driver route choice behavior in the connected vehicle environment. A dynamic process of commuter day-to-day route choice behavior under the connected vehicle environment was proposed, the driving experience and the real-time information that affect the driver route choice were taken into considered simultaneously. The authors conducted a series of simulation experiments under the different percentages of drivers who paid enough attention to fuel consumption, and then simulation results were compared. The simulation results demonstrated that the performance of traffic state was better when enough drivers put emphasis on fuel consumption, and the travel time was more sensitive to the change of traffic state than fuel consumption.

A route-choice experiment was conducted in Ben-Elia et al. (2013) to investigate the impact of information accuracy on route choice behavior. 36 participants, involving 20 repetitions under three different levels of information accuracy participated in the experiment. Aggregate analysis using non-parametric statistics and disaggregate analysis using a mixed logit choice model were applied. The results suggested that decreasing accuracy shifts choices not only from the riskier to the reliable route but also to the useless alternative. Prescriptive information had the largest behavioral impact followed by descriptive and experiential feedback information. Liao and Chen (2015) applied the concept of a Bayesian game to the route choice problem when travelers were maximizing their degree of satisfaction by choosing routes, and a Bayesian model was used to analyze the impact of this heterogeneity on travelers' route choices. The results suggested that the use of ATIS exposes certain heterogeneities in traveler types and beliefs.

A learning-based model of route-choice behavior when information was provided in real time was presented in Ben-Elia and Shiftan (2010). Participants made majority of binary route-choice trials relying on real-time information and learning from their personal experience reinforced through feedback in a laboratory-controlled experience. A discrete choice model with a mixed logit specification was estimated based on the experiment's data accounting for panel effects. The results showed that information and experience had a combined effect on drivers' route-choice behavior. Informed participants tended to base their decisions on memorization relating to previous outcomes with faster learning rates and had greater sensitivity to travel time variability.

Changes in traveler's route choice behavior in response to pre-planned events such as constructions or special events that lead to road capacity reductions and create bottlenecks in the traffic network was studied in Hu et al. (2018a, b). High-resolution vehicle trajectory data were collected via a smartphone app "Metropia," which was capable of keeping track of individual driver's behavior before and after road capacity reduction, to investigate travelers' behavioral responses to pre-planned events and the contribution factors. A functional data analysis (FDA) approach-based clustering method was proposed to cluster trajectory data and identify detour patterns, and two logistic and a least absolute shrinkage and selection operator (LASSO) regression models were used to explain drivers' detour behavior choice for each pattern with spatial and temporal features of interest. A case study based on a lane closure event on MoPac expressway in

Austin, TX was used as an example. The case study demonstrated that: (1) the freeway capacity reduction triggered heterologous behavior responses, (2) driver detour behavior exhibited three major patterns, and (3) each detour pattern highly depended on spatial features such as trip length, distance to freeway entrance and distance to other alternative freeways, in addition to the temporal features when the trip happens.

Apart from private vehicles, taxis also play an important role in providing on-demand mobility and their route choice behavior has also been extensively studied. Traditionally, vacant taxis cruise on roads searching for customers. In recent years, thanks to the proliferation of GPS-enabled smartphones, e-hailing applications (e.g., Uber, Lyft, and Didi Chuxing) are widely adopted by ride-sourcing drivers and in some cases, traditional taxi drivers to receive requests from nearby customers. The driver of a hired taxi usually aligns his/her routing objective with the passenger's, given the paramount importance of customer service (taking a detour to get higher fare is unprofessional and rare), and such a problem has been well studied. The interesting question is how to route vacant taxis. Taxis cruising on roads not only result in wasted gas and time for taxi drivers but also generate additional traffic in a city. Therefore, how to improve the utilization of taxis is of importance to both taxi drivers and the society. In an earlier study, Hu et al. (2012) proposed a dynamic programming model of routing vacant taxis to depict the decisions at intersections according to the passenger arrival rate. Taxi drivers were assumed to minimize the expected search time for customers when making routing decisions at intersections. However, the expected search time was only minimized for the next customer, which might be inefficient in the long run. For this reason, experienced taxi drivers would not simply make their customer search decisions depending on the current searching time/profit, but would also consider the subsequent possible states that could be encountered. The majority of vacant taxi routing studies in the literature, in fact, only considers an optimization problem until meeting the next customer (e.g., Huang et al., 2015; Qu et al., 2014), and in some cases, the revenue from the next customer (e.g., Yuan et al., 2013). Yu et al. (2018) formulated the vacant taxi routing problem as a Markov Decision Process (MDP) so that long-term objectives can be taken into account instead of the immediate one of meeting the next customer. The proposed model and solution algorithm in Yu et al. (2019) were tested in a case study with parameters derived from GPS trajectories of over 12,000 taxis in Shanghai, China for a study period of 5:30–11:30 a.m. on a typical weekday. The optimal routing policy was compared with three heuristics based on simulated trajectories. Results showed that the optimal routing policy improved average unit profit by 23.0% and 8.4% over the random walk and local hotspot heuristic, respectively; and improved occupancy rate by 23.8% and 8.3%, respectively.

A comparison of the reviewed route choice behavior research is summarized in Table 3, in chronological order. The comparison is based on the model developed, source of data (field data versus survey), size of data used (high, medium or low), provision of information or incentives, contributing factors it focused on, and the type of trips it investigated.

5. Mode choice and destination choice behavior

Mode choice and destination choice were found to change less as compared to departure time and route choice, according to a user satisfaction survey conducted in the Greater Cincinnati and northern Kentucky area (Aultman-Hall et al., 2000). Users were asked what portion of the time the traffic information affected their travel behavior. They reported that after the callers received information from a traffic advisory telephone service, 71% of the time their route taken cane be adjusted, and 34% of the time they can leave at a different time. On the other hand, they were willing to change their destination only for 25% of the time, and adjusted their mode merely for 5.7% of the time. The study also showed a total of 65% of users indicated they would be willing to pay for the service. On average, the maximum amount people would pay per call was $0.25.

Abdel-Aty and FathyAbdalla (2006) collected and analyzed data that can be used to model mode choice paradigms using same subjects and same experiments. The effect of advanced traveler information systems (ATIS) on the mode choice was considered. A travel simulator was used as a dynamic data collection tool. The simulator used a realistic network, two modes of travel, real historical volumes, and different weather conditions. It provided five different levels of traffic information/advice, one at a time, and collected dynamic mode choices and pre-trip (long-term) and enroute (short-term) route choices. The results showed that education level did not affect the mode compliance and providing pre-trip or enroute traffic information assisted travelers and drivers in their mode decisions. As the level of information/advice increased, the benefits increased. One interesting finding was that developing in-vehicle information devices may lead to a less transit usage in some cases, which indicated a potential drawback of this technology.

Table 3 Comparison of route choice behavior research.

Research	Date	Data source	Size of data	Provision of information, incentives	Major contributing factors	Type of trips	Model developed
Abdel-Aty and FathyAbdalla (2006)	2006	Field	Medium	Traffic information/ advice	Age, gender, income, driving experience, and frequency usage of the expressways	Morning–week–day trips	Binomial and multinomial generalized model
Ben-Elia and Shiftan (2010)	2010	Survey	Medium	Information	Travel time variability, risk taking	24-h trips	Discrete choice model
Lu et al. (2011)	2011	Survey	Small	Ex post information	Average travel times, route shares, and route switches	Work to home trips	Block bootstrap method
Shiftan et al. (2011)	2011	Survey	Medium	Pre-trip travel time information	Drivers' personal characteristics	Morning peak-hour trips	Combined RP-SP route-choice model
Kusakabe et al. (2012)	2012	Survey	Medium	Traffic incident information	Off-ramp choice behavior	24-h trips	Multinomial logit model
Razo and Gao (2013)	2013	Survey	Medium	Traffic information	Travelers' risk attitudes	24-h trips	Latent-class mixed logit model
Ben-Elia et al. (2013)	2013	Survey	Small	Information	information accuracy	24-h trips	Mixed logit model
Lindsey et al. (2014) and Rapoport et al. (2014)	2014	Survey	High	Pre-trip information	Travel condition	Peak-hour trips	Experience-weighted attractions learning model
Djavadian et al. (2014)	2014	Survey	Medium	Incentives	Social navigation route guidance	From Delft or Gouda to Dordrecht	Dynamic descriptive behavioral model
Liao and Chen (2015)	2015	Survey	Small	Information	Travel time	24-h trips	Bayesian game
Zhang et al. (2018a, b)	2018	Survey	Medium	Friends' travel information	Social interactions	Daily commute trips	Cumulative prospect theory-based day-to-day route-choice model
Dai et al. (2018)	2018	Survey	Small	Information	Fuel consumption, traffic condition	24-h trips	Linear utility maximization weighted model

Chicago Metropolitan Agency for Planning (CMAP)'s Travel Tracker Survey, which is a household travel diary survey including both GPS and non-GPS components, was used to estimate a mode choice model for work trips to explore the influence of unreliability on travel behavior (Sweet and Chen, 2011). The results suggested that unreliable auto travel conditions induce mode switching to transit and that the influence was strongest when service by train was already faster than by car. The results suggested that auto travel unreliability may have the strongest influence in metropolitan regions with highly-competitive transit systems, which triggered the mode choice change most effectively. Nevertheless, the influence of travel unreliability was limited and was not the underlying driver of travel decision making.

Carsharing programs have been deployed in North America in 1994 and the organizations provided members access to a fleet of shared vehicles on an hourly basis, reducing the need for private vehicle ownership and encouraging members to make greater use of alternative modes of travel (Katzev, 2003; Shaheen et al., 2009). Katsev et al. (2001) analyzed the effect of CarSharing Portland (CSP) on travel behavior. The results showed that carsharing led to significant changes in the use of alternative transportation. After joining CSP, individuals took the bus more often, rode their bicycle more and did more walking than they had before. Martin and Shaheen (2011) evaluated the travel patterns' shift toward and away from public transit and non-motorized modes based on a 6281 respondent survey completed in late-2008 by member of major North American carsharing organizations. The results showed an overall decline in public transit use that was statistically significant, as 589 carsharing members reduced rail use and 828 reduced bus use, while 494 increased rail use and 732 increased bus use. At the same time, members exhibited a statistically significant increase in travel by walking, bicycling, and carpooling. Data collected on the commute distance of respondents found that carsharing members tend to have shorter commutes than most people living in the same zip code. Costain et al. (2012) presented a comprehensive investigation of the behavior of carsharing members through the analysis of administrative datasets of a dominant carsharing program in Toronto. The dataset was collected from AutoShare, a Toronto based Carsharing Company, and included monthly transaction and membership directory data from 2008 to 2010. In 2010, a total of 84,773 trips were made by 6085 active members. Results showed that carsharing was most often used for off-peak period travel or on weekends, when transit service was poor and traffic congestion was low. The free-floating carsharing systems (FFCS) car2go and DriveNow were offered by companies that possessed the organizational capabilities, technical knowledge and financial resources to roll-out carsharing systems large scale (Firnkorn, 2012). The new free-floating carsharing systems operated with more cars per city than most traditional carsharing organizations offer in total in all cities. Kopp et al. (2015) analyzed the travel behavior based on substantial data that were collected with an innovative survey design based on a GPS tracking smartphone application. They contrasted the core group of members of FFCS model DriveNow (male, 25–45 years old) with people who did not use car sharing. The results showed that FFCS reported more trips, which covered shorter distances, and differed substantially in their mode choice behavior. It also demonstrated that FFCS were more intermodal and multimodal in their behavior and they choose bikes significantly more and motorized private transport modes less.

Models were built to understand the determinants of shopping destination choice in Scott and He (2012). A total of 616 shopping trips were selected from a travel survey conducted in five counties of the Louisville KY-IN MSA in 2000, and shopping opportunities were aggregated to traffic analysis zones (TAZs) for analysis. Multinomial logit models were developed to estimate the determinants of shopping destination choice and potential path area to determine an individual's destination choice set given their spatio-temporal constraints. In this way, the destination choice set was a more realistic representation of the shopping alternatives available to the individual. The results suggested that constrained models were better predictors of destinations than unconstrained models. The advances in GPS and GIS technologies provide new opportunities for collecting travel data.

A research investigated how land use, road network structure, and axis of travel influenced home-based, non-work destination choice based on in-vehicle GPS travel data in the Minneapolis-St. Paul Metropolitan Area in 2008 (Huang and Levinson, 2015). In-vehicle GPS travel data were used to model non-work destination choice, and a new approach combining survival analysis and random sampling to form choice sets was proposed. The results suggested that a non-work destination closer to the axis of home and work was more attractive to auto users, a non-work destination closer to downtown was less attractive, and a non-work destination reached by a route with greater changes of speed per unit time or more turns per unit time was less attractive.

Given the real-time trip origin and destination information, Huang and Levinson (2017) adopted mixed-effects logit models to model home-based trip chains with two destinations and collected in-vehicle GPS travel data which recorded 141 participants' vehicle trips including origins, parking destinations, and travel routes during a study period of 5 months. Three alternatives of building choice sets where various relationships of the two destinations (such as major–minor destinations, selecting one first, and selecting two concurrently) were considered, proposed and compared. The hypothesis had been tested that not only the spatial relationship but also the land use relationship of the destinations in a trip chain affect the decision-making process. The results suggested that trip-chaining behavior was shaped by the features of retail clusters, spatial patterns of clusters, transportation networks, and the axis of travel. It also reveals that not only the spatial relationship but also the land use relationship of the destinations in a trip chain affected the decision-making process.

6. Driving behavior

Traditional driving risk analysis is usually performed based on crash history data or survey results, and uses this information to identify hazardous locations or driving risk factors contributing to the crash events. Research in this type reveals driving risk factors based on the correlation analysis at the aggregate level, and typically does not go down to the individual level due to the absence of personalized driving data. An emerging stream of research has been applying the latest Information and Communication Technology in data collection and driving behavior evaluation and adjustment in the last decade. Such data usually include not only vehicle spatial-temporal dimension location, but more importantly also speed, acceleration, and deceleration, which are frequently used to evaluate a driver's driving behavior.

6.1 The 100-car naturalistic driving study

The 100-Car Naturalistic Driving Study was the first instrumented vehicle study undertaken with the primary purpose of collecting large-scale naturalistic driving data. 100 participants (40 women and 60 men) between the ages of 18 and 64 years old from the Washington, DC, area were recruited and In-Vehicle Data Recorders (IVDR) was instrumented to continuously measure the vehicle's position, speed and acceleration using GPS and accelerometers as well as video cameras. Drivers were given no special instructions, no experimenter was present, and the data collection instrumentation was unobtrusive. Four levels of driving events—crash, near-crash, incidents, and baseline—were classified from the video by trained video reductionists.

The resulting database contained many extreme cases of driving behavior and performance, including severe drowsiness, impairment, judgment error, risk taking, willingness to engage in secondary tasks, aggressive driving, and traffic violations. The dataset included approximately 2,000,000 vehicle miles, almost 43,000 h of data, 241 primary and secondary drivers, 12–13 months of data collection for each vehicle, and data from a highly capable instrumentation system including 5 channels of video and many vehicle state and kinematic sensors (Dingus et al., 2006).

Based on such a dataset, a list of studies was performed. Significant risk factors were identified in Guo and Fang (2013) via a negative binomial regression model. High- and moderate-risk drivers were predicted with two logistic models. The cluster analysis identified approximately 6% of drivers as high-risk drivers, with average crash and near-crash (CNC) rate of 3.95 per 1000 miles traveled, 12% of drivers as moderate-risk drivers (average CNC rate = 1.75), and 84% of drivers as low-risk drivers (average CNC rate = 0.39). The results indicated that crash and near-crash risk for individual drivers was associated with critical incident rate, demographic, and personality characteristics. Differences in braking behavior between age and gender groups in car-following scenarios were characterized in Montgomery et al. (2014), in which the mixed model analysis of variance was used to examine the differences. The results showed that males age 18–20 had the lowest average minimum time to collision (TTC) at braking of 2.5 ± 0.8 s, and females age 31–50 had the highest average minimum TTC at braking of 6.4 ± 0.9 s. Age was found to be a statistically significant factor for TTC at braking between participants under 30 and participants over 30, with the latter braking 1.7 s on average before the former.

Klauer et al. also used such dataset to study the relationship between the performance of secondary tasks, including cell-phone use, and the risk of crashes and near-crashes (Klauer et al., 2014). A mixed-effects linear-regression model was used to assess trends for performance of a secondary task over time by both novice and experienced drivers. Results suggested that inattention contributed to 78% of all crashes collected over the 12-month data collection period, and specifically, the risk of a crash or near-crash among novice drivers increased significantly if they were dialing a cell phone, reaching for a cell phone, sending or receiving text messages, reaching for an object other than a cell phone, looking at a roadside object, or eating. Driver distraction was also studied in Liang et al. (2012) which predicted crash and near-crash risk on the basis of driver glance behavior and demonstrated that distraction estimated from driver eye-glance patterns was positively associated with crash risk. A variety of publications also took advantage of such dataset and focused on other aspects of driving behavior, such as seat belt use (Reagan et al., 2013), lane-change behavior (Fitch et al., 2009), run-off-road crash (McLaughlin et al., 2009), real-end crashes and near-crashes (Jonasson and Rootzén, 2014), and individual driver risk assessment (Guo and Fang, 2013).

6.2 Pay-as-you-drive-and-you-save insurance actuarial study

Traditional insurance models are based on a combination of static factors such as the driver's socio-demographic profile and vehicle information in conjunction with driving history. With the advent of new mobile technologies, some insurance companies have begun exploring a new auto insurance model known as Usage-Based-Insurance [UBI] or Pay-As-You-Drive-And-You-Save [PAYDAYS], which aims to incorporate individualized, real-world dynamic driving patterns into actuarial pricing. In 2013, the Federal Highway Administration contracted a research project to prove their PAYDAYS theory and study the implications of such an approach to insurance companies' premium calculation model. The motivation behind this project was that while most existing UBI or PAYDAYS efforts can be considered a major leap forward, the majority of researchers and insurers relied solely on user GPS trajectories, which only measured the specific driver's performance—such as the number of miles driven, traveling speeds, and hardness of braking—without considering other critical risk factors in the surrounding environment that may also contribute to crash risk, i.e. the contextual-sensitive risk factors. A total of 131,537 trips taken by 503 panel members over an 18-month period was collected in this study, which corresponds to 1,090,136 miles traveled. Individualized driving behavior data were collected from the driver's smartphone GPS module, and combined with geographical network information and dynamic traffic conditions to identify driving risk factors and evaluate driving behaviors under various contexts (Hu et al., 2018a, 2018b).

The benefits of utilizing context-relevant information in the driving behavior assessment process, i.e. contextual driving behavior assessment approach, were evaluated in Zhu et al. (2017a, b). A Bayesian Network (BN) model that investigated the relationships between GPS driving observations, individual driving behavior, individual driving risks, and individual crash frequency was developed. In contrast to prior studies without context information (i.e. non-contextual approach), the data used in the BN approach was a combination of contextual features in the surrounding environment that may contribute to crash risk, such as road conditions surrounding the vehicle of interest and dynamic traffic flow information, as well as the non-contextual data such as instantaneous driving speed and the acceleration/deceleration of a vehicle. The analysis results showed that the contextual model had significantly better performance than the non-contextual model, and that drivers who drove at a speed faster than others or much slower than the speed limit at the ramp, and with more rapid acceleration or deceleration on freeways were more likely to be involved in crash events. In addition, younger drivers, and female drivers with higher VMT were found to have higher crash risk.

Hu et al. further examined the relationship between the driving performance measurements and accident rate, which was verified by combining the crash history of the drivers. A total of five measurements were defined to capture the driving performance at the trajectory and link level, including relative speed, contextual speeding, smoothness, hard brake and hard start. Based on those performance measurements, trip level performance was then aggregated for each trip from the trajectory and link level measures. Numeric analysis on the trip level demonstrated that driving behavior was context sensitive, and the principal component analysis performed at the driver level showed that pedal operation and driving speed were the two most important performance measurements to characterize an individual's driving pattern. The subsequent correlation analysis of crash history and driving performances verified both pedal operation and driving speed were significantly related to more at-fault accidents (Hu et al., 2015a, b, 2018a; Zhu et al., 2013).

Ma et al. demonstrated how second-by-second GPS data can be integrated into existing or new auto insurance pricing structures in Ma et al. (2018). Two types of data, real-time GPS trajectory data collected from the PAYDAYS project, as well as survey data were used. Vehicle trajectories and accident data were incorporated to quantify the relationship between driving hazard and accidents with the goal of establishing the linkage between driving risks and accident costs. GPS data considered in this study included not only tradition UBI factors, but also the unique contextual-based risk measurements that compared the driving speed of the vehicle with other drivers on the same road segment. It was found that hard brakes, hard starts, peak-time travel, speeding as well as driving at a speed significantly different from traffic flow were highly correlated with accident rate. The potential underwriting loss an insurer may incur resulting from adverse selection if omitting pertinent risk factors was illustrated. The results were helpful for insurance companies that are interested in getting into the UBI area to set up their auto insurance premium rates.

7. Conclusions and discussions

This manuscript reviewed the state-of-the-art research on the impact of ICT on triggering traveler behavior changes. The use of dynamic traffic information and incentives, two most commonly seen means, are frequently used to effectively influence people's travel behavior. The review started from a review of system development and current practices, followed by behavior changes in the form of departure time choice, route choice, destination choice and mode choice, and driving behaviors.

Transportation technologies have been and will continue to advance rapidly, and as such, traveler's pre-trip decision making and enroute experience will continue to be assisted with the new technologies. The transportation data to be collected will also be greatly expanded not only in volume but also in velocity and variety. It will facilitate researchers in developing new and better models and algorithms to investigate traveler's behavior, and study what it takes to influence the decision-making process. The advancement of ICT will also facilitate the real-time or near real-time behavioral interactions, to design behavior experiments by presenting information and incentives/cost to the users, and observe how their behavior may adjust with a very short implementation cycle. Such efficient experiment design of having the human in the loop is another promising research direction to go. Last but not the least, how to further behavior change and make it a habit has not been well studied. While the offering of incentives has been proven to be effective, the hope is the behavior change can last even if the incentives are withdrawn, and the travelers have formed the habit of making informed and better choices of trip making. Interdisciplinary research combining traffic safety, psychology, economics and researchers from the other areas will be beneficial to advance behavior research to the exciting future.

References

Abdel-Aty, M.A., FathyAbdalla, M., 2006. Examination of multiple mode/route-choice paradigms under ATIS. IEEE Trans. Intell. Transp. Syst. 7 (3), 332–348.

AENEAS, 2010. New Dedicated Innovative Services—TELE-BUS. Krakow, Poland. From, http://www.eltis.org/index.php?id=13&study_id=2840.

Ajzen, I., 1991. The theory of planned behavior. Organ. Behav. Hum. Decis. Process. 50 (2), 179–211.
An, K., Xianbiao, H., Chiu, Y.-C., Chen, X., 2016. A network partitioning algorithm to support macroscopic fundamental diagram based network modeling. In: 96th Annual Meeting of the Transportation Research Board, Washington, DC.
Arian, A., Ermagun, A., Zhu, X., Chiu, Y.-C., 2018. Chapter six—An empirical investigation of the reward incentive and trip purposes on departure time behavior change. In: Shiftan, Y., Kamargianni, M. (Eds.), Advances in Transport Policy and Planning. In: vol. 1. Academic Press, pp. 145–167.
ARPA-E, 2018. University of Maryland (Transnet): Incentivizing Individual Travel Behavior Changes for System-Level Energy Savings. From, https://arpa-e.energy.gov/?q=impact-sheet/university-maryland-transnet.
Aultman-Hall, L., Bowling, S., Asher, J.C., 2000. ARTIMIS telephone travel information service: current use patterns and user satisfaction. Transp. Res. Rec. 1739 (1), 9–14.
Bamberg, S., Ajzen, I., Schmidt, P., 2002. Choice of travel mode in the theory of planned behavior: the roles of past behavior, habit, and reasoned action. Basic Appl. Soc. Psychol. 25 (3), 175–187.
Bamberg, S., Daniel, R., Christoph, W., 2003. Does habitual car use not lead to more resistance to change of travel mode? Transportation 30, 97–108.
Bauer, J., Bedsole, L.K., Snyder, K., Neuner, M., Smith, M.C., 2018. Expanding Traveler Choices Through the Use of Incentives: A Compendium of Examples. Federal Highway Administration.
Ben-Elia, E., Ettema, D., 2011. Rewarding rush-hour avoidance: a study of commuters' travel behavior. Transp. Res. A Policy Pract. 45 (7), 567–582.
Ben-Elia, E., Shiftan, Y., 2010. Which road do I take? A learning-based model of route-choice behavior with real-time information. Transp. Res. A Policy Pract. 44 (4), 249–264.
Ben-Elia, E., Bierlaire, M., Ettema, D., 2010. A behavioural departure time choice model with latent arrival time preference and rewards for peak-hour avoidance. In: European Transport Conference. Citeseer.
Ben-Elia, E., Boeije, H., Ettema, D., 2011. Behaviour Change Dynamics in Response to Rewarding Rushhour Avoidance: A Qualitative Research Approach. Transportation Research Board.
Ben-Elia, E., Di Pace, R., Bifulco, G.N., Shiftan, Y., 2013. The impact of travel information's accuracy on route-choice. Transp. Res. Part C Emerg. Technol. 26, 146–159.
Bhat, C.R., Steed, J.L., 2002. A continuous-time model of departure time choice for urban shopping trips. Transp. Res. B Methodol. 36 (3), 207–224.
Burris, M., 2001. Lee County Variable Pricing Project: Evaluation Report. Center for Urban Transportation Re-search.
Costain, C., Ardron, C., Habib, K.N., 2012. Synopsis of users' behaviour of a carsharing program: a case study in Toronto. Transp. Res. A Policy Pract. 46 (3), 421–434.
Currie, G., 2011. Free fare incentives to shift rail demand peaks—medium-term impacts. In: Transportation Research Board 90th Annual Meeting. Washington, DC, USA.
Dai, R., Lu, Y., Ding, C., Lu, G., Wang, Y., 2018. A simulation-based approach to investigate the driver route choice behavior under the connected vehicle environment. Transport. Res. F: Traffic Psychol. Behav. in press, https://www.sciencedirect.com/science/article/pii/S1369847816304454.
Dingus, T.A., Klauer, S.G., Neale, V.L., Peterson, A., Lee, S.E., Sudweeks, J., Hankey, J., Perez, M.A., Ramsey, D., Gupta, S., Bucher, C., Doerzaph, Z.R., Knipling, R.R., Jarmeland, J., 2006. The 100-car naturalistic driving study. In: Phase II—Results of the 100-Car Field Experiment. National Highway Traffic Safety Administration (NHTSA).
Djavadian, S., Hoogendoorn, R.G., Van Arerm, B., Chow, J.Y.J., 2014. Empirical evaluation of drivers' route choice behavioral responses to social navigation. Transp. Res. Rec. 2423 (1), 52–60.

Dong, H., Cirillo, C., 2018. A dynamic approach toward stochastic departure time choices using a linked data set. In: Transportation Research Board 97th Annual Meeting.

Ettema, D., Tamminga, G., Timmermans, H., Arentze, T., 2005. A micro-simulation model system of departure time using a perception updating model under travel time uncertainty. Transp. Res. A Policy Pract. 39 (4), 325–344.

Ettema, D., Knockaert, J., Verhoef, E., 2010. Using incentives as traffic management tool: empirical results of the "peak avoidance" experiment. Transport. Lett. 2 (1), 39–51.

Firnkorn, J., 2012. Triangulation of two methods measuring the impacts of a free-floating carsharing system in Germany. Transp. Res. A Policy Pract. 46 (10), 1654–1672.

Fitch, G.M., Lee, S.E., Klauer, S.G., Hankey, J., Sudweeks, J., Dingus, T., 2009. Analysis of Lane-Change Crashes and Near-Crashes. National Highway Traffic Safety Administration.

Fujii, S., Kitamura, R., 2003. What does a one-month free bus ticket do to habitual drivers? An experimental analysis of habit and attitude change. Transportation 30, 81–95.

Fujii, S., Gärling, T., Kitamura, R., 2001. Changes in drivers' perceptions and use of public transport during a freeway closure: effects of temporary structural change on cooperation in a real-life social dilemma. Environ. Behav. 33 (6), 796–808.

Gadda, S., Kockelman, K.M., Damien, P., 2009. Continuous departure time models: a Bayesian approach. Transp. Res. Rec. 2132 (1), 13–24.

Guo, F., Fang, Y., 2013. Individual driver risk assessment using naturalistic driving data. Accid. Anal. Prev. 61, 3–9.

Hu, X., 2013. Developing the analysis methodology and platform for behaviorally induced system optimal traffic management. PhD, University of Arizona.

Hu, X., Chiu, Y.-C., 2015. A constrained time-dependent K shortest paths algorithm addressing overlap and travel time deviation. Int. J. Transp. Sci. Technol. 4 (4), 371–394.

Hu, X., Gao, S., Chiu, Y.-C., Lin, D.-Y., 2012. Modeling routing behavior for vacant taxicabs in urban traffic networks. Transp. Res. Rec. 2284 (1), 81–88.

Hu, X., Chiu, Y.-C., Ma, Y.-L., Zhu, L., 2015a. Studying driving risk factors using multi-source mobile computing data. Int. J. Transp. Sci. Technol. 4 (3), 295–312.

Hu, X., Chiu, Y.-C., Zhu, L., 2015b. Behavior insights for an incentive-based active demand management platform. Int. J. Transp. Sci. Technol. 4 (2), 119–134.

Hu, X., Chiu, Y.-C., Shelton, J., 2017a. Development of a behaviorally induced system optimal travel demand management system. J. Intell. Transp. Syst. 21 (1), 12–25.

Hu, X., Chiu, Y.-C., Villalobos, J.A., Nava, E., 2017b. A sequential decomposition framework and method for calibrating dynamic origin-destination demand in a congested network. IEEE Trans. Intell. Transp. Syst. 18 (10), 2790–2797.

Hu, X., Yuan, Y., Zhu, X., Yang, H., Xie, K., 2018a. Behavioral responses to pre-planned road capacity reduction based on smartphone GPS trajectory data: a functional data analysis approach. J. Intell. Transp. Syst. 23 (2), 133–143.

Hu, X., Zhu, X., Ma, Y.-L., Chiu, Y.-C., Tang, Q., 2018b. Advancing usage based insurance—a contextual driving risk modeling and analysis approach. IET Intell. Transp. Syst. 13, 453–460.

Hu, X., Zhu, X., Chiu, Y.-C., Tang, Q., 2019. Will information and incentive affect traveler's day-to-day departure time decisions?—An empirical study of decision making evolution process. Int. J. Sustain. Transp. in press, https://www.tandfonline.com/doi/abs/10.1080/15568318.2019.1570402?af=R&journalCode=ujst20.

Huang, A., Levinson, D., 2015. Axis of travel: modeling non-work destination choice with GPS data. Transp. Res. Part C Emerg. Technol. 58, 208–223.

Huang, A., Levinson, D., 2017. A model of two-destination choice in trip chains with GPS data. J. Choice Model. 24, 51–62.

Huang, J., Huangfu, X., Sun, H., Li, H., Zhao, P., Cheng, H., Song, Q., 2015. Backward path growth for efficient mobile sequential recommendation. IEEE Trans. Knowl. Data Eng. 27 (1), 46–60.

Jonasson, J.K., Rootzén, H., 2014. Internal validation of near-crashes in naturalistic driving studies: a continuous and multivariate approach. Accid. Anal. Prev. 62, 102–109.

Katsev, R., Brook, D., Nice, M., 2001. The effects of car sharing on travel behaviour: analysis of CarSharing Portland's first year. World Transport Pol. Pract. 7 (1).

Katzev, R., 2003. Car sharing: a new approach to urban transportation problems. Anal. Soc. Issues Public Policy 3 (1), 65–86.

Khattak, A.J., Schofer, J.L., Koppelman, F.S., 1995. Effect of traffic information on commuters' propensity to change route and departure time. J. Adv. Transp. 29 (2), 193–212.

Klauer, S.G., Guo, F., Simons-Morton, B.G., Ouimet, M.C., Lee, S.E., Dingus, T.A., 2014. Distracted driving and risk of road crashes among novice and experienced drivers. N. Engl. J. Med. 370 (1), 54–59.

Knockaert, J., Tseng, Y.-Y., Verhoef, E.T., Rouwendal, J., 2012. The Spitsmijden experiment: a reward to battle congestion. Transport Policy 24, 260–272.

Kopp, J., Gerike, R., Axhausen, K.W., 2015. Do sharing people behave differently? An empirical evaluation of the distinctive mobility patterns of free-floating car-sharing members. Transportation 42 (3), 449–469.

Kusakabe, T., Sharyo, T., Asakura, Y., 2012. Effects of traffic incident information on drivers' route choice behaviour in urban expressway network. Procedia Soc. Behav. Sci. 54, 179–188.

Land Transport and Authority, 2014. Travel Early Travel Free on the MRT. Land Transport and Authority. Accessed Nov, 15, from, https://www.lta.gov.sg/apps/news/page.aspx?c=2&id=c3983784-2949-4f8d-9be7-d095e6663632.

Lee, C., Winters, P., Pino, J., Schultz, D., 2013. Improving the Cost Effectiveness of Financial Incentives in Managing Travel Demand Management (TDM). National Center for Transit Research (US).

Lemp, J., Kockelman, K., 2010. Empirical investigation of continuous logit for departure time choice with Bayesian methods. Transp. Res. Rec. 2165, 59–68.

Lemp, J.D., Kockelman, K.M., Damien, P., 2010. The continuous cross-nested logit model: formulation and application for departure time choice. Transp. Res. B Methodol. 44 (5), 646–661.

Liang, Y., Lee, J.D., Yekhshatyan, L., 2012. How dangerous is looking away from the road? Algorithms predict crash risk from glance patterns in naturalistic driving. Hum. Factors 54 (6), 1104–1116.

Liao, C.-H., Chen, C.-W., 2015. Use of advanced traveler information systems for route choice: interpretation based on a Bayesian model. J. Intell. Transp. Syst. 19 (3), 316–325.

Lindsey, R., Daniel, T., Gisches, E., Rapoport, A., 2014. Pre-trip information and route-choice decisions with stochastic travel conditions: theory. Transp. Res. B Methodol. 67, 187–207.

Liu, W., Li, X., Zhang, F., Yang, H., 2018. Modeling evolution of mode and departure choices in a bi-modal network with user inertia and information provision. In: Transportation Research Board 97th Annual Meeting, Washington, DC, USA.

Lu, X., Gao, S., Ben-Elia, E., 2011. Information impacts on route choice and learning behavior in a congested network: experimental approach. Transp. Res. Rec. 2243 (1), 89–98.

Luten, K., Binning, K., Driver, D., Hall, T., Schreffler, E., 2004. Mitigating Traffic Congestion: The Role of Demand-Side Strategies. FHWA, Office of Transportation Management, Washington, DC.

Luten, K., Binning, K., Driver, D., Hall, T., Schreffler, E., 2006. Mitigating Traffic Congestion: The Role of Demand-Side Strategies. FHWA, Georgia Power Company, Atlanta, GA.

Ma, Y.-L., Zhu, X., Hu, X., Chiu, Y.-C., 2018. The use of context-sensitive insurance telematics data in auto insurance rate making. Transp. Res. A Policy Pract. 113, 243–258.

Martin, E., Shaheen, S., 2011. The impact of carsharing on public transit and non-motorized travel: an exploration of North American carsharing survey data. Energies 4 (11), 2094–2114.

McLaughlin, S.B., Hankey, J.M., Klauer, S.G., Dingus, T.A., 2009. Contributing Factors to Run-Off-Road Crashes and Near-Crashes: Final Report. The National Highway Traffic Safety Administration.

Merugu, D., Prabhakar, B.S., Rama, N., 2009. An incentive mechanism for decongesting the roads: a pilot program in Bangalore. In: Proc. ACM NetEcon Workshop, Citeseer.

Montgomery, J., Kusano, K.D., Gabler, H.C., 2014. Age and gender differences in time to collision at braking from the 100-car naturalistic driving study. Traffic Inj. Prev. 15 (sup1), S15–S20.

National Research Center, 2016. Modal Shift in the Boulder Valley. City of Boulder.

Nurul Habib, K.M., 2013. A joint discrete-continuous model considering budget constraint for the continuous part: application in joint mode and departure time choice modelling. Transportmetrica A: Transp. Sci. 9 (2), 149–177.

Nurul Habib, K.M., Day, N., Miller, E.J., 2009. An investigation of commuting trip timing and mode choice in the Greater Toronto area: application of a joint discrete-continuous model. Transp. Res. A Policy Pract. 43 (7), 639–653.

Podobnik, B., 2002. New urbanism and the generation of social capital: evidence from Orenco station. Natl. Civ. Rev. 91 (3), 245–255.

Qu, M., Zhu, H., Liu, J., Liu, G., Xiong, H., 2014. A cost-effective recommender system for taxi drivers. In: Proceedings of the 20th ACM SIGKDD International Conference on Knowledge Discovery and Data Mining. ACM.

Rapoport, A., Gisches, E.J., Daniel, T., Lindsey, R., 2014. Pre-trip information and route-choice decisions with stochastic travel conditions: experiment. Transp. Res. B Methodol. 68, 154–172.

Razo, M., Gao, S., 2013. A rank-dependent expected utility model for strategic route choice with stated preference data. Transp. Res. Part C Emerg. Technol. 27, 117–130.

Reagan, I.J., McClafferty, J.A., Berlin, S.P., Hankey, J.M., 2013. Using naturalistic driving data to identify variables associated with infrequent, occasional, and consistent seat belt use. Accid. Anal. Prev. 50, 600–607.

Saleh, W., Farrell, S., 2005. Implications of congestion charging for departure time choice: work and non-work schedule flexibility. Transp. Res. A Policy Pract. 39 (7), 773–791.

Scott, D.M., He, S.Y., 2012. Modeling constrained destination choice for shopping: a GIS-based, time-geographic approach. J. Transp. Geogr. 23, 60–71.

Shabanpour, R., Golshani, N., Derrible, S., Mohammadian, A., Miralinaghi, M., 2017. Joint discrete-continuous model of travel mode and departure time choices. Transp. Res. Rec. 2669, 41–51.

Shaheen, S., Cohen, A., Chung, M., 2009. North American carsharing: 10-year retrospective. Transp. Res. Rec. 2110, 35–44.

Shiftan, Y., Bekhor, S., Albert, G., 2011. Route choice behaviour with pre-trip travel time information. IET Intell. Transp. Syst. 5 (3), 183–189.

Stanford University, 2012. Congestion and Parking Relief Incentives (CAPRI). From, https://stanfordcapri.org/welcomeinfo.php.

Sweet, M.N., Chen, M., 2011. Does regional travel time unreliability influence mode choice? Transportation 38 (4), 625–642.

The Washington Post, 2018. This App Wants to Reward You for Smart Commuting Choices. The Washington Post.

Thorhauge, M., Cherchi, E., Rich, J., 2016a. How flexible is flexible? Accounting for the effect of rescheduling possibilities in choice of departure time for work trips. Transp. Res. A Policy Pract. 86, 177–193.

Thorhauge, M., Haustein, S., Cherchi, E., 2016b. Accounting for the theory of planned behaviour in departure time choice. Transport. Res. F: Traffic Psychol. Behav. 38, 94–105.

Thorhauge, M., Cherchi, E., Walker, J.L., Rich, J., 2017. The role of intention as mediator between latent effects and behavior: application of a hybrid choice model to study departure time choices. Transportation 1–25. https://link.springer.com/article/10.1007/s11116-017-9839-2.

University of Washington, 2002. Looking Both Ways:The Past and the Future. 2001–2002 U-PASS Annual Report. .

US National Park Service, 2003. Draft Report on Air Emissions Inventory for Zion National Park. National Park Service.

Wang, J.J., 1996. Timing utility of daily activities and its impact on travel. Transp. Res. A Policy Pract. 30 (3), 189–206.

Xiao, Y., Lo, H.K., 2016. Day-to-day departure time modeling under social network influence. Transp. Res. B Methodol. 92, 54–72.

Xiong, C., Shahabi, M., Yin, Y., Zhou, X., Zhang, L., 2018. Integrated, personalized, real-time traveler information and incentive technology for energy-efficient mobility systems. In: Transportation Research Board 97th Annual Meeting, Washington, DC, USA.

Yang, N., Long Lim, Y., 2018. Temporary incentives change daily routines: evidence from a field experiment on Singapore's subways. Manag. Sci. 64 (7), 3365–3379.

Yang, L., Zheng, G., Zhu, X., 2013. Cross-nested logit model for the joint choice of residential location, travel mode, and departure time. Habitat Int. 38, 157–166.

Yang, Y., Steiner, R.L., Srinivasan, S., 2016. The impact of flexible work hours on trip departure time choices in metropolitan Miami. In: CICTP 2016, pp. 2215–2229.

Yen, B.T.H., Tseng, W.-C., Chiou, Y.-C., Lan, L.W., Mulley, C., Burke, M., 2015. Effects of two fare policies on public transport travel behaviour: evidence from South East Queensland, Australia. J. East Asia Soc. Transp. Stud. 11, 425–443.

Yu, X., Gao, S., Hu, X., 2018. Optimizing vacant taxis' routing decisions: model-based and model-free approaches. In: Transportation Research Board 98th Annual Meeting, Washington, DC, USA.

Yu, X., Gao, S., Hu, X., Park, H., 2019. A Markov decision process approach to vacant taxi routing with e-hailing. Transp. Res. B Methodol. 121, 114–134.

Yuan, N.J., Zheng, Y., Zhang, L., Xie, X., 2013. T-finder: a recommender system for finding passengers and vacant taxis. IEEE Trans. Knowl. Data Eng. 25 (10), 2390–2403.

Yue, J.S., 2014. Nudging Drivers: Sensing, Smartphone Apps and Incentives. Stanford University.

Yue, J.S., Chinmoy, V.M., Deepak, M., Hossein, K.A., Balaji, P., 2015. Reducing road congestion through incentives: a case study. In: Transportation Research Board 94th Annual Meeting, Washington, DC.

Zhang, C., Liu, T.-L., Huang, H.-J., Chen, J., 2018a. A cumulative prospect theory approach to commuters' day-to-day route-choice modeling with friends' travel information. Transp. Res. Part C Emerg. Technol. 86, 527–548.

Zhang, L., Yang, D., Ghader, S., Carrion, C., Xiong, C., Rossi, T.F., Milkovits, M., Mahapatra, S., Barber, C., 2018b. An integrated, validated, and applied activity-based dynamic traffic assignment model for the Baltimore-Washington region. Transp. Res. Rec. 2672 (51), 45–55.

Zhu, X., Hu, X., Chiu, Y.-C., 2013. Design of driving behavior pattern measurements using smartphone global positioning system data. Int. J. Transp. Sci. Technol. 2 (4), 269–288.

Zhu, X., Yuan, Y., Hu, X., Chiu, Y.-C., Ma, Y.-L., 2017a. A Bayesian network model for contextual versus non-contextual driving behavior assessment. Transp. Res. Part C Emerg. Technol. 81, 172–187.

Zhu, Z., Chen, X., Xiong, C., Zhang, L., 2017b. A mixed Bayesian network for two-dimensional decision modeling of departure time and mode choice. Transportation 45 (5), 1499–1522.

CHAPTER NINE

Travel modeling under foreseeable communications-and-mobility technologies: Part I (short-term view)

Yupo Chan*
University of Arkansas at Little Rock, Little Rock, AR, United States
*Corresponding author: e-mail address: yxchan@ualr.edu

Contents

Advances in Transport Policy and Planning, Volume 3
ISSN 2543-0009
https://doi.org/10.1016/bs.atpp.2019.07.003

Abstract

In recent years, one has witnessed rapid advances in communications and mobility technologies. These include breakthroughs in information and communications technology (ICT) on the one hand, and connected vehicles (CVs) on the other. I will review and track the evolution of these advances. Most importantly, I wish to map out the corresponding implications for travel modeling-and-simulation. The discussions will be carried out in two chapters. The current Part I chapter will paint a plausible projection of how the travel modeling community will respond to ICT and CVs as we see it today. The projection is based on existing data and observations, thus lending some credibility to the conjecture. The Part II chapter will speculate on the long-term view, where there is a lot more uncertainty when automated vehicles (AV) join the vehicular fleet. Together, the two chapters offer solid guidelines to deal with what is coming and to deal with uncertainties that are yet to come.

Keywords: Information and communications technology, Connected vehicles, Advanced-traffic management systems, Dynamic traffic assignment, Multiple-discrete-continuous extreme value model

Abbreviations

ATC	air traffic control
AV	automated vehicle
CAV	connected and automated vehicle
CV	connected vehicle
DAPP	dynamic adaptive pathways planning
DOT	decreasing-order-of-time (algorithm)
DRO	distributionally robust optimization
DSRC	dedicated short-range communications
DSS	decision support system
DTA	dynamic traffic assignment
EMGSS	entropy-maximization-with-golden-section-search
FDTF	fundamental diagram of traffic flow
FIFO	first-in, first-out
GEV	generalized-extreme value
ICT	information and communications technology
MDC	multiple-discrete-continuous (model)
MDCEV	MDC extreme value (model)
MNL	multinomial-logit (model)
NHTS	national household travel survey
PRSN	policy-based routing in stochastic networks
RDM	robust decision-making
SDOT	subnet-division-decreasing-order-of-time (algorithm)
TMC	traffic management center
TNCs	transportation network companies
ZOV	zero-occupant vehicles

1. Scope

Communications and mobility technologies are fundamental to today's daily life, from information sharing to economic transactions, and to the execution of leisure activities. Smartphones, the Internet, real-time driving directions, social media, shared mobility services and connected and automated vehicles (CAVs) have increasingly combined mobility with communications in ways that profoundly affect our daily activities, travel, commerce, employment, and housing/industrial locational choices—just to name a few. A connected vehicle (CV) has internal devices that enable it to communicate wirelessly with other vehicles, as in vehicle-to-vehicle (V2V) communication, or with an intelligent roadside unit, as in vehicle to infrastructure (V2I) communication. V2V applications enable crash prevention, and V2I applications enable telecommunication, safety, mobility, and environmental benefits. In contrast, a fully automated vehicle (AV), all driving functionality is handled through onboard computers, software, maps, radar and light detection and ranging (lidar) sensors.

The goal of this chapter is to

- explore the emerging capabilities of ICT, CV and related technologies,
- perform a policy analysis of their mobility implications, and
- identify key transport modeling-and-simulation challenges and opportunities in light of this coming trend.

For the purpose of this and the following chapter, I would like to differentiate between the information part and the communications part lumped under ICT. In our usage of ICT, information technology (IT) goes well beyond its computational connotation and includes innovative enterprise analytical procedures and software to solve mobility problems. Communications technology is also broadly interpreted to include not only advances in telecommunications, but also new ways to facilitate the exchange of information between people, thus paving the way to embrace emerging disruptive technologies.

Following a typical typology in the transportation literature, I will discuss emerging versions of "supply" and "demand" travel models. These include urban and regional traffic management, urban and regional activity-based demand modeling, and urban and regional land-use models. To focus our discussions, we concentrate only on agent-based (AB), disaggregate and microsimulation models, which are judged to be the constructive tools of the future.

As there is a great deal of uncertainties in the future direction of the current technological revolution, there is no axiomatic way to "derive" future modeling guidelines. The default option is through selected "case studies."

Here is how the current chapter is organized. I start with how existing ICT has influenced the way we manage today's travel, illustrating with tangible examples in urban incident traffic management. To most of us, these ICT influences have already been felt, or they are at the verge of implementation. Based on existing practice, I also configure an architecture of how urban and regional traffic will be managed in the age of ICT. Next, I examine the ongoing developments that are yet to be fully accounted for in our modeling efforts, starting with a telecommuting example of a dual-earner family. Discussions focus on changing auto ownership needs in light of CVs, as the family's activity pattern change as a result of telecommuting. I conclude the chapter with a projection on how ICT and CVs will provide shared mobility services for the changing labor demographics such as a dual-earner family, and how it might influence the modeling communit.

2. Instant information

Let me start with reviewing a somewhat familiar example to appreciate the power of today's ICT. New data sources from smartphone applications ("apps" for short) offer the opportunity to revolutionize our modeling efforts. Here, I will point to an example wherein one can study public-transportation travel patterns at very little cost using an app available on smartphones. Many smartphone apps integrate other shared mobility services, such as bike-sharing, car sharing, and ride hailing, thus providing a multimodal perspective not easily captured in traditional data sets. Brakewood et al. (2017) examined such an existing data source from user interactions with a smartphone app called "TRANSIT app." It provides real-time information about existing public-transportation and shared mobility services.

Because TRANSIT app covers more than 125 metropolitan regions, its dataset can be used to identify intercity travelers (in addition to urban travelers). It helps to understand how they use public-transportation in metropolitan areas other than their home city. A simple example of this is shown in Fig. 1. Data from the "locations table" of a 2014-data sample are displayed graphically, showing how an individual traveler used the app in Los Angeles, California; Houston, Texas; and New York City over the course of 5 days. Each colored circle in Fig. 1 represents that individual's interactions with the app on a specific day.

Fig. 1 Example of an individual's multicity transit travel: (A) first day to third day, (B) fourth day, and (C) fourth and fifth days (Brakewood et al., 2017)—Permission Granted.

It can be seen that on the first day (light blue), the app user is observed in the vicinity of the Ontario International Airport near Los Angeles, California. On the following 2 days, this individual uses the app in various areas of the Los Angeles metropolitan region. On the fourth day (pink), the app user has its records in the vicinity of Houston Hobby Airport and subsequently New York LaGuardia Airport. These records imply that she has traveled from Los Angeles to New York and has transferred planes in Houston on the way. On the fifth day, this user has the app records in the Bronx, which is her self-reported home location in the "place marks" table of the app.

The above visualization exercise was conducted to demonstrate three unique aspects of this TRANSIT app dataset. First is the ability to study multicity public-transportation travel. Second is the ability to study multi-agency urban-transit travel including underground rail and buses across jurisdictions (even though not shown explicitly in Fig. 1), and the third is the ability to study multi-modal travel, such as taking bike share to access transit (even though not shown in the give example). While initiated by the user rather than passively generated, these three aspects of the Transit-app dataset have the potential to provide unique travel behavior information that is not easily captured in traditional public-transportation datasets such as travel surveys and automated-fare-collection data.

3. Urban traffic incident management

How do we take full advantage of this type of rich information base? Chan (2017) outlined how ICT-enabled information could respond to current developments in traffic incident management, i.e., managing nonrecurrent traffic surges. Chan identified that arising from ICT is the availability of real-time information from crowd sourcing of information, commensurate with the challenges of big data. Illustrations were drawn from these four core functions of an urban traffic management center (TMC), tasked with resolving any traffic disruptions such as road accidents, fire or chemical spills, and congestion due to sports events:

(a) detecting and resolving an incident (facilitated by crowdsourcing),
(b) monitoring and forecasting traffic (facilitated by CVs serving as sensors),
(c) advising motorists about routing alternatives (facilitated by real-time information), and
(d) configuring traffic control strategies and tactics (facilitated by big data).

I will provide four analytical models that will support the above four functions of a TMC.

Model 1—Stochastic incident management: This model uses a decision algorithm to respond to incidents as soon as an incident is reported, including by crowd sourcing.

Model 2—Microstate spatial inference: This model uses a monitoring (and potentially a prediction) algorithm for inferring traffic along roadways with limited number of sensors or in the absence of sensors, based on information reported on major roadways covered by sensors, including CVs.

Model 3—Dynamic shortest-path algorithm: This model is a way to advise motorists about path choices on the basis of real-time traffic condition, irrespective of the rate of receiving such information and the means by which real-time information is transmitted. This differs from other route guidance systems such as WAZE in that the algorithm is independent of the refreshing rate of transmission.

Model 4—Policy-based routing in stochastic networks: Afforded by the wealth of information source including "big data," this model assists in traffic control by advising motorists about judicious decisions in route choice and travel itinerary. Included in the itinerary advisory are a commuter's best departure time from home and any justifiable en-route wait time on the roadside.

Table 1 illustrates how all four TMC analytical models can take advantage of these ICT advances productively. It focuses on the specific ways these

Table 1 Opportunities arising from modeling-technology synergy.

	"Disruptive" technologies					
	ICT				Transportation	
Model	Real time info	Crowd sourcing	Big data	Data quality	AVs & CVs	Shared mobility services
Stochastic Incident Management Model						
Microstate Spatial Inference Model						
Dynamic Shortest Path Algorithm						
Policy-based Routing in Stochastic Networks model						

models take advantage of the information enabled not only by today's ICT but also by emerging CAVs as well. In the following sections, let us describe each of the four models in some detail, focusing on their analytical innovations as show cases for the IT side of ICT.

3.1 Model 1: Stochastic incident management of asymmetrical network workloads

A study of incident management in central Arkansas was performed by Hu and Chan (2013). Under the current contractual agreement with the state police, towing companies are called on alphabetically to respond to traffic incidents. This practice is followed in the spirit of fairness to all contractors. However, such a practice may result in undue delay in clearing an incident if an unsuitable or distant company is called upon to respond to an accident. Rather than response time, on-scene service time is one of the most useful measures of the effectiveness of incident management. The sooner an incident is cleared, the less the delay to motorists. Aside from speedy reporting an accident, the instant availability of clearance information will—in combination—allow better operational efficiency. In this regard, social media data can be useful for more effective real-time incident response, so is an automated congestion-monitoring method via CVs. INRIX or smartphone-related algorithms can also be used to evaluate realtime travel-time effects of incidents on traffic.

The Hu and Chan stochastic-incident management (SIM) model uses an innovative dispatching policy that employs a linearized, stochastic mixed-integer-programming model, based upon the availability of instant information. In addition to dispatching the required service to a reported (primary) incident, the incident manager at the TMC is now responsible for the optimal allocation of the response vehicle fleet as a whole. This task includes reusing response vehicles (on the road) in addition to dispatching a new vehicle from a garage or a depot. Aside from getting away from an alphabetical assignment of dispatches, this new policy suggests that response vehicles dispatched to reported incidents can, when available, be reused to take care of potential or secondary incidents—or additional incidents triggered by the primary incident—that are reported by crowd sourcing or CVs. The use of such resources is referred to as the proper handling of an "asymmetrical network workload," with asymmetric workload consisting of both primary and secondary incidents.

For a uniform fleet stationed among multiple depots in the study area, suppose an active response vehicle dispatched to a reported incident has finished its assignment and is available to clear a potential incident that has just arisen. The SIM model suggests that an operator should not dispatch another response vehicle from a depot when the (newly) dispatched vehicle's travel time to an incident would be no better than the work time required by the available vehicle to clear the incident onsite. Otherwise, an additional (new) vehicle should be dispatched. In short, a response vehicle can take care of additional incidents (an asymmetric workload) on its way back to the depot after it has cleared a reported incident, thereby relaxing the one-stationed-vehicle, one-incident assumption.

The SIM model is a two-stage stochastic optimization model, where the first-stage decision variables are often referred to as here-and-now decisions and second-stage decisions are referred to as wait-and-see decisions. It consists of an iterative simulation-and-optimization sequence, where the simulation is used to evaluate the existing incident management scheme while the cost-minimization optimization is used to evaluate the proposed scheme in response. The simulation-optimization result shows that, through this new (proposed) policy, the delay cost to the motorists and work time for the contractors were reduced by about 20%. Although the workload decreased, the total number of vehicle dispatches remained the same, since an individual dispatch is accounted for whenever each primary accident occurs. This says that the amount of business (measured in dispatches) given to contractors remain the same. Surprisingly, the model also distributes business among all contractors equitably (measured in work hours). In other words, the number of vehicle dispatches and work time of each of the garages are comparable, no matter where the garage is located and irrespective of the whereabouts of potential incidents. Most importantly, the public is served better and with less inconvenience from delays and it incurs less expenditure by the state police (from whom the towing contractors are paid by their work time instead of by the number of dispatches). The takeaway from this case study is that timely detection and reporting is the key in handling asymmetrical workloads—an aspect that the new ICT/CV technologies can certainly help to provide.

3.2 Model 2: Microstate spatial inference model for network traffic estimation

It is common practice for traffic sensors such as cameras to be deployed on major highways and arterials to monitor heavily-traveled corridors. This practice leaves smaller roads unattended. These minor roadways, however, could very well become important as traffic on major highways is diverted during peak hours and as a result of highway incidents. It is counter-productive to channel traffic from a congested highway to an equally congested side street. Using more cameras, an attempt was made by Castillo et al. (2008) and others to monitor traffic more comprehensively—including on side-streets. Instead of additional cameras, Fowe and Chan (2013) proposed an efficient estimating procedure based on *existing* traffic counts (using existing sensors) on major highways. In addition, one can take advantage of the integration of CV infrastructure and data into existing advanced-traffic management systems (ATMS), with CVs acting as probes for data gathering, instead of the traditional cameras. At the same time, ATMS can mine pooled, big data collected over the network for a rich set of information that was inconceivable in the past.

Based on the *entropy* measure, a model was constructed to define a possible range of traffic volumes considering all the possible turning movements of vehicles when they enter the link and exit from the link. Then a search was conducted within this range following the rule of *golden sections*. Fowe and Chan's entropy-maximization-with-golden-section-search (EMGSS) model was subsequently applied in a central Arkansas case study in at the intersection of Colonel Glenn Road and Interstate 430 in Little Rock—a major shopping area. The Little Rock Traffic Engineering Department provided a 24-h traffic count at 15-min time intervals. These were obtained by seven camera detectors located at the indicated major road segments. It was shown that when some traffic-observing sensors were removed, the estimated traffic volumes were still competitive with the link-volume estimates when all the sensors were present. This finding helps to distinguish between redundant sensors and critical sensors in a network and thus provides a way to economize on the number of sensors. In addition to validation of the algorithm by field data in Little Rock, a controlled experiment with a randomly generated 100-node, 522-link grid network was conducted, and this experiment led to similar results. The derived traffic volumes (on the side streets where no sensors are present) now go into a pool, forming a rich set of "big data" for all to share.

3.3 Model 3: Dynamic shortest-path algorithm for continuous information updates

Real-time traffic management requires accurate information on travel times around the network on a continuous basis. However, the reality is that existing technology falls short of delivering such up-to-date information. As a result, we are unable to measure the point-to-point shortest paths around the network accurately. To achieve the desired computational speed, existing algorithms for time-dependent (or real-time) shortest-path computation call for the unrealistic aggregation of travel time as multiples of a given time increment. In other words, if the refreshing rate of receiving real-time traffic conditions is a 5-min increment, road travel times are estimated at multiples of 5; that is, the travel time on a roadway is either 5 min, or 10 min, or 15 min, and so on. Any fractional travel time, or a more precise travel time estimate, will destroy a dynamic-programming recursion operation. Under this scenario, it is implicitly assumed that within a predefined time increment, such as 5 min, travel speed remains uniform. Admittedly, such a time increment can be varied—for example, between peak and off-peak periods—with a shorter increment for peak travel and a longer increment for off-peak travel. However, this method still has limitations on granularity, which is dictated by the refreshing rate of receiving incoming traffic conditions.

Hu and Chan (2008) proposed an improved solution algorithm for the all-to-one or one-to-all time-dependent versions of the shortest-path calculation. The algorithms are solidly founded on Bellman's principle of optimality (Bellman, 1958) and apply to continuous or real-value link travel-times (rather than the current practice of discrete-time specifications). In other words, the two versions the shortest-path algorithms so employed are shown to yield optimal results. Moreover, by partitioning the task of shortest-path computation into two logical parts as explained below, the fidelity of the travel times so obtained is greatly enhanced. Without loss of generality, suppose time increments are one unit (say one minute) long in a network. We wish to find the time-dependent shortest path between an origin-destination pair. As a first step, we divide the original network into two subnets $P(t)$ and $Q(t)$. $P(t)$ consists of the collection of links with link travel times less than unity. $Q(t)$ consists of the collection of arcs with link travel times greater than or equal to unity. (Notice subnets need not be contiguous.) Chabini's Decreasing Order of Time (DOT) algorithm is applied toward subnet $P(t)$ (Chabini, 1998). A regular static shortest-path algorithm is applied to subnet $Q(t)$. The results are then combined together. The new algorithms are practical in computational speed, and as a result they capture a more realistic and accurate metric for route choice. Most important, a relatively coarse refreshing time increment can be used throughout the analysis and yet be compatible with any continuous or real-value link travel-times, thus providing the finest granularity as required. To support these claims, computational results that considered various network sizes, densities, and numbers of time increments were provided. It was found that the Hu and Chan subnet-division-decreasing-order-of-time (SDOT) algorithm is competitive with the traditional Chabini decreasing-order-of-time (DOT) algorithm (Chabini, 1998) in terms of run time, and can be used in real time for route guidance.

In short, no longer do we need to worry about the traffic information being dated by the time it is received. The accuracy of such real-time information will have profound implication on not only judicious route choice, but also on scheduling much more realistic carpooling arrangements as required in shared mobility services in general. Aside from computer-aided-dispatch sharing, such synergies can also cross fertilize integrated corridor management.

3.4 Model 4: Policy-based routing in stochastic networks with incident risks

The fourth model assists in traffic control by advising motorists about judicious decisions not only in route choice but also travel itinerary which could include an en-route wait time in addition to a delayed departure as speculated by dynamic traffic assignment (DTA). Recognizing the commuters wish to arrive at work by a particular time, an *advanced traveler information system* (ATIS) was used to map a driver's time constraints and risk-taking behavior to real-time routing decisions in a probabilistic time-dependent network (or stochastic network) (Chan et al., n.d.). Thus a risk-averse driver will be directed to a "safer" route away from potential traffic accidents, often incurring a longer travel time by paying a "risk premium." When en-route delays and alternate routings are taken into account, ATIS networks have been shown to exhibit other than the first-in, first-out (FIFO) property; that is, drivers who depart earlier may not arrive ahead of those who depart later. The key is to explicitly consider wait times both at the origin and en-route in order to avoid congestion delays. This generalization of en-route wait time should not come as a surprise, as the DTA literature (Wirtz et al., 2005) clearly shows that delaying one's departure time during rush hours has the potential of avoiding unnecessary delays in a journey to work (Long et al., 2016).

Many ATIS algorithms assume perfect information is available at any time for route guidance. This is no longer a wild assumption today, as we can conveniently rely on private traffic-information services such as INRIX, instead of the capital-intensive, infrastructuarl alternative that involves committing huge public-agency resources to obtain such data.[a] In addition, the Model 3 described above will ensure accurate travel-time information independent of the communications transmission rate. Empirical results were

[a] As of 2007, over 94 U.S. metropolitan markets and 50,000 miles of roads as well as 12 markets and 5000 miles of roads available in the U.K. select INRIX traffic for integration across their navigation and traffic applications (http://inrix.com/press-releases/2598/).

obtained from a central Arkansas highway network that showed the different route choice decisions reflecting the work time constraint and risk-taking attitude of a driver (Chan et al., n.d.). The algorithm was also tested on a randomly generated network of 520 nodes with 1667 links (for a sparse network) and 2990 links (for a dense network). Clock time (*t*) was defined at discrete points as integers 1, 2, 3, etc., for each time increment during which no perceptible change in traffic conditions occurred. The total study-time period (*T*) was varied from 60 min (1 h) to 340 min (approximately 6 h). The proposed behavioral algorithm, solidly founded on Bellman's optimality condition, the fundamental diagram of traffic flow (FDTF), and multi-attribute utility theory, was shown to be operationally feasible for real-time applications. Given the instant information afford by today's technology, this algorithm paves the way for a quality future travel-control-system. This applies to not only conventional vehicles such as the ones in the Central Arkansas study, but also a future network with the presence of CVs.

3.5 Advanced traveler information system (ATIS): An architecture

I will now portray a TMC architecture, built upon the above four models serving as core IT algorithms, and assisted by advances in ICT and CVs. It is organized around three basic building blocks: the input functions, the output functions, and the core IT modeling functions performed by the TMC. Let us describe these three blocks in terms of functions that are performed real-time vs. those that are performed offline.

Real-time module. Through a variety of sensors and input formats, including traffic cameras, cellular floating vehicle data, GPS, social media, satellite surveillance, geographic information system, and crowdsourcing, the TMC is provided instantaneously with travel time, vehicular speed, traffic density, incidents, and weather information (Gong et al., 2015; Zhang et al., 2015). After execution of the four model algorithms, the output from the TMC advises motorists about existing and forecast traffic condition, redirection advisories (if any), issuing alerts and outright commands when necessary. All these are facilitated by variable message signs (VMSs), traffic lights, real-time maps, short message service, interactive voice response and radio—not to mention the Internet.

Offline training module. The efficiency of the above real-time module is assisted by a set of parameters that are calibrated offline, thus freeing the calibration task during actual operations. Based on the relatively low density of the study area, the traffic incidents at both peak hours and off-peak hours are assumed to be Poisson processes (Birst and Smadi, 2000). Based on the 2000–03 dataset, Chan et al. (n.d.) and Hu and Chan (2013) used linear regression to compute the incident occurrence rate. Here the dependent variable is the average number of incidents and the independent variable is the time duration. The 4-year worth of data is ample for estimating the Poisson distributions stratified by the five levels of incident severities. Also calibrated offline is the risk metric for each arc/link. For an ATIS, Chan et al. (n.d.) derived incident-risk probability-metrics separately for peak and off-peak periods. As applied in the FDTF, a binary switch (peak vs. off-peak) will be triggered by the critical concentration at which traffic switch from stable to unstable or meta-stable traffic conditions, resulting in a three-phase determination that includes the meta-flow regime. This is amply reflected in the final probability of incident equation for the risk metric. Again, this was facilitated by the 2000–03 historical data.

Before leaving this section on Urban Traffic Incident Management, I would like to leave the readers with this thought. If the changes in ICT cause work trip patterns to change significantly, such as the rise of telecommuting, the peak travel demands could be defined differently, perhaps based on non-recurrent activities such as sporting events, festivals, holiday periods, or emergency evacuations in locations that are vulnerable to weather emergencies. Modeling incident management now becomes even more important.

4. Regional traffic management

Following the above train of thought, Han (2017) also focused on real-time traffic management of *recurrent* traffic flows, as facilitated by advances in ICT and CVs. Instead of focusing on an existing network, he took a more global view by examining a region-wide network, both for surface transportation and air transportation. Similar to the previous TMC study, his traffic management architecture could conceivably include INRIX and CVs serving as probes for data gathering, and harnessing pooled big databases. In short, much of the ICT/CV opportunities shown in Table 1 can also be exploited in Han's model. Similarly, Han's model can also be a blue print to guide CV implementation at the appropriate time, recognizing that CVs have to be coordinated by a network control system. In fact, the future controlled CV network is really the ATIS of the future. While the Chan study above focuses on incident management, the control-theoretic scheme proposed by Han was applied to two case studies, one in responsive region-wide traffic-signal control and another on air traffic management.

4.1 Offline and online modeling

Han's discussion of real-time traffic management starts with a recent European project, CARBOTRAF (Litzenberger et al., 2012). In addition to relieving congestion, that project aims to adaptively influence traffic in real time to reduce carbon dioxide, nitrogen oxides and black carbon (BC) emissions caused by road transportation in urban and interurban areas. A decision support system (DSS) was developed to use real-time and simulated traffic and emissions data for predicting congestion and emission levels and suggesting appropriate intelligent-transportation-system (ITS) actions, including VMSs and coordinated signal control. Similar to the incident management study above, there is the offline module and an online module—a typical demarcation of computational tasks required for real-time execution efficiency. The CARBOTRAF system has an offline module that performs extensive traffic microsimulation (using S-Paramics and Vissim), emissions estimation (Herrera et al., 2010; Jiang et al., 2013) and pollutant dispersion modeling (Wolf et al., 2014). Input data from the test site in West End of Glasgow, Scotland, include network characteristics, demand profile, meteorological conditions, and so forth. At the outset, Han identified suitable ITS actions with the potential to reduce harmful emissions while maintaining efficient traffic flow. These actions are incorporated in the traffic simulation. The offline module provides a look-up table containing the interrelationship of traffic states, emissions, congestion, and ITS actions.

At the same time, the online module of the CARBOTRAF system serves two main purposes:

- to provide access to real-time data through traffic, meteorological, and air quality sensors and online databases (including big data) and
- to determine in real time the optimal traffic control measure(s) for an effective reduction of congestion and emissions.

The data collection for CARBOTRAF in Glasgow, UK, was performed via the AQWEB Internet-based data collection and management system. It has been deployed in the Glasgow air quality network and across Scotland. The system allows air quality and meteorology sensors to be connected wirelessly to a cloud network through a gateway that standardizes data formats.

A Decision Support System (DSS) combines streaming data and data from the look-up table to rank different candidate ITS actions and makes suggestions to the traffic operator accordingly. The following information is required by the DSS in operation:

- the current ITS action being deployed,
- the probability distributions of traffic-emission objectives for the complete set of alternative actions, which are derived from the look-up table, and
- operational constraints on the set of ITS actions.

However, the application of this approach has the following potential issues and challenges. First, the look-up table is sparsely populated because of limited data or computational resources and could render the generation of an effective statistical model infeasible. In this case, no additional insights beyond simple interpolation are available, and the model objective function reduces to a weighted average between operation cost and the compromised air quality due to congestion. Second, the use of expectation in the stochastic optimization may be susceptible to outliers in the model prediction, and at the same time, sensing data and is not robust enough to handle unknown probability distributions. Third, solving stochastic optimization is computationally expensive and causes operational delays. This is on top of the delays caused by current data-communication latency. In combination, it may render the suggested ITS action sub-optimal when executed in real time. Finally, the current DSS has an inventory of a finite number of ITS actions without more refined decision resolution (for example, incomplete control parameters governing those ITS actions). In the following section, Han illustrated a more general decision support architecture that (partially) addresses these challenges.

4.2 Analytical model for real-time operation

For more general real-time control, a class of *learning-based* models was considered by Han. The decision rule (DR) approach relies on predefined functional forms (either explicit or implicit) to convert real-time traffic states to traffic control parameters. Insurance of the optimality of an arbitrarily defined DR may be achieved by offline training with historical data. Unlike the look-up table approach, the DR approach is based on a continuous interpretation of the response surface in the state-control-objective space. Another important distinction is that the DR approach requires no substantial computation in real time, as all the learning, training, and optimization are conducted offline. Finally, model uncertainties or sensing errors may be accounted for in the offline training phase of the DR in such a way that the robustness of the resulting control is ensured. It is important to note that these DRs, unlike the DSS, are derived methodologically rather than intuitively.

The DR approach can yield a timely decision that allows real-time operation, and its efficacy can be improved to a target degree of optimality through the offline training of the calibrated parameters if desired. The offline training of the DR may be conceptually formulated as an optimization problem with uncertainties. The uncertainties can be handled by robust optimization, in which performance bounds are provided, including the worst case scenarios. However, the proposed *distributionally robust optimization* (DRO) is not based on the worst case parameters. The distributional robustness method is based on a family of probability distributions, the ambiguity set, instead of simply the worst parameters. DRO can be used not only to provide a distributionally robust solution to a problem when the true distribution is unknown, but also to give a general solution taking into account some risk. In short, DRO addresses the inexact nature of the knowledge of the underlying probability distributions in a robust way to ensure sound performance of the resulting decisions. The goal of DRO is to minimize the expectation of a performance function, such as delay or total emission, under the most adversarial realization of the uncertain distribution. Performance optimization is performed during the offline training phase of the DR approach, when a computationally expensive optimization problem needs to be solved. This leaves the online operation rather simple, as it only involves analytical transformation from flow, density, speed, air quality to DR and the performance of such a DR is guaranteed by offline training.

4.3 Regional and air traffic applications

The first application of the DR approach was a responsive signal control strategy for a subnetwork of the Glasgow test site that included five signalized intersections. For this application, the link-transmission model was used to describe traffic dynamics. Historical data on traffic flow and vehicle turning movements were used to conduct a data-driven calibration of the uncertain distribution set. The study period spanned 1 h during the morning peak (8:00–9:00 a.m.). The objective was to maximize the throughput of the entire test network, given real-time vehicle-flow data collected in the network.

The second application implemented the DR approach for online signal control in a synthetic 2 × 2 grid network that was set up in the S-Paramics microsimulation software. The objective was to simultaneously reduce total travel time and total carbon emissions on the network. Average *dynamic* demands for 28 origin-destination (O-D) pairs that were randomly perturbed in multiple simulation runs were prescribed. This allows testing the robustness of the DRO approach. As this was a *multicriteria optimization* problem, the following were considered using responsive signal control:

- minimizing average vehicle travel time,
- minimizing network-wide total carbon emissions, and
- minimizing a weighted sum of travel time and emissions.

As a control experiment, the Webster formula was used to calculate the optimal cycle time and green splits with the aim of minimizing vehicle delays at individual intersections. Being a non-responsive signal control strategy, this serves as a datum for comparison with the other three responsive signal-control alternatives.

I will now discuss a little bit about regional traffic management as pertains to truck traffic. In the longer term, when CV technology enables the following trucks in a platoon to be driven without a driver onboard. As a result, the driver labor costs could be eliminated, leading to a significant operating cost saving (Shladover, 2019). However, this concept has further implications for modeling not only platoons moving on highways, but also staging areas at major freeway entry and exit points (analogous to railroad marshaling yards). It is at these entries and exits that the platoons would be assembled and disassembled and where control would be transferred between drivers and the automation system. Remember that drivers are also needed to perform the local pickup and delivery functions. This is a phenomenon that has not been addressed in classic traffic flow literature and advanced modeling research is recommended.

The final application of the DR framework addresses air traffic management. Han focused on multi-airport systems, which serve air traffic demand in large metropolitan areas (such as New York City). Owing to the spatial proximity of the airports, multi-airport-system airspaces are characterized by heavy demand and enormous complexity. An ongoing project (Sidiropoulos et al., 2015, 2017) seeks to implement the dynamic route service policy (as opposed to the static route structure) for terminal airspaces by designing three-dimensional and conflict-free dynamic routes that accommodate time-varying and uncertain air traffic demands throughout the day. The goal is to reduce delay, fuel consumption, and controller workload—making this a multicriteria optimization problem. Doing this involves (a) the spatial-temporal characterization and clustering of dynamic traffic demand, (b) the prioritization of flight groups in case of conflict, and (c) the design of three-dimensional routes by multicriteria optimization (Sidiropoulos, 2016). With the help of subject matter experts, feasible policies are determined offline in a set of design control parameters, which may be deployed on a pre-tactical level (e.g., 24 h in advance) or operational level (e.g., up to 2 h in advance). This is similar to the DSS approach for regional traffic management described above.

On the operational level, even with traffic demand prediction 2 h in advance, the computational burden does not allow the optimization of design control parameters in real time, especially when prediction errors are considered. To address these issues, a *conceptual* DR approach was considered, in lieu of the DSS-like approach mentioned above. Adaptive control is employed consisting of clustering threshold control, route priority control, and optimization parameters. This has proven to be responsive to the demand prediction. It was applied to different stages of the design, and this process resulted in the key performance indicators including delay, fuel consumption, and controller workload. The error between the predicted and realized demand was factored into the performance objective function.

The main source of uncertainty lies in the traffic demand forecast, which encompasses numerous attributes, including operation type (arrival vs. departure), O-D airport, weight class (small, large, heavy vs. super-heavy), user type (passenger vs. cargo), O-D type (domestic vs. international), and flight direction. It is extremely difficult to estimate the marginal or joint distribution of the prediction error associated with these attributes. To resolve this problem, the DRO approach was again invoked by calibration of the uncertainty set for the objective function through simulation. Han reported a case study using historical, time-based flow management data provided by the Port Authority of New York and New Jersey.

4.4 Summary

In sum, Han (2017) presented a general methodology framework for real-time regional traffic management, based on the state-of-the-art, current driver behavior and current ATC practice. In the surface transportation application, the motivation for the study was the eventual implementation of CAVs, which will be ultimately controlled by an automated traffic management scheme. The DR approach combined with DRO offers a range of solutions for tackling some of the challenges of the real-time DSS approach. First, the DR approach approximates the response surface with linear or nonlinear forms and when combined with DRO yields more reliable decisions as compared with a possibly sparse look-up table with a finite number of scenarios. Second, the DRO is a very effective approach to handling uncertainties not only in the variables but also in their distributions, which cannot be accurately estimated in practice because of an insufficient sample or complex dependence structure, particularly in air traffic control (ATC). The DR framework allows all the expensive computations to be done offline, which makes on-line decision rather efficient and suitable for real-time operation. In addition, the issue of delays in transmitting data in real time can be addressed by a careful design of the DR.

There is only a major and significant unknown left. For the Glasgow study and the TMC study, it is the behavior of drivers after the introduction of CVs, which results in a mixed vehicular fleet. For the ATC study, it is the implementation of new ATC strategies, which shifts the burden from centralized control to *human coordination* among aircraft. In the United States, for example, the Next-Generation Air-Transportation-System (NextGen) examines how to overhaul the United States national airspace system. *Free flight* is a developing air traffic control method that uses no centralized control by air traffic controllers. Instead, parts of airspace are reserved dynamically and automatically in a distributed way among aircraft using computer communication to ensure the required separation between aircraft. Similarly, the Single-European-Sky ATM Research program plans to develop new methods, technologies, procedures, and systems to accommodate air traffic needs in Europe for 2020 and beyond.

In order to design the right modeling-and-simulation tools, let us ask ourselves several thought-provoking questions based on the discussion up to this juncture. In our past modeling efforts, one often spent more time in data collection than in analysis. Obviously, this has changed with the advent of ICT and CVs wherein data is plentiful. A question remains as to whether activity/travel information given nearby land-use information can be facilitated with as much ease as regular travel information to pave the way for the next generation of activity-based demand models? Second, using accelerometers and gyroscopes from two smartphone platforms as well as two reference points, one can currently determine the optimal number of driving-behavior clusters for traffic management. However, is there a way to predict the behavior of drivers after the introduction of CVs, which get mixed into the traffic stream? Would the physics of traffic flow still work? Third, can the above analysis tools identify for us the full range of benefits we can expect to reap from traffic management systems (TMS) of the future—including TMCs, real-time regional traffic control, and ATC? I are talking about benefits through integration of new IT (e.g., stochastic optimization, DRO, and most critically offline and online demarcation of computational tasks), and use of new sources of ICT/CV data. More importantly, can these models help pinpoint the new TMS functions to be developed, the new services to be provided, or the improvements in performance to be achieved? We will keep this questions in mind as we move from traffic operations management (the supply side) to demand modeling.

5. Urban activity-based demand modeling

Having discussed traffic management in some depth, I will now identify some desired properties of an urban travel model under emerging ICT and CVs, with the latter playing an increasingly influential role for urban travel. With tremendous uncertainty facing the modeling community, however, I will start with a simple example just to initiate some thoughts. As motivated by ICT advances and the changing demographics of the workforce, telecommuting is in the increase, as one can work remotely as much as at the traditional work place for most service industries (Paleti and Vukovic, 2017). Let us examine the associated telecommuting behavior, concentrating on a growing number of *dual-earner* households in recent decades due to the demographic shift in the labor force. Given the rise of telecommuting, choices in multi-worker households become more complex, including the related activity-time-use choices of all members of the household. In other words, what do the household members do with the extra time a bread earner (or both bread earners) saved by telecommuting? The authors developed an innovative model for analyzing the frequency of telecommuting in dual-earner households. A companion model studied activity-time-use decisions while accounting for household-level interaction effects (Paleti and Vukovic, 2017).

Data from the 2009 National Household Travel Survey (NHTS), which collected detailed demographic and travel-diary information from a representative population in the United States, were used to undertake the empirical analysis. The responses to the following question in the survey formed the basis for explaining the telecommuting choice in this study: "How many times in the last month did you work only at home for an entire work day instead of traveling to your usual workplace?" The survey recorded travel-diary information at a very *disaggregate* activity-purpose segmentation. For the purposes of this study, these activity-purpose alternatives were aggregated into eight broad categories: home, work, escort, shopping, maintenance, eating out, visiting, and discretionary. A host of explanatory variables was considered in the analysis, including the following:

- demographic characteristics (age, gender, educational attainment, immigration status, disability status, and attitudinal variables),
- work characteristics (degree of work flexibility, part-time work status, work industry, and commute distance), and
- household characteristics [income, housing tenure, presence of children in three age groups (0–5, 6–10, and 11–15 years), and auto ownership].

5.1 Effects of ICT

The Paleti and Vukovic study developed generalized-extreme value (GEV) models that are consistent with the random-utility-maximization (RUM) framework—the prevailing modeling approach for travel-demand modeling (Bhat, 2002).[b] Furthermore, such an approach will cut across a spectrum of familiar activity-based models, including the multinomial-logit, the nested logit and the cross-nested logit. *Activity-based (AB) models* are based on the principle that travel demand is derived from people's daily activity patterns. Activity-based models predict which activities are conducted when, where, for how long, for and with whom, and the travel choices people will make to complete those (Chu et al., 2012). Having this type of detailed model at their disposal allows researchers, practitioners, and policy makers to evaluate the effect of alternative policies on individuals travel behavior at a high level of spatial and temporal resolution and select the best policy alternative considering a potential wide range of performance indicators. The activity-time-use preferences were modeled by Paleti and Vukovic as multiple-discrete-continuous (MDC) in nature because each worker, having more discretionary time from telecommuting, can choose to invest time in a

[b] The GEV distribution is a family of continuous probability distributions developed within extreme value theory to combine the Gumbel, Fréchet and Weibull families, which are also known as type I, II and III extreme-value distributions. Extreme value theory or extreme value analysis deals with the extreme deviations from the median of probability distributions. It seeks to assess, from a given ordered sample of a given random variable, the probability of events that are more extreme than any previously observed. By the extreme value theorem—which states that a real-valued function must attain a maximum and a minimum—the GEV distribution is the only possible limit distribution of properly normalized maxima of a sequence of independent and identically-distributed random variables.

different combination of activities (e.g., shopping, social, active recreation) for a different duration. The study used the MDC extreme value (MDCEV) model that has served as the standard workhorse for analyzing such MDC choices within the RUM framework (Enam, 2017).

Several consumer demand choices are characterized by the choice of multiple alternatives simultaneously. An example of such a choice in activity-travel analysis is the type of discretionary (or leisure) activity to participate in and the duration of the participation. In this context, within a given time period (say a day or a week), an individual may decide to participate in multiple types of activities (for example, in-home social activities, out-of-home social activities, in-home recreational activities, out-of-home recreational activities, and out-of-home non-maintenance shopping activities). Bhat (2005) derived and formulated a utility theory based model for discrete/continuous choice that assumes diminishing marginal utility as the level of consumption of any particular alternative increases. In other words, the satisfaction slopes off after overindulging in an activity. This assumption yields a multiple discreteness model (i.e., choice of multiple alternatives can occur simultaneously). This is in contrast to the standard discrete-choice model that assumes the absence of any diminishing marginal utility, leading to the commitment of a particular activity. We refer to it as the case of strictly single discreteness. The multiple discreteness model so formulated, the MDCEV model, has a surprisingly simple and elegant closed-form for the discrete-continuous probability of not consuming certain activities and consuming given levels of the remaining alternatives. The MDCEV model has the appealing property that it collapses to the familiar multinomial-logit (MNL) choice model in the case of single discreteness. Finally, heteroscedasticity and/or correlation in unobserved characteristics affecting the demand of different alternatives can be easily incorporated within the MDCEV model framework using a mixing approach.

Under this scheme, Paleti and Vukovic proposed these two models—based on the final sample size after extensive data cleaning—of 2111 dual-earner households:

(a) A GEV-based joint count model of the monthly telecommuting frequencies of workers in dual-earner households.

(b) A panel MDCEV model of the activity-time-use decisions of the two workers in the family conditional on their telecommuting choices.

The NHTS questionnaire was administered to respondents continuously throughout the year, so the telecommuting frequency data do not correspond to the same calendar month for all workers. During the model estimation, therefore, the statistical significance of 12 monthly indicator variables for the month of the survey day was checked. However, none of these dummy variables was significant in the telecommuting frequency model. It was concluded that a random set of 30 days is adequate for understanding long-term telecommuting patterns.

Here are the findings related to model (a). The calibrated model suggests that men were less likely to telecommute than women. Age did not have an influence on telecommuting frequency choices. Workers born in the United States tended to telecommute less frequently than immigrants. Workers who had significant concerns regarding safety were more inclined to telecommute than those who did not. Workers with a bachelor's or a higher degree telecommuted more frequently than other workers. Part-time workers telecommuted more frequently than full-time workers. Workers employed in manufacturing and construction, administration, and professional fields were found to telecommute less frequently than workers employed in other types of industries. Now consider workers in households in which there were more cars than adults of driving age. These workers telecommuted less frequently than workers in households in which the number of cars owned was the same as or less than the number of adults of driving age. Overall, the results indicate the ability of a GEV-based joint-count modeling framework to better explain telecommuting frequency data, compared with a majority of other mixed discrete-choice models (Bhat, 2003). The Paleti and Vukovic findings suggest superior data fit in the GEV version of the count models and strong evidence for the presence of intra-household interactions in decisions about telecommuting frequency. In turn, telecommuting frequency determines the discretionary activity and travel patterns of members of the household, including the type of activity to participate in and the duration of the participation.

Here are the findings related to model (b). The home activity was chosen as the reference alterative for the baseline marginal utility specification. Relative to home activity, workers were least likely to invest time in visiting activities and most likely to invest time in work activity. This translates to telecommuting, wherein work is performed at home rather than at the regular work location. Men were found to be more likely to go into work than women, even though both had the option to telecommute. Men were also more likely to eat out and spend time in discretionary activities, but they were less inclined to partake in shopping, maintenance, and escort activities. Older workers were more likely to avail themselves of their option to telecommute and not go to the workplace, but they tended to undertake more escort, shopping, and maintenance activities. Workers with a disability were less likely to participate in work, escorting, and discretionary activities but were more prone to invest time in maintenance activities. This is understandable, given that hospital and personal care are sub-activities under maintenance. Higher educational attainment was associated with higher likelihood of participation in non-mandatory activities and lower inclination to go into work. Workers who considered safety to be a big issue were more likely to invest time in escorting. This is probably indicative of parents who are concerned with safety decide to escort their children to and from school. Workers born in the United States were more likely to invest time in discretionary activities than were immigrants. Paleti and Vukovic's independent MDCEV model indicates that telecommuting choices have considerable influence on the discretionary activity-time-use patterns of workers. This underlines the importance of accounting for intra-household interaction effects in activity-time-use choices.

In sum, here are the merits of the methodological framework developed in the Paleti and Vukovic study in light of advances in the IT part of ICT:

- Unlike past studies, the modeling components for telecommuting and time-use choice were consistent with the RUM theory, which is the commonly used decision-making mechanism in choice modeling in spite of some of the implicit assumptions (Cascetta, 2009).
- The study findings confirm the presence of strong intra-household interaction effects in both the telecommuting choices and the activity-time-use choices in the new demographic labor force consisting of dual-income households. Bernardo et al. (2015) corroborated the importance of considering household structure in activity-based travel demand models, as well as re-designing work policies in the United States to facilitate a reduction in work-family conflict in dual-earner families.
- Also, telecommuting was found to have a significant effect on time-use decisions in both mandatory and non-mandatory activities. This reflects a widespread influence of the effect of ICT not only on inducing telecommuting, but also in its fallouts to other non-work activities.

There are several avenues for possible modeling improvements in the future. First, the present study analyzed monthly telecommuting choices as opposed to the decision to telecommute on a given day—mainly due to data availability. Panel surveys (or the equivalent data gathered by ICT means) that record telecommuting and activity-travel choices over multiple days can significantly enhance the understanding of interactions between telecommuting and time-use decisions. It will allow a more disaggregate level of analysis.

Second, households who prefer telecommuting can relocate to suburban locations further out from the city in the long term, which will lead to changes in residential location patterns. The Paleti and Vukovic study did not have the longitudinal data to account for these potential interaction effects between a telecommuting and residential location preference—a topic I will pick up later in the following chapter.

Third, the MDCEV model requires the time budget as an external input.[c] In the study, the available time for activity participation was assumed to be known and fixed before running the model. Therefore, the allocation of the total available time to different activities could change, but not the total available time itself. Recently, researchers developed supplementary log-linear regression and *stochastic frontier models*[d] to estimate the budget for MDC models on the basis of the idea that people work with *latent* budgets (Augustin et al., 2015; Pinjari et al., 2016), or a more flexible budget that is based on the circumstance. These methods can be used to resolve the endogenous budget problem of the MDCEV model.

Fourth, the time-use component currently takes the form of a panel MDCEV model that operates at the person level. A better modeling framework to account for intra-household interactions is a household-level formulation that accommodates multiple budget constraints (or two constraints in the case of dual-earner households) (Bhat et al., 2013; Castro et al., 2012).

Fifth, Ben-Elia et al. (2014) studied interrelationships between ICT, activity fragmentation and travel behavior. The concept of fragmentation relates to how activities are spatially and temporally reorganized—by subdividing activities into smaller components that are then performed at different times and/or locations. Their results demonstrate that these interrelationships are quite complex. ICT and fragmentation apparently have a reciprocal relationship with mobile ICT use influencing the degree of spatial fragmentation. In other words, increased usage will result in less fragmentation. At the same time, the usages of sedentary ICT are influenced by the degree of temporal fragmentation. The more one's time is fragmented, the more usage of sedentary ICT. Person-ICT attributes and ICT use mediate the participation in nonwork activities, and can replace work and

[c] Golob et al. (1981) proposed a model of traveler behavior that suggests urban travelers expend average daily amounts of time and money on travel with stable regularities. This time budget is found to be consistent among urban areas and over time in the same area.

[d] The stochastic frontier model was first proposed in the context of production-function estimation to account for the effect of technical inefficiency. The inefficiency causes actual output to fall below the potential level (that is, the production frontier) and also raises production cost above the minimum level (that is, the cost frontier).

nonwork travel. Between spatial and temporal fragmentation, work trips are reduced, nonwork personal travel possibilities are restricted, and time could reallocated for leisure activity and travel. Back to telecommuting, Ben-Elia and Ettema (2011) found out that—well beyond the factors that were unveiled by Paleti and Vukovic—the way to change commuting behavior is influenced by such additional factors as education, scheduling, habitual behavior, attitudes, and travel information availability.

5.2 Foreseeable effects of CV

Driven by ICT, the Paleti and Vukovic model is a very specific travel estimation model based on several assumptions. First, multi-vehicle ownership refers to a fleet of conventional vehicles, mainly due to the database that was employed. However, the modeling analysis could easily include ownership of a mixed fleet of conventional and CVs, as long as we can characterize the attributes of a CV in an MDCEV model. Second, the example models only the interactions among wage earners within the family. In a more general context, car sharing can involve other families, such as by carpooling or by commercial means, including today's active transportation network companies (TNCs) such as Uber and Lyft (Fagnant et al., 2015). Third, Paleti and Vukovic focused on telecommuting and its fallouts. It is obvious that other daily activities—setting aside telecommuting—could be the fallout of ICT, now a business or social meeting can be conducted via the Internet instead of face-to-face. In short, one should really view the above modeling effort with a much broader lens, as I am trying to do immediately above and again reexamine below.

In addition to ICT, I will now discuss the introduction of a fleet of privately-owned or commercial CVs on urban travel, with CVs arriving in the near future. Disaggregate modeling systems such as the MDCEV and AB models in general are suited to evaluating a mixed fleet of conventional vehicles and CVs with some modifications (Zmud et al., 2018). The following structure of a disaggregate modeling chain focuses on individual characteristics of the people and vehicles in the system tracing from demand modeling to route choice, paving the way to examine the immediate future:

Synthetic population → Long-Term Choices → Mobility Choices → Daily Activity Patterns → Tour and Trip Details → Trip Assignment → Dynamic Traffic Assignment (DTA).

An attractive feature of AB models (such as the Paleti and Vukovic study) is the feasibility of using a large number of household and person characteristics in the models. Because each household and person is simulated separately, each can have its own set of socio-demographic characteristics. To operate an activity-based microsimulation model, information at this level of detail—although collected in a population census—has not been made available in the public domain due to privacy and confidentiality reasons.[e] To fulfill this fundamental data requirement, population can alternatively be synthesized using various techniques. The distribution of those characteristics across the population is controlled through population synthesis. In the synthesis process, distributions of key variables such as income, household size, number of workers, and age group are controlled at a detailed geographic level such as census tract, census block group, or traffic analysis zone. Many software applications for population synthesis have been developed over the years (Moeckel, 2017; Zhu and Ferreira, 2014).

While construction of a synthetic population is the first step in the above modeling chain, DTA is the last step in this chain. In DTA methods, the trend is toward microscopic dynamic-assignment that simulates each vehicle's trajectory and each driver's behavior on the network (as discussed in the "Policy-Based Routing in Stochastic Networks (PRSN)" model under Section 3). Rather than using fixed lane capacities and speed-flow relationships, DTA reveals traffic congestion levels and effective capacities through the simulation of vehicles navigating the roads and intersections. Because no observed data exist on how the introduction of CVs will affect aggregate speed-flow relationships, as represented in the FDTF, the use of a simulation method that can represent detailed differences in the ways that human drivers and CVs will navigate road networks together may be the most promising approach of learning how CVs will influence traffic. Use of DTA methods for region-wide long-range forecasting is still in the initial implementation stages, but combining DTA with AB demand models may become more widespread as the methodology matures and ICT-enhanced network data become more plentiful and accessible, as was discussed in Section 3.4.[f]

The infiltration of CVs into the existing vehicle fleet will be under the "Mobility Choices" step of the above modeling chain. To represent private CV ownership, an auto ownership model can be enhanced to predict

[e] This picture is changing with the emergence of new data sources such as mobile phones, call detail records and smartcard transactions (see Brakewood et al., 2017; Chan, 2017).

[f] The Multiagent Transport Simulation (MATSim) model [http://www.matsim.org] uses agent-based and activity-based microsimulation to model traffic and transportation dynamics based on daily activity-travel plans. Given the microscopic nature of MATSim, the travel behavior of individuals who have access to communications technologies can be modeled conceivably in a future version of the model. Recently, it has been successful in modeling emerging modes such as TNC and AV.

both the number and type of vehicles—CV or conventional. The simplest approach is to make it an all-or-nothing choice between owning CVs and conventional vehicles, in which a household first chooses what type of vehicle to buy and then how many. A more complex approach would be mixed ownership, in which a household first chooses how many vehicles to purchase and then what type. Most current AB models used in practice enforce travel schedule consistency for persons but not for vehicles. Remember that the latter case needs to be considered for telecommuting and carpooling situations that include today's TNCs. As a result, these new data on vehicle ownership could be used to influence travel behavior rather than constrain individual travelers to specific vehicles, as I have illustrated in the multi-vehicle family with the Paleti and Vukovic model.

The types of variables that can be used to model the choice between CVs and conventional vehicles may include:

- Socio-demographics such as age and income,
- Relative purchase costs of CVs vs. conventional vehicles,
- Incentive policies to encourage CV ownership, including conventional vehicle trade-in,
- Relative operating costs of CVs vs. conventional vehicles,
- Accessibility/utility difference of using a CV for home-work commutes and other destinations—for example, a reduced disutility of in-vehicle time for CVs would make it more attractive for long trips, and,
- Parking costs that might be avoided with a self-parking or TNC-owned CV. Here, self-parking includes "Trained Parking" in which a car can be "taught" to find a parking place.

Transportation planners might also consider an interaction between the number and type of vehicles owned. For example, planners could assume that households choosing to purchase a CV would be more likely to own one vehicle rather than two vehicles, because the CV—with its highly automated communication features—could serve as a private taxi to take both would be drivers to their destinations. I will come back to this point in more detail in Section 6. (It will certainly influence the telecommuting choices of a dual-earner household.) This assumption, along with most of the assumptions used to represent CVs in the models, is clearly speculative and not based on any real data. Thus, it is important to use the models initially in an *exploratory* way to investigate the implications of different assumptions. It is also important to refine the assumptions over time as new data become available from stated-preference data and (eventually) actual-purchase decisions of CVs.

For the other types of mobility models, planners could consider modeling membership in a CV-sharing club or group. The high purchase cost and taxi-like usage of CVs may encourage shared ownership across households that uses some type of shared scheduling app similar to taxis and TNCs but is limited to a small set of owners—and at the limiting case, a multiple-earner household. This would presumably offer a lower shared purchase-and-maintenance cost, but with the inconvenience of not having the vehicle at hand all the time (Viegas and Martinez, 2017).[g]

Remember that our discussion on PRSN has generalized DTA to en-route waiting, well beyond waiting at home before (say) a morning commute. PRSN can identify different vehicle-following distance and speed characteristics, depending on the level of vehicle automation. If these vehicles are traveling in mixed traffic, then overall travel times are generated for all vehicles. If separate facilities—such as roadside units—are considered for CVs, then it is important to separately track the travel times for CVs and conventional vehicles.

Another area in which PRSN models can provide insight is the repositioning of CVs when not in use. This is also referred to as zero-occupancy vehicles (ZOVs) when traveling without a passenger.[h] This repositioning will occur for both privately-owned and fleet-operated CVs. Repositioning to pick up another passenger can be directly simulated from the drop-off and pick-up locations of each passenger. (The scheduling task can be accomplished by the SIM model under Section 3) Repositioning that is used to avoid parking costs can be more difficult, as the parking locations for these trips may not be predetermined. Nonetheless, the inclusion of these ZOV trips is critical to understanding congestion in the system. These PRSN and SIM simulations can offer insight into the performance impact on the transportation system and, in turn, the impact on traveler behavior.

---

[g] Carrying this concept further is shared Mobility as a Service (MaaS). Ultimately, we bring together individual MaaS options—both public and private—in one place. These options include trains, buses, ride hailing and sharing schemes for cars, bikes and scooters, taxis, and shuttles/pods for first and last mile connections to high-capacity, fixed-route service or point-to-point service when fixed-route service does not exist or is infrequent. In this way, we leverage the latest digital innovations to provide an integrated point-to-point service to users accessible via a single mobile application (app) and payment channel similar to today's TNCs.

[h] In the context of PRSN here, CVs (or AVs) waiting to pick up new riders will add "deadheading" miles. If a single-occupant vehicle is to be blamed for traffic congestion, think twice about a zero-occupant vehicle! Putting the picture together, this means CAVs will likely increase vehicle-miles traveled, energy use, and emissions (https://mobility21.cmu.edu/what-is-our-plan-for-zero-occupancy-vehicles/—accessed 15 July, 2019).

6. Modeling implications of connected (and automated) vehicles

The above discussions focused on how one might take advantage of ICT (and CV) introduction to further our existing travel modeling effort, and how to structure future models to include ICT/CV. The two modeling examples cited above on traffic management and telecommuting give some guidelines on how to do this. However, they beg the question of how *emerging* ICT and CAVs in combination might impact the prevailing travel modeling paradigms *in general*. The most speculative aspect will be predicting travel behavior in the context of CAVs, thus presenting a fundamental framework for travel modeling; and presenting approaches for planning under the many other uncertainties that surround CAVs. In a recent study, Zmud et al. (2018) studied the challenge of describing the emerging CAV technologies and their likely influences upon their adoption timelines. Shladover (2019) discussed the implications that development and deployment of CAV technology could have for the future of the Interstate Highway System. Based on these studies, let us translate their findings into modeling implications, paving the way for our discussion in the next chapter, entitled "Travel Modeling under Emerging Communications and Mobility Technologies: Long-Term View."

Looking through and beyond the short term, a framework for travel modeling in the presence of CVs (and AVs) includes five elements: (1) data, (2) planning context, (3) model configuration, (4) CV/AV adoption timeline, and (5) communication of uncertainty to decision makers. Traditionally speaking, the first three elements—data, planning, and model configuration—combine to create a prediction environment. Such a prediction environment includes developing a vision for transportation in a region, setting target goals and performance measures, collecting available data, building models from the data, and using models in either a predictive or an exploratory mode to evaluate alternative transport investments. By having control of (1), (2) and (3), our premise is that we can have a handle on planning the future, although its execution is by no means straightforward. The fourth element—CV/AV adoption timeline—concerns the timeline for the advancement and adoption of CAVs, much of it are factors exogenous to the modeling community. Following the CV and AV adoption timeline as promulgated by the Society of Automotive Engineers, I have conceptualized in Table 2 the likely travel impacts at each level of automation (from "Level 0—No Automation" through "Level 5—Full

Table 2 Impact of each automation level.

<table>
<tr><th colspan="2" rowspan="2">Automation scenario</th><th>Level 0</th><th>Level 1</th><th>Level 2</th><th>Level 3</th><th>Level 4</th><th>Level 5</th></tr>
<tr><th>No automation</th><th>Driver assistance</th><th>Partial automation</th><th>Conditional automation</th><th>High automation</th><th>Full automation</th></tr>
<tr><td colspan="2">Definition</td><td>The driver performs all driving tasks</td><td>Some driving-assist features may be included in the vehicle design</td><td>Vehicle has combined automated functions, such as acceleration and steering</td><td>Driver is a necessity, but is not required to monitor the environment</td><td>Vehicle is capable of performing all driving functions under certain condition</td><td>Vehicle is capable of performing all driving functions under all condition</td></tr>
<tr><td colspan="2">Example automation features</td><td>Automatic emergency braking; blind spot warning; lane departure warning</td><td>Lane centering OR adaptive cruise control</td><td>Lane centering AND adaptive cruise control</td><td>Traffic jam chauffeur</td><td>Local driverless taxi; pedals/ steering wheel may or may not be installed</td><td>Same as level 4, but feature can drive everywhere in all conditions</td></tr>
<tr><td rowspan="5">Impacts</td><td>Cost</td><td></td><td></td><td></td><td colspan="3">Distributed vehicle ownership?</td></tr>
<tr><td>Safety</td><td></td><td></td><td colspan="4">Some safety issues remain elusive</td></tr>
<tr><td>Operations</td><td></td><td colspan="5">Coordination of flow may reduce queuing and congestion</td></tr>
<tr><td>Fuel</td><td></td><td></td><td></td><td></td><td colspan="2">Shared AV will alter infrastructure</td></tr>
<tr><td>Mobility</td><td></td><td colspan="5">Mobility-limited persons gain increased mobility</td></tr>
</table>

Automation"). These impacts, to be discussed in detail, will have profound implications on modeling.

Expected areas of impact of CV-and-AV adoption on travel are critical considerations for modelers as explained below:

Transportation cost impacts. There are two types of costs associated with automation. The first is the increased manufacturing cost, and the second is the infrastructure cost to support the introduction of automation, such as roadside units. While cost of CVs in the short run, through "Level 2—Partial Automation" is likely to be borne by the individual owners, costs of vehicles that include highly automated technology will need to be recouped by manufacturers. As a result, the ownership cost per vehicle is likely to increase, particularly starting at "Level 3—Conditional Automation." However, the cost per trip may decline if fleet services of driverless vehicles prevail in the market, as may be the case at "Level 5—Full Automation." Thus, the overall transportation cost to the consumer is uncertain and is most likely tied to private vehicle ownership vs. distributed vehicle ownership, vehicle club membership, or ride sharing. As cost is a key input to any travel model, this cost uncertainty has to be explicitly factored into future travel models.

Transportation safety impacts. CVs at Level 0 have been around for quite some time, and they have been assimilated into the auto fleet. Projecting from this experience into Levels 1 and 2, it is likely that such features as "lane centering" and "adaptive cruise control" will be accepted by the public. However, going beyond Level 2, it is critical that the CVs and AVs have to be proven totally safe before any adoption can take place—as debates are continuing on the elusiveness of safety assurance. No doubt, a reduction in crashes would improve the reliability of travel times and reduce property damage, injuries, and fatalities. Improved reliability, in turn, would increase the utility of CVs and AVs, growing their market share. As reliability—particularly travel time reliability—is a key input to today's travel models, the safety factor must be carefully included in the next generation of travel models.

Vehicle operations impacts. Much research has focused on connecting vehicles—both passenger vehicles and freight vehicles—through dedicated short-range communications (DSRC) or wireless technology into platoons of vehicles, which would dramatically shorten headway space and thereby improve coordinated acceleration/deceleration and vehicle throughput. The overall impact would be to increase capacity, with most estimates arriving at a doubling of existing roadway capacities. However, platooning requires increased space to be executed, particularly at staging areas at major freeway entry and exit points. As a result, the prospect of increased capacity may be diminished where formation and dissolution of platoons are frequent. In the longer term, however, the prospects of positive impacts from vehicle operations of an automated fleet are expected to be impressive. While groups of platooned vehicles may or may not improve intersection and freeway operations, the coordination of flow through synchronized arrivals and reserved time and space (such as dedicated lanes during morning or evening commutes) may indeed prove to reduce queuing and congestion.

Fuel impacts. As indicated in Table 2, there is likely minimal fuel impact on CVs (through Level 3). Beyond that we are transitioning into AVs. AVs of the future are likely to be electric vehicles. An AV that runs autonomously and is shared in a public-transport mode is called a shared autonomous vehicle (SAV). If SAVs are used, the individual user would not need to be concerned with charging/refueling the vehicle, a "nagging" feature of electric vehicles. The burden would fall upon the fleet owner/operator, who would use optimizing algorithms to reduce cost. The introduction of AVs into the vehicular fleet would not only have an enormous impact on the petroleum industry, but also on fuel-delivery services, gas-station land-use, and the need for strategically-located electric-refueling stations. This would in turn have profound implication on land-use modeling, setting aside modeling SAV operations.

Personal mobility and convenience impacts. If CVs and AVs prevail in the marketplace as the U.S. population ages, the prospect of older adults, young teens, and mobility-limited persons gaining increased transportation freedom could greatly improve. Such benefits would be felt as early as Level-1 automation, when lane centering or adaptive cruise control will relief the driver of some burden of driving. In the long run, these individuals could also benefit in a scenario of privately-owned AVs if the cost of the vehicles is not prohibitive. Relieving a driver from the monotonous task of driving will free up the commuting time for more productive and creative activities. In this light, the (dis)utility and (in)convenience of commute time—through which the value/worth of travel time is typically imputed—is going to decrease. A key modeling issue is how the perception of the cost of travel time will change if today's drivers become passengers in SAVs and if the capital cost of vehicle ownership is replaced by paying capital, maintenance, and operations costs on a per-trip basis.

The last element in framing future travel-modeling effort is communication. This refers to person-to-person communication, rather than "telecommunications." It involves the need for the analyst to convey the level of uncertainty associated with the modeling results to decision makers and stakeholders, given hard data are yet to be available. A situation that modelers/analysts commonly face is a de facto interpretation of analysis results as predictive. A better method is to determine at initial project scoping whether the analysis is going to be based on predictive, data-supported modeling (where data is available for some CV operations) or on exploratory techniques, which is different from prediction. Going beyond the short term, the context of planning for CAV technology is one of deep uncertainty about the impacts, infrastructure needs, deployment timeline, market penetration, design, engineering, and many more aspects associated with such automation. CAVs are expected to be disruptive, but that is the only certainty about which the modeling community generally agrees.

7. Summary

There have been advocacies for advancing modeling techniques to anticipate ICT and CVs. Similarly, the current chapter paints a plausible near-term projection of how the travel modeling-and-simulation community will respond to ICT and CVs as we see it today. Since there is no axiomatic way to "derive" the modeling strategies for the future, I adopted a case study approach. Citing an urban and a regional traffic management case study and a telecommuting effort—representing a supply model and a demand model—I illustrated how such a projection could be done based on existing data and observations, thus lending some credibility to the conjecture. To build a model, the first requirement is data availability. The state-of-the-art in keeping and searching data is progressing by leaps and bounds. With improved ITS infrastructure and communications technology, hot-spot analyses performed with incident management data for freeway networks and arterials have become a much more promising alternative, particularly in conjunction with spatial statistics, which provide better insights into spatio-temporal information (Songchitruksa and Zeng, 2010). Aside from using such data for monitoring *nonrecurrent* traffic patterns, I also showed how innovative modeling practices can be equally adept in monitoring *recurrent* (commuting) traffic. I emphasized the use of *offline* training of the calibrated parameters to supplement an *online* tracking of traffic. The end result is an *agile* model that can be executed on a real-time basis. However, it is clear that no one has the complete data that accurately describe the future, even the near term when ICT and CV data are available. A significant unknown is the behavior of drivers after the introduction of CVs in the traffic stream. We would hope that the physics of traffic flow still holds for us to analyze vehicular flow. Let us put ourselves in the future tense when CVs are already part of the vehicular fleet, together with private ride sharing companies, they collect granular data (e.g., exact volume, time of day, O-D, length, speed) that can better inform important urban and regional transportation planning or modeling stakeholders. But, from the private-sector perspective, sharing this level of detail might jeopardize not only the individual's privacy but also the firm's business practices and intellectual property. Balancing these factors is a distinct challenge to public-/private-sector data sharing. In a nutshell, it reflects the many non-technological challenges modelers face (National Academies of Sciences, 2018).

Supplementing the supply models is a demand model on telecommuting, reflecting the demographic changes in today's workforce when there is more than one bread earner in the family, in addition to the prevalence of ICT. Consistent with random utility models, the extreme value modeling components used to analyze telecommuting among households found out some interesting results. First, there is presence of strong intra-household interaction effects in both the telecommuting choices and the activity-time-use choices. Second, telecommuting has a significant effect on time-use decisions in both mandatory and non-mandatory activities. Third, such a model requires the time budget as an external input. A more prudent approach is to estimate the budget on the idea that people work with latent budgets. To better account for intra-household interactions is a household-level formulation that accommodates separate budget constraints of dual-earner households. These findings have profound implications on the future generation of activity-based modeling.

As a two-chapter sequence, I wish to examine the modeling efforts in a much broader scope than just anticipating technological changes and carrying out these efforts all the way from model construction to calibration. The point has been mentioned previously, but it deserves to be mentioned again under a different lens. For our modeling suggestions regarding the advent of ICT, included in IT is not only computation, but also innovative modeling techniques. Included in communications are person-to-person dialogs to convey the level of uncertainty associated with any modeling recommendations. This is in addition to the conventional "communication devices" such as smartphones, computers, Internet, CVs and radio, etc. By these expanded definitions, the reader can see how different the way of thinking has to be in coming up with guidelines for future travel modeling efforts in light of emerging technologies—i.e., we have to think "outside the box."

As we progress with our discussions in this chapter, we introduced an increasing level of uncertainties as we moved from a short-term view to a longer-term view, paving the way for the following chapter. As pointed out by Shladover (2019), we should remember that we are dealing with a complicated mix of information technology, vehicle technology, and infrastructure technology. These three domains are radically different in their product life cycles and investment horizons. Although information technology is on the fast track, with product functional lifetimes measured in months, vehicles are designed for functional lifetimes of years, and civil infrastructures must be designed to last for decades. These differences are to a large extent inherent in the capital intensity of the products and production processes associated with each industry, so we should not expect vehicles and civil infrastructures to change as rapidly as mobile phones and their application software. This incongruity poses further uncertainty regarding how the mix will fit together, and how one can model travel in the future.

Acknowledgments

The author wishes to acknowledge the intellectual stimulations received from participating in the Chan Wui and Yunyin Rising Star Workshop in June 2016 on board the MS Queen Mary 2, focusing on the subject of the "Analytical Relationship between Mobility and Communications" (https://commons.ualr.edu/chanrsworkshop/). This chapter synthesizes and expands the 2017 journal papers of the eminent participating Workshop scholars that span North America and Europe. The synthesis is supplemented by the latest thoughts and literature up to, 2019, the time of this writing. As seen by the references, much of the material contained in this chapter is borrowed from the writings of the various participants of this Workshop, including C. Brakewood, G. Erhardt, K. Han, E. Miller, R. Moeckel, and R. Paleti. Last but not least, I owe deep gratitude to E. Ben-Elia, editor of this volume, for his many insightful suggestions during my writing. Obviously, the author alone bears any self-generated errors while composing this chapter. Funding of this study came from the anonymous foundation that supported the Workshop.

References

Augustin, B., Pinjari, A.R., Eluru, N., Pendyala, R.M., 2015. Estimation of annual mileage budgets for a multiple discrete-continuous choice model of household vehicle ownership and utilization. Transp. Res. Rec. 2493, 126–135. https://doi.org/10.3141/2493-14.

Bellman, R., 1958. On a routing problem. Q. Appl. Math. 16, 87–90.

Ben-Elia, E., Alexander, B., Hubers, C., Ettema, D., 2014. Activity fragmentation, ICT and travel: an exploratory path analysis of spatiotemporal interrelationships. Transport. Res. A Policy Practice 68, 56–74.

Ben-Elia, E., Ettema, D., 2011. Changing commuters' behavior using rewards: a study of rush-hour avoidance. Transp. Res. F 14 (5), 354–368.

Bernardo, C., Paleti, R., Hoklasc, M., Bhat, C., 2015. An empirical investigation into the time-use and activity patterns of dual-earner couples with and without young children. Transp. Res. A 76, 71–91.

Bhat, C.R., 2002. Random utility-based discrete choice models for travel demand analysis. In: Goulias, K.G. (Ed.), Transportation Systems Planning: Methods and Applications, first ed. CRC Press, Boca Raton, FL, pp. 25–61. (Chapter 10).
Bhat, C.R., 2003. Econometric choice formulations: alternative model structures, estimation techniques, and emerging directions. In: Resource Paper for Workshop Entitled "Econometric Models of Choice: Formulation and Estimation" 2003 International Association for Travel Behaviour Research Conference, Lucerne, Switzerland.
Bhat, C.R., 2005. A multiple discrete–continuous extreme value model: formulation and application to discretionary time-use decisions. Transport. Res. B Methodol. 39 (8), 679–707.
Bhat, C.R., Goulias, K.G., Pendyala, R.M., Paleti, R., Sidharthan, R., Schmitt, L., Hu, H.-H., 2013. A household-level activity pattern generation model with an application for Southern California. Transportation 40 (5), 1063–1086. https://doi.org/10.1007/s11116-013-9452-y.
Birst, S., Smadi, A., 2000. An application of ITS for incident management in second-tier cities: a Fargo, ND case study. In: Proceeding of Mid-Continent Transportation Symposium. Iowa State University, Ames, Iowa.
Brakewood, C., Ghahramani, N., Peters, J., Kwak, E., Sion, J., 2017. Real-time riders—a first look at user interaction data from the back end of a transit and shared mobility smartphone app. Transp. Res. Rec. 2658, 56–63.
Cascetta, E., 2009. Transportation Systems Analysis: Models and Applications, second ed. Springer, Berlin, New York.
Castillo, E., Conejo, A.J., Menendez, J.M., Jimenez, P., 2008. The observability problem in traffic network models. Comput. Aided Civ. Inf. Eng. 23 (3), 208–222. https://doi.org/10.1111/j.1467-8667.2008.00531.x.
Castro, M., Bhat, C.R., Pendyala, R.M., Jara-Díaz, S.R., 2012. Accommodating multiple constraints in the multiple discrete–continuous extreme value (MDCEV) choice model. Transp. Res. B Methodol. 46 (6), 729–743. https://doi.org/10.1016/j.trb.2012.02.005.
Chabini, I., 1998. Discrete dynamic shortest path problems in transportation applications: complexity and algorithms with optimal run time. In: Transportation Research Record 1645. TRB, National Research Council, Washington, D.C., pp. 170–175.
Chan, Y., 2017. Telecommunications- and information technology–inspired analyses—review of an intelligent transportation systems experience. Transp. Res. Rec. 2658, 44–55.
Chan, Y., Fowe, J.A. , Arani, M., n.d. (forthcoming). Routing in a stochastic network with non-recurrent incidents: a behavioral interpretation of dynamic traffic assignment, *ASCE ASME J. Risk Uncertain. Eng. Syst. A Civ. Eng.*
Chu, Z., Cheng, L., Chen, H., 2012. A review of activity-based travel demand modeling. In: Proceedings: The Twelfth COTA International Conference of Transportation Professionals. ASCElibrary.org. https://doi.org/10.1061/9780784412442.006.
Enam, A., 2017. Development and application of advanced econometric models for exploring activity-travel behavior. In: A Dissertation Submitted in Partial Fulfillment of the Requirements for the Degree of Doctor of Philosophy at the University of Connecticut, Storrs, Connecticut.
Fagnant, D.J., Kockelman, K.M., Bansal, P., 2015. Operations of shared autonomous vehicle fleet for Austin, Texas, Market. Transp. Res. Rec. 2536, 98–106. https://doi.org/10.3141/2536-12.
Fowe, A., Chan, Y., 2013. A microstate spatial inference model for network traffic estimation. Transport. Res. C Emerg. Technol. 36, 245–260. https://doi.org/10.1016/j.trc.2013.08.011.

Golob, T.F., Beckmann, M.J., Zahavi, Y., 1981. A utility-theory travel demand model incorporating travel budgets. Transp. Res. B 15B (6), 375–389.

Gong, Q., Adams, T.M., Wang, X.B., 2015. Estimating link travel time with sparse GPS data on highway corridors. Transp. Res. Rec. 2477, 7–17. https://doi.org/10.3141/2477-02.

Han, K., 2017. Framework for real-time traffic management with case studies. Transp. Res. Rec. 2658, 35–43.

Herrera, J.C., Work, D.B., Herring, R., Ban, X.J., Jacobson, Q., Bayen, A.M., 2010. Evaluation of traffic data obtained via GPS-enabled mobile phones: the mobile century field experiment. Transport. Res. C Emerg. Technol. 18 (4), 568–583. https://doi.org/10.1016/j.trc.2009.10.006.

Hu, J., Chan, Y., 2008. Dynamic shortest path algorithm for continuous arc travel times: implication for traffic incident management. Transp. Res. Rec. 2089, 51–57. https://doi.org/10.3141/2089-07.

Hu, J., Chan, Y., 2013. Stochastic incident management of asymmetrical network workloads. Transport. Res. C Emerg. Technol. 27, 140–158.

Jiang, S., Fiore, G.A., Yang, Y., Ferreira, Jr., J., Frazzoli, E., González, M.C., 2013. A review of urban computing for mobile phone traces: current methods, challenges and opportunities. In: Proceedings of the 2nd ACM SIGKDD International Workshop on Urban Computing. Association for Computing Machinery, New York. https://doi.org/10.1145/2505821.2505828.

Litzenberger, M., Ponweiser, W., Schramm, M., Paukerl, A., Marcinek, M.-S., 2012. CARBOTRAF—a decision support system for reducing CO2 and black carbon emissions by adaptive traffic management. In: Schrenk, M., Opovich, V.V. (Eds.), Proceedings REAL CORP 2012 Tagungsband 14–16 May 2012, Schwechat. http://www.corp.at ISBN 978 – 3 – 9503110 – 2 - 0 (CD-ROM); ISBN 978 – 3 – 9503110 – 3 - 7 (Print).

Long, J., Szeto, W.Y., Gao, Z., Huang, H.J., Shi, Q., 2016. The nonlinear equation system approach to solving dynamic user optimal simultaneous route and departure time choice problems. Transp. Res. B Methodol. 83, 179–206. https://doi.org/10.1016/j.trb.2015.11.005.

Moeckel, R., 2017. Modeling the impact of communications technologies on travel behavior and land use. Transp. Res. Rec. 2658, 8–16.

National Academies of Sciences, Engineering, and Medicine, 2018. Socioeconomic Impacts of Automated and Connected Vehicles. The National Academies Press, Washington, DC. https://doi.org/10.17226/25359.

Paleti, R., Vukovic, I., 2017. Telecommuting and its impact on activity–time use patterns of dual-earner households. Transp. Res. Rec. 2658, 17–25.

Pinjari, A.R., Augustin, B., Sivaraman, V., Faghih Imani, A., Eluru, N., Pendyala, R.M., 2016. Stochastic frontier estimation of budgets for Kuhn–Tucker demand systems: application to activity time use analysis. Transp. Res. A Policy Pract. 88, 117–133. https://doi.org/10.1016/j.tra.2016.03.013.

Shladover, S.E., 2019. Connected and automated vehicle technology impacts on future interstate highway system. In: National Academies of Sciences, Engineering, and Medicine. Appendix F in Renewing the National Commitment to the Interstate Highway System: A Foundation for the Future. The National Academies Press, Washington, DC. https://doi.org/10.17226/25334.

Sidiropoulos, S., 2016. A Framework for the Optimization of Terminal Airspace Design in Multi-Airport Systems. PhD dissertation, Imperial College, London.

Sidiropoulos, S., Majumdar, A., Han, K., Schuster, W., Ochieng, W.Y., 2015. A framework for the classification and prioritization of arrival and departure routes in multi-airport systems terminal maneuvering areas. In: Presented at 15th AIAA Aviation Technology, Integration, and Operations Conference, Dallas, Texas. https://doi.org/10.2514/6.2015-3031.

Sidiropoulos, S., Han, K., Majumdar, A., Ochieng, W.Y., 2017. Robust identification of air traffic flow patterns in metroplex terminal areas under demand uncertainty. Transport. Res. C Emerg. Technol. 75, 212–227. https://doi.org/10.1016/j.trc.2016.12.011.

Songchitruksa, P., Zeng, X., 2010. Getis-ord spatial statistics to identify hot spots by using incident management data. Transp. Res. Rec. 2165, 42–51. https://doi.org/10.3141/2165-05.

Viegas, J., Martinez, L., 2017. Transition to shared mobility: how large cities can deliver inclusive transport services. In: Corporate Partnership Board Report. International Transport Forum. OECD. https://www.itf-oecd.org/transition-shared-mobility.

Wirtz, J.J., Schofer, J.L., Schulz, D.F., 2005. Using simulation to test traffic incident management strategies: the benefits of preplanning. Transp. Res. Rec. 1923, 82–90. https://doi.org/10.3141/1923-09.

Wolf, J., Bachman, W., Oliveira, M., Auld, J., Mohammadian, A.K., Vovsha, P. Zmud, J., 2014 *NCHRP Report 775: Applying GPS Data to Understand Travel Behavior, Vol. II. Guidelines*, Transportation Research Board of the National Academies, Washington, DC, https://doi.org/10.17226/23436.

Zhang, S., Tang, J., Wang, H., Wang, Y., 2015. Enhancing traffic incident detection by using spatial point pattern analysis on social media. Transp. Res. Rec. 2528, 69–77. https://doi.org/10.3141/2528-08.

Zhu, Y., Ferreira Jr., J., 2014. Synthetic population generation at disaggregated spatial scales for land use and transportation microsimulation. Transp. Res. Rec. 2429, 168–177. https://doi.org/10.3141/2429-18.

Zmud, J., Williams, T., Bradley, M., Kalra, N., Row, S., 2018. Updating Regional Transportation Planning and Modeling Tools to Address Impacts of Connected and Automated Vehicles. Volume 1: Executive Summary and Volume 2: Guidance. NCHRP Research Report 896, Transportation Research Board, Washington, DC.

Further reading

Mobility 21, 2019. What is our plan for zero-occupancy vehicles? accessed 15 July 2019. https://mobility21.cmu.edu/what-is-our-plan-for-zero-occupancy-vehicles/.

CHAPTER TEN

Travel modeling under emerging communications and mobility technologies: Part II (long-term view)

Yupo Chan*
University of Arkansas at Little Rock, Little Rock, AR, United States
*Corresponding author: e-mail address: ychan@alum.mit.edu

Contents

Advances in Transport Policy and Planning, Volume 3
ISSN 2543-0009
https://doi.org/10.1016/bs.atpp.2019.07.004

Abstract

In recent years, one has witnessed rapid advances in telecommunications and mobility technologies. These include breakthroughs in information and communications technologies (ICT) on the one hand, and connected and automated vehicles (CAVs) on the other. I will review and track the evolution of these advances. Most importantly, I wish to map out the corresponding implications for travel modeling-and-simulation. The discussions were carried out in two chapters. In contrast to the Part-I chapter which focuses on the short-term view, the current Part-II chapter is much more speculative, as I dive into the unknowns of the future. The unknowns pertain particularly to the alternate future scenarios and how stakeholders respond under them, representing the most tenuous aspect of analysis. Aimed at stimulating more thoughtful discussions, I include "visioning," which includes not only exploring where modeling-and-simulation is heading, but also guiding where we should be going.

Keywords: Information and communications technology (ICT), Connected and automated vehicles (CAV), Agent-based (AB), disaggregate and microsimulation models, Vissim micro-simulation tool, Activity generation-and-scheduling, Scenario based analysis

Abbreviations

A&E	adoption and engagement
ACC	adaptive-cruise-control
AGS	activity generation and scheduling
AV	automated vehicle
CACC	cooperative adaptive cruise control
CAV	connected and automated vehicle
CV	connected vehicle
DL	dedicated lane
DSH	dynamic speed harmonization
DTA	dynamic traffic assignment
DSRC	dedicated short-range communications
FDTF	fundamental diagram of traffic flow
GPL	general purpose lane
HOV	high occupancy vehicle
ICT	information and communications technologies
I2V	infrastructure-to-vehicle
IoT	internet of things
IDM	intelligent driver model
LDT	long-distance travel
IPF	iterative-proportional-fitting
MATSim	multiagent transport simulation
MITO	microsimulation transportation orchestrator
NLDTM	national long-distance travel model
PRSN	policy-based routing in stochastic networks
PDF	probability density function
PMF	probability mass function

S&P social & professional
TGS tour generation and scheduling
TNCs transportation network companies
V2I vehicle-to-infrastructure

1. Scope

While the Part-I chapter highlighted the existing influence of ICT and connected vehicles (CVs) on transportation modeling, the current Part-II chapter outlines the likely implications for future efforts. While the previous chapter concentrates mainly on ICT, which has been around for quite some time, this chapter will focus more on connected and automated vehicles (CAV), still an incoming technology at the time of writing. In other words, ICT has already established a partial history, making it more tractable. Even with the introduction of Connected Vehicles, CAV is still much under development in general, and accordingly a majority of its travel implications are still unknown. Again, I wish to comment on both supply and demand models—as I did in the previous chapter—ending with urban and regional development models that require a really long-term outlook.

Traffic management models (or supply models) in part build upon some physical laws, such as the theory of traffic flow. By contrast, demand models are built upon behavioral sciences, which are by far less precise. Most researchers tend to agree that ICT and CAVs are disruptive technologies[a] that could change travel behavior dramatically. The combined ICT/CAV implications would ultimately determine the directions toward which both travel supply and demand models are heading. At the same time, one should also be mindful of the demographic changes that are occurring worldwide, including the composition of the labor force, life time expectancy, and life style changes. Anticipating these potential changes, I configure—to the extent possible—some strategies for traffic-management and travel-demand modeling. In the current Part-II chapter, I put forth more nebulous predictions and exploratory discussions on future supply-and-demand modeling in general.

[a] In 2009, Milan Zeleny described high technology as disruptive technology. Disruptive technology refers to any enhanced or completely new technology that replaces an existing technology, rendering it obsolete. Because disruptive technology is new, it has certain advantages, enhancements and functionalities over competitors. As an unused, unapplied and untested alternative, it takes time for disruptive technology to be dominantly deployed, ultimately degenerating into an existing technology. Such an evolutionary life cycle occurs in the use and development of any technology.

While the traffic-management recommendations in the Part-I chapter are mainly based on existing ICT and CV impacts, I will start here with an exploration to include CAV impacts on dedicating lanes for their priority or exclusive use in the near future. Since I have already discussed *urban* travel demand models under the telecommuting example, I choose to follow up with *regional* demand models in the current chapter. This is motivated by the fact that the full impact of ICT is likely to be felt not necessarily by urban/short-distance travel, but by regional/long-distance travel. It is in long distance travel that the full "substitutional" and "complementary" effects between physical and virtual travel come about (Larsen et al., 2006). In other words, ICT enables virtual travel that replaces some physical travel. At the same time, virtual presence in an attractive destination could stimulate more physical travel to such an attractive place. Notice that such effects are gradually unfolding as the population gets to assimilate not only ICT, but also CAVs. Setting aside other costs, the advantages of AVs are fully felt in long distance travel, when the transit time, a "sunk cost" in conventional automobile travel, can now become productive in performing meaningful activities. By contrast, such effects are much muted in urban travel, showing up mainly in the form of telecommuting and shared mobility modes. Parenthetically, long-distance travel modeling is by far is much more challenging considering the scarcity even of current data, not to say future data.

Based on my observations on both urban and long distance travel, a "second generation" of activity-based models is then proposed. To the extent that the two chapters are geared toward structuring future modeling efforts to respond to the rapid changes in technologies, I have answered this call in proposing a future generation of activity-based *demand* models. Upon completing this mission, I moved onto urban and regional development models, visioning not only the presence of Internet-of-Things (IOT), but also the emerging Smart Cities of the future, where CAVs morph into shared mobility services, which is regarded by many as the transportation system of the future, when passengers simply "hail a ride" and shippers depend solely on vehicles that move by themselves to deliver shipments. The current chapter ends with a possible architecture for modeling-and-simulation in the long run. With the fast pace of technological developments and its uncertain impacts upon travel behavior, however, the architecture I lay out is by no means definitive. While carefully thought out, my observations and recommendations have plenty of room for further discussions and refinement by the professional community.

2. Methods for managing deep uncertainty

Given the uncertainty that surrounds the introduction of CAVs, how do we prepare for its eventual implementation? Following Zmud et al. (2018) and Shladover (2019), I will describe both a qualitative method and a quantitative method below. The most common qualitative method for addressing uncertainty is scenario planning.

Scenario planning constructs diverse and often divergent narratives about the long-term future. A family of scenarios aims to span the range of plausible futures relevant to the decision at hand. The aim is for planners to use those scenarios to consider how near-term policies might shape and be shaped by those futures.

Assumption-based planning hinges on identifying load-bearing assumptions, defined as assumptions that, if broken, would require major revision of the course of action. Obviously, we are most interested in the vulnerability of those load-bearing assumptions. For example, a plan for shared automated vehicles (SAVs) hinges on the assumption that it will save ownership cost. This assumption might be vulnerable if the price of a CAV becomes affordable due to mass production. Assumption-based planning guides organizations in determining a course of action to deal with the vulnerability of load-bearing assumptions once they are identified.

In response to the difficulty of linking scenarios to policy choices when applying qualitative methods, many have turned to quantitative methods for decision making under deep uncertainty.

Robust decision making (RDM) rests on a simple concept. Rather than using models and data to assess decision options under a single set of assumptions, RDM runs models over a large number of assumptions to describe how plans perform in many plausible conditions. Unlike Monte Carlo analysis, which attaches probabilities to those assumptions to estimate expected outcomes, RDM uses simulations and other tools to stress-test strategies and helps decision makers identify robust strategies—those that perform well regardless of the assumptions or future conditions—and unveil the key trade-offs among them. Under the broad category of RDM may be the specific example of distributionally robust optimization (DRO) that I discussed in the section entitled "Regional Traffic Management" (Section 4 of the chapter "Travel modeling under-foreseeable communications-and-mobility technologies"), where explicit stage-wise optimal decisions are obtained.

Info-gap theory also helps decision makers identify robust options, but it takes a somewhat different tack from RDM. Remember that RDM uses models to assess the performance of options in a wide range of potential future conditions and then identifies conditions to which the system is vulnerable. In contrast, info-gap uses models to compute how options perform as a function of uncertainty. An info-gap analysis produces a graph showing the performance that planners can robustly achieve on one axis as a function of uncertainty on the other axis. In these graphs, the options plotted at the upper right part are less plausible, as it is associated with a high degree of uncertainty. By contrast, the lower left part is more reliable. Info-gap does not provide decision makers with the solution; rather, it informs decision makers on risks, vulnerabilities and trafeoffs by examining the option plotted out by these graphs.

A third quantitative method is Dynamic adaptive pathways planning (DAPP). With the DAPP approach, a plan is conceptualized as a series of actions over time. These are called "pathways" in response to how the future actually unfolds. The DAPP approach recognizes that policies or decisions have a design life and might fail as the operating conditions change. Once actions fail, other actions are needed to achieve the stated objectives, and a series of pathways emerges one after another. At predetermined trigger points, the course can change while the objectives are still to be achieved. By exploring different pathways and considering the path-dependency of actions, planners can design an adaptive plan that includes short-term actions and long-term options.

I will illustrate how these can be implemented by using several case studies, ranging from dedicating lanes for priority and exclusive use by AVs, to Orlando I-4 Express lanes application. Recognizing the profound and highly unpredictable implications of ICT and CAVs on future travel, the goal is to identify implications on future travel modeling strategies to anticipate the future, rather than simply predicting the future outright. However, the uncertainty surrounding the evolution of ICT and CAVs is acute enough, setting aside the even more unpredictable reaction of the traveling public to these technologies. Aimed at the modeling-and-simulation communities, some plausible recommendations will be provided on future analytical efforts on developing the responsive travel analysis tools to "crystal ball" the future.

3. Traffic management for connected and automated vehicles

There has been a lot of talk about CAVs, commensurate with a flurry of activities worldwide in testing their implementation in selected sites and applications. CAVs are developing rapidly, and manufacturers and shared fleet operators suggest that fully automated CVs will not likely be present on the highway system in significant numbers until the year 2038 (Shladover, 2019). In other words, there will be quite some time before CAVs will replace the traditional automobile fleet that has dominated the human landscape for decades. Aside from passenger traffic, CAV technology will produce a variety of innovations in urban freight distribution, especially with the potential for smaller and more specialized delivery vehicles that could operate without drivers under certain operational design domains restrictions (Shladover, 2019). These will probably have more of an impact on local urban traffic than on highway operations, although there could be some impacts on metropolitan highways near goods distribution hubs. With the eminence of such emerging retail giants as Amazon, modeling such traffic cannot be ignored.

In the near future, however, one of the incentives for greater market penetration of CAVs is dedicating lanes for their priority or exclusive use. To prepare for this change, some guidance is needed related to

- the implications in terms of safety, mobility, and environmental and societal considerations,
- the conditions amenable to dedicating lanes for priority and exclusive use by CAVs, and
- the laws and regulations regarding dedicating lanes.

To arrive at this guidance, we need an analytical procedure, or a model, to trace out the impact on high-occupancy-vehicle (HOV) lanes by the introduction of CAVs.

3.1 The analysis

To respond to the requirement, Booz Allen Hamilton et al. (2018) began with a literature review to identify categories of benefits and dis-benefits when dedicating lanes to a special category of vehicles. The literature review also identified the stakeholders who benefit (or do not benefit) from dedicating lanes to CAVs, factors influencing these benefits, and the performance measures: (1) mobility, (2) safety, (3) environmental considerations, and (4) societal equity. Building on that review, the team used an analytical process that applied computer-based simulation models—rather than field testing—to identify variables and measures sensitivity of dedicating lanes to CAV users. Booz Allen Hamilton et al. formulated a simulation-based analysis of two CAV applications: Cooperative Adaptive Cruise Control (CACC) and Dynamic Speed Harmonization (DSH).

In response to the objectives of these two book chapters, I focus on the modeling-and-simulation part of the Booz Allen Hamilton et al. study. The project team utilized modeling-and-simulation-based analysis to evaluate potential benefits and parametric sensitivity of CAV penetrations on overall traffic efficiency and safety. Six frameworks were evaluated for CACC modeling, and eight frameworks were evaluated for DSH modeling. This helped to identify appropriate algorithms for use. Accordingly, the team selected the CACC model by Lee et al. (2014) and the DSH model by Ma and Li (2016). Both models were developed for the PTV Vissim micro-simulation tool—a commercial, off-the-shelf, multimodal microscopic traffic-simulation software in which each entity (e.g., a car, train, pedestrian) is simulated individually. For this study, they were integrated into a unified programming interface so that they could work together or in isolation.

Vissim's ability to isolate the behavior of each entity is one of the most crucial elements for CACC-concept implementation. Lee et al. (2014, 2016) used a customized version of Vissim to conduct evaluations of the impact of CACC dedicated-lane (DL) on traffic flow. In their 2014 study, Lee et al. focused on DL uses for CACC-equipped vehicles, with a set of lane-changing models for the interactions between the CACC lane and adjacent general-purpose-lane (GPL). The simulation was conducted using Vissim and its Application Programming Interface (API) and Component Object Model (COM) modules. For their 2016 research, Lee et al. developed a CACC add-on package made up of three major modules—a Vissim Network module, a Simulation Manager module, and a customized API module.

Lee et al. used these types of car-following behavior for their analysis:

- Vissim's default car-following model consisting of psycho-physical car-following for non-CACC drivers.
- The Intelligent Driver Model (IDM) for adaptive-cruise-control (ACC) vehicles to represent the lead vehicle of a CACC platoon.
- A customized IDM to manage CACC longitudinal maneuvers.

Both the ACC and CACC models were based on the collision-free IDM and were implemented using Vissim's driver-behavior API. Compared to other models, Lee's Vissim-CACC model can assess the potential system-wide benefits, such as total travel time, total throughput, total delay, and average speed, under a wide range of traffic conditions. In addition to the network-wide performance evaluation, it can also evaluate the localized impacts of CACC, such as mainline travel time and headway distribution at a certain location for safety analysis. In the Booz-Allen-Hamilton et al. study, CAV DLs were deployed on a multilane freeway corridor with multiple interchanges producing the wide variety of lane-changing activities (see below for further details). Such a corridor would have existing dedicated/exclusive lane facilities, such as an HOV/HOT lane with a barrier and HOV/High-Occupancy-Toll (HOT)-dedicated access ramp. It is necessary to examine the collective impacts of CAV/DL strategies on adjacent corridors.

Depending on the benefit/dis-benefit categories examined, evaluations of CAV/DL strategies can incorporate a wide spectrum of performance measures. Producing proper performance measures is the most critical requirement for the modeling tools for CAV/DL analysis. Qualitative performance measures for societal justice such as equity and perception of exclusivity were excluded from the forthcoming summary-evaluation table. By contrast, almost all mobility measures are available through the selected modeling tool.

Combining Vissim tools with external environmental models such as MOVES (U.S. EPA, 2016) and the VT-Micro Model (Rakha and Ding, 2003) could enable estimation of the environmental impacts of CAV DL strategies. Obtaining safety measures appeared challenging, however, as Vissim could not generate the necessary number of crashes and crash severity. Methods such as the Safety Impact Analysis (SAI), developed by Carter et al. (2009), could be used to enhance these tools to account for safety. The SIA is a systematic approach for evaluating the safety impacts of a new vehicle system by incorporating historical crash, driver performance, and system performance data to enable a rigorous comparison between baseline and treatment vehicle crash conflicts. SIA has been used to assess the safety impacts of vehicle-to-vehicle (V2V) technologies (Harding et al., 2014). As Harding et al. had already used SIA in assessing safety impacts, the project team could use the Surrogate Safety Assessment Model (FHWA, 2008) in this study by integrating it with Vissim modeling tools. This would provide estimates of surrogate measures such as time to collision, post encroachment time, and speed difference. Other measures, mainly required for planning purposes, were unavailable from the selected modeling tool.

The next task included development of case-study models to conduct simulation-based analysis of CAV applications to evaluate their impacts on DL scenarios. The project team conducted a four-step process to utilize the models to conduct the simulation-based analysis: (1) develop baseline models, (2) integrate CAV application models, (3) develop scenarios for the simulation-based assessment, and (4) measure the performance of the applications.

Development of the baseline models involved a calibration of Vissim-based models to represent real-world operational conditions and certain hypothetical operational conditions. Integration of CAV application models required the development of CACC and DSH models to work within Vissim's API, along with conducting preliminary testing to compare and calibrate the vehicle behavior to field data. Based on the following six research issues, the research team then developed a list of scenarios to develop DL guidance for local agencies–following the qualitative "scenario planning" option of managing deep uncertainty. The impacts of the following scenarios were assessed:

- priority lane use with CAVs permitted on HOV lanes, vs. exclusive lane use with CAVs having exclusive access to DLs;
- different market penetration rates, assessed under both DL and non-DL scenarios;
- various combination of CAV applications;
- varying demand and changing operational conditions on the CAV/DL benefits;
- various access restrictions to the DL under exclusive CAV lane situations; and
- hypothetical scenarios such as an incident-related lane closure or moving bottlenecks (i.e., incident management applications).

3.2 Results of the analysis

Potential sites for the *virtual* case studies were evaluated based on their overall characteristics (e.g., geography, operational conditions, modes, and presence of managed lanes); their managed lane characteristics (e.g., geometry, allowed users, operating rules, access point configurations); and the feasibility of modeling CAV applications. Based on these criteria, Booz Allen Hamilton et al. selected and developed simulation models for two case study sites: I-66 in Northern Virginia and US-101 in San Mateo, California. The modeling-and-simulation activity helped the project team identify factors that are sensitive to dedicating lanes to CAV users. It also unveils expected impacts under various conditions of lane dedication, market penetration, demand conditions, combined deployment of applications, and so on.

For CACC/DLs, it is advisable to have shared DLs with HOVs at low market penetration (10%) condition, exclusive DLs at medium market penetration (20–45%), and no DLs for higher market penetration (greater than 50%). The effects of various stratifications between CACC and DSH introduction

Table 1 Virtual case-study results.

	Market	Low penetration	Higher penetration
CACC	Shared DL conditions	Slight mobility benefits for both DL users and GPL users	• Moderate to significant mobility and energy/ environmental benefits to DL users • Slight to moderate benefits to GPL users
	Exclusive DL conditions	Significant mobility and energy/environmental benefits to DL uses, at the expense of GPL users	
DSH	Shared DL conditions	Slight safety benefits for both DL and GPL users	• Moderate to significant improvement in safety • Slight improvement in energy/environmental performance for DL users; GPL users would remain unaffected
	Exclusive DL conditions	• Slight safety benefits for DL users • Significant safety benefits for GPL users (at the expense of their mobility performance).	

under low- vs.high penetration markets are summarized in Table 1. These include mobility, safety and energy/environmental benefits for DL and GPL users, respectively.

It was found out that combining DSH-enabled vehicles with CACC-enabled vehicles will improve safety, in addition to mobility and energy/environmental performance. In particular, CACC/DLs can provide mobility benefits (in terms of throughput improvement), when the corridor is subject to peak or higher-than-peak demand. Mobility benefits are more when there is continuous access to the DLs because even vehicles taking shorter trips can utilize the DLs. Speed differential between DLs and GPLs increases with restricted access to DLs, wherein DLs with exclusive access for CAVs will have a much higher travel speed than GPLs and average travel speed on GPLs reduces significantly. This is because the demand on GPLs will be higher when compared to continuous access, as vehicles taking

Table 2 Lane friction guidance.

CAV Market	Low penetration	High penetration
Shared DL with HOVs	• Lowest lane friction • Does not warrant lane separation barriers or restricted lane access	
Exclusive DL	• Highest lane friction (on the order of 30 mph) • Warrants physical separation for enforcement purposes as well as for safety purposes	• Medium lane friction—speeds of the DL and the adjacent GPL differed by 10–15 mph • Warrants separation devices between toll Lanes and free lanes • Does not warrant physical separators, but rather buffer-separated double solid lines

shorter trips cannot use the DLs. Where there is speed differential between DL and adjacent GPL–or when "lane friction" exists—Table 2 provides the guidance as to when barrier separated lanes are needed.

The above represents an agent-based micro-simulation analysis on traffic management on a corridor, representing the first detailed description of such an IT tool. In many ways, it is an adaptation of an existing tool, Vissim, although it is an innovative adaption. The Vissim-based CACC modeling tool has been applied only for evaluating the impact of a CACC lane on a single corridor with multiple interchanges. Looking toward the future, measuring region- and state-wide effectiveness of CAV/DL strategies is equally crucial for planning purposes. As summarized in the above-mentioned statements and Tables, the resulting guidance list must be used in conjunction with the assumptions and conditions under which the conclusions were drawn. Being a scenario-based analysis, scenarios may occur that fall outside of the scope of the analysis conducted in the Booz-Allen-Hamilton et al. study. In such case, there is a need to enhance or change this guidance to incorporate these additional scenarios. With the uncertainties surrounding the implementation of CAVs, such necessities are inevitable.

4. Regional demand modeling

Having now covered a "supply" model, I will move on to demand modeling. In the Paleti and Vukovic model, I discussed how ICT could reduce urban travel demand if people substitute virtual for physical travel in the form of telecommuting. This models a phenomenon that is already occurring. I extended this scenario to include the introduction of CAVs at least for the traffic management case, and acknowledged that effect is highly speculative. Echoing this point, Erhardt (2017) supplemented the Paleti and Vukovic study with a regional long-distance travel model, rather than short-distance urban travel. He emphasized that when the effects of future technology were considered, data collected in the past—when such technology did not exist—are inherently limited. In such situations, *assumption-based planning* models can be used to explore a range of reasonable outcomes. Let us now use regional travel as a case study (to supplement the urban travel discussion above in the Part-I chapter). Unlike urban travel, regional travel involves long-distance where the effects of CVs and AVs are most pronounced as passengers reap the full benefits of attention-free "driving." Such travel modeling effort is generally regarded as more challenging, as the data base is typically sparse. Rapidly evolving ICT and CAVs pose additional risk to the accuracy of long-distance travel (LDT) demand prediction when much is unknown about the future, making real data even scarcer if not totally absent.

4.1 Different types of ICT effects

The nature of this modeling risk is multifaceted: In addition to the *substitution* of on-site work with telecommuting, Erhardt (2017) suggested that ICT could also serve be *complement*ary and thereby generate more demand. For substitution, there are some more moderate forms than telecommuting. These include phone calls, e-mails, video-conference sessions (including options such Skype or FaceTime), desktop-sharing applications (such as GoToMeeting), virtual private networks to access a computer remotely, social-media applications (such as Facebook or Twitter), and socially-networked video games. Irrespective of the degree of substitution, one can model LDT as an alternative in a travel-telecommunications mode-choice model. Given the multitude of telecommunications options and the challenge of predicting how the technology will change in the future, it may be appropriate to represent the ICT alternative as a single mode (i.e., "electronic means") with a utility term representing the overall quality and cost of the ICT options available. This term would be a candidate for sensitivity testing based on the assumed levels of ICT development in the future. Another advantage of this approach is that it is sensitive to the cost of the physical modes in the future, including CAVs. For example, if the cost of fuel were to increase dramatically in the future, the substitution of ICT and CAVs for conventional travel could be expected to increase, provided that there are ways to mitigate the high cost of owning a CAV (such as through joint ownership or shared rides).

According to Erhardt, those who advocate complementarity effects between ICT/CAV and LDT would point to the following motivations:

- Extended social and professional network effect: ICT may facilitate geographically extended social and professional networks. By virtue of these new friendships, these extended networks could induce additional LDT because there would be more people to visit in far-away places (Larsen et al., 2006).
- Desire effect: It may be that by making information about possible (attractive) destinations more readily available, people are spurred to travel to destinations or engage in activities that they otherwise would not have thought of (Mokhtarian, 1990).
- Reduced burden effect: As people's lives become more connected, that connectedness could serve to reduce the burden of LDT, as distance no longer stands in the way of friendship. A similar effect would occur for CAVs, where the travel time is freed up for more productive or more attractive activities (compared with the monotonous task of driving). In short, reduced burden means a smaller disutility associated with travel time or less disassociation from being away from home, which results in more traveling (Mokhtarian and Tal, 2013).
- Backfill effect: When telecommuting via ICT is substituted for travel in conventional vehicles, the additional time freed up can be used to engage in other more appealing activities. This can be thought of as freeing up commuting time for shopping, recreational, social or other leisure activities. However, this complementary effect is somewhat uncertain—certainly not as dramatic as from substitution.
- Land use effect: ICT and long-distance commute by CAVs may influence long-term land-use patterns by enabling more dispersed residential and employment locations. This might result in more travel between distant locations in the long run (Mokhtarian, 2009).

Since we have no knowledge on the prevalence of substitutional vs. complementary effects due to ICT, we are adapting the qualitative "assumption-based planning" method in managing such deep uncertainty.

4.2 Modeling implications

As noted above, estimating the effect of future technology from past data is problematic because the technology is not present at the time of data collection. While ICT clearly exists in the present day, the challenge is in estimating the moving target effect of a *changing* technology, both in information and transportation technology. This could potentially be done with a well-designed stated-preference survey. It would be necessary to structure the experiments such that the respondents could reasonably grasp what was being asked and were not simply choosing randomly. While it may be possible to design a survey that is robust enough to support model estimation, getting reliable data from such a survey could be very challenging. Therefore, an alternative approach, albeit more conceptual, is proposed, as described below.

A key challenge in understanding the effect of ICT on LDT is that ICT is evolving on a faster time scale than transportation infrastructures, with CAVs being somewhere in the middle. Major infrastructure projects can easily take 10–20 years to plan and construct, whereas over that same time frame, ICT can go through several evolutions. If ICT were constant, it would be less important to model it explicitly, because its effect would have already been priced into the trip rates and cost constants derived from existing data. Given the rapid change of ICT and CAVs, however, even current data are irrelevant because the technologies are expected to continue to change, and change rapidly. This problem is compounded by the challenges of collecting LDT data in the first place, as most modelers will agree. Because long-distance trips are less frequent, a longer data-collection window is needed to capture a sufficient number of observations, which makes valid data gathering even more difficult.

Given data limitations, I wish to contribute to the body of knowledge by considering the problem from a theoretical perspective. Let us propose an *assumption-based* approach as a structured means of considering the possible effects from ICT/CAV. The focus is on proposing a model structure that could realistically be applied to generate predictions of LDT. The starting point for this assessment is the United States National Long-Distance Travel Model (NLDTM) (Erhardt, 2017; Outwater et al., 2015), both because it represents current thinking on how to model LDT and because it is susceptible to integration with ICT/CAV. In the development of the NLDTM, both aggregate and disaggregate model structures were considered. The research ultimately implemented a modified structure that primarily followed the disaggregate structure, with some compromises to reduce computational times (Outwater et al., 2015). When I wrote this chapter, I decided to start from the fully disaggregate structure because it excludes details outside the current discussion. The approach can be extended in future work to modify the model structure as desired.

As illustrated in the Input/Output Model columns in Fig. 1, the NLDTM model operates on three inputs. The first is a "synthetic population," which is derived from micro-simulation (Erhardt, 2017).[b] The other two inputs include "zonal land use," and "zone-to-zone level-of-service" for all modes. There are four core-model components: "auto ownership," "aggregate mode–destination choice," "disaggregate tour generation and scheduling (TGS)," and "disaggregate mode–destination choice." The purpose of the "aggregate mode–destination choice" model is to generate accessibility log-sums,[c] which are used in the TGS models. The use of accessibilities in TGS models allows the model to capture an induced-demand effect in which improving long-distance level-of-service can lead to an increase in the number of long-distance tours. The TGS step uses a series of logit models to predict whether a long-distance tour occurs on the travel day, the duration of that tour, and the number of people in the party. The disaggregate mode–destination choice step then predicts those choices for the simulated travelers. The final output is a list of individual tour records with the specified attributes such as origin, purpose, etc. In Fig. 1, as adapted from Erhardt (2017), the related inputs and model components of the NLDTM are highlighted by the black circled outlines.

4.4 Long-distance-travel model-structure with implicit and explicit ICT/CAV effects

By modifying the NLDTM, one can account for the ICT/CAV effect *implicitly* (Erhardt, 2017). Fig. 1A shows a conceptual model for how the NLDTM can be adapted to implicitly capture the effect of ICT/CAV without too many changes. Compared with an *explicit* model (to be discussed in the sequel), it is simple but less directly aligned with the expected underlying behavior. For example, this implicit model does not include a separate model of ICT/CAV adoption and engagement (A&E). Instead, ICT/CAV availability and A&E would be treated as model *inputs*. It would be treated as an *aggregate* metric that captures the overall level of availability and A&E by the population, rather than modeling values for individual travelers (as in the explicit model). This implicit approach provides different ICT/CAV penetration levels that can be tested for future years for alternative scenarios.

[b] As indicated previously, more explanation on how to derive a synthetic population will be presented in a subsequent section of this chapter, Section 6.

[c] Aside from the division and addition of constants, expected consumer surplus in a logit choice model is simply the log of the denominator choice probability, or ln $[\sum_j \exp(V_j)]$. This is often called the "log-sum" term.

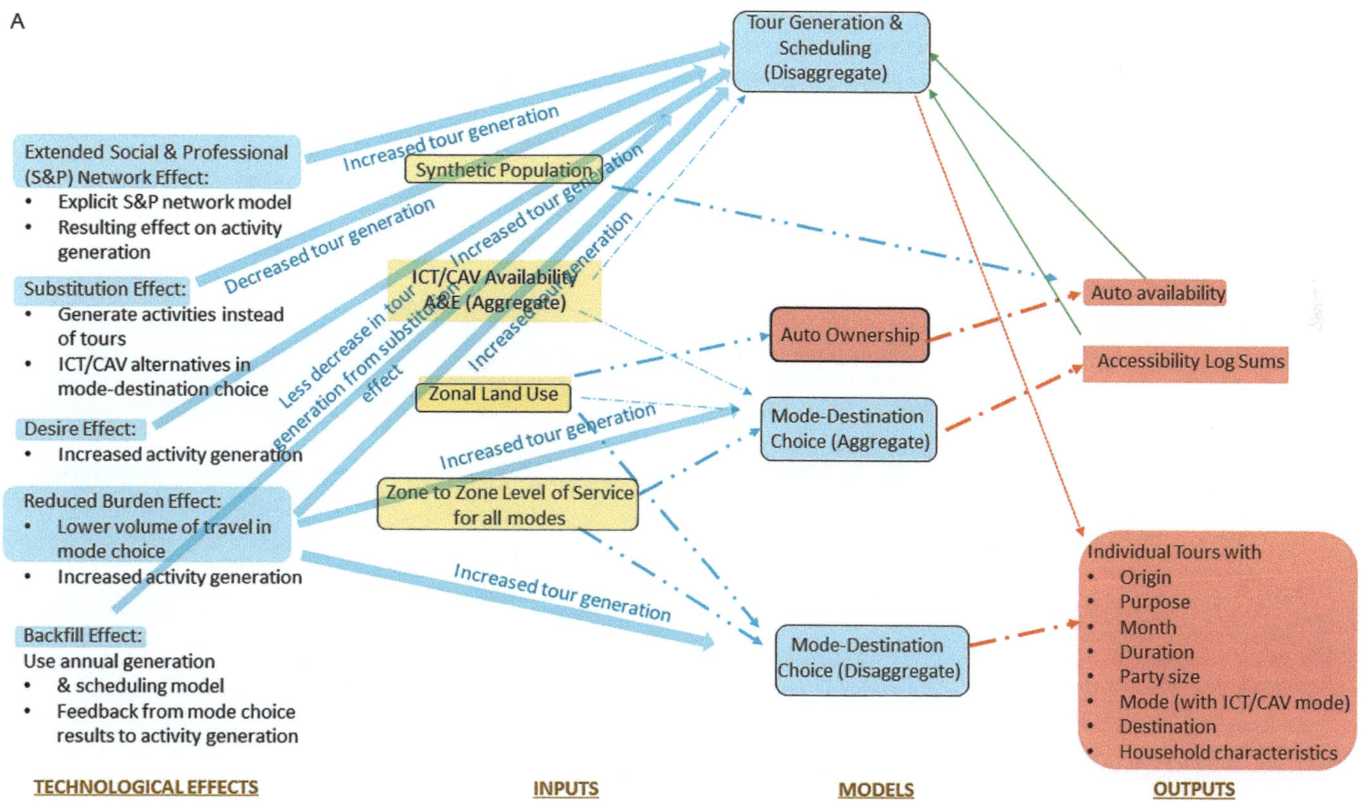

Fig. 1 (A) Implicit LDT model structure with ICT/CAV effects.

(Continued)

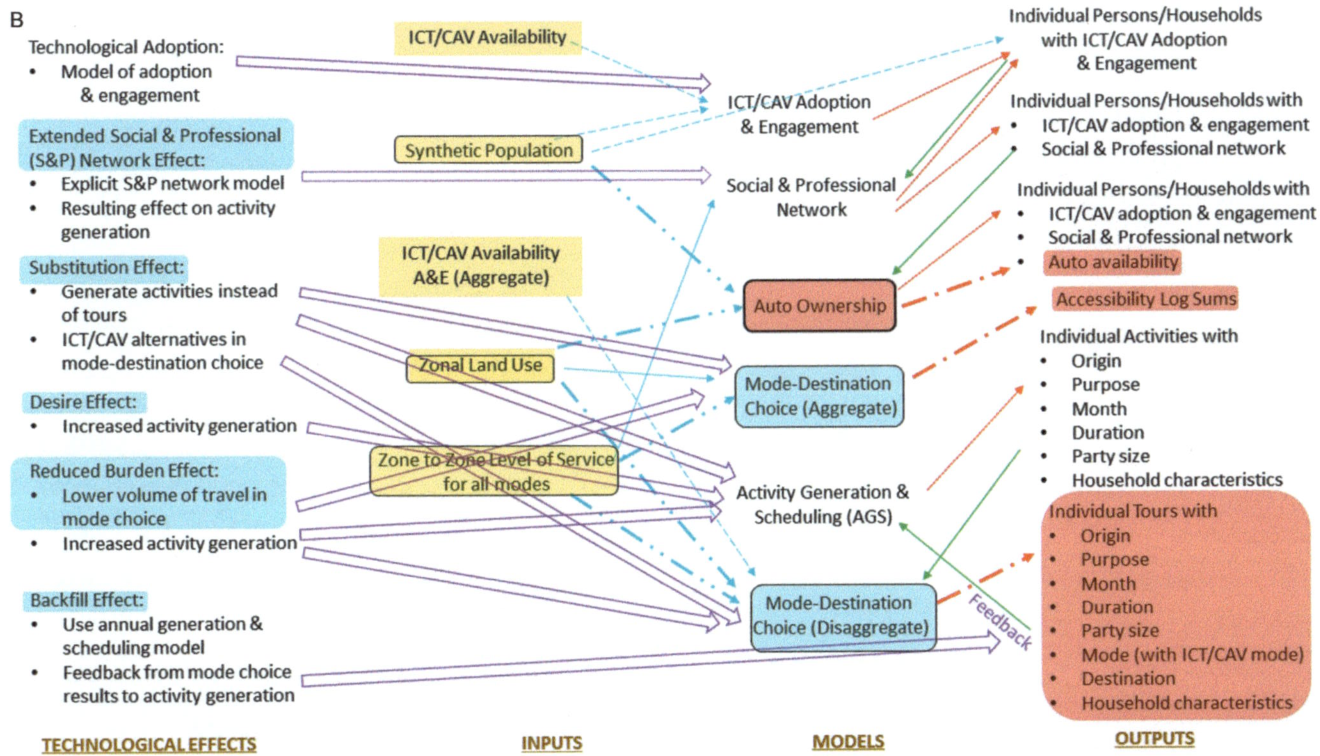

Fig. 1—Cont'd (B) Explicit LDT model structure with ICT/CAV effects. Note: The elements in the implicit model (IM) are a subset of the Explicit Mode [EM]; its elements are highlighted in blue in the 1st and 3rd columns. In the 2nd column, the 3 common elements between IM and EM are shown in yellow with an outline, with the remaining "ICT/CAV Availability" element split between EM and IM in two separate yellow labels. In the 3rd column, "auto ownership" is shared between EM and IM. In the last column, the IM elements are highlighted in red.

For example, these different levels of penetration will feed into the disaggregate tour generation and scheduling model as well as the aggregate mode-destination choice model, as shown by the thin blue arrows in "dashed" lines. Accompanying these thin blue arrows are the thicker blue arrows in "dash dot dot" lines showing how the other inputs feed into the models. A thicker blue is used to denote that the same effects are also considered in the forthcoming explicit model, while a thinner blue denotes either IM or EM (but not both).

We also add another set of inputs—all highlighted in blue shade—under the label of "Technological effects" as shown for extended social & professional (S&P) network effect, substitution effect, desire effect, and backfill effect. Implementation of these ICT/CAV effects is shown as thick (blue) arrows without outlines. Notice that these are not model steps themselves but are instead included in Fig. 1A to highlight which model components would change to capture each effect. Again, such technological inputs are highlighted by blue-shaded boxes, being a subset of the elements in the Technological Effects column, with the accompanying shaded arrows showing the implications of these technologies. Of particular interest are these three models that are most affected: Tour Generation and Scheduling (TGS), Mode-Destination Choice (Aggregate), and Mode-Destination Choice (Disaggregate). Tracing all the way through the outputs, the thin and thick red arrows (in "dot" and "dash dot" lines, respectively) show how an output is being affected by a particular model. For example, the "Mode-Destination Choice (Disaggregate)" model results in the "individual tours" output complete with origin, purpose, all the way to destination and household characteristics. Among these arrows, the heavier ones (in "dash dot" lines) account for both the current implicit model (IM) as well as the forthcoming explicit model (EM). For example, the arrow pointing from "aggregate mode–destination choice" to "accessibility log sums," being a heavy red arrow (in "dash dot" line), applies to both the IM and EM.

It can be seen that the "extended S&P network," the "desire," and the "reduced burden" effects are each captured in the Tour Generation and Scheduling (TGS) model by increasing the likelihood of making long-distance tours when ICT/CAV availability and A&E increase. Similarly, the stimulation of the "reduced burden" effect would be reflected in the aggregate and disaggregate mode–destination choice models as a result of the decreased valuation of time. These effects would be uniform across the population or segmented by specific groups, rather than a function of the ICT/CAV A&E of the individual or the modeled social and professional network of the individual (as will be shown in the EM below). Finally, notice there are a couple of "feedback" arrows (in solid lines) that show the auto availability and accessibility log sum outputs of the respective models will affect TGS. As I have mentioned above, the outputs of the "auto availability" and "aggregate mode-destination choice" models serve as inputs to the TGS model.

As alluded to earlier, Fig. 1B also shows a conceptual model for how the NLDTM can be adapted to *explicitly* capture the effect of ICT and CAVs. Accordingly, the inputs, models, outputs, and flows of information are adapted to reflect the proposed model structure (Erhardt, 2017). Being more comprehensive, the EM structure would include quite a few more labels across the four columns, which are not highlighted in color shading. For example, there is explicitly one new input: a measure of "ICT/CAV availability," as highlighted in the first yellow label in the second column labeled "Inputs." This would be measured as a single population-level value based on the metric of technological development. The purpose is to provide an explicit lever with which a higher level of ICT/CAV availability can be tested for future years or alternative scenarios. This metric, along with the synthetic population, would feed a model of ICT/CAV A&E that predicts the *individual-level* use of the technology. It is this individual-level factor that affects all downstream models, such that there may be a large effect on travel for heavy users of the technology but no effect on travelers who do not use the technology. For example, the "synthetic population" input feeds into "Individual Persons/Households with ICT/CAV A&E," which in turn feeds into "S&P network" and so on. The former also serves as input to the "auto ownership" model, which in turn produces outputs in the "Individual persons/households" block complete with "auto availability." The input is shown in a heavier blue arrow (in "dash dot dot" line), showing the commonality with the IM. This is to be distinguished from the lighter blue arrows (in "dash" lines) for either the IM or EM (but not both).

Unlike the IM, the "extended S&P network effect" in the "Technological Effects" column would be obtained by *explicitly* simulating the "S&P networks" in an exogenous model. The effect is input to the "social & professional network" model, as suggested by a violet hollow arrow that points toward S&P Network. Such an S&P Network model has already been described; it starts from the "synthetic population" and model links between individuals in that population. The probability of linking up in an S&P network would be a function of the physical distance, as measured by the "zone-to-zone level-of-service" matrices (serving as input), and the virtual distance, as measured by the individual/household's ICT/CAV engagement (through a backward pointing green arrow in solid line) and by other factors such as socioeconomic and demographic similarities (not shown in the figure). In the IM, by comparison, the presence of these links would subsequently produce a variable in the "generation and scheduling" model to increase the likelihood of travel to destination zones where a person has strong S&P ties.

The "substitution effect" would be modeled by adding a virtual travel alternative to the mode-choice model. Again, the effect is shown as a hollow arrow with a violet outline in Fig. 1B, pointing toward the "Mode-Destination Choice (Aggregate)" model. This would allow the probability of that alternative to be affected both by the ICT/CAV alternatives available to the traveler and by the generalized cost of physical modes, as represented by the "Level of service for all modes" input. This structure also requires that the TGS model (formerly used in the IM) be replaced with an "activity generation and scheduling (AGS)" model that includes not only physical but also virtual long-distance activities, accounting for those generated by the substitution, desire and reduced burden effects. In Fig. 1B, this is again illustrated by the three wide-arrow outlined in violet bearing upon AGS.

Through a violet wide-arrow, the "desire effect" would be captured by a term in the AGS model that increases long-distance activity generation with increased ICT/CAV A&E. Similarly, the "reduced burden effect" would be captured with a second term in the AGS model that makes long-distance activities more likely, with a larger possible effect considered for trips of longer duration (duration in terms of number of days away). The second component of the "reduced burden effect" would be the "values of time" that are lower for passenger modes in which ICT/CAV A&E is higher. This reflects the potential to use the travel time more productively with better connectivity and without the burden of driving. The result is shown in mode-destination choice.

Finally, the "backfill effect" on "individual tours" is captured by adding a feedback loop (shown as a backward pointing green arrow in solid line) from the final tours back to the AGS model. This way, if some of the tours choose a virtual mode, there will be room for additional physical tours to be scheduled. It is important to note that this feedback structure is predicated on the AGS model using an annual scheduling approach similar to that of LaMondia et al. (2008). The NLDTM as currently implemented does not use this approach, but annual scheduling models were estimated during the course of that research (Outwater et al., 2015). In sum, all the above five technological effects are shown in Fig. 1B as wide arrows with violet outlines bearing upon the models (except for the additional "feedback" green arrow in solid line). Without a detailed discussion here, the other outputs from the EM model are amply illustrated in Fig. 1B, complete with other feedback arrows in green solid line.

5. General demand modeling

In light of the above observations, Miller (2017) noted that while travel demand modeling had made very significant strides over the past 20 years, considerable need, opportunity, and scope exist for the development of significantly more powerful second-generation agent-based micro-simulation models that build upon emerging big data and high-performance computing. This task, however, will involve the development of new behavioral representations and computational algorithms that fully exploit new ICT and new transportation modes and services such as CAVs.

5.1 State of the art in activity-based modeling

The AB model is a computational framework for exercising disaggregate modes of system behavior. It is the only computational structure developed that is capable of dealing with these important aspects of travel demand, as amply mentioned above:

- Tour-based modeling,
- Within-household interactions (as discussed in Section 5.1, entitled "Effects of ICT" section under the "Urban Activity-Based Demand Modeling" section of the previous chapter),
- Efficiently dealing with between-agent heterogeneities in preferences, such as the interactions between the two bread winners in a family regarding telecommuting, and
- Complex en-route traveler experiences and dynamic decision-making (as discussed in Section 3.4. entitled "Policy-Based Routing in Stochastic Networks" (PRSN) model under the "Incident Traffic Management" section in the previous chapter).

In this section, I wish to provide the means to quantify these demand-model performance measures for both existing and new transportation networks, thus allowing the desired level of modeling service to be rendered. To do this Miller first identify the many well-recognized weaknesses of existing AB models, including computational intensity, rigidity in decision structures, and software complexity. In addition, these AB models are overly procedural in nature, strongly static-equilibrium based, and require maintaining information concerning the individual trip-maker throughout the decision chain.

At the same time, we need to observe these emerging developments: Real-time information flows are most important to make timely decisions, but they lie completely outside of current AB models, which are typically calibrated offline. As shown above, daily shared-mobility service—both within a household and between households—is emerging with the availability of CAVs. Modeling these extra household-passenger modes in real time is extremely problematic within the current generation of AB models. With the forthcoming "backfill effect," more time is available to engage in activities other than employment or school. However, current AB models do not handle nonwork or non-school trips well. Beyond a multi-earner family, demographic changes suggest a deferred retirement age, making an elderly worker a more prominent part of the labor force. CAVs make the commuting trip a lot more convenient for these elderly workers, thus further extending their working life. Such changes in the labor force are eroding the way the daily work commute is currently represented in AB models. In light of the above, Miller offer some possible suggestions of a second generation of operational AB models, each of which will be explained further below:

- adoption of a more event-driven modeling structure (i.e., being more responsive to a real-time activity),
- development of more dynamic, disequilibrium, evolutionary models (which suggests that the model may learn and adapt itself to changing scenarios),
- greater attention to capturing behavior in parsimonious formulations (which will ease the task of model calibration),
- much more flexible, generic design (to accommodate technological changes in an agile fashion), and
- much more exploitation of cloud–cluster computing for computational efficiency (which is needed in the era of "big data").

Aside from being a "tall order," we will remember that there is no certainty on how the technology will evolve, setting aside the more taxing question of how people will react to these technological changes. In response to this demanding list of requirements, we shall follow a quantitative "robust decision making" method of managing deep uncertainty—as suggested in Section 2. This way, even though we do not know what really lies ahead, still we could come out with a plan that will work under a variety of plausible conditions.

5.2 An example of emerging activity-based models

A potentially more flexible and extensible modeling of activity and travel is provided by a "project-based" approach to the generation and scheduling of activity episodes in response to the various events that occur, say, in a day (Miller, 2005a,b,c). In this conceptual framework, a potentially universal set of projects exists that generates activity episodes of various types and attributes that achieve the projects' goals. Here is a familiar example. Let us take the "activity" of "work." Under this activity, there are several categories of work. Such a "categorization" might include desk-based, which reflect the conventional environment where work is distributed among members of an organization to be accomplished independently in an office. This is to be contrasted with work that is done "on the road," such as the typical work of a traveling salesperson. Also, there are several modes to carry out work. These "modes" might include the office which is the usual place of work for service-oriented jobs, or the work can be done at home, as the case of telecommuting. Likewise, a "shopping" activity might involve picking up "grocery" among other shopping trips. If it is grocery shopping, there are several modes for it to be executed, two common ones would be to pick up the grocery physically in a supermarket or to have the grocery be delivered by ordering through the Internet.

For our daily, repetitive activities, it is further argued that such activity types are generic (e.g., work, shopping), with each activity type (say "shopping") potentially having some well-defined categories and modes (e.g., in-store vs. Internet shopping). Notice that each mode is defined by a combination of technology (such as a private car driving to the store vs. via public transportation), service attributes (such as the shopping "experience" at the mall vs. simply scrolling through an online catalog on the computer), and so forth. It is argued, therefore, that the familiar concept of mode of travel (auto vs. transit) can be readily generalized and extended to all activity types. This broadened approach again facilitates the development of more generic models and computer codes, with new technologies and services being presented to the decision-making agents for possible choice within their behavioral decision-making processes, in much the same way as a new para-transit mode is presented to trip makers for possible use in current travel models.

Fig. 2 combines the above concept into an illustration. On top of the figure is a tabular display of generic activities, in this case the "work" activity, under which Miller has listed the different categories of work and for each

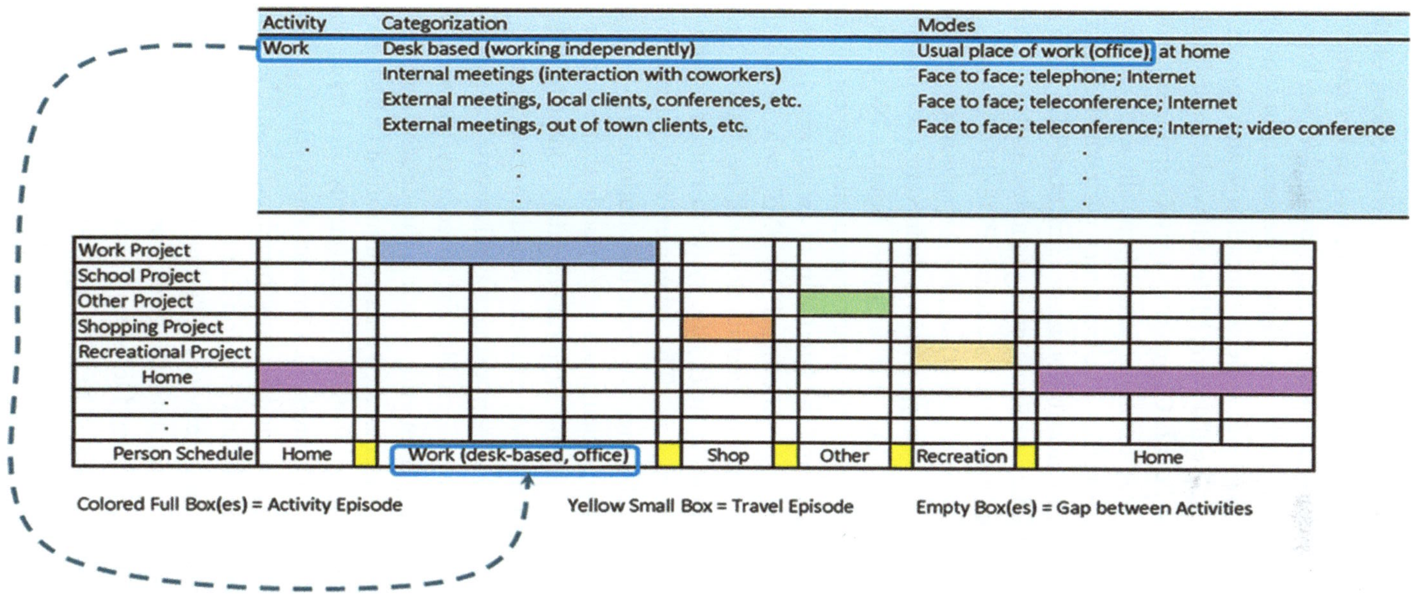

Fig. 2 Scheduling activity episodes.

category the different modes of execution. At the bottom of the figure is how a particular worker will execute the activity in her own style, which we call an "activity episode." What is an *activity episode*? An activity episode is an instance of engagement by one or more persons in an activity of a given type (e.g., shopping, work) at a specific location with a specific start time, duration, and end time. To illustrate, Miller showed a typical daily schedule generated this way in Fig. 2. Competing activity episodes are selected for execution within a given planning period (typically a given day or week), as illustrated in the same figure. The frequency with which an activity is executed is represented in a probability density function (PDF) or a probability mass function (PMF). Let us denote such a function as $P_X(x)$. The probable start time of an activity is specified as another PDF/PMF, denoted by $P_Y(y)$. Combining the two functions $P_X(x)$ and $P_Y(y)$ results in a joint PDF or PMF function, denoted by $P_{XY}(x, y)$, which is defined in a feasible region characterized by a lower-bound and an upper-bound. Now let us define the lowest frequency x_L vs. the highest frequency of execution x_U, and the earliest start time y_L and the latest start of an activity y_U, we can write $x_L \leq x \leq x_U$, $y_L \leq y \leq y_U$. Another PDF/PMF will define the activity duration, $P_Z(z)$. Another joint distribution will be defined between start time and duration, resulting in $P_{YZ}(y, z)$, with similar bounds defined as $y_L \leq y \leq y_U$ and $z_L \leq z \leq z_U$. The scheduler will generate from the set of projects as defined by the two joint distributions, $P_{XY}(x, y)$ and $P_{YZ}(y, z)$, the number of a particular activity episode that a person (or household) might engage in during a typical weekday, complete with start time and duration. It is in this way that the scheduler proceeds to build each person's daily schedule. Please note that travel is inserted as part of the scheduling process, serving as the enabler for an activity. As such, traveling is merely a means to deliver an end, which is the desired activity.

Miller proposed an agent-based micro-simulation (ABM) model, which simulates the scheduling of out-of-home activity-and-travel episodes for each individual within a household. Decision about which activity episodes to engage in, when, where, and for how long depends on the *agent's* (household's) preferences, needs, and decision rules, as well as the resources available for undertaking these activities including time, money, car ownership, information. For each household (agent), more than one person can be involved in decision making. Decisions concerning the allocation of personal and household resources to activity episodes can be made by a *resource manager* (say, the head of household). A *scheduler* (say, the spouse or the head of household) may also get involved, who determines which of the activity episodes being proposed by the projects will actually be scheduled for execution. Trips emerge naturally out of this scheduling process in order for the subject person to move from one activity-episode location to the next, including home, as illustrated in Fig. 2.

5.3 Some observations

This approach potentially provides a much more generic, abstract representation of activity–travel behavior decision-making than many current models. It might permit a more flexible basis for modeling new services and modes as well as for more dynamic models. In other words, this approach provides a generic, modular representation of activity–travel options and decision rules that is independent of what these options or rules are. This generic, modular representation can be contrasted with many current models that begin with a random-utility model design, which then typically imposes a relatively rigid computational and behavioral structure on the model system (as illustrated by the MDCEV model under Section 5, entitled "Urban Activity-Based Demand Modeling" in the previous chapter. Stated in another way, both the decision rules and options to which they are applied are hardwired into the model design, which makes any extension to the model challenging. In the proposed approach, one begins with an object-oriented (one might also say potentially ontological) representation of activities and the activity generation-and-scheduling process. This process might be then operationalized by the use of a variety of modeling methods, including, where appropriate, the familiar random-utility-based models.

Although experience to date is still limited, the framework does seem to facilitate simpler, more generic parameterizations of utility functions than comparable AB models. It also produces a much more simplified and computationally-efficient software than many other current models, which results in the ability to model 24-h travel behavior for the entire Greater Toronto–Hamilton Area (consisting of 6.5–8.5 million people, depending on the year being modeled) in approximately 2 h of computer time on a reasonably powerful server. Since the framework became fully operational in early 2016, the City of Toronto has undertaken more than 1000 model system runs—something that one suspects is not conceivable with most other model systems in current operational or research use. It is also noteworthy that at least 90% of this 2-h run time is dedicated to performing static equilibrium auto and transit assignments for five time periods within the 24-h day being modeled, which is an indication of the need for more efficient models of network path-choice for use in such applications. (Please revisit Section 3.3, entitled "Dynamic Shortest-Path Algorithm for Continuous Information Updates" section under "Incident Traffic Management.")

Having said all that, one should be mindful that the generic list of universal activities as proposed by Miller is really not so "generic" given the emergence of ICT and CAVs. For example, the presence of substitution and complementarity effects suggest that there are interactions between activities. I have already talked about substituting a work trip with telecommuting in the previous chapter. Now take the "information gathering" activity (which is a generic activity among others). It can be accomplished in many ways in the digital age. Aside from the traditional modes such as newspapers, radio, or television, I mentioned the "extended social and professional network effect" within "Different types of ICT effects" under Section 4. This is certainly a new form of information gathering, as one gets exposed to places and activities that are revealed through social networking, creating the want to explore exotic places to fulfill a brand new "Entertainment or recreation" activity that was not "in the books." Now let us revisit Fig. 2, which shows the "travel episode" sandwiching an activity, namely one typically drives to the mall to shop and then travels back home with the merchandise. The mode of travel will be greatly expanded with the introduction of CAVs, wherein many share-mobility services now prevail in addition to a privately owned vehicle or conventional public transportation. SAVs will have very different service attributes than a conventional automobile. This suggests that while the Miller proposal has its merits, there are certainly many "wrinkles" to be worked out before Miller's ABM model can be implemented in the presence of a rapidly evolving ICT/CAV scene.

6. Emerging urban and regional development models

Along this line of thought on future modeling paradigms under emerging ICT and CAV trends, Moeckel (2017a,b) offered a comprehensive framework for analyzing the impact of ICT and CAVs on auto ownership, housing search, workplace choice, in addition to travel behavior such as activity generation, destination choice, or mode choice. In other words, he offered a future generation of urban and regional development models.

6.1 Modeling

In his analysis, Moeckel outlined the implications of auto-ownership and locational choices on travel, as illustrated partly in Fig. 3. As shown in the feedback cycle in the figure, land use and transport are closely connected (Wegener, 2004), reflecting a well-known fact. The transport system (shown at the top left of the figure) provides travel times under current traffic condition, which are used, along with other locational factors, in land-use models (top right of the figure) to assess the desirability of various locations. Demand for work travel is derived on the basis of where people live and where firms locate, and this demand then leads to updated traffic congestion level and, therefore, travel times. At the bottom of the circle I have explicitly inserted the ICT/CAV sector that includes all the respective components, including GPS, smart phones, social networks, crowd sourcing, shared mobility services, big data, and e-commerce. Following the theme of the current and the previous chapter, this speaks for the important role ICT/CAV now plays in the classic interaction between transport and land use. Each of these ICT/CAV components have profound effects on activities, trip decision, mobility, destination choice, mode choice, route choice, and ultimately land use–just to name a few. Represented generally in a clockwise circle by the arrows, these interactions—complex as they may be–have been discussed previously in this chapter, in the prevailing literature, and will be further elaborated below in Section 7.1.

Here are some existing models that simulate these interactions on a *global* scale, albeit excluding the ICT/CAV interactions. Microsimulation

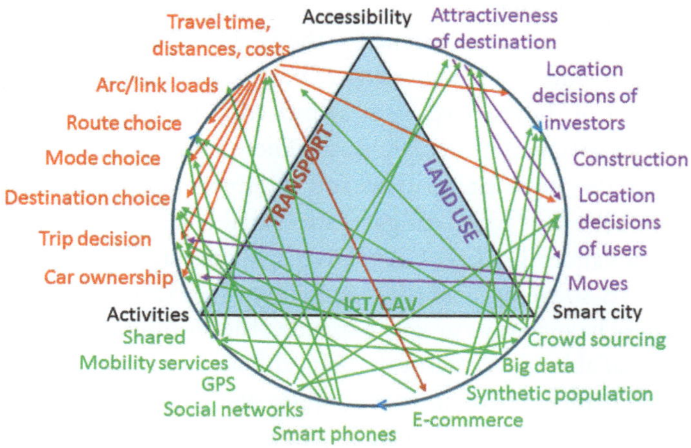

Fig. 3 Integration of transport, ICT/CAV and land use.

Transportation Orchestrator (MITO) is a model used to generate travel demand. It is designed as a microsimulation and generates travel demand microscopically for every household represented in a synthetic population. Traffic assignment is modeled by MATSim (Multiagent Transport Simulation, http://www.matsim.org). Given the microscopic nature of MATSim, the travel behavior of individuals who have access to communications technologies can be modeled conceivably in a future version of the model, perhaps capitalizing on our discussions in Section 3.4 on PRSN model under the "Urban Traffic Incident Management" section of the previous chapter. Locational choices are represented by the microscopic discrete-choice model SILO (http://www.silo.zone) (Moeckel, 2017a,b). The model consists of the household-relocation, demography, and real-estate modules. Currently, SILO focuses on simulating population only. Zonal employment by industry is provided as an exogenous input. Following traditional modeling paradigms, the output of a land-use model feeds into a travel-demand model, and a travel-demand model feeds into traffic assignment. In its current implementation, the model will miss the impact of ICT and CAVs on firm location choice. In Section 7.1, I will further discuss ways to incorporate ICT/CAV into the modeling framework, as illustrated in Fig. 3.

7. Synthetic population data

In the above discussions, we have observed that several modeling procedures start with a synthetic population dataset. It is not surprising, commensurate with the development of disaggregate modeling and AB micro-simulation, the requirement for the accuracy and spatial resolution of a synthetic population is increasing (Zhu and Ferreira, 2014). The relationships between different types of agents within a synthetic population also need to be specified in realistic ways. These requirements make it necessary to consider new data sources and interpolation methods to enable population synthesis at more disaggregate spatial levels.

Recent advances in ICT/CAV have spawned additional web-based services, crowd-sourcing, and the availability of geographically registered datasets. These have in turn greatly expanded the amount of relevant, independently available data that can help in constructing a disaggregate synthetic population. Mining these public and private big-data sources can identify spatial and socioeconomic patterns across households, individuals, jobs, and so forth that can make it practical to construct synthetic populations at the household and building scale. These new data sources can also support urban micro-simulations by enriching models with more realistic heterogeneous behaviors and spatial details. However, those readily available data sets are very often not perfect for the research at hand. The barriers include the quality of the data resulting from incompleteness, privacy, cross-referencing difficulties, and other technical issues, as alluded to in Section 5.2, entitled "Foreseeable effects of CV," under the "Urban Activity-Based Demand Modeling" section. Finding ways to enhance the value of traditional surveys and methods through the use of these new datasets and computational techniques is challenging but timely and valuable.

Zhu and Ferreira (2014) presented a new population-synthesis approach aimed at improving the spatially-disaggregated accuracy of population generation by using limited micro-data and rich/diverse sets of aggregated marginal data.[d] A general iterative-proportional-fitting (IPF) method was used to estimate the joint distribution of households' and individuals' characteristics. This is performed under multiple levels of constraints at the level of planning districts for which certain marginal constraints are available. To improve the spatial detail of the synthetic population, additional building location, attribute, and occupancy information was collected from multiple sources. The information is used to constrain housing locations by using a second IPF procedure that addresses building capacity as well as spatial-demographic patterns estimated by using a discrete choice model. The procedure yields realistic spatial heterogeneity while preserving some of the joint distribution of household and locational characteristics.

More than once, we have discussed social networks as a key feature of today's ICT. As it turned out, there is a definite relationship between a social network and a synthetic population that can be exploited. This is illustrated in Table 3. In a social network, every person is in fact represented individually in a synthetic population, which is made possible by the fabric of such a network. As to which social network(s) an individual belongs is another attribute in the synthetic population that is added to every person. Persons of the same household will be assigned to the same social network(s) a priori, as it is assumed that information is shared between family members. People living in the same neighborhood are given a higher likelihood of sharing the

[d] The marginal distribution of a subset of a collection of random variables is the probability distribution of the variables contained in the subset. It gives the probabilities of various values of the variables in the subset without reference to the other variables. This contrasts with a conditional distribution, which gives the probabilities contingent upon the values of the other variables.

Table 3 Example of synthetic population that includes information on social networks (Moeckel, 2017a,b).

Person ID	Household ID	Age	Gender	Family Status	Occupation	Driver's License	Workplace or School ID	Income	Smart-phone	Telework (%)	Social Netw. ID1	Social Netw. ID2	Social Netw. ID
1	1	40	2	Married	Empl.	Yes	2020433	55,000	Yes	0	5384	632	215
2	1	44	1	Married	Empl.	Yes	3339031	61,000	Yes	50	5384	9821	
3	1	8	2	Single	Student	No	3896097	0	No	0	5384	2394	
4	2	75	1	Married	Retired	Yes	0	26,000	No	0	139	681	
5	2	73	2	Married	Retired	No	0	8,000	No	0	139		
6	3	38	1	Married	Empl.	Yes	2298203	125,000	Yes	20	6147	4260	37
7	3	39	2	Married	Home	Yes	0	0	Yes	0	6147	6604	
8	3	4	2	Single	Student	No	527084	0	No	0	6147	219	
9	3	2	1	Single	Home	No	0	0	No	0	6147		
10	4	56	2	Single	Empl.	Yes	2729405	94,000	Yes	100	1647	5507	
11	…												

same social network(s) than other people. Working at the same workplace or attending the same school is another circumstance that increases the likelihood of being a member of the same social network(s). With such information, one can construct a synthetic population—possibly using the IPF procedure–that is required for disaggregate modeling, and an example is shown in Table 3. The main idea is to differentiate spatially and at the same time maintain the relationship between household and locational features. In fact, one can argue that a "community" is now not only defined as a village, a town or a city, but also a "social network."

7.1 Urban and regional development implications

Let us examine Fig. 3 further, concentrating on the highlighted triangle with "ICT/CAV," "transport" and "land use" on each side. The triangle has its corners anchored at "activities," "accessibility" and "smart city," representing the linkage between "transport" and "land use," between "land use" and "ICT/CAV," and between "ICT/CAV" and "transport." In other words, executing the desired activities results in travel (or transport), transport provides the accessibility that allows locational decisions to be made. These locational decisions, with the advent of ICT/CAV, organize themselves ultimately to form a smart city.

Let us now focus on the interactions of ICT/CAV with "transport and land use," as the interactions between "transport" and "land use" has been discussed above and amply documented elsewhere, notably by Wegener (2004) and Chan (2005). It is now our job to highlight the importance of including the ICT/CAV side of the triangle in a future urban and regional development model. Let us start from the left with GPS. It is clear that GPS will allow precise identification of locations. Given such information, it is equally clear that it allows—through a number of intermediate decisions including destination and mode choice–to ultimately arrive at an informed route choice. This is facilitated by ICT/CAV that combines GPS shortest-path information with actual traffic conditions that are reported either passively by mobile-phone users or actively by congestion reports. GPS devices often result in shortened travel times for the drivers, particularly under congested conditions. Improved accessibility will result, in the long run, in the relocation of business and households.

Now imagine we are living in a "smart city," where every component of it is interconnected through Internet of Things (IoT). IoT has assisted in the assembly of "big data" through "crowding sourcing." This is amply illustrated by our discussion in the "Instant Information" section, where the "Transit app" allows tracking of all these data. The availability of big data has facilitated "E-commerce," featuring business transactions through the Internet. More than once, we have also featured ICT by the pervasive use of smart-phones, which have affected which activities a person conducts and with whom. Individuals who own a smart-phone will have better information on where their friends are and on the activities they conduct. Smart-phone owners, through the embedded GPS, will be more likely to join people in their social network for activities. Also, smart phones form the basis of shared mobility services such as Uber and Lyft.

I have, by "judgment call," place a number of "arrows" that crisscross the circle of Fig. 3. I paid particular attention to the ICT/CAV part of the circle, for obviously reasons. For example, I have drawn an arrow from "social network" to the attractiveness of a destination. As explained in the LDT demand model, the choice of a vacation spot could very well be influenced by the information exchange between "close friends." Likewise, I have drawn an arrow to "location decision of users" to show the long term possibilities that one might reside close to these friends by becoming neighbors. As pointed out previously, it is unclear that data will be available to model whether a household chooses to be an owner of a CAV, or it would consider co-ownership for cost considerations. Irrespective, I have grouped these interested owners or co-owners under the "shared mobility" label, and I have attributed their choice of shared mobility services to social networks (by which friends decide to carpool) as well as the availability of "big data." It is attributed to big data because the purchase of a CAV might be driven by the tradeoff between the consequences of sole ownership and shared ownership, a piece of data that can only be available from pooling various sources of information together. More importantly, how the availability of shared mobility services changes travel demand is largely unknown, as represented by the arrow pointing toward "trip decision." The topic will require additional research to better reflect the impact of such new mobility services. As discussed, owners of CAVs will be assumed to have a reduced travel-time burden, which will soften their desire to live within a reasonable distance to work. This will be achieved, in part, by the alternate activities that can be conducted while traveling. Someone working while traveling may need to spend less time in the office and may gain some time for other activities. If users of CAVs can do regular work while they commute, longer commute times will be acceptable.

In the previous chapter, I discussed "crowd sourcing" in Section 3.1, "Stochastic Incident Management model," under the "Urban Incident Traffic Management" section in the chapter "Travel modeling under-foreseeable communications-and-mobility technologies." I pointed out that crowd sourcing enables detection of a traffic incident and monitoring the traffic-clearance duration, which ultimately allows a more informed route choice based on more accurate real-time reading of travel cost/time. When combined with the attractiveness of a destination on the clockwise circle itself, this in turn allows determination of accessibility.

Over the past decades, ICT has spawned the rapid rise of E-commerce. With E-commerce, shopping patterns have been dramatically altered, and will continue to be altered. With such conglomerates as Amazon, a large portion of the current and emerging world economy is arguably pivoted by E-commerce. (See the arrow pointing toward "trip decision," or whether a shopping trip is to be executed at all given the convenience of shopping online.) At the same time, E-commerce can be described as a double-edged sword. On the one hand, many individual shopping trips may be replaced with more efficient package-delivery tours. However, the closure of physical stores that cannot compete with online stores may trigger longer shopping trips for those items that are difficult to shop online, or for those who do not want to order online. (See the "arrow" pointing from "Travel time, distance, costs" back to "E-commerce," showing the two-way interaction between the two.) An example can be drawn from shopping for expensive jewelry for sentimental reasons, where a physical visit to a jewelry store is part of the experience. Suffice to say that E-commerce has dramatically changed the idea of a set of fixed "generic activities," as I alluded to under Section 5.3.

With the advance of ICT/CAV, we are blessed with a rich set of information, ready to be harnessed. Labeled with the name of "Big Data," this set of information has many, many applications. Some of them have been discussed in the above sections entitled "Urban Incident Traffic Management" (Section 3 in the chapter "Travel modeling underforeseeable communications-and-mobility technologies"), "Regional Traffic Management" (Section 4 of the chapter "Travel modeling underforeseeable communications-and-mobility technologies"), and "General Demand Modeling" (Section 5). For traffic management as discussed in the previous chapter, it is applied toward route choice in ATMS, and for "General Demand Modeling," it is applied toward a second-generation agent-based micro-simulation models. I represent them in two arrows in Fig. 3, one pointing toward "route choice" and the other pointing to "travel time," respectively—the two key variables in the respective subjects. While the first arrow is self-explanatory, the second one simply facilitate "activity episodes" more expeditiously as the travel activity is required for the execution of all other activities, as illustrated in Fig. 2. For Fig. 3 in general, it is obvious that I might have left as many arrows out as I have put in. For that reason Fig. 3 is merely a work in progress.

With the drastic redefinition of the "generic activities" under ICT/CAV, the theory of constant travel-time budgets suggests that many could use the time saved through online shopping or telework to engage in alternate activities, or to execute other trips, such as driving a longer distance to a preferred grocery store or making additional leisure trips. Workers who only need to visit the office 1 or 2 days per week may decide to move farther away from their workplace to enjoy lower housing costs or a larger house, which may offset any travel savings from telecommuting. Finally, social networks will greatly enlarge one's vision of "proximity" to travel much further for pleasure.

The above discussion is to provide a framework for a modeling suite that is capable of assessing the impacts of ICT/CAV on both transport and land use. It is clear from Fig. 3 that the introduction of ICT/CAV will have pervasive influence on not only mobility, but also land use. At the same time, with the imminent arrival of CAVs, the existing transport system will be revolutionized in the future. Although it is generally accepted that impacts on both transport and land use will be substantial, remarkably little is known about the magnitude of these impacts.

The modeling of technologies that do not yet exist or that are not yet widespread involves a lot of uncertainty. For example, the extent to which people will travel greater distances in CAVs is unknown. Most believe that travel demand will increase because travel time may be used for other activities. However, how much the travel demand will increase is unknown. Simulation models cannot predict how attitudes will change in the future, but such models can help in assessing the impact of various assumptions on attitudes, as discussed. These what-if scenarios help in framing possible and likely futures of travel demand and land use under various scenarios. The model results could show, for example, that increased travel demand is dampened by increased congestion. Such hidden relationships sometimes can be revealed with models. By testing a large number of assumptions, a range of possible and likely future development can be identified, as I will discuss immediately below.

7.2 Policy analysis of regional development

Let me now divert away from traditional land-use models and paint a broader picture through the viewing glasses of the policy analysis community (Shladover, 2019). Although CAVs, once becoming available, are available for use by travelers throughout the United States, the roadway infrastructure is likely to be diverse, due to the disparity between well-to-do states and the less endowed ones. Available knowledge suggests that this disparity is likely to become even more diverse across the regions and between urban and rural area than it is today. Focusing on the subject of CAV, the future operations of the highway network will be highly dependent on the cooperation between in-vehicle and infrastructure systems, given the growing importance of infrastructure-to-vehicle (I2V) and vehicle-to-infrastructure (V2I) CV systems to enable the vehicles and the roadway infrastructure to function as a well-integrated system. This requires extra effort to make the National Highway System function as a single consistent system.

However, there are forces working against national consistency, and they are several and powerful. Let us lay them out one by one below:

1. There are differing affinities of the populace for reliance on new vehicle technology and different levels of resources available to be early adopters. These differences exist not only between the sun-belt vs. rust-belt region or coastal vs. inland regions, but also tied to the urban vs. rural divide.
2. There are different financial and human resources available to public agencies in different parts of the United States to develop and operate I2V and V2I cooperative systems. These could represent differences between high-tax and low-tax states, prosperous vs. depressed metropolitan regions, urban vs. rural counties.
3. There are trends that will be amplified by the growing digital divide within the U.S. population, which already tends to be correlated with the above regional differences.

The likely differences in economic growth in high-tech regions and rust-belt regions are only going to exacerbate these forces at the national level. To plan for the future, such quantitative methods as "*dynamic adaptive pathways planning*" might become very useful to map out actions over time in response to how the future unfolds. The one significant advantage that the less prosperous locations have is better availability and lower cost for new right-of-way that could be used for new transportation facilities or expansions of existing facilities. The development of these new highway facilities that are designed specifically for use by more highly automated vehicles could be a major factor in "leveling the playing field" nationally in favor of the less prosperous locations that want to enjoy the transportation benefits from higher levels of road vehicle automation. I have yet to see any literature that models this phenomenon and provide a policy analysis on how to effect the desired location-based economic development.

8. Adapting a strategic and visioning approach

It is clear from the above discussions that a *strategic* approach is required to welcome the forthcoming ICT and CAV *interventions*. Strategic models for planning have existed in various forms for a long time. Several forms of strategic models for transportation planning have been developed in recent years to address a gap in the technical understanding of an uncertain future. These models are intended for use as *visioning* tools, specifically to help guide policies and investments. Accordingly, planners have adopted a revised name, "strategic visioning frameworks," to emphasize this purpose. Current strategic visioning frameworks have been developed to address specific policies, such as green-house-gas reduction strategies or smart growth policies (Zmud et al., 2018).

8.1 Background

Current visioning frameworks were designed to be faster in execution, thus allowing for extensive scenario testing. The processing speed is accelerated by excluding detailed network representations and instead describing the built environment, transportation supply and ICT/CAV by using aggregate measures. This is consistent with the advocacy of much more flexible, generic design (to accommodate technological changes in an agile fashion) as discussed under Section 5.1. Following the thrust of this chapter, these models are also developed and applied as AB, disaggregate, micro-simulation models, maintaining detailed personal, household, and firm characteristics that influence travel demand, combined with aggregate transport-supply, ICT/CAV measures and land-use. The models allow for many scenarios to be processed quickly, after which visualizers can help interpret the scenarios interactively for a thorough understanding of the impacts of various combinations of policies and investments. In the previous chapter, I have ascribed this methodology as *robust decision making*.

Another important feature of strategic visioning frameworks is ensuring that the interaction between different policies or future scenarios is integrated so that transport supply, ICT/CAV, travel behavior, population, employment, and land use are linked, as illustrated in Fig. 3. These linkages are important to comprehend how the combination of technologies, policies, or demographics can influence travel demand and beyond. Transport and ICT/CAV policies in combination can target similar demographic populations and be effective in combination with other policies. This is illustrated by the increasingly large number of multi-earner families, which might very well adopt shared-mobility CAV services under Section 5.1, "Effect of CAV," in the section entitled "Urban Activity-Based Demand Modeling" of the chapter "Travel modeling underforeseeable communications-and-mobility technologies." Without our discussions in this chapter, however, the target might be missed. The transport, ICT/CAV and land-use interactions (as shown in Fig. 3) are used to quantify any induced travel demand, which is a critical aspect of uncertain futures. Like AB models, strategic models are structured to be able to include ICT/CAV policy analysis, but it requires some modifications depending on the questions being asked. Strategic models are currently sensitive to many of the behavioral impacts and can be further adapted to represent changing behaviors.

8.2 Model system

VisionEval (http://visioneval.org) is an example (among many others) of a strategic modeling framework that has been used to represent emerging travel modes. Strategic models have several components that are relevant to CAV ownership and availability, including representing vehicle ownership costs (purchase, insurance, operating), bike ownership, vehicle age, and fuel efficiency. In addition, these components can be easily adapted to include car-share and bike-share—which I include under the term of "shared mobility services." Strategic models also incorporate household budgeting (both time budget and monetary budget), allowing the introduction of CAVs into the household budget decisions.

Urban form is currently represented in strategic models as a combination of development and area type (e.g., transit-oriented development in a residential area[e]). These models can be adjusted to incorporate place types that are important for CAVs, such as the replacement of recharging station

[e] A transit-oriented development is a type of urban land use that maximizes the amount of residential, business and leisure space within walking distance of public transport. The objective is to increase public-transport ridership by reducing the use of private cars, thus promoting sustainable growth in the long run.

for regular gas station, and the replacement of parking-constrained areas for extensive parking structures. Life-cycle variables that define modality choice for young single adults, multi-earner families, elderly workers, and retirees can also be incorporated into the urban form, commensurate with an aggregate representation of network and AB travel models.

Most strategic models estimate vehicle-miles-of-travel (VMT) directly, and adjustments for different policies are provided through empirical research. In a very tangible case study by Adler et al. (2014), for example, their forecasting model was a regional travel demand model used to create the desired travel demand forecasts. Irrespective of the forecasting method used, however, there are uncertainties in the model parameters and structure and uncertainties in inputs of future conditions. Probability distributions were developed for all of these uncertain factors. They showed that a travel demand forecasting model could be synthesized by using response surface methods[f] in an analytically tractable model that can then be imbedded in a Monte Carlo simulation to generate distributions of the outputs of interest. One can ascribe this approach to illustrate the quantitative method of "*info-gap theory*" to manage deep uncertainty, as described in Section 2. The method was applied to Orlando I-4 Express lanes application, where a planning-level study was undertaken to evaluate the traffic and revenue that could be expected for the proposed managed lanes.

In general, the VMT so obtained by strategic models can be adjusted by a number of ways. In the context of our discussions in this chapter, these adjustments can be included for households that optimize their travel with CAVs or adjust their trip chaining because the CAV can be used to pick up and deliver multiple household members. A new model component for estimating the VMT associated with deadheading (i.e., cars with no occupants that are repositioned or sent to pick up another passenger) could be developed for both privately owned CAVs and for-hire CAVs. Strategic models also currently evaluate induced demand, but this impact may need to be re-evaluated once empirical evidence on CAV and for-hire-CAV use is documented.

To be simple, strategic models do not typically include a traditional mode-choice model. Instead, modal shares of interest are directly modeled on the basis of characteristics of supply and demographics. Models can be constructed to directly estimate VMT from for-hire services (e.g., car-share,

[f] In the previous chapter, we have also employed offline "response surface analysis" in coming out with "Decision Rules" used in "Regional Traffic Management" (Section 4 of the chapter "Travel modeling underforeseeable communications-and-mobility technologies").

bike-share, or Transportation network companies [TNCs]) or other modes that may emerge. This does not necessarily mean the replacement of random-utility–based models, as the RUM framework remains important in household travel-time budgeting.

9. Conclusions

Among many, the "AV-Ready Transport Models and Road Infrastructure for the Coexistence of Automated and Connected Vehicles" project, funded under Horizon 2020, aims to increase the knowledge of road authorities in transitioning toward a shared road network with increasing levels of AVs using the same road network as conventional vehicles. The project entails (1) transport modeling, (2) tool building, and (3) simulated-use cases in four road authorities (Gothenburg, Helmond, Milton Keynes, and Stuttgart, see https://www.h2020-coexist.eu/). Recognizing the profound implications of ICT and CAVs on future travel, our two-chapter sequence also tries to identify as many plausible implications on future travel modeling as possible. However, the uncertainty surrounding the evolution of ICT and CAVs is acute enough, setting aside the even more unpredictable reaction of the traveling public to these technologies. Aimed at the modeling-and-simulation communities, this chapter and the previous chapter laid out some plausible recommendations on future analytical efforts on developing the responsive travel analysis tools. Since there is no axiomatic way to "derive" prescriptions for these future analytical procedures for travel supply/demand models, I adopted an alternate way, mainly based on selected case studies. Recognizing that we are laying out a future direction for the modeling community, I focused specifically on AB, disaggregate and micro-simulation models, rather than the traditional "four-step" model of trip generation, trip distribution, modal split and traffic assignment. This effort is complemented with urban and regional development models that take full advantage of disaggregate, household-level of analysis. I am happy to report partial success in formulating some definitive guidelines for my colleagues to ponder. To do this, I first concentrated on transportation supply models. Specifically, I traced the ICT/CAV impacts on today's intelligent traffic-management practice, when such practice has already taken advantage of some ICT innovations. Assuming that the physics underlying traffic flow theory as we know today is likely to prevail in the future, I speculated how the future intelligent traffic-management scheme should look like, including after the introduction of CAVs on a partial scale, starting with CVs. This is an important first step, as it is our belief that the future ITS scheme is likely to reflect how CAVs operate in the future. More than that, we would like the prescriptions to apply to regional transportation systems, including air traffic, as civil aviation evolves with the NextGen automation in the United States, which is similar to the automation by ICT/CAVs on the ground.

While today's traffic operations in the presence of ICT are observable, we must admit that tomorrow's travel pattern is certainly not. Obviously, much of the unobservable is due to the unknown reactions of the traveling public to the introduction of new ICT/CAV technologies. For the observable traffic operations, even though the physics governing traffic-flow theory might still prevail in the future, the calibration of empirical parameters for such basic principles as the FDTF and instrument-flight-rule/visual-flight-rule will certainly need to be revisited. Any projection of how a mixed traffic stream will flow in the presence of CAVs has to be taken in the context of the scenario under which such flows are simulated, as pointed out by the Booz-Allen-Hamilton traffic-corridor study. For demand modeling, which is much more behavioral in nature, I had far fewer observations at hand to even speculate, when much of it depends on how people react to the introduction of ICT/CAVs and other forms of automation. The only way is to rely on such analysis tools as scenario planning and strategic visioning. Fortunately, under such broad strokes analyses some limited detailed examinations can be conducted, as afforded by our case studies. One example is the travel choices of a multi-vehicle, multi-wage-earner families, which are likely to be the trend of future workforce demographics. Here, "multi-vehicle" refers to not necessarily just owning more than one car, but rather owning a mixed fleet of conventional and CAVs, which can be shared in private or in public.

With the partial study of the telecommuting case study in an urban setting, I moved onto regional travel modeling. I focused on a case study of long-distance travel, which has a different set of attributes compared with urban travel. For one, the effect of ICT/CAV is likely to be felt in full force in long-distance travel compared with urban/short-distance travel. Also, data is scarce for analyzing long distance travel today, setting aside for tomorrow with the unknown development of ICT/CAV. After diving into the analysis, it was clear that–in the progression of transport modeling from traffic management to urban travel to regional travel– we have to rely tools ranging from "scenario planning" to "dynamic adaptive pathways planning" at this "bifurcation" point of our future telecommunication and mobility technologies. Having gone through five case studies, by adapting some recommended strategic and visioning approaches, I capped our model "crystal balling" by examining future land-use models that should address the implied locational and spatial development patterns after the implementation of ICT/CAVs. After pointing out some logical conjectures, the only place we can all agree is that there will be some profound implications on not only on travel, but also our life styles, not to mention the broader economic and non-economic consequences.

10. Prospects

I am happy to report several takeaways from our analyses. With so many moving pieces in this era of disruptive technologies, it is clear that disaggregate, AB and micro-simulation modeling is a promising path to follow, based on the case studies on traffic management and telecommuting, which were discussed in some depth in these two chapters. Using such tools as "dynamic adaptive pathways planning," agility is arguably the key to succeed in an ever-evolving ICT/CAV scene, particularly the life-cycle time-frame incongruity between ICT, CAV and infrastructures. Accordingly, a case is built for dynamic, disequilibrium, evolutionary models with a more flexible and generic design. Such agile analysis tools range from real-time traffic operations to the way we explore the demand for CAV-based private-and-shared mobility-services in the future, and to future urban and regional development. These include the agile adaption of existing state-of-the-art tools, including Vissim for traffic management and NLDTM for long-distance travel. While the advance in computation helps, there is a need to demarcate between *online* vs. *offline* analysis modules in our models for real-time operations. In general, offline modules will house the bulk of calibrated parameters, including such parameters as the calibrated FDTF, the list of "universal" activities, and scenario-based synthetic populations. On the other hand, online modules will include real-time traffic control, tour-episode construction, and strategic smart-growth management. The readers will discern from the discussions that these offline and online tools are to be developed and applied as disaggregate models, maintaining detailed personal, household, and firm characteristics that influence travel. However, it does not preclude combining with aggregate representation of transport-supply, ICT/CAV measures and land-use where appropriate for scenario and assumption exploration—the only universal tool to model the highly uncertain future.

As illustrated by the various case studies presented in these chapters, perhaps the solid basic-building-block remains innovative and rigorous analytic procedures that will help unveil at least some of the unanticipated consequences. In this regard, we should celebrate our advances in such IT tools as stochastic optimization, distributionally robust optimization, multicriteria optimization, metaheuristics, behavioral sciences in decision making, and MDC extreme-value model within the RUM framework—just to name a few. In the author's opinion, there is always room for further modeling-and-simulation innovations, including greater attention to capturing behavior in parsimonious formulations (which will ease the task of model calibrations). Just to repeat for emphasis, the biggest challenges and opportunities remain in how to explore the unknowns, including strategic and visioning approaches to examine the future. Obviously, the exercise performed here in these two chapters is aimed at stimulating more thoughtful discussions on *visioning*, which includes not only exploring where modeling-and-simulation is heading, but also guiding where we should be going.

While such visions as the Internet of Things (IoT) is often offered as a panacea of the future, ensuring sufficient cybersecurity protection to repel the large majority of cyberattacks is also a real challenge (Shladover, 2019). In the context of the current writing about the vulnerability of ICT and CAV, this is already becoming a challenge for modern non-automated vehicles because of their dependence on electro-mechanical actuation (such as engine, brake, and steering control) and in-vehicle networks. The temptation for attackers is likely to be greater for highly automated vehicles, whose occupants are less likely to notice and respond quickly to an attack (because they are not doing the driving). Modeling cybersecurity, particularly how to guard against such events to ensure a safe and streamline traffic flows, remains a subject that I found sorely lacking in the literature, since the subject has not been in the mainstream of traditional travel modeling.

Looking way ahead, how about envisioning a Smart City of the future, as illustrated in Fig. 3? A smart city is defined here as a community that provides advanced applications and services to its dwellers through cutting-edge ICT and CAVs (among other modern day conveniences including IoT), thus delivering a better way of living by making services–not only transportation services–available to everyone anywhere at any time. At the time of writing, 20 smart city projects have been awarded by the United States Department of Transportation, spearheaded by the Columbus, Ohio, challenge. It can be seen therefore that while the conceptual advantages of the ideas discussed in these two chapters are many, the biggest modeling-and-simulation challenge remaining is the broader unknown future that lies ahead (well beyond the interface between mobility and communications discussed in these two chapters), when today's brick-and-mortar community may be wired from east to west, from north to south, and from any point to another point!

Acknowledgments

The author wishes to acknowledge the intellectual stimulations received from participating in the Chan Wui and Yunyin Rising Star Workshop in June 2016 on board the MS Queen Mary 2, focusing on the subject of the "Analytical Relationship between Mobility and Communications" (https://commons.ualr.edu/chanrsworkshop/). This chapter synthesizes and expands the 2017 journal papers of the eminent participating Workshop scholars that span North America and Europe. The synthesis is supplemented by the latest thoughts and literature up to 2019, the time of this writing. As seen by the references, much of the material contained in this chapter is borrowed from the writings of the various participants of this Workshop, including C. Brakewood, G. Erhardt, K. Han, E. Miller, R. Moeckel, and R. Paleti. Last but not least, I owe deep gratitude to E. Ben-Elia, editor of this volume, for his many insightful suggestions during my writing. Obviously, the author alone bears any self-generated errors while composing this chapter. Funding of this study came from the anonymous foundation that supported the Workshop.

References

Adler, T., Doherty, M., Klodzinski, J., Tillman, R., 2014. Methods for quantitative risk analysis for travel demand model forecasts. Transp. Res. Rec. (2429), 1–7.

Booz Allen Hamilton, WSP, New Jersey Institute of Technology, 2018. Dedicating Lanes for Priority or Exclusive Use by Connected and Automated Vehicles. *NCHRP Research Report*. Transportation Research Board, Washington, DC, p. 891.

Carter, A.A., Burgett, A., Srinivasan, G., Ranganathan, R., 2009. Safety impact methodology (SIM): evaluation of pre-production systems. In: Proceedings of the 21st International Technical Conference on the Enhanced Safety of Vehicles (June 2009). Paper No. 09-0259. National Highway Traffic Safety Administration, Washington, D.C.

Chan, Y., 2005. Location, *Transport and Land-Use: Modeling Spatial-Temporal Information*. Springer, Berlin, New York, p. 930. With Web-based Instructor's Manual and Software, Second Edition in preparation.

Erhardt, G.D., 2017. Conceptual models of the effect of information and communications technology on long-distance travel demand. Transp. Res. Rec. 2658, 26–34.

FHWA, 2008. Income-Based Equity Impacts of Congestion Pricing: A Primer. Federal Highway Administration, U.S. Department of Transportation, Washington, DC.

Harding, J., et al., 2014. Vehicle-to-Vehicle Communications: Readiness of V2V Technology for Application. Report No. DOT HS 812 014. National Highway Traffic Safety Administration, Washington, DC.

LaMondia, J., Bhat, C.R., Hensher, D.A., 2008. An annual time use model for domestic vacation travel. J. Choice Model. 1 (1), 70–97. https://doi.org/10.1016/S1755-5345(13)70023-X.

Larsen, J.K., Axhausen, W., Urry, J., 2006. Geographies of social networks: meetings, travel and communications. Mobilities 1 (2), 261–283. https://doi.org/10.1080/17450100600726654.

Lee, J., Shladover, S.C., Rakha, H.A., Lu, X.-Y., Jagannathan, R., Dailey, D.J., 2014. Mobility impacts of cooperative adaptive cruise control (CACC) under mixed traffic conditions. In: Proceedings of the 21st ITS World Congress (September 7–11, 2011, Detroit, MI). ITS America, Washington, D.C.

Lee, J., et al., 2016. Simulation of Evolutionary Introduction of Cooperative Adaptive Cruise Control Equipped Vehicles into Traffic. Federal Highway Administration, U.S. Department of Transportation, Washington, D.C.

Ma, J., Li, X., 2016. Freeway speed harmonization. In: IEEE Transactions on Intelligent Vehicles. vol. 1(1). Institute of Electrical and Electronics Engineers, New York, NY, pp. 78–89.

Miller, E.J., 2005a. Propositions for modelling household decision-making. In: Lee-Gosselin, M., Doherty, S.T. (Eds.), Integrated Land-Use and Transportation Models: Behavioural Foundations. Elsevier, Oxford, pp. 21–60.

Miller, E.J., 2005b. An integrated framework for modelling short- and long-run household decision-making. In: Timmermans, H. (Ed.), Progress in Activity-Based Analysis. Elsevier, Oxford, pp. 175–202.

Miller, E.J., 2005c. Project-based activity scheduling for household and person agents. In: Mahmassani, H.S. (Ed.), Transportation and Traffic Theory, Flow, Dynamics and Human Interaction: Proceedings of the 16th International Symposium on Transportation and Traffic Theory. Elsevier, Oxford, pp. 565–584.

Miller, E.J., 2017. Modeling the demand for new transportation services and technologies. Transp. Res. Rec. 2658, 1–7.

Moeckel, R., 2017a. Constraints in household relocation: modeling land-use/transport interactions that respect time and monetary budgets. J. Transp. Land Use 10 (1).

Moeckel, R., 2017b. Modeling the impact of communications technologies on travel behavior and land use. Transp. Res. Rec. 2658, 8–16.

Mokhtarian, P.L., 1990. A typology of relationships between telecommunications and transportation. Transp. Res. A 24 (3), 231–242. https://doi.org/10.1016/0191-2607(90)90060-J.

Mokhtarian, P.L., 2009. If telecommunication is such a good substitute for travel, why does congestion continue to get worse? Transp. Lett. 1 (1), 1–17.

Mokhtarian, P.L., Tal, G., 2013. Impacts of ICT on travel behavior: a tapestry of relationship. In: Rodrigue, J.-P., Notteboom, T., Shaw, J. (Eds.), The SAGE Handbook of Transport Studies. SAGE, London.

Outwater, M., Bradley, M., Ferdous, N., Pendyala, R., Garikapati, V., Bhat, C., 2015. Foundational knowledge to support a long-distance passenger travel demand modeling framework: final report. FHWA, U.S. Department of Transportation. http://www.rsginc.com/sites/default/files/publications/Long%20Distance%20Model%20Framework%20Final%20Report.pdf.

Rakha, H., Ding, Y., 2003. Impact of stops on vehicle fuel consumption and emissions. J. Transp. Eng. *129* (1), 23–32American Society of Civil Engineers, Reston, VA.

Shladover, S.E., 2019. Connected and automated vehicle technology impacts on future interstate highway system. In: National Academies of Sciences, Engineering, and Medicine. Appendix F in Renewing the National Commitment to the Interstate Highway System: A Foundation for the Future. The National Academies Press, Washington, DChttps://doi.org/10.17226/25334.

U.S. EPA, 2016, https://www.epa.gov/moves/september-2016-moves-model-review-work-group-meeting-materials (accessed 14 August 2019).

Wegener, M., 2004. Overview of land use transport models. In: Hensher, D.A., Button, K.J., Haynes, K.E., Stopher, P.R. (Eds.), Handbook of Transport Geography and Spatial Systems, Handbooks in Transport. In: vol. 5. Elsevier, Amsterdam, Netherlands, pp. 127–146. https://doi.org/10.1108/9781615832538-009.

Zhu, Y., Ferreira Jr., J., 2014. Synthetic population generation at disaggregated spatial scales for land use and transportation microsimulation. Transp. Res. Rec. 2429, 168–177. https://doi.org/10.3141/2429-18.

Zmud, J., Williams, T., Bradley, M., Kalra, N., Row, S., 2018. Updating Regional Transportation Planning and Modeling Tools to Address Impacts of Connected and Automated Vehicles. Volume 1: Executive Summary and Volume 2: Guidance. NCHRP Research Report 896Transportation Research Board, Washington, DC.

Further reading

Bhat, C.R., 2005. A multiple discrete–continuous extreme value model: formulation and application to discretionary time-use decisions. Transp. Res. B Methodol. 39 (8), 679–707.

Castillo, E., Conejo, A.J., Menendez, J.M., Jimenez, P., 2008. The observability problem in traffic network models. J. Comput. Aided Civ. Infrastruct. Eng. 23 (3), 208–222. https://doi.org/10.1111/j.1467-8667.2008.00531.x.

Fowe, J.A., 2009. Road-Traffic Monitoring and Routing: Stochastic Algorithms for Safety and Efficiency. MS thesisUniversity of Arkansas at Little Rock.

Herrera, J.C., Work, D.B., Herring, R., Ban, X.J., Jacobson, Q., Bayen, A.M., 2010. Evaluation of traffic data obtained via GPS-enabled mobile phones: the mobile century field experiment. Transp. Res. C 18 (4), 568–583. https://doi.org/10.1016/j.trc.2009.10.006.

Jiang, S., Fiore, G.A., Yang, Y., Ferreira Jr., J., Frazzoli, E., González, M.C., 2013. A review of urban computing for mobile phone traces: current methods, challenges and opportunities. In: Proceedings of the 2nd ACM SIGKDD International Workshop on Urban Computing. Association for Computing Machinery, New Yorkhttps://doi.org/10.1145/2505821.2505828.

Wolf, J., Bachman, W., Oliveira, M., Auld, J., Mohammadian, A.K., Vovsha, P., Zmud, J., 2014. NCHRP Report 775: Applying GPS Data to Understand Travel Behavior, Vol. II. Guidelines. Transportation Research Board of the National Academies, Washington, D.Chttps://doi.org/10.17226/23436.

Zhang, S., Tang, J., Wang, H., Wang, Y., 2015. Enhancing traffic incident detection by using spatial point pattern analysis on social media. Transp. Res. Rec. 2528, 69–77. https://doi.org/10.3141/2528-08.

FSC
www.fsc.org
MIX
Papier | Fördert gute Waldnutzung
FSC® C083411

Kolibri 360 GmbH
Ferdinand-Jühlke-Straße 7
99095 Erfurt, Deutschland
produktsicherheit@kolibri360.de